Advanced Oracle DBMS Packages
The Definitive Reference

Oracle In-Focus Series

Paulo Portugal

I dedicate this book to my parents and siblings that have always supported me in my professional life. Also thanks to friends Michael Bell, Gabriel Rosales and the Burleson team with their valuable help on this project.

In particular, I dedicate this book to my daughter Maria Clara and my dear wife Simone who are the people that bring me balance, motivation, inspiration, joy and an eternal desire to live alongside them.

Thanks to God for having given me all this achievement.

Paulo Portugal

Advanced Oracle DBMS Packages
The Definitive Reference

By Paulo Portugal

Copyright © 2012 by Rampant TechPress. All rights reserved.
Printed in the United States of America.
Published in Kittrell, North Carolina, USA.
Oracle In-focus Series: Book 41
Series Editor: Donald K. Burleson
Production Manager: Robin Rademacher and Jennifer Stanley
Production Editor: Valerre Aquitaine
Cover Design: Janet Burleson
Printing History: October 2012 for First Edition

ISBN 10: 0-9844282-2-4
ISBN 13: 978-0-9844282-2-9
Library of Congress Control Number: 2011937947

Table of Contents

Using the Online Code Depot

Purchase of this book provides complete access to the online code depot that contains sample code scripts. Any code depot scripts in this book are located at the following URL in zip format and ready to load and use:

rampant.cc/dbms_packages.htm

If technical assistance is needed with downloading or accessing the scripts, please contact Rampant TechPress at rtp@rampant.cc.

Conventions Used in this Book

It is critical for any technical publication to follow rigorous standards and employ consistent punctuation conventions to make the text easy to read. However, this is not an easy task. With database terminology there are many types of notation that can confuse a reader. For example, some Oracle utilities such as STATSPACK and TKPROF are always spelled in CAPITAL letters, while Oracle parameters and procedures have varying naming conventions in the database documentation. It is also important to remember that many database commands are case sensitive, are always left in their original executable form and never altered with italics or capitalization. Hence, all Rampant TechPress books follow these conventions:

- **Parameters:** All database parameters will be lowercase italics. Exceptions to this rule are parameter arguments that are commonly capitalized (KEEP pool, TKPROF); these will be left in ALL CAPS.

- **Variables:** All procedural language (e.g. PL/SQL) program variables and arguments will also remain in lowercase italics (*dbms_job*, *dbms_utility*).

- **Tables & dictionary objects:** All data dictionary objects are referenced in lowercase italics (*dba_indexes*, *v$sql*). This includes all *v$* and *x$* views (*x$kcbcbh*, *v$parameter*) and dictionary views (*dba_tables*, *user_indexes*).

- **SQL:** All SQL is formatted for easy use in the code depot, and all SQL displayed in lowercase. The main SQL terms (select, from, where, group by, order by, having) will always appear on a separate line.

- **Programs & Products:** All products and programs that are known to the author are capitalized according to the vendor specifications (CentOS, VMware, Oracle, etc.). All names known by Rampant TechPress to be trademark names appear in this text as initial caps. References to UNIX are always made in uppercase.

Acknowledgements

This type of highly technical reference book requires the dedicated efforts of many people. Even though I am the author, my work ends when I deliver the content. After each chapter is delivered, several Oracle DBAs carefully review and correct the technical content. After the technical review, experienced copy editors polish the grammar and syntax.

The finished work is then reviewed as page proofs and turned over to the production manager, who arranges the creation of the online code depot and manages the cover art, printing distribution, and warehousing.

In short, the author plays a small role in the development of this book, and I need to thank and acknowledge everyone who helped bring this book to fruition:

- **Robin Rademacher and Jennifer Stanley** for the production management including the coordination of the cover art, page proofing, printing, and distribution.

- **Valerre Q Aquitaine** for help in the production of the page proofs.

- **Janet Burleson** for exceptional cover design and graphics.

- **John Lavender** for assistance with the web site, and for creating the code depot and the online shopping cart for this book.

- **Don Burleson** for providing me with the opportunity to write this book.

With my sincerest thanks,

Paulo Portugal

Preface

This book is geared to present the main packages used in the Oracle Database and their usage by database administrators and developers. Like many of you, throughout my career I have faced difficulties in finding information about the Oracle DBMS packages. In the course of this relentless and exhausting pursuit, I have collected the most useful packages for this book. I'm also providing practical examples on the application of these tools (which are also notoriously difficult to find).

After 30 years, Oracle has slowly evolved into 11g, and with each new version of Oracle, new DBMS packages are created to ease the Titanic job of administrating the database. Many of those DBMS packages are extremely specialized and do not become well-known to Oracle professionals. Other DBMS packages are under-documented requiring creativity to find out how they work.

Many of the graphic tools of database management like OEM and Oracle Grid Control, make use of the DBMS packages. Notwithstanding, most modifications made available by these graphic tools usually run in the background, and therefore the user ends up not knowing exactly what is going on in the inner workings of their Oracle database.

This is only one reason why a senior DBA never relies on a GUI and takes the time to understand the command-line interfaces to all of the important DBMS packages.

But even when there exists a graphic tool to replace a package, for some mission critical databases, running a "UI Wizard" application against the production database is never advisable. Directly calling a DBMS package is simply the best way, the only way, a "best practice" to do some important task.

Besides, GUI tools are more susceptible to malfunctions due to incorrect configurations or software/hardware conflicts. So they frequently prevent correct operations, sometimes without even returning an error message, thereby leaving the user in an uncomfortable situation. Those are just some of the scenarios where a solid knowledge of Oracle DBMS Packages will certainly be invaluable for any Oracle professional.

Among the advantages of running DBMS packages from SQL*Plus is that they provide complete information to the DBA and developers of all of the intermediate stages of a procedure. Moreover, direct invocation of the DBMS packages allows us to quickly and easily access or alter database information without the use of flawed or unsecure graphic tools, or when a GUI tool is simply not available.

Remember, OEM only generates the native commands, and it is most popular as a crutch for the beginner.

Code Depot Username = reader, Password = dbms

Another very important advantage is that DBMS packages can be combined and some of them can also be edited, serving as a basis to perform extremely complex tasks; for example, when the functionality needed is not exactly the same but is close to what one package offers by itself. That is something usually not possible with most GUI tools.

The packages are organized in the following chapters:

- *Table, Index and Tablespace Management*
- *Oracle Security*
- *Oracle File Management and Network*
- *Oracle Concurrency Management*
- *Oracle Tuning*
- *Oracle Backup and Recovery*
- *Management and Monitoring*
- *Data Warehouse*
- *RAC and Distributed Transactions*
- *Data Guard*
- *Streams and HS*
- *HTML DB and XDB*

The days of the generic DBA have been long gone, and the huge scope of Oracle technology makes it impossible for any DBA to know all areas of database administration., Some DBA's specialize if Oracle tuning, others in Oracle security, others in backup and recovery and stilll others in high availability and replictation.

Nowadays, the speed at which Oracle professionals must do their tasks as well as the excess of information they are exposed to prevents them from learning all the packages and their different usage alternatives by heart.

Therefore, by organizing the book by job function, I hope that the readers will be able to make use of it as a practical guide to learn about the packages, see which packages are the most useful to them and use our book as a reference book to be kept on your desks, hopefully making your grueling daily routines a little easier!

I am always looking to improve the content of this book, so if you find any paackages that neeed additional information or errata, I'd love to correct it in a futire edition.

Please send all improvement requests and errata to errata@rampant.cc.

Introduction to Oracle DBMS Packages

Oracle Packages

In this first chapter, we will review the history of Oracle packages and describe the advantages and benefits of their use by database administrators and application developers.

History of Packages with PL/SQL Language

Since every DBMS package is embedded into the PL/SQL language, let's explain the history of DBMS packages and get an idea of the possibilities available within each different version of Oracle. The evolution of PL/SQL is tied to the evolution of the DBMS packages and this section starts with a brief introduction to the history of the PL/SQL language.

PL/SQL is an acronym for Programming Language/Structured Query Language, and like any procedural language, PL/SQL exists in order to support Boolean IF logic, looping, assignment statements, and data access methods, structires that you cannot use in SQL alone..

PL/SQL supports three types of code constructs:

- **Procedures:** A named or un-named (anonymous) listing of PL/SQL statements.

- **Functions:** Just like a procedure, but a function must return a value.

- **Packages:** A package is a named collection of functions and procedures. It is the packages that are pinned into the SGA for faster execution and reusability (using *dbms_shared_pool.keep*)

The PL/SQL language was introduced in Oracle 6 and has its origins in the 3rd generation language syntax of ADA and Pascal languages. Despite the creation of PL/SQL language version 1.0 as an Oracle 6 option, it was not until Oracle 7 with PL/SQL version 1.1 that many of PL/SQL's more representative characteristics where introduced including features such as PL/SQL packages, functions, procedures, user-defined record types and PL/SQL tables.

Before the introduction of the PL/SQL language, the only way to use procedure constructs with SQL was through the PRO*Cobol, Pro*Fortran and Pro*C languages where the procedural logic was coded in C language, but Oracle SQL instructions could be added.

At compile time, the entire code had to be precompiled to interpret the Oracle SQL instructions and convert them into the native language library calls. The precompiler then created a file, written entirely in the language, which finally could be compiled using the regular language compiler.

Here follows a summary of the evolution and relevant functionalities of each PL/SQL version.

- **Oracle6:** With Oracle 6 came the first version of PL/SQL (1.0) which was very limited in its capabilities. Still, even in Oracle 6, the beginning of PL/SQL version 1.1 gave support to the client/server architecture.

- **Oracle7:** Versions PL/SQL 2.0, 2.1, 2.2, and 2.3 were released respectively with Oracle 7.0, 7.1, 7.2, and 7.3. They introduced many characteristics such as stored procedures support, packages, functions, PL/SQL tables; built-in packages such as *dbms_output*, *dbms_pipe*, and *dbms_sql* amongst others; the PL/SQL wrapper to protect source codes and file I/O within the PL/SQL code.

- **Oracle8:** Support for functionalities such as nested tables, LOBS and VARRAYS began with Oracle 8. In version 8i with PL/SQL 8.1 came native dynamic SQL, autonomous transactions and new types of triggers such as startup, logon and logoff triggers.

- **Oracle9i:** Introduced in PL/SQL 9.0 with Oracle 9i came functionalities such as PL/SQL CASE expressions, native compilation of PL/SQL and globalized datatypes.

- **Oracle10g:** Oracle versions 10g Release 1 and 10g Release 2 represented a great leap forward. In an effort to make Oracle 10g a truly self-managed database made for grid computing, Oracle included a very good set of data movement and self-tuning/self-diagnosing features, adding new components such as ADDM, AWR and Data Pump. This also brought many new and very useful packages like *dbms_db_version*, *dbms_errlog*, *dbms_tdb*, *dbms_advisor*, *dbms_monitor*, *dbms_scheduler*, *dbms_service*, *dbms_sqltune*, *utl_compress* and others.

Lastly, in version 11g it came up with more than 40 new packages which shall be presented later in this book.

Advantages and Benefits of the Use of Packages

One of the main advantages and benefits of using Oracle Packages is better performance. Before the existence of PL/SQL, the applications connecting to Oracle needed to submit each SQL command individually. Thus, each SQL command resulted in a call to Oracle that responded with data that was then processed elsewhere, resulting in a high use of server resources as data kept moving to and from the external application doing the processing.

With the advent of PL/SQL, SQL commands could be placed inside a PL/SQL block that ran inside the same Oracle server with minimum overhead.

With PL/SQL, it became possible to recompile one package body without the need to recompile the package specification, resulting in less impact to the database. Also, by placing SQL: inside PL/SQL with stored procedures and functions that use bind variables, SQL statements can reside inside the library cache of Oracle and be fully reentrant, avoiding the need to repeated hard parsing.

The perils of Non-Use of Bind Variables in Oracle

The biggest problem in many applications is the failure to usilize bind variables. Oracle bind variables are a super important way to make Oracle SQL reentrant.

Oracle uses a signature generation algorithm to assign a hash value to each SQL statement based on the characters in the SQL statement. Any change in a statement (generally speaking) will result in a new hash and thus Oracle assumes it is a new statement. Each new statement must be verified, parsed and have an execution plan generated and stored, all high overhead procedures.

Ad-hoc query generators (Crystal Reports, Oracle Discoverer, Business Objects) do not use bind variables, a major reason for Oracle developing the cursor_sharing parameter to force SQL to use bind variables (when *cursor_sharing=force*).

When SQL is placed within PL/SQL, the embedded SQL never changes and a single library cache entry will be maintained and searched, greatly improving the library cache hit ratio and reducing parsing overhead. Here are some particularly noteworthy advantages of placing SQL within Oracle stored procedures and packages:

- **High productivity:** PL/SQL is a language common to all Oracle environments. Developer productivity is increased when applications are designed to use PL/SQL procedures and packages because it avoids the need to rewrite code. Also, the migration complexity to different programming environments and front-end tools will be greatly reduced because Oracle process logic code is maintained inside the database with the data, where it belongs. The application code becomes a simple "shell" consisting of calls to stored procedures and functions.

- **Improved Security:** Making use of the "grant execute" construct, it is possible to restrict access to Oracle, enabling the user to run only the commands that are inside the procedures. For example, it allows an end user to access one procedure that has a command *delete* in one particular table instead of granting the *delete* privilege directly to the end user. The security of the database is further improved since you can define which variables, procedures and cursors will be public and which will be private, thereby completely limiting access to those objects inside the PL/SQL package. With the "grant" security model, back doors like SQL*Plus can lead to problems; with "grant execute" you force the end-user to play by your rules.

- **Application portability:** Every application written in PL/SQL can be transferred to any other environment that has the Oracle Database installed regardless of the platform. Systems that consist without any embedded PL/SQL or SQL become "database agnostic" and can be moved to other platforms without changing a single line of code.

- **Code Encapsulation:** Placing all related stored procedures and functions into packages allows for the encapsulation of storage procedures, variables and datatypes in one single program unit in the database, making packages perfect for code organization in your applications.

- **Global variables and cursors:** Packages can have global variables and cursors that are available to all the procedures and functions inside the package.

Packages Internals

During the installation of Oracle, several built-in DBMS packages are included in order to extend Oracle's core functionality. These packages are referred to as built-in packages. The built-in packages are installed by the scripts *catproc.sql* and *catalog.sql* located in the directory *$ORACLE_HOME/rdbms/admin*. If Oracle Universal Installer is used to install the database (Oracle's recommended method), the installer will run the built-in scripts automatically. These scripts call many other individual scripts that refer to each package that is being created in the database.

PL/SQL on the client or the server

It is worth mentioning that PL/SQL is a core part of Oracle and PL/SQL can exist either on the client side in an anonymous PL/SQL block or in the server side as a stored procedure of function. In both environments, the PL/SQL engine is responsible for the processing of the PL/SQL blocks and subroutines as well as the sending of the SQL commands to the SQL processor.

When the PL/SQL engine resides inside a stored procedure of function the PL/SQL blocks are sent to the PL/SQL engine in the Oracle server. On the client PC, the PL/SQL engine is located in the client side, the PL/SQL processing is done at the client.

This way, all the SQL commands inserted in the PL/SQL block are sent to the Oracle server for processing, but the PL/SQL logic gets processed on the client, thus diminishing the server overhead. In some cases, when the PL/SQL block does not have any SQL statement, it can be processed entirely on the client's side.

Introduction to the DBMS packages

The DBMS packages all begin with the name *dbms_*; for example, *dbms_trace* or *dbms_monitor*. There are packages named with other initials such as *utl_file* and *html_util*, but far and away the most are named with the DBMS prefix The DBMS packages offer us a storage method for the procedures, functions, variables and other package constructions, all put within a single unit within the database.

Inside the shared pool

An area of the Shared Pool called library cache holds an important area named shared SQL area that holds DBMS package code, as well as control structures such as locks and library cache handles.

There is also another important area, the private SQL area, which holds information specific for each user session and Oracle allocates a private SQL area to store specific values of a session.

However, the code itself is stored in the shared SQL area. When more than one user runs the same program unit, a single, shared copy of the unit will be used by both users. This enables Oracle not to waste memory, allowing the database to perform more efficiently.

The private SQL area is always stored in an area named User Global Area (UGA). However. the location of the UGA depends on the type of connection that is established with the database.

If you have a dedicated connection, the UGA will be located entirely inside the PGA, while in the case of a shared connection, a fixed part of the UGA will be located in the Shared Pool, and the variable part of the UGA which contains all the private SQL areas will be located in the Large Pool or Shared Pool (if the large pool is undefined).

The private SQL area is split into two areas:

- **Persistent area:** The persistent area contains the bind variable values and this area is released only when the cursor is closed.

- **Runtime area:** The runtime area contains information about an executed query, including the progress of a full table scan and the current state of the SQL work areas. These PGA areas are allocated to run RAM intensive operations such as sorting and hash-joins. For DML operations, a runtime area is released when the command completes.

Another internal characteristic of Oracle is the use of the LRU (least recently used) algorithm for maintaining compiled codes in the shared memory. To prevent a particularly large or time-bound object from leaving memory and forcing Oracle to read it from disk again, it is possible to "pin" the package into the memory or pin it as it is frequently referred, using a package named *dbms_shared_pool*. This will be covered more in Chapter 8, *Management and Monitoring*.

At the time of the creation of a PL/SQL package, Oracle automatically stores the following information in the database: the name of the object in the schema, the source code, the parse tree and the error messages. The storage of this information inside Oracle avoids unnecessary re-compilations being made in the database.

In the process of running a procedure within a package, Oracle checks the security to see if the user that is running the procedure is the owner of the package or whether he has permission to run this package or procedure. Next, Oracle checks the data dictionary so as to verify whether the package is valid or invalid and, finally, Oracle executes the procedure.

In order to run the select command in a view defined with a PL/SQL function, there needs to be access to select, just in this view; it is not necessary to have access to execute the function.

Invalid packages

A package may become invalid for various reasons such as in the following cases:

- **Table Invalid:** One or more objects referred by the procedure or package has been altered the procedure wil be marked as invalid. For example, this can happen when one column has been added in a table referred to inside the package.

- **Privilege Revoked:** If a system privilege needed by the procedure or package has been revoked from the owner of the procedure or package; or one object privilege accessed by the procedure or package has been revoked from the owner of the procedure or package.

Every time that procedure marked as invalid is called before its execution, Oracle tries to recompile it, running it if successful or returning an error message otherwise.

After a brief description of the relevant internal aspects, we will proceed with a presentation of the specific packages which are the central point of this book.

Table, Index and Tablespace Management

One of the primary jobs of the Oracle DBA is to manage the data as it resides in rows within tables; the data which, in turn, reside within our tablespaces.

The DBA is also responsible for managing indexes, ensuring that the SQL workload has all of the indexes that are required for optimal query completion, and deploying indexes as a shortcut to fetch the rows with the least amount of database I/O and resource consumption.

Traditionally, he DBA relied solely on the SQL*Plus command line interface, and it has only been recently that Oracle has provided DBMS packages to make it easier to manage tables, tablespaces and indexs storage. Oracle also offers the Oracle Enterpise Manager Grid Control GUI (called OEM), but it is extremely limited when compared to the command-line invocation.

This chapter will show us useful DBMS packages for managing tables, indices and tablespaces.

The beauty of the Oracle DBMS packages is that the end-user does not need knowledge that limits the awareness of the procedure being executed.

In order to approach this subject in a practical manner, it is necessary to analyze the most important procedures of each package, including a brief description, followed by practical examples. Let's start with *dbms_errlog*, a handy package for logging DML insert errors.

Package *dbms_errlog*

When doing a batch insert you may receive data from a host of external locations. While it's nice to assume that the data has been scrubbed and validated, there is always a chance that you will have invalid numeric and character data. The problem is how to deal with large volumes of errors and that is what the *dbms_errlog* package does for us.

This *dbms_errlog* package allows DML operations to continue working properly despite errors that might occur during the procedure.

To do this, *dbms_errlog* creates a table called an "error log" table. Any records not processed by the DML operation due to errors will be inserted into this table allowing any problems in the operation to be analyzed and fixed later on.

When doing massive DML operations, problems like these may arise:

- Data values that are too large for the column (e.g. inserting 40 characters into a varchar2(20).

- Partition mapping errors happen (No partition exists)

- Errors during triggers execution occur (mutating table error)

- Constraint violations (check, unique, referential and NOT NULL constraints) occur

- Type conversion errors (numeric with alpha characters, invalid dates) happen

For these cases, the *dbms_errlog* package can be used to create a table that will store details about all DML operations that present errors.

The following script demonstrates its use as seen in the package. DML errors of operation are simulated, then they are inserted in the log table that was created for the package under analysis. First, the main user is created which will be used throughout this book.

Note: This script will create a DBA user with a weak password what is not recommended for any production environment.

🖫 Code 2.1 – dbms_errlog.sql--Create user

```
create user
   pkg
identified by
   pkg#123
default tablespace
   users
temporary tablespace
   temp;

grant dba to pkg;
```

Next, a test table is created. Just for fun, we decided to name it *tb_dbms_errlog* as that is the name of the package that is being studied. Finally, our test table is also given a primary key.

```
--Create a test table
create table tb_dbms_errlog
as
select
    *
from
    dba_objects
where
    rownum < 1;

alter table
    tb_dbms_errlog
    add constraint
        pk_obj_id10 primary key (object_id);
```

After executing this DDL, our error log table is created using the package *dbms_errlog* and rows are inserted to simulate constraint errors.

To create an error log table, we specify both the name and location where it should be created as well as the name of the table it is intended to deal with, i.e. the table whose DML will be logged into it.

```
--Create an error log table

exec dbms_errlog.create_error_log(
    dml_table_name          => 'tb_dbms_errlog',
    err_log_table_name      => 'tb_log',
    err_log_table_owner     => 'pkg',
    err_log_table_space     => 'users');
```

Now, we insert rows into the *tb_dbms_errlog* table, logging any errors. Also specify an optional tag that can be used to identify errors more easily, and an unlimited reject limit to ensure the operation succeeds no matter how many records present errors.

```
select
    count(*)
from
    tb_dbms_errlog;


  COUNT(*)
----------
         0

insert into
```

```
   tb_dbms_errlog
select
   *
from
   dba_objects
      log errors into
         tb_log('tag_27042009')
      reject limit unlimited;


49742 rows created.

commit;


Commit complete.

select
   count(*)
from
   tb_dbms_errlog;


  COUNT(*)
----------
     49742
```

Next, we select data from the *tb_log* table and confirm that no errors exist.

```
select
   count(*)
from
   tb_log;



COUNT(*)
----------
         0
```

Next, we delete some rows from the test table. This will be needed in the next step to simulate some records failing because of the primary key constraint while the others are successfully inserted.

```
delete
from
   tb_dbms_errlog
where
   object_id between 2354 and 4598;


2228 rows deleted.
```

```
commit;

Commit complete.
```

Now, let's insert all the rows again using the *log errors into table_name* syntax. As some rows exist with the same *object_id*, some errors will be generated.

```
insert into
   tb_dbms_errlog
select
   *
from
   dba_objects
      log errors into
         tb_log('tag_27042009_1')
      reject limit unlimited;


2228 rows created.

commit;

Commit complete.
```

Now it is possible to check errors generated by the *insert* command in our error log table. In this example, the ROWNUM clause was used to return less than 10 rows.

```
col "err msg"  for a60
col "err type" for a1
col "err tag"  for a15
col "obj id"   for a10

select
   t.ora_err_mesg$   "err msg",
   t.ora_err_optyp$  "err type",
   t.ora_err_tag$    "err tag",
   t.object_id       "obj id"
from
   tb_log t
where
   rownum < 10;
```

```
Err Msg                                                      E Err Tag        Obj ID
------------------------------------------------------------ - -------------- -----
ORA-00001: unique constraint (pkg.pk_obj_id10) violated      I tag_27042009_1  176
ORA-00001: unique constraint (pkg.pk_obj_id10) violated      I tag_27042009_1  177
ORA-00001: unique constraint (pkg.pk_obj_id10) violated      I tag_27042009_1  178
ORA-00001: unique constraint (pkg.pk_obj_id10) violated      I tag_27042009_1  179
ORA-00001: unique constraint (pkg.pk_obj_id10) violated      I tag_27042009_1  180
ORA-00001: unique constraint (pkg.pk_obj_id10) violated      I tag_27042009_1  181
ORA-00001: unique constraint (pkg.pk_obj_id10) violated      I tag_27042009_1  182
ORA-00001: unique constraint (pkg.pk_obj_id10) violated      I tag_27042009_1  184
ORA-00001: unique constraint (pkg.pk_obj_id10) violated      I tag_27042009_1  185
```

As seen in this *insert* operation, all the valid records have been inserted into the table and any records breaking the constraint have been automatically sent to the log table, saving both time and resources on large DML operations.

Package *dbms_iot*

Oracle Index-organized tables (IOTs) are a unique style of table structure, an alternative to the traditional "heap structure" tables. An IOT is equivalent to the highly normalized fourth-normal-form (4NF), where every row in the table is indexed.

Whenever all rows in a table are indexes, the table itself becomes redundant and the entire table data can be stored within the B-tree index structure.

Besides storing the primary key values of an Oracle indexed-organized tables row, each index entry in the B-tree also stores the non-key column values.

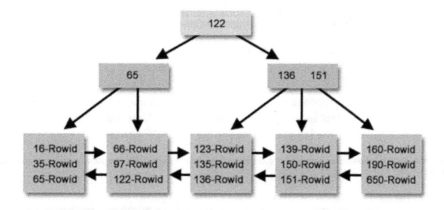

Oracle Indexed-organized tables provide faster access to table rows by the primary key or any key that is a valid prefix of the primary key. Because the non-key columns of a row are all present in the B-tree leaf block itself, there is no additional block access for index blocks.

This improves I/O, especially when the IOT is placed in a tablespace with a 32k blocksize.

For the installation of *dbms_iot*, it is necessary to execute the script *dbmsiotc.sql*. This script can be found in the *$ORACLE_HOME/rdbms/admin* directory. This package contains two procedures:

- *build_chain_rows_table*

- *build_exceptions_table*

Procedure *dbms_iot* .build_chain_rows_table

When an existing row within a table expands (from an *update* SQL statement) to the point of passing the PCTFREE threshold or *db_block_size*, another block is needed to store the row fragment. This event is called row chaining or row migration.

In order to identify these chained rows in an IOT (Index Organized Tables), we use the command *analyze* together with the package *build_chain_rows_table*. Procedure *build_chain_rows_table* creates a table to hold information about these chained rows.

Finding and repairing chained rows is an important part of the Oracle administration. When an Oracle row expands, it sometimes chains onto multiple data blocks.

> Note: Excessive row chaining can cause a dramatic increase in disk I/O because several I/Os are required to fetch the block instead of one single I/O.

This extra disk I/O dramatically affects performance. This procedure is used to create a table that will hold information about the chained rows.

Chained rows are a symptom of suboptimal IOT settings, where not enough room has been left on the data block for the rows ro grow. You must also ensure that the bocksize is larger than the largest row length for the IOT entries.

> 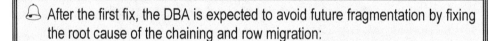 After the first fix, the DBA is expected to avoid future fragmentation by fixing the root cause of the chaining and row migration:

- *alter table … move,*
- Increase PCTFREE,
- Use IMP/EXP and do not create tables with more than 255 columns.
- Increase the tablespace *db_block_size (db_16k_block_size, db_32k_block_size)*

Some articles about how to prevent and monitor chained rows can be used at www.dba-oracle.com.

Here is an example showing a table that contains chained rows. First, the IOT table is created and rows are inserted.

Code 2.2 – dbms_iot.sql

```
conn pkg/pkg#123


connected.


create table tb_dbms_iot (
    col1 char(100) primary key,
    col2 char(100),
    col3 char(100),
    col4 char(100),
    col5 char(100))
organization index
including col2
pctthreshold 5
overflow tablespace users;


table created.


insert into
    tb_dbms_iot
        (col1)
    values
        ('a')
/


1 row created.


insert into
    tb_dbms_iot
        (col1,col2)
    values
        ('a1','b2')
    /


1 row created.


insert into
    tb_dbms_iot
        (col1,col2,col3)
    values
        ('a3','b3','c3')
/


1 row created.


insert into
    tb_dbms_iot
```

```
      (col1,col2,col3,col4)
   values
      ('a4','b4','c4','d4')
/


1 row created.


insert into
   tb_dbms_iot
      (col1,col2,col3,col4,col5)
   values
      ('a5','b5','c5','d5','e5')
/


1 row created.


commit;
```

Next, statistics are collected for this table followed by information about chained rows. Note that the *"compute statistics"* command populates the *chained_rows* column in the dba_tables view.

```
analyze table tb_dbms_iot compute statistics;

Or

exec dbms_stats.gather_table_stats (tabname => 'tb_dbms_iot');


Table analyzed.


--Information about chained rows
select
   chain_cnt,
   round(chain_cnt/num_rows*100,2) pct_chained,
   avg_row_len, pct_free , pct_used
from
   user_tables
 where
    table_name = 'tb_dbms_iot';


CHAIN_CNT PCT_CHAINED AVG_ROW_LEN   PCT_FREE   PCT_USED
--------- ----------- ----------- ---------- ----------
        3          60         313          0          0

select
   num_rows,
   chain_cnt
```

```
from
   dba_tables
where
   table_name='tb_dbms_iot';


 NUM_ROWS  CHAIN_CNT
---------- ----------
        5          3
```

Now, using package *dbms_iot*, (the table that records chained rows) is created and then their statistics are collected.

```
execute dbms_iot.build_chain_rows_table(
   owner                   => 'pkg',
   iot_name                => 'tb_dbms_iot',
   chainrow_table_name     => 'tab_iot_chained_rows');


.


-- Populate chained rows table

analyze table tb_dbms_iot list chained rows into tab_iot_chained_rows;


Table analyzed.
```

Finally, the information about chained rows is collected with the query below.

```
col owner name for a10
col col1 for a10
col cluster_name for a10
col partition_name for a10
col subpartition_name for a10
set linesize 200
set pagesize 100

select
   owner_name,
   table_name,
   timestamp,
   col1
from
   tab_iot_chained_rows;
```

OWNER_NAME	TABLE_NAME	TIMESTAMP	COL1
pkg	tb_dbms_iot	4/26/2009 1	a3
pkg	tb_dbms_iot	4/26/2009 1	a4

Remember, locating and repairing chained rows fixes a symptom and it does not fix the root cause of the row chaining. Remember, in order to eliminate and prevent chained rows and migration rows, you need to execute one of the following procedures to adjust for anticipated future row expansion:

- *alter table ... move*

- Increase PCTFREE

- Move table into a tablespace with a larger blocksize

- Imp/Exp

- Avoid tables with more than 255 columns

- Take advantage of *utlchain* or *dbms_iot*, select chained records into a temporary table, delete them, and insert them back.

Procedure *dbms_iot build_exceptions_table*

When a referiential integrity constraint is created or enabled in a table, the process will abort if one of the rows violates the constraint. In order to prevent an operation such as *alter table ... enable/add constraint* from failing with a runtime exception, we can use the *build_exceptions_table* procedure. This procedure creates an error table where records that violate a constraint being created/enabled are held. That makes it easier to fix the bad data and re-load it later.

A very common scenario where an exceptions table is very useful is when a batch load needs to be put into an IOT table. Before that, the decision may be made to disable some constraints to boost the performance of this process. At the time of enabling these constraints, after the load this procedure could be used to record rows that had violated any constraints that were being enabled.

Thus, check this exception table to gather more information about these rows. Let's create the test table named *tb_dbms_iot_excpt* and populate it with some rows to simulate the constraint error.

🖫 Code 2.3 – dbms_iot_build_exceptions_table.sql

```
conn pkg/pkg#123

Connected.

create table
    tb_dbms_iot_excpt (
```

```
   object_id    number,
   object_name    varchar2(128),
   object_type    varchar2(20),
   status varchar2(10),
   primary key(object_id, object_name))
   organization index pctthreshold 10 overflow;

Table created.

insert into
   tb_dbms_iot_excpt
select
   object_id,
   object_name,
   object_type,status
from
   dba_objects
where
   rownum < 1000;

999 rows created.

commit;

Commit complete.
```

Now, let's invalidate some rows so the constraint that is added will have some errors.

```
update
   tb_dbms_iot_excpt
set
   status='invalid'
where
   rownum < 100;

99 rows updated.

commit;

Commit complete.
```

Next, the package *build_exceptions_table* is executed and table exceptions named *tab_iot_exceptions* are created to store the exceptions rows.

```
exec dbms_iot.build_exceptions_table(
   owner                   => 'pkg',
   iot_name                => 'tb_dbms_iot_excpt',
   exceptions_table_name   => 'tab_iot_exceptions');
```

```
select
   count(*)
from
   tab_iot_exceptions;

  COUNT(*)
----------
         0
```

Below, the check constraint fails and the rows responsible for this failure are inserted into the *tab_iot_exceptions* table.

```
alter table
   tb_dbms_iot_excpt
add constraint
   ck_stat
check (status='valid')
exceptions into
   tab_iot_exceptions;

alter table tb_dbms_iot_excpt add constraint ck_stat check (status='valid')
exceptions into  tab_iot_exceptions


ERROR at line 1:

ORA-02293: cannot validate (pkg.ck_stat) - check constraint violated
```

Finally, see the failure rows in exceptions table *tab_iot_exceptions*.

```
col owner        for a10
col table_name   for a20
col constraint   for a10
col object_id    for 9999
col object_name  for a30

set linesize 200
set pagesize 100

select
   *
from
   tab_iot_exceptions;

ROW_ID       OWNER      TABLE_NAME           CONSTRAINT OBJECT_ID OBJECT_NAME
---------- ---------- -------------------- ---------- --------- --------------
             pkg        tb_dbms_iot_excpt    ck_stat         248 i_rgchild
             pkg        tb_dbms_iot_excpt    ck_stat         249 duc$
             pkg        tb_dbms_iot_excpt    ck_stat         250 i_duc
             pkg        tb_dbms_iot_excpt    ck_stat         251 c_obj#_intcol#
    .
    .
    .
```

The table *tab_iot_exceptions* has information about rows that have violated some constraint of the *tb_dbms_iot_excp* table.

Package *dbms_lob*

Starting in Oracle8, Oracle recognized that a tablespace mist be able to store much more than just text and numbers. A sophisticated database must also be able to store images, videos, maps; all tyes of unstructured data.

The LOB data type allows holding and manipulating unstructured data such as texts, graphic images, video sound files. The *dbms_lob* package was designed to manipulate LOB data types. Oracle provides the *dbms_lob* package which is used to access and manipulate LOB values in both internal or external storage locations.

With this package *dbms_lob*, it is possible to read and modify given BLOB, CLOB and NLOB types as well as effecting operations of reading in BFILEs. The types of data used for package *dbms_lob* include:

- BLOB
- RAW
- CLOB
- VARCHAR2
- INTEGER
- BFILE

It is important to remember that the maximum size for a data type LOB is 8 TB for databases with blocks of 8k, and 128 TB for databases configured with blocks of 32k. Package *dbms_lob* contains procedures that are used to manipulate segments of type LOB (BLOBs, CLOBs and NCLOBs) and BFILEs.

The two different types of LOBs are:

- **Internal LOBs (inline):** They are the LOBs stored inside of the database in a way that optimizes performance and supplies an efficient access environment, taking advantage of Oracle Database security and reliability features. These can be persistent or temporary types.
- **External LOBS (BFILE):** LOBs stored in an external location, as in an operating system file. The database itself holds an internal reference to the

external file(s), enabling access to each external file's data via SQL (data type BFILE).

Below is a list containing some of the main procedures and functions that are presented in this package and what they do.

- **isopen:** This function checks to see if the LOB was already opened using the input locator.

- **createtemporary:** The procedure *createtemporary* creates a temporary CLOB or BLOB and its corresponding index in the user default temporary tablespace.

- **instr:** Used to return the matching position of the nth occurrence of the pattern in the LOB.

- **getlength:** Used to get the length of specified LOB.

- **copy:** Copies part or all of a source internal LOB to a destination internal LOB.

- **writeappend:** Writes a specified amount of data to the end of an internal LOB.

- **trim:** Trims the value of the internal LOB to the length specified by the *newlen* parameter.

Here is how to perform, search and replace in a CLOB with some procedures of the *dbms_lob* package. First, create the test table and insert some rows.

⊞ Code 2.4 – dbms_lob.sql

```
Conn pkg/pkg#123

Connected to Oracle 11g Enterprise Edition Release 11.1.0.6.0
Connected as pkg

drop table
    tab_dbms_lob_search
purge
/

Table dropped

create table tab_dbms_lob_search(
    clob_id number,
    c clob
);

Table created

insert into
    tab_dbms_lob_search
values
    (1,'Oracle Database 7i,8i,9i and 10g')
/
```

```
1 row inserted
insert into
   tab_dbms_lob_search
values
   (2,'Oracle Database 7i,8i,9i and 10g')
/

1 row inserted

commit
/

Commit complete
```

Let's create a procedure that uses the *dbms_lob* package to search and replace text within a LOB (CLOB, BLOB).

🖫 Code 2.5 – search_n_replace_text_lob.sql

```
create or replace procedure
   proc_dbms_lob_search_rep(
lob_local    in out clob,
      srch_string varchar2,
      rep_string  varchar2) as
temp_clob       clob;
end_offset      integer := 1;
start_offset    integer := 1;
nth      number := 1;
rep_string_len number := length(rep_string);
temp_clob_len  number := 0;
lob_local_len  number := 0;

begin
    if lob_local is NULL then
      raise_application_error(-20001, 'LOB is empty. You need to execute
inserts first!');
    end if;


    --The function isopen check to see if the LOB was already opened using
the input locator
    if dbms_lob.isopen(
         lob_local) = 0
    dbms_output.put_line(' LOB is open!');

    then
      null;
    dbms_output.put_line(' LOB is closed!');

    end if;

    --The procedure create temporary creates a temporary CLOB
    dbms_lob.createtemporary(
```

```
        temp_clob,
        TRUE,
        dbms_lob.session);

LOOP
        -- The function instr returns the matching position of the nth
occurrence of
        --the pattern in the LOB, starting from the offset you specify.

        end_offset := dbms_lob.instr(lob_local, srch_string, 1, nth);
        if end_offset = 0
    then
        temp_clob_len := dbms_lob.getlength(temp_clob);
        lob_local_len := dbms_lob.getlength(lob_local) - start_offset + 1;

        if lob_local_len > 0
        then
        --The procedure copy copies all, or a part of, a source internal
LOB to a destination internal LOB.
            dbms_lob.copy(
                temp_clob,
                lob_local,
                lob_local_len,
                temp_clob_len + 1,
                start_offset);
        end if;
        exit;
        end if;
        --The function getlength gets the length of the specified LOB.
        temp_clob_len := dbms_lob.getlength(temp_clob);
        if (end_offset - start_offset) > 0
        then
          dbms_lob.copy(
                temp_clob,
                lob_local,
                (end_offset - start_offset),
                temp_clob_len + 1,
                start_offset);
        end if;
        start_offset := end_offset + length(srch_string);
        nth     := nth + 1;

        if rep_string is not null then

    --The procedure writeappend writes a specified amount of data to the end
of an internal LOB.

        dbms_lob.writeappend(
            temp_clob,
            rep_string_len,
            rep_string);
        end if;
    end loop;
    if length(srch_string) > length(rep_string) then
        --The procedure trim trims the value of the internal LOB to the
length you specify in the
        --newlen parameter
        dbms_lob.trim(
          lob_loc => lob_local,
```

```
            newlen  =>  dbms_lob.getlength(
                          temp_clob)
         );
      end if;
      dbms_lob.copy(
          lob_local,
          temp_clob,
          dbms_lob.getlength(temp_clob), 1, 1);
   end;
 /

Procedure created

--Check for errors
show errors

No errors for procedure pkg.proc_dbms_lob_search_rep
```

This procedure executed the following steps:

1. First, it finds the position of the first occurrence of the searched text.

2. Then it creates a temporary NCLOB, copies everything from the original NCLOB to it up to the point where it found the text to be replaced, and appends the new text.

3. Now, it trims the temporary NCLOB to keep only what came after the word to replace.

Now let's look at the table results to see how they are before the search and replace process.

```
select
   *
from
   tab_dbms_lob_search;

   CLOB_ID C
---------- ------------------------------------------------------------
         1 Oracle Database 7i,8i,9i and 10g
         2 Oracle Database 7i,8i,9i and 10g
```

Call the procedure to change the value for the first row only (*clob_id*=1).

```
declare
     lob_local clob;
   begin
     select c
         into lob_local
     from
tab_dbms_lob_search
```

```
      where
clob_id = 1
      for update;
      proc_dbms_lob_search_rep(
          lob_local   => lob_local,
          srch_string =>  ' and 10g',
          rep_string  =>  ' ,10g and 11g ');
      commit;
  end;
 /
```

The results below show the new replaced text.

```
select
    *
from
    tab_dbms_lob_search
 /


CLOB_ID   C
------ ------------------------------------------------------------
      1 Oracle Database 7i,8i,9i ,10g and 11g
      2 Oracle Database 7i,8i,9i and 10g
```

In the preceding example, the following procedures and functions were used: *isopen, createtemporary, instr, getlength, copy* and *trim*.

Package *dbms_lob dbms_pclxutil*

Creating an index on large tables is a slow operation that can take days on a non-partitioned table. In order to expedite this process, the *dbms_pclxutil* package was created to offer the creation of local indexes in partitioned tables using a high degree of parallelism. On server with 16, 32, 64 or 128 CPU's, *dbms_pclxutil* greatly improves the performance of the index building process.

The *dbms_pclxutil* procedure is used in cases where there are large partitioned tables and local indices need to be created on these tables. Through the *build_part_index* procedure, the user can create these indexes using parallelism. The *dbms_pclxutil* is an alternative to a *parallel* hint.

With today's RAID-0+1 standard, the optimal degree of parallelism is impossible to prredict and the faster resinse rime with different DEGREE settings musty be determined by testing. A suggested starting value for parallel degree is *cpu_count-1*, which saves one background process for the parallel query coordinator. The *cpu_count* parameter is set at installation time when Oracle checks the number of processors on the database server.

Because of Oracle's commitment to be first to market, many new Oracle features, they are introduced far ahead of their time. Oracle Parallel Query (OPQ) was introduced over a decade ago, back in the stone age of data processing when few servers had symmetric multiprocessing (SMP) capabilities, and a server with 4 or more CPU processors was very rare.

Parallelism was first created to accelerate the operations performed in large partitioned tables. The use of parallelism in the creation of local indices of partitioned tables saves the DBA time because several parallel processes are executed in the creation of an index rather than only one process.

Below is an example indicating how to use the *build_part_index* procedure. First, create a partitioned table.

🖫 Code 2.6 – dbms_pclxutil.sql

```
conn pkg/pkg#123

create table pkg.table_partition(
    owner           varchar2(30),
    object_name     varchar2(128),
    subobject_name  varchar2(30),
    object_id       number,
    data_object_id  number,
    object_type     varchar2(19),
    created         date,
    last_ddl_time   date,
    timestamp       varchar2(19),
    status          varchar2(7),
    temporary       varchar2(1),
    generated       varchar2(1),
    secondary       varchar2(1)
    )
    storage ( initial 5120 k ) nologging parallel 2
    partition by range (created)
    (
  partition ar_t01 values less than (to_date('01-dec-2004','dd-mon-  yyyy'))
tablespace users,
  partition ar_t02 values less than (to_date('01-dec-2005','dd-mon-yyyy'))
tablespace users,
  partition ar_t03 values less than (to_date('01-dec-2006','dd-mon-yyyy'))
tablespace users,
  partition ar_t04 values less than (to_date('01-dec-2007','dd-mon-yyyy'))
tablespace users,
  partition ar_t05 values less than (to_date('01-dec-2008','dd-mon-yyyy'))
tablespace users,
  partition ar_t06 values less than (to_date('01-dec-2009','dd-mon-yyyy'))
tablespace users,
  partition ar_t07 values less than (to_date('01-dec-2010','dd-mon-yyyy'))
tablespace users
);
```

Now we populate the table with sample data.

```
insert into
```

```
    pkg.table_partition
select
    *
from
    dba_objects;
```

Now, we create an index using the *unusable* option just to add index information to the dictionary.

```
drop index pkg.idx_tab_1
/
create index
    pkg.idx_tab_1
on
    pkg.table_partition (created)
tablespace
    users
local unusable;

--If the index already exists, change this to unusable
alter index
    pkg.idx_tab_1
unusable;

--Check status of index created
select
    index_name,
    status,
    last_analyzed
from
    dba_ind_partitions
where
    index_name = 'idx_tab_1';
```

Next, let's rebuild the index using four jobs with the procedure *build_part_index*.

```
exec dbms_pclxutil.build_part_index(
        jobs_per_batch     => 2,
        procs_per_job           => 4,
        tab_name           => 'table_partition',
        idx_name           => 'idx_tab_1',
        force_opt          => FALSE)
/

--Look at job created
select
    log_user,
    schema_user,
    what
from
    dba_jobs;
```

```
LOG_USER    SCHEMA_USER    WHAT
--------    -----------    -----------------------------------------
pkg         pkg            dbms_utility.exec_ddl_statement('alter index
"pkg"."idx_tab_1" rebuild partition "ar_t01" parallel (degree 4)');


--Check status of index again
select
    index_name,
    status,
    last_analyzed
from
    dba_ind_partitions
where
    index_name = 'idx_tab_1'
```

As we see when rebuilding indexes in partitioned tables, package *dbms_pclxutil* provides faster response time by allowing the use of a high degree of parallelism in this task.

Of course, to experience the most benefits from this technique, the server must have enough free spare resources to physically perform this task in parallel.

To get the most from it, it is desirable to have at least as many CPU cores as processes as are intended to run in parallel, and to have the index and table data stored over several hard drives.

Be careful because if the server does not have enough resource parallelism, it may indeed adversely affect performance. Remember, parallelism only works with Enterprise Edition databases.

Package *dbms_lob dbms_redefinition*

Back in the 1990's DBA's has the luxury of taking a database offline to reorganize the tables. However, in today;'s 24x7 environment, we need tools to do maintenance while the database remains available.

The package *dbms_redefinition* allows the redefinition and/or the reorganization of tables while the database remains online and accepting updates.

Rebuilding a table while it is accepting updates is a complex task, and the *dbms_redefinition* package uses materialized views and snapshot logs in order to maintain the updates while the redefinition operation is being executed.

The reorganization process is illustrated here:

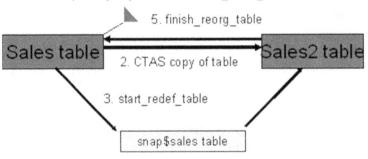

Figure 2.1: *Reorganization Process*

It is important to note that the package *dbms_redefinition* may be used to redefine the structure of a table while simultaneously arranging for its reorganization online when DML operations are executed on the package.

Lastly, this information is used by the *dbms_redefinition* package to refresh the synchronization by applying the snapshot logs to maintain both the changes related to the reorganization and any changes other sessions may have requested to the table during the online reorganization process. Sure, it may seem complex at first.

Fortunately, the *dbms_redefinition* package provides a very simple and useful front end and internally performs most of these tasks. thus saving the user from having to do any complex manual intervention. Unfortunately, it is only available with Enterprise Edition.

There has been an ongoing debate about the value of periodic rebuilding of tables and indexes along two dimensions:

1. **Reclaimed storage:** The Oracle 10g segment advisor identifies tables and indexes that have become sparse as a result of high DML as a candidate for rebuilding.

2. **Improved speed:** There are documented cases where rebuilding a table or index reduces consistent gets and makes the SQL run faster, but this workload feature is not yet in the Oracle 10g segment advisor.

There are eight procedures in the package *dbms_redefinition*:

- *abort_redef_table*

- *can_redef_table*

- *copy_table_dependents*

- *finish_redef_table*

- *register_dependent_object*

- *start_redef_table*

- *sync_interim_table*

- *unregister_dependent_object*

The *dbms_redefinition* package allows copying a table using Create Table As (CTAS), creating a snapshot on the table, enqueuing changes during the redefinition, and then re-synchronizing the restructured table with the changes that have accumulated during reorganization.

The following is a practical example presented to make a reorganization using the package *dbms_redefinition*. Create the table *table_redefinition* to be used as an example and an index named *idx_tab_redef*.

🖫 Code 2.7 – dbms_redefinition.sql

```
conn pkg/pkg#123

Connected to Oracle 11g Enterprise Edition Release 11.1.0.6.0
Connected as pkg

create table pkg.table_redefinition
tablespace
   pkg_data as
 select
    prod_id,
    prod_name,
    prod_desc,
    prod_category,
    prod_subcategory,
    prod_category_id
 from
    sh.products;

Table created

create index
   idx_tab_redef
on
   table_redefinition (prod_category)
tablespace
   pkg_idx;

Index created
```

The procedure *can_redef_table* is used to check whether the table can be redefined or reorganized. Note that error *ORA-12089* appears because the table does not have a primary key yet.

```
execute dbms_redefinition.can_redef_table(
      uname => 'pkg',
      tname => 'table_redefinition');

begin dbms_redefinition.can_redef_table(
      uname => 'pkg',
      tname => 'table_redefinition');
end;

ORA-12089: cannot online redefine table "pkg"."table_redefinition" with no
primary key
ORA-06512: at "sys.dbms_redefinition", line 139
ORA-06512: at "sys.dbms_redefinition", line 1766
ORA-06512: at line 1
```

Create a primary key and now the package will work on this table.

```
alter table
   pkg.table_redefinition
add constraint
   pk_obj_id
primary key
   (prod_id)
;
```

Next, we execute the check again.

If it completes successfully, the table is available to reorganize.

```
exec dbms_redefinition.can_redef_table(
      uname => 'pkg',
      tname => 'table_redefinition');
```

Now we create the temporary "snapshot" table that will receive changed data during the redefinition process using different column names for the example and another tablespace (reorg).

```
create table pkg.temp_redefinition (
      prod_id_diff            number(6)       NOT NULL,
      prod_name_diff          varchar2(50)    NOT NULL,
      prod_desc               varchar2(4000)  NOT NULL,
      prod_category           varchar2(50)    NOT NULL,
      prod_subcategory_diff   varchar2(50)    NOT NULL,
      prod_category_id        number          NOT NULL
   )
   partition by list (prod_category_id)
   (
   partition p1 values (201),
   partition p2 values (202),
   partition p3 values (203),
   partition p4 values (204),
   partition p5 values (205))
```

```
tablespace pkg_data_32m;


Table created
```

Now we are ready to start the *redefinition* process.

```
execute dbms_redefinition.start_redef_table(
        uname              => 'pkg',
        orig_table  => 'table_redefinition',
        int_table   => 'temp_ redefinition ',
        col_mapping        => 'prod_id prod_id_diff,prod_name
prod_name_diff,
prod_desc prod_desc,prod_category prod_category,prod_subcategory
prod_subcategory_diff,prod_category_id prod_category_id ',
        options_flag       => dbms_redefinition.cons_use_pk);
```

The commands being internally executed by the *dbms_redefinition* package can be checked in the *v$sqlarea* view.

```
select
   sql_text
from
   v$sqlarea
where
   sql_text like '%temp_redefinition%';
```

```
SQL_TEXT
--------------------------------------------------------------------------------
insert into "pkg"."temp_redefinition"("prod_id_diff","prod_name_diff","prod_desc
select sql_text from v$sqlarea where sql_text like '%temp_redefinition%'
begin dbms_redefinition.finish_redef_table(uname => 'pkg',orig_table => 'table_r
insert /*+ bypass_recursive_check append */ into "pkg"."temp_redefinition"("pro
begin dbms_redefinition.start_redef_table(uname => 'pkg',orig_table => 'table_re
update "pkg"."temp_redefinition" set "prod_id_diff" = :1,"prod_name_diff" = :2,"
insert into "pkg"."temp_redefinition"  ("prod_id_diff","prod_name_diff","prod_de
delete from "pkg"."temp_redefinition" snap$ where "prod_id_diff" = :1
lock table "pkg"."temp_redefinition" in exclusive mode  nowait

9 rows selected
```

To see which objects are being reorganized, use the sample below.

```
select
   *
from
   dba_redefinition_objects;
```

```
OBJECT_TYPE  OBJECT_OWNER
OBJECT_NAME                  BASE_TABLE_OWNER            BASE_TABLE_NAME
INTERIM_OBJECT_OWNER                                            INTERIM_OBJECT_NAME
EDITION_NAME
-----------  --------------------------------------------------------------------- -------
-------------------- -------------------------- ------------------------------- ---------------
------------------------------------------------------------- ------------------------------- ----
--------------------------
```

```
table          pkg
table_redefinition          pkg                    table_redefinition          pkg
temp_redefinition
```

Now, let's check the interim table and the original table.

```
select
   count(*)
from
   pkg.temp_redefinition;

  COUNT(*)
----------
        72

select
   count(*)
from
   pkg.table_redefinition;

  COUNT(*)
----------
        72
```

To ensure that the redefinition is including changed rows, let's make some changes to the original table.

```
delete
from
   pkg.table_redefinition
where
   prod_id=33
/

1 row deleted

commit
/

Commit complete

select
   count(*)
from
   pkg.temp_redefinition
/

  COUNT(*)
----------
        72

select
   count(*)
from
   pkg.table_redefinition
/
```

```
   COUNT(*)
----------
        71

commit
/

Commit complete
```

Alternately, intermediate changes can be synced with the interim table.

```
exec dbms_redefinition.sync_interim_table(
     uname          => 'pkg',
     orig_table     => 'table_redefinition',
     int_table      => 'temp_redefinition');


--Check count(*) rows again
select
   count(*)
from
   pkg.temp_redefinition
/

   COUNT(*)
----------
        71
select
   count(*)
from
   pkg.table_redefinition
/

   COUNT(*)
----------
        71
```

The final step performs one of the most critical and easily forgotten steps, to create any required triggers, indexes, materialized view logs, grants, and/or constraints on the newly reorganized table, probably using the *dbms_metadata*, package to generate the DDL for these ancilliary objects.

Using *dbms_metadata*, look how easy it is to copy all dependent objects with just a single call to *dbms_redefinition*.

```
declare
     num_err pls_integer;
     begin
```

```
    num_err := 0 ;
    dbms_redefinition.copy_table_dependents(
        uname              => 'pkg',
        orig_table             => 'table_redefinition',
        int_table          => 'temp_ redefinition ',
          copy_indexes   => 1,
          copy_triggers  => TRUE,
          copy_constraints        => TRUE,
          copy_privileges         => TRUE,
          copy_statistics         => TRUE,
          copy_mvlog              => TRUE,
          num_errors              => num_err);
 end;
/

declare
  num_err pls_integer ;
  begin
  num_err := 0 ;
  dbms_redefinition.copy_table_dependents (uname => 'pkg',orig_table => '
table _ redefinition ',int_table => 'temp_ redefinition ',copy_indexes =>
1,copy_triggers => TRUE,copy_constraints => TRUE,copy_privileges =>
TRUE,copy_statistics => TRUE,copy_mvlog => TRUE,num_errors => num_err);
  end;


ORA-00904: "prod_id": invalid identifier
ORA-06512: at "sys.dbms_redefinition", line 1361
ORA-06512: at "sys.dbms_redefinition", line 2009
ORA-06512: at line 5
```

To see the redefinition errors, use the following sample.

```
select
    *
from
    dba_redefinition_errors
/
```

```
OBJECT_TYPE  OBJECT_OWNER
OBJECT_NAME                   BASE_TABLE_OWNER            BASE_TABLE_NAME              DDL_TXT
EDITION_NAME
------------ --------------------------------------------------------------------------------- -------
-------------------- ----------------------------- ----------------------------- ---------------
----------------------------------------------------------------- -----------------------------
index       pkg
pk_obj_id               pkg                              table_redefinition          create
unique index "pkg"."tmp$$_ pk_obj_id0" ON "pkg"."temp_ redefinition " ("prod
index       pkg
pk_obj_id               pkg                              table_ redefinition         create
unique index "pkg"."tmp$$_pk_obj_id0" ON "PKG"."temp_ redefinition " ("prod
```

Here, we create an index and constraint on an interim table.

```
alter table
    temp_redefinition
add constraint
```

```
   ck_price
check (prod_id_diff > 0);

Table altered

create index
   idx_prod_sub
on
   temp_redefinition (prod_subcategory_diff)
tablespace
   pkg_idx_32m;

Index created
```

Next we create the same primary key, but with a different name.

```
alter table
   pkg.temp_redefinition
add constraint
   pk_obj_id1
primary key (prod_id_diff);
```

And here we finish the reorganization process with the *finish_redef_table* procedure.

```
exec dbms_redefinition.finish_redef_table(
   uname          => 'pkg',
   orig_table     => 'table_redefinition',
   int_table      => 'temp_ redefinition ');

--Check new table redefined
desc table_redefinition
```

Name	Type	Nullable	Default	Comments
prod_id_diff	number(6)			
prod_name_diff	varchar2(50)			
prod_desc	varchar 2(4000)			
prod_category	varchar 2(50)			
prod_dubcategory_ diff	varchar 2(50)			
prod_category_id	number			

```
select
   owner,
   segment_name,
   tablespace_name
from
   dba_segments
where
   segment_name in ('table_redefinition','idx_prod_sub')/
```

```
OWNER                       SEGMENT_NAME              TABLESPACE_NAME
--------------------------- ------------------------- -------------------------------------------
pkg                         id_prod_sub               pkg_idx_32M
pkg                         table_redefinition        pkg_data_32M
pkg                         table_redefinition        pkg_data_32M
pkg                         table_redefinition        pkg_data_32M
pkg                         table_redefinition        pkg_data_32M
pkg                         table_redefinition        pkg_data_32M
```

```
select
   index_name
from
   dba_indexes
where
   table_name='table_redefinition'
/

select
   index_name
from
   dba_indexes
where
   table_name='table_redefinition';
```

ORA-00942: table or view does not exist

```
select
   owner,
   constraint_name,
   constraint_type,
   table_name,
   search_condition,
   index_name
from
   dba_constraints
where
   table_name='table_redefinition'/
```

```
OWNER       CONSTRAINT_NAME      CONSTRAINT_TYPE TABLE_NAME        SEARCH_CONDITION INDEX_NAME
----------- -------------------- --------------- ----------------------------- -
pkg         ck_price    C table_redefinition      prod_id_diff > 0
pkg         SYS_C009932 C table_redefinition      "prod_category_id" is not NULL
pkg         SYS_C009931 C table_redefinition      "prod_subcategory_diff" is not NULL
pkg         SYS_C009930 C table_redefinition      "prod_category" is not NULL
pkg         SYS_C009929 C table_redefinition      "prod_desc" is not NULL
pkg         SYS_C009928 C table_redefinition      "prod_name_diff" is not NULL
pkg         SYS_C009927 C table_redefinition      "prod_id_diff" is not NULL
pkg         pk_obj_id1  P table_redefinition       pk_obj_id1

8 rows selected
```

```
select
   index_name
from
   dba_indexes
where
   table_name= table_redefinition'
/
```

```
select
   index_name
from
   dba_indexes
where
   table_name='table_redefinition';

ORA-00942: table or view does not exist

select
   index_name
from
   dba_indexes
where
   table_name='table_redefinition'
/


INDEX_NAME
------------------------------
idx_tab_redef
idx_prod_sub
pk_obj_id1
```

If the reorganization fails, you will need to take special steps to restart it. Because the redefinition requires creating a snapshot, upon an abort you need to execute *dbms_redefinition.abort_redef_table* to release the snapshot to restart the procedure. The *dbms_redefinition.abort_redef_table* procedure accepts three parameters, e.g. schema, original table name, and holding table name, and "pops the stack", allowing the DBA to start over.

Package *dbms_rowid*

The *dbms_rowid* package allows us to create *rowid*s and obtain information about *rowid*s that are already created. This might include the object number or the data block number, and the *dbms_rowid* package allows us to see this information without having to write any additional code.

Displaying a *rowid* is useful for identifying which row is being locked by a session and not just the object that is being locked, which is information usually acquired through views such as *v$lock*, *v$locked_objects*, the script *utllockt.sql* and others.

> **Beware:** Oracle *rowid*'s are not permanent, and they may change as a result of table reorganization, table coalescing, and row relocation.

All tables of the Oracle database have one pseudo column called *rowid*.

Just like your home address indicates where you live, a unique address call a *rowid* is used for each row of each table of the database is created, using the file number, data block number and offest into the data block.

The *rowid* column holds the data block that contains definitive information, the line inside of the data block, the database file that has the line and the data object number. The *rowid* can be easily manipulated with the Oracle *dbms_rowid* package.

There are also "old rowids", leftovers from Oracle when a change was mnade to the roiwid storage method. Old *rowid*s, also called *restricted rowid*s, will be automatically converted to the new *rowid* format if:

- Export/import is used to move data
- The migration utility is used
- The ODMA is used to upgrade to 9i

If *rowid*s are used in an Oracle 7 application and stored as columns in other tables, then these columns will have to be manually changed to the new format using the Oracle *dbms_rowid* package. If a column in a table has been designated as a datatype of *rowid*, it will be altered to accept the new format during migration; this will not affect the data in the column.

When an index in a table is created, the Oracle database uses *rowid* to construct the index, using pairs of symbolic keys and *rowid's*.

Each key of the index points to one definitive *rowid* associated to the address of a line in the table, supplying fast access to the register. *rowid* also can be used for tasks such as access to particular lines (rows); verification of how the table is organized; exportation of lines specified in the set with the *export* (*expdp*) utility; verification of which line is being locked for a session; and verification of the space really used by one table.

The code of this package is found in the *dbmsutil.sql* script and it is called by *catproc.sql* in the creation of the database. A public synonym is created for the package by this script and the *execute* privilege is granted to *public*. The package *dbms_rowid* contains only one procedure and ten functions. The following are examples on how to make use of the functions and procedures of the package *dbms_rowid*.

So, how can we find the block number of a row? This information is useful when the block that is corrupted is known and from which line this block belongs needs to be found.

For example, some advanced recovery techniques from 10g and beyond allow the DBA to easily recover corrupt blocks from a backup using RMAN while the rest of the database remains open, and then apply all redo information to make these blocks consistent, all with minimum impact to the end users.

If a situation like this ever comes up where a few blocks are corrupt, Oracle will provide the block information along with the error message so that information is actually present. RMAN manuals can be found at tahiti.oracle.com.

However, for the purpose of this example, a sample block address is obtained with the following procedure just to show what it is like. First, the block number of a single row using *rowid_block_number* will be returned by this query.

🖫 Code 2.8 – dbms_rowid.sql

```
conn pkg/pkg#123

Connected to Oracle 11g Enterprise Edition Release 11.1.0.6.0
Connected as pkg

select
   dbms_rowid.rowid_block_number(rowid)
from
   table_redefinition
where
   prod_id_diff=14;

DBMS_rowid.rowid_BLOCK_NUMBER(
------------------------------
                          8267
```

Once the *rowid_block_number* procedure shows the block number, use the *rowid_object* procedure to get the *rowid* of the object. The query below shows all of the *rowid* information including object, file, block and row:

```
select
   substr(rowid,1,6)  "object",
   substr(rowid,7,3)  "file",
   substr(rowid,10,6) "block",
   substr(rowid,16,3) "row"
from
   table_redefinition;

object file block  row
------ ---- ------ ---
AAARbV AAJ  AAAABL AAM
AAARbV AAJ  AAAABL AAD
AAARbV AAJ  AAAABL AAE
AAARbV AAJ  AAAABL AAF
 ...
 ...
 ...
```

Then the *rowid* object number is determined by using the procedure *rowid_object* of the package *dbms_rowid*.

```
set serveroutput on
  declare
     object_no integer;
     row_id    rowid;
  begin
     select
        rowid
     into
        row_id
     from
        table_redefinition
     where
        prod_id_diff = 13;
     object_no := dbms_rowid.rowid_object(row_id);
     dbms_output.put_line(
        'Here is the object rowid number: ' || object_no);
  end;
/

Here is the object rowid number: 71384
```

The example above shows the object number. We can check it using the query below to compare the values.

```
col object_name for a20
select
   object_id,
   data_object_id,
   object_name,
   object_type
from
   dba_objects
where
   data_object_id=71384;

OBJECT_ID  DATA_OBJECT_ID OBJECT_NAME          OBJECT_TYPE
---------- -------------- -------------------- --------------------
    71384          71384 table_redefinition   table partition
```

An alternate way to get *rowid_object* is shown below:

```
   select
      dbms_rowid.rowid_object(rowid)
   from
      table_redefinition
   where
      prod_id_diff = 14;

DBMS_rowid.rowid_OBJECT(rowid)
------------------------------
```

Next, a *rowid* is created for test purposes only. Note that this should not be used because the Oracle server will create valid *rowid*s automatically.

```
--Restricted rowid - binary format (row_type=0)

  --Check the objeto_id
select
  owner,
  object_name,
  object_type,
  object_id
from
  dba_objects
where
  object_id='71385';
OWNER                        OBJECT_NAME             OBJECT_TYPE                          OBJECT_ID
---------------------------- ----------------------- -------------------------------------------------pkg
table_redefinition    table partition                     71385


    select dbms_rowid.rowid_create(rowid_type    => 0,
                                   object_number => 71385,
                                   relative_fno  => 9,
                                   block_number  => 16393,
                                   row_number    => 1)
    from dual;

DBMS_rowid.rowid_CREATE(rowid_
------------------------------
00004009.0001.0009

  --Extended rowid - Hexadecimal format(row_type=1)
    select
       dbms_rowid.rowid_create(
          rowid_type     => 1,
          object_number  => 71385,
          relative_fno   => 9,
          block_number   => 16393,
          row_number     => 1)
    from
       dual;

DBMS_rowid.rowid_CREATE(rowid_
------------------------------
AAARbZAAJAAAEAJAAB
```

The *dbms_rowid* procedure *rowid_info* can be used to return information like *rowid* type, *object_id*, datafile number, block id and row number. One example of *rowid_info* is shown below:

```
  declare
     row_id        rowid;
     rowid_type    number;
     object_id     number;
```

```
        datafile_num number;
        block_id     number;
        row_number   number;
     begin
        row_id := dbms_rowid.rowid_create(1, 71385, 9, 16393, 1);
        dbms_rowid.rowid_info(row_id,
                              rowid_type,
                              object_id,
                              datafile_num,
                              block_id,
                              row_number);
        dbms_output.put_line('rowid:           ' || row_id);
        dbms_output.put_line('Object ID:       ' || object_id);
        dbms_output.put_line('Datafile Number:' || datafile_num);
        dbms_output.put_line('Block ID:        ' || block_id);
        dbms_output.put_line('Row Number:      ' || row_number);
     end;
/
```

```
rowid:            AAARbZAAJAAAEAJAAB
Object ID:        71385
Datafile Number:9
Block ID:         16393
Row Number:       1
```

Note that the above procedure returns the datafile where the object is located using the function *rowid_relative_fno*.

```
  select
     dbms_rowid.rowid_relative_fno(rowid)  "Datafile Number"
  from
     table_redefinition
  where
     prod_id_diff = 14;
```

```
Datafile Number
---------------
              9
```

Return the row number of *rowid* using the function *rowid_row_number*.

```
  select
     dbms_rowid.rowid_row_number(rowid)
  from
     table_redefinition
  where
     prod_id_diff = 14;
```

```
DBMS_rowid.rowid_ROW_NUMBER(rowid)
----------------------------------
                                 0
```

Below we see that the PL/SQL returns the absolute file number from a *rowid* using the function *rowid_to_absolute*.

```
--Using query
select
   dbms_rowid.rowid_to_absolute_fno(
       row_id       => rowid,
       schema_name        => 'sh',
       object_name        => 'products') "Absolute file number"
from
   sh.products
where
   rownum <2;
```

```
Absolute file number
--------------------
                   5
```

```
--Using PL/SQL Code
 declare
     absolute#   integer;
     row_id       char(18);
     object_name varchar2(20) := 'table_redefinition';
 begin
     select
         rowid
     into
         row_id
     from
         table_redefinition
     where
         prod_id_diff = 14;
     absolute# := dbms_rowid.rowid_to_absolute_fno(
             row_id            => row_id,
             schema_name   => 'PKG',
             object_name   => object_name);

     dbms_output.put_line(
         'Absolute file number: ' || absolute#);
 end;
/
```

Absolute file number: 9

Starting with Oracle 8, information about *rowid*s such as the object number, relative file number, block and row were added. When an Oracle migration from Oracle 7 to Oracle 8 is completed, the extension of the *rowid* process is done automatically. However, for single columns of a *rowid* data type, this extension is not automatically done, so the function *rowid_to_extended* needs to be used.

Convert a restricted *rowid* to an extended *rowid* using the function *rowid_to_extended*.

```
--Converting restricted internal rowid to extended format
select
   dbms_rowid.rowid_to_extended(
           old_rowid         => dbms_rowid.rowid_to_restricted(rowid,0),
           schema_name       => 'pkg',
           object_name       => 'table_redefinition',
           conversion_type   => 0) "Extended rowid"
from
   table_redefinition
where
   prod_id_diff=14;
```

```
Extended rowid
------------------
D/////AAJAAACBLAAA
```

```
  --Converting restricted internal rowid to extended format (without
  -- specifying schema and table name)

select
   dbms_rowid.rowid_to_extended(
      old_rowid         => dbms_rowid.rowid_to_restricted(rowid,0),
      schema_name       => NULL,
      object_name       => NULL,
      conversion_type   => 0) "Extended rowid"
from
   table_redefinition
where
   prod_id_diff=14;
```

```
Extended rowid
------------------
AAARbXAAJAAACBLAAA
```

```
  --Converting restricted external rowid to extended format
 select
    dbms_rowid.rowid_to_extended(
       old_rowid     => '00000BF5.0000.0005',
       schema_name   => 'pkg',
       object_name   => table_redefinition,
       conversion_type => 1)
 from
    table_redefinition
  where
     prod_id_diff=14;
```

```
DBMS_rowid.rowid_TO_EXTENDED(O
-----------------------------
D/////AAFAAAAv1AAA
```

```
--Converting extended rowid to restricted rowid using function
rowid_to_restricted
```

```
--Restricted rowid is BBBBBBB.RRRR.FFFFF where BBBBBBB is the block and RRRR
is the te row in the block and FFFFF is the datafile
```

```
select
   dbms_rowid.rowid_to_restricted(
      old_rowid => rowid,
      conversion_type => 1) "Restricted rowid"
from
   table_redefinition
where
   prod_id_diff = 14;
```

```
Restricted rowid
-----------------
0000204B.0000.0009
```

```
--Return the type of rowid using function rowid_type
   select
      dbms_rowid.rowid_type(
         row_id => rowid) "rowid type"
   from
      table_redefinition
   where
      prod_id_diff = 14;
```

```
rowid Type
----------
        1
```

```
  --In Oracle 7 rowids were restricted format
   select
      dbms_rowid.rowid_type(
         chartorowid('00000BF5.0000.0005')) "rowid type"
   from
      table_redefinition
   where
      prod_id_diff = 14;
```

```
rowid Type
----------
        0
```

Verify whether a restricted *rowid* can be converted to an extended format using the function *rowid_verify*.

```
--The column should be rowid type or character string
   select
      rowid, prod_category
   from
      pkg.table_redefinition
   where
      dbms_rowid.rowid_verify(
         rowid_in        => prod_category,
         schema_name     => 'pkg',
         object_name     => 'table_redefinition',
```

```
          conversion_type => 0) = 1;
```

```
rowid              PROD_CATEGORY
-----------------  --------------------------------------------------
AAARbVAAJAAAABLAAA Electronics
```

A useful function of this package is the ability to export only one line of a table, a set of lines or just a block using the *export (exp)* utility. Below is a demonstration of how to execute such procedures.

The example below is just a simple task to show what this package can do but, of course, a lot of things can be done with this package. Some other examples can be found at www.dba-oracle.com.

🖫 Code 2.9 – dbms_rowid_exp_row_block.sql

```
conn pkg/pkg#123

create table
   tab_rowid_exp
tablespace
   pkg_data_32m as
select
   *
from
   dba_tables;
```

Exporting specific blocks

Below we choose which blocks are desired by using the procedure *rowid_block_number*.

```
select
   distinct
      dbms_rowid.rowid_block_number(
         rowid)
from
   tab_rowid_exp;
```

```
DBMS_rowid.rowid_BLOCK_NUMBER(
-----------------------------
                        20561
                        20573
                        20577
                        20588
            ..........  . .
            ..........  . .
            ..........  . .
```

Get the row count in each block chosen (20567,20632).

```
select
    dbms_rowid.rowid_block_number(rowid) "block number",
    count(1) "num rows in block"
from
    tab_rowid_exp
where
    dbms_rowid.rowid_block_number(rowid)
in
    (20567,20632)
group by
    dbms_rowid.rowid_block_number(rowid);
```

```
Block Number Num Rows in block
------------ -----------------
      20632                29
      20567                41
```

Show some data from the rows that are inside the blocks that will be exported.

```
select
    dbms_rowid.rowid_block_number(rowid) "block number",
    table_name "part of row to be exported"
from
    tab_rowid_exp
where
    dbms_rowid.rowid_block_number(rowid)
in
    (20567, 20632)
group by
    dbms_rowid.rowid_block_number(rowid),
    table_name;

Block Number Part of Row To be Exported
------------ ------------------------------
      20567 logmnr_indsubpart$
      20567 logmnr_ccol$
      20567 logmnr_col$
.............
.............
```

```
Choose which blocks to export.

exp pkg/pkg#123@ora11g tables=tab_rowid_exp query=\"where
dbms_rowid.rowid_block_number\(rowid\) \in \(20567,20632\)\"
file=tab_rowid_exp_blocks.dmp log=exp_tab_rowid_exp_blocks.log
statistics=none

[ora11g@dbms ~]$ exp pkg/pkg#123@ora11g tables=tab_rowid_exp query=\"where
dbms_rowid.rowid_block_number\(rowid\) \in \(20567,20632\)\"
file=tab_rowid_exp_blocks.dmp log=exp_tab_rowid_exp_blocks.log
statistics=none
```

```
Export: Release 11.1.0.6.0 - Production on Mon May 4 07:30:34 2009
Connected to: Oracle 11g Enterprise Edition Release 11.1.0.6.0 - Production
With the Partitioning, OLAP, Data Mining and Real Application Testing options
Export done in US7ASCII character set and AL16UTF16 NCHAR character set
server uses WE8MSWIN1252 character set (possible charset conversion)
About to export specified tables via Conventional Path ...
. . exporting table                    tab_rowid_exp          70 rows exported
Export terminated successfully without warnings.
```

Next to be shown is how to export specific rows of a table. First, choose which rows will be exported.

```
select
    rowid,
    table_name,
    owner
from
    tab_rowid_exp
where
    table_name in('promotions','countries','products')
and
    owner='SH';
```

```
rowid              TABLE_NAME                        OWNER
-----------------  -----------------------------     -----------------
AAARbyAAJAAAFBQAAS products                          SH
AAARbyAAJAAAFBQAAX countries                         SH
AAARbyAAJAAAFBQAAa promotions                        SH
```

Then use *exp* again to export these specific rows.

```
exp pkg/pkg#123@ora11g tables=tab_rowid_exp query= \"where rowid in
\(\'AAARbxAAJAAAFBQAAS\'\,\'AAARbxAAJAAAFBQAAX\'\,\'AAARbxAAJAAAFBQAAS\'\)\"
file=tab_rowid_exp_rows.dmp log=tab_rowid_exp_rows.log statistics=none

[ora11g@dbms ~]$ exp pkg/pkg#123@ora11g tables=tab_rowid_exp query= \"where
rowid in
\(\'AAARbxAAJAAAFBQAAS\'\,\'AAARbxAAJAAAFBQAAX\'\,\'AAARbxAAJAAAFBQAAS\'\)\"
file=tab_rowid_exp_rows.dmp log=tab_rowid_exp_rows.log statistics=none
```

```
Export: Release 11.1.0.6.0 - Production on Mon May 4 07:30:41 2009
Connected to: Oracle 11g Enterprise Edition Release 11.1.0.6.0 - Prod
With the Partitioning, OLAP, Data Mining and Real Application Testing options
Export done in US7ASCII character set and AL16UTF16 NCHAR character set
server uses WE8MSWIN1252 character set (possible charset conversion)
About to export specified tables via Conventional Path ...
. . exporting table                    tab_rowid_exp           2 rows exported
Export terminated successfully without warnings.
```

The following is another function of this *dbms_rowid* package. In cases where there is a lock in objects, generally a search is done in the SGA v$ views, such as *v$lock*, *v$locked_object*, or *v$dml_locks*, trying to find which object is being locked at any given time.

This *dbms_rowid* package simplifies determining which records are being locked. See below we used the "*select xxx for update*" command to hold a long term lock.

⊟ Code 2.10 – dbms_rowid_row_lock.sql

```
conn pkg/pkg#123
--Now a lock will be simulated
--Creating table
  create table tab_rowid_lock(
     col1 number
  );

Table created

  --Populating table
    begin
       for x in 1 .. 50 loop
          insert into
             tab_rowid_lock
          values (x);
       end loop;
    end;
  /
commit;

  --Generating lock
    --Open a session (session1)
       select
          *
       from
          tab_rowid_lock
       where
          col1=2
       for update;

    --Open another session (session2)
       update
          tab_rowid_lock
       set
          col1 = 10
       where
          col1=2;
```

Now lets use the "select for update" clause to simulate a long-term locked rowset. To release these locks, we use a variety of queries against v$views and then use *dbms_rowid.rowid_create* to find the specific row numbers being locked.

⊟ Code 2.11 – dbms_rowid_find_locked_rows.sql

```
--We can get the lock here
        col owner            format a12  heading 'owner'
        col session_id       format 9999 heading 'sid'
        col object_name      format a30  heading 'object'
        col oracle_username  format a15  heading 'username'
```

```
      col os_user_name    format a15  heading 'os user'
      select l.session_id,
             o.owner,
             o.object_name,
             o.object_id,
             l.oracle_username,
             l.os_user_name
      from
        gv$locked_object l,
        dba_objects       o
      where
        l.object_id = o.object_id
      order by
        o.object_name;
```

```
SESS OWNER         OBJECT_NAME                       OBJECT_ID ORACLE_USERNAME OS_USER_NAME
---- -----------   -----------------------------     --------- --------------- ---------------
 135 pkg           tab_rowid_lock                        71414 pkg             Paulo
 155 pkg           tab_rowid_lock                        71414 pkg             Paulo
```

```
   --Get rowid information of the locked object
     select
       sid,
       row_wait_obj# "object rowid",
       row_wait_file# "datafile",
       row_wait_block# "block number",
       row_wait_row# "row wait number"
     from
       v$session
     where
       row_wait_obj# = 71414;
```

```
SID Object Rowid   Datafile Block Number Row Wait Number
---------- ------------ ---------- ------------ ---------------
       135          71414        4         9740               1
```

```
  --Return which row is locked in that table
     select
       *
     from
       tab_rowid_lock
     where
       rowid = dbms_rowid.rowid_create(
         rowid_type    => 1,
         object_number       => 71414,
         relative_fno  => 4,
         block_number  => 9740,
         row_number    => 1);
```

```
COL1
----------
         2
```

It becomes easy to find which row is locked in a table by using the *dbms_rowid* package.

Package *dbms_space*

The *dbms_space* package contains five procedures and two functions that serve to analyze the object growth and the space used by tables and indexes. The *dbms_space* package gives us the following additional information:

- **Cost:** To determine the cost to create an index
- **Management:** To find recommendations on management of segments
- **Verify:** To verify information on free blocks in an object
- **List:** To return a list of objects that are associated to one specific segment
- **Gowth:** To verify the growth of one definitive object in a given time Space: To verify space made unusable in a table, index or cluster.

The *dbms_space* package is created by the script *dbmsutil.sql* which, in turn, is executed by another script called *catproc.sql*. The user must have the *analyze* privilege in objects to be able to execute this package.

Following is the list of subprograms of the *dbms_space* package:

- *asa_recommendations (function)*
- *create_index_cost* (procedure)
- *create_table_cost* (procedure)
- *free_blocks* (procedure)
- *object_dependent_segments* (function)
- *object_growth_trend* (function)
- *space_usage* (procedure)
- *unused_space* (procedure)

Function dbms_space *asa_recommendations*

The Oracle Segment Advisor, created with Oracle 10g Release 2, can identify objects that have space for reclamation or objects that have too much row chaining. The process is run automatically by Oracle using the *dbms_advisor* package.

Use the function *asa_recommendations* to verify if there are recommendations for improvement in a particular segment. See an example in the code below:

🖫 Code 2.12 – dbms_space_asa_recomm.sql

```
conn pkg/pkg#123
--Show tablespace reclaimable space
select
   tablespace_name,
   allocated_space,
   used_space reclaimable_space
from
   table(dbms_space.asa_recommendations('TRUE', 'TRUE', 'ALL'));
```

```
TABLESPACE_NAME   ALLOCATED_SPACE   RECLAIMABLE_SPACE
----------------  ----------------  -----------------
sysaux            292627118         205913743
ts_sa1            229874497         213349934
ts_sa2            4389377192        3465313855
ts_sa3            4853596429        3902675147
```

```
--Show index, table and lob reclaimable space
select
   tablespace_name,
   segment_owner,
   segment_name,
   segment_type,
   allocated_space,
   used_space,
   reclaimable_space
from (
   select
      *
   from
      table(
         dbms_space.asa_recommendations(
            all_runs         => TRUE,
            show_manual      => TRUE,
            show_findings    => ALL);
```

```
TABLESPACE_NAME                SEGMENT_OWNER              SEGMENT_NAME
SEGMENT_TYPE       ALLOCATED_SPACE USED_SPACE RECLAIMABLE_SPACE
----------------------------- ---------------------------- ---------------------------- --------
---------- --------------- ---------- -----------------
ts_sales02_acom_wlp_data_m    sales102_acom_wlp            ad_bucket                     table
65536     8192            57344
ts_sales02_acom_wlp_data_m    sales102_acom_wlp            ad_count                      table
65536     8192            57344
TS ts_sales02_acom_wlp_data_m sales102_acom_wlp            bt_event                      table
65536     8192            57344
```

Procedure *dbms_space create_index_cost*

This *create_index_cost* procedure accepts the DDL for a *create index* statement and outputs the storage needed to create the index. This approach of using *dbms_space.create_index_cost* is useful because it allows the DBA to adjust some storage parameters before creating an index. The *create_table_cost* procedure for table space size estimates is also available within the *dbms_space* package.

This *create_index_cost* procedure shows the cost of the creation of an index in a particular table. For in this, it is enough to pass the DDL of the index and then the result of the procedure becomes the necessary space for the creation of this index. A single prerequisite is necessary: The table must have been recently analyzed with *dbms_stats*.

To see how this works, let's create an example table and then gather statistics of this table. Next, simulate the creation of an index in this table using the procedure *create_index_cost*. This will show how much space is needed on the index tablespace to create this index.

Below is an illustration of this procedure.

🖫 Code 2.13 – dbms_space_create_idx_cost.sql

```
conn pkg/pkg#123
--Creating table
  create table tab_dbms_space
  tablespace
    pkg_data_32m
  as
  select
    *
  from
    dba_objects;

--Actualizing table statistics
  exec dbms_stats.gather_table_stats(
        ownname  => 'pkg',
        tabname  => 'tab_dbms_space',
        degree   => 4);


--Estimating index size
  set serveroutput on

  declare
    used_bytes          number;
    alloc_bytes_on_tbs  number;
  begin
    dbms_space.create_index_cost(
```

```
      ddl                  => 'create index idx_obj_name ON
tab_dbms_space(object_name)',
      used_bytes => used_bytes,
alloc_bytes          => alloc_bytes_on_tbs,
plan_table  => '');
    dbms_output.put_line('Index Used Bytes: ' || used_bytes);
    dbms_output.put_line('Allocated Bytes on Tablespace: ' ||
alloc_bytes_on_tbs);
  end;
/
```

```
Index Used Bytes:             1723300
Allocated Bytes on Tablespace: 3145728
```

For *dbms_space.create_index_cost*, the procedure accepts the DDL for a "create index" statement and outputs the storage needed to create the index. The Oracle documentation notes these input parameters for *dbms_space.create_index_cost:*

- **ddl:** The create index DDL statement

- **used_bytes:** The number of bytes representing the actual index data

- **alloc_bytes:** Size of the index when created in the tablespace

- **plan_table:** Which plan table to use, default NULL

> **Note:** Using *dbms_space.create_index_cost* requires that the table already exist and that the table have current metadata statistics (as computed with *dbms_stats*).

Procedure *dbms_space create_table_cost*

Oracle provides the *dbms_space* built-in package to facilitate computing and estimating the space used by database objects, i.e. tables and indexes. Take a close look at how you can use the *dbms_space* package to estimate the required storage for tables.

The *create_table_cost* procedure allows the user to identify the amount of space the table to be created in the database will occupy. The procedure bases its calculation on either the information of the columns of the table, or the information on the average size of each row of the table.

The example below shows a simulation of a table creation using the *create_tab_cost* procedure. Note that it is necessary to input some parameters like *avg_row_size* (in bytes), *row_count*, and *pct_free* so the calculation of table size can be done when the procedure is executed.

Using the dbms_space create_table_cost procedure

The *dbms_space.create_table_*cost procedure is used for estimating the final size of a table or index (with *dbms_space.create_index_cost*) by accepting input sizing parameters and computing the estimated used bytes and allocated bytes for a table or index. Here are the sizing input columns for *create_table_cost*:

- **avg_row_size:** The anticipated average row size in the table

- **colinfos:** The description of the columns

- **row_count:** The anticipated number of rows in the table

- **pct_free:** The percentage of free space in each block for future expansion of existing rows due to updates

- **used_bytes:** The space used by user data

- **alloc_bytes:** The size of the object taking into account the tablespace extent characteristics

Here is an example invocation of *dbms_space.create_table_cost:*

🖫 Code 2.14 – dbms_space_create_tab_cost.sql

```
conn pkg/pkg#123

--Estimating table size before creation
set serveroutput on
declare
   used_bytes  number;
   alloc_bytes number;
begin
   dbms_space.create_table_cost(
      tablespace_name => 'SYSTEM',
      avg_row_size    => '1500',
      row_count       => '100000',
      pct_free        => '10',
      used_bytes      => used_bytes,
      alloc_bytes     => alloc_bytes);
   dbms_output.put_line(Table Used Megabytes:' ||
                      (used_bytes / 1024 / 1024));
   dbms_output.put_line('Allocated Megabytes on Tablespace: ' ||
                      (alloc_bytes / 1024 / 1024));
end;
/
```

```
Table Used Megabytes:            195.3125
Allocated Megabytes on Tablespace: 200
```

As we see, the *dbms_space.create_table_cost* procedure gives us an estimate of the used and allocated space for the target table.

Procedure *dbms_space free_blocks*

The *dbms_space free_blocks* procedure returns information on free blocks in objects as tables, indexes and clusters. This can be used to let DBAs know if they need to recreate a table that does not have enough free space, thereby preventing an out-of-space error such as an error *ORA-01631: max # extents (1) shown in table XXX*. The *dbms_space free_blocks* procedure only works in objects with manual segment space management. (no *segment space management auto*) clause, so bitmap freelists are 'not allowed if you use this package.

Locally managed tablespaces do provide an unlimited number of extents. Even if dictionary managed tablespaces are used, newer versions of Oracle allow altering of an object and setting an unlimited number of extents for it.

If the database uses manual segment space management, i.e. for LOBs, and they are stored in a dictionary managed tablespace, there may be a limit on the maximum number of extents. However, in this case, monitoring free blocks in order to avoid out of space errors is a task that all DBAs should do in their day-by-day work.

In the next example, a table is created on a tablespace with the *segment space management manual* and then the *free_blocks* procedure is executed to show how many free blocks this table has.

🖫 Code 2.15 – dbms_space_free_blocks.sql

```
conn pkg/pkg#123            .
--User needs to have the following privilege "analyze any"
grant analyze any to pkg;
--Create a tablespace with "segment space management manual"
 create tablespace pkg_data_32m_manual
     datafile '/oracle/app/oradata/ora11g/pkg_data_32m_manual.dbf'
     size 20m segment space management manual;
--Create example table
create table pkg.tab_dbms_space_1
tablespace
   pkg_data_32m_manual
as
select
   *
from
   dba_objects;


--Get free blocks
set serveroutput on
```

```
declare
  free_blks number;
  begin
  dbms_space.free_blocks(
     segment_owner  => 'pkg',
     segment_name   => 'tab_dbms_space_1',
     segment_type   => 'table',
     freelist_group_id =>  0,
     free_blks =>  free_blks);
    dbms_output.put_line('Free Blocks: ' || to_char(free_blks));
  end;
/
```

Function *dbms_space object_dependent_segments*

The function *object_dependent_segments* returns a list with the segments associated the input parent segments. The *dbms_space object_dependent_segments* helps to reduce the impact on some DBA tasks like disabling constraints, and rebuilding tables or indices. It helps by seeking objects that may become invalid or that are in an unusable state when the master object is deleted ad re-created.

For the parameter, *objtype* must be specified by one of the following numbers:

- *object_type_table = 1*

- *object_type_nested_table = 2*

- *object_type_index = 3*

- *object_type_cluster = 4*

- *object_type_table_partition = 7*

- *object_type_index_partition = 8*

- *object_type_table_subpartition = 9*

- *object_type_index_subpartition = 10*

- *object_type_mv = 13*

- *object_type_mvlog = 14*

The example below demonstrates how to use *object_dependent_segments* to get all objects that have some dependency with the table used by variable *objname* (products).

🖫 Code 2.16 – dbms_space_obj_depend_seg.sql

```
conn pkg/pkg#123
set linesize 200
col segment_owner format a25
```

```
col segment_name format a25
col segment_type format a20
col tablespace_name format a20
col partition_name format a20
col lob_column_name format a12
set serveroutput on
  select
    segment_owner,
    segment_name,
    segment_type,
    tablespace_name
  from
    (table(dbms_space.object_dependent_segments(
            objowner      => 'sh',
            objname       => 'products',
            partname      => NULL,
            objtype       => 1)));
```

```
SEGMENT_OWNER    NAME                     SEGMENT_TYPE          TABLESPACE_NAME
-------    -------------------------    --------------------    --------
sh         products                     table                   example
sh         products_prod_status_bix     index                   example
sh         products_pk                  index                   example
sh         products_prod_subcat_ix      index                   example
sh         products_prod_cat_ix         index                   example
```

Function *dbms_space object_growth_trend*

One of the most important features of Oracle 11g and beyond is its ability to predict the growth of the segments. The *object_growth_trend* prediction mechanism is based on data collected and stored by the AWR, and the growth trend reporting is also built into the Oracle database kernel and is available by default.

The active space monitoring of individual segments in the database gives the up-to-the-minute status of individual segments in the system available to the database. This provides sufficient information over time to perform growth trending of individual objects in the database as well as the database as a whole.

You can use the *object_growth_trend* function to verify space used for a certain object in different spaces of time. It is used quite often to create capacity planning and ensure that there is always enough space in tablespaces for tables and indexes.

Most production databases grow over the course of time and planning for growth is a very important task of every professional Oracle DBA. If resources are carefully planned out well in advance, such problems as the system being out of space can be avoided and hence, using the *object_growth_trend* procedure is indespensible for capacity planning.

Of course, alerts will be generated when the space utilization crosses established alert thresholds, but a proactive approach is always preferred over a reactive approach..

In the example below, the size of the table products over time is shown and can predict the growth and deduce the capacity planning for this table.

🖫 Code 2.16 – dbms_space_obj_growth_trend.sql

```
conn pkg/pkg#123
set linesize 200

col timepoint     for a40
col space_usage for a20
col space_alloc for a20
col quality       for a30

select
    *
from
        table(dbms_space.object_growth_trend(
            object_owner => 'SH',
            object_name => 'products',
            object_type => 'table'))
where
   space_usage > 0;
```

```
TIMEPOINT                      SPACE_USAGE   SPACE_ALLOC   QUALITY
------------------------------ ------------- ------------- ------------
11-APR-09 12.52.04.849170 PM   1186955951    1744830464    interpolated
12-APR-09 12.52.04.849170 PM   1186955951    1744830464    interpolated
13-APR-09 12.52.04.849170 PM   1186955951    1744830464    interpolated
```

The result of this query shows the time when the statistics were collected, the space used for the data of the object, the space allocated by the object and the quality of the result.

Procedure *dbms_space space_usage*

The *space_usage* procedure returns the total used space within a table of index, all rows up to the High Water Mark (HWM). The *space_usage* procedure can only be used in tables/indexes that have been created in a tablespace with auto segment space management (ASSM or "bitmapped freelists). The types of segments that can be analyzed by the *space_usage* procedure include:

- Table
- Table partition
- Table subpartition

- Index

- Index partition

- Index subpartition

- Cluster

- LOB

- LOB partition

- LOB subpartition

To understand how the *space_usage* procedure works, consider a table called *tab_dbms_space_usage* which receives many *insert* and *delete* operations.

Because the delete operations leave empty space, the *space_usage* procedure can be used to verify the lost space in this table and justify as reorganization of the table. A table can be reorganized in a variety of ways:

- *alter table ... shrink space.*

- CTAS copy of the table

- The dbms_redefinition package

There are many ways to count row space used within a table:

- **Count:** You can count the rows and multiply by *dba_tables.avg_row_len*.

- **dbms_space:** We can see percentages of spaced used with data blocks using the *space_usage* procedure.

- **Blocks:** Some rough estimates of rows space in a table can be computed by gathering *dba_tables.blocks* and subtract the value of PCTFREE.

- **File size:** One way of looking at total consumed space within a table is to map the table to a single tablespace and the tablespace to a single data file. You can then check *dba_segments* to see the total file size for the table rows.

The following is an example of collecting actual spaced used within a table. A table is created and some operations performed to simulate changes.

At this time, all blocks are full, so check it by running the *dbms_space.space_usage* procedure. The results below:

💾 Code 2.17 – dbms_space_space_usage.sql

```
conn pkg/pkg#123
create table tab_dbms_space_usage
tablespace
```

```
   pkg_data_32M
as
select
   *
from
   dba_objects;

set serveroutput on
declare
   v_unformatted_blocks number;
   v_unformatted_bytes  number;
   v_fs1_blocks         number;
   v_fs1_bytes          number;
   v_fs2_blocks         number;
   v_fs2_bytes          number;
   v_fs3_blocks         number;
   v_fs3_bytes          number;
   v_fs4_blocks         number;
   v_fs4_bytes          number;
   v_full_blocks        number;
   v_full_bytes         number;
 begin
   dbms_space.space_usage('pkg',
                          'tab_dbms_space_usage',
                          'table',
                          v_unformatted_blocks,
                          v_unformatted_bytes,
                          v_fs1_blocks,
                          v_fs1_bytes,
                          v_fs2_blocks,
                          v_fs2_bytes,
                          v_fs3_blocks,
                          v_fs3_bytes,
                          v_fs4_blocks,
                          v_fs4_bytes,
                          v_full_blocks,
                          v_full_bytes);
   dbms_output.put_line('Unformatted Blocks = ' || v_unformatted_blocks);
   dbms_output.put_line('Unformatted Bytes = ' || v_unformatted_bytes);
   dbms_output.put_line('FS1 Bytes (at least 0 to 25% free space) = ' || v_fs1_bytes);
   dbms_output.put_line('FS1 Blocks(at least 0 to 25% free space) = ' || v_fs1_blocks);
   dbms_output.put_line('FS2 Bytes (at least 25 to 50% free space)= ' || v_fs2_bytes);
   dbms_output.put_line('FS2 Blocks(at least 25 to 50% free space)= ' || v_fs2_blocks);
   dbms_output.put_line('FS3 Bytes (at least 50 to 75% free space) = ' || v_fs3_bytes);
   dbms_output.put_line('FS3 Blocks(at least 50 to 75% free space) = ' || v_fs3_blocks);
   dbms_output.put_line('FS4 Bytes (at least 75 to 100% free space) = ' || v_fs4_bytes);
   dbms_output.put_line('FS4 Blocks(at least 75 to 100% free space)= ' || v_fs4_blocks);
   dbms_output.put_line('Full Blocks in segment = ' || v_full_blocks);
   dbms_output.put_line('Full Bytes in segment  = ' || v_full_bytes);
 end;
/


Unformatted Blocks = 0
Unformatted Bytes = 0
FS1 Bytes (at least 0 to 25% free space) = 0
FS1 Blocks(at least 0 to 25% free space) = 0
FS2 Bytes (at least 25 to 50% free space)= 0
FS2 Blocks(at least 25 to 50% free space)= 0
FS3 Bytes (at least 50 to 75% free space) = 0
FS3 Blocks(at least 50 to 75% free space) = 0
FS4 Bytes (at least 75 to 100% free space) = 0
FS4 Blocks(at least 75 to 100% free space)= 0
```

Package dbms_space

```
Full Blocks in segment = 1015
Full Bytes in segment  = 8314880
```

By deleting some rows and checking the available space again, some newly freed-up blocks can be seen.

```
Unformatted Blocks = 0
Unformatted Bytes = 0
FS1 Bytes (at least 0 to 25% free space) = 0
FS1 Blocks(at least 0 to 25% free space) = 0
FS2 Bytes (at least 25 to 50% free space)= 0
FS2 Blocks(at least 25 to 50% free space)= 0
FS3 Bytes (at least 50 to 75% free space) = 0
FS3 Blocks(at least 50 to 75% free space) = 0
FS4 Bytes (at least 75 to 100% free space) = 155648
FS4 Blocks(at least 75 to 100% free space)= 19
Full Blocks in segment = 996
Full Bytes in segment  = 8159232
```

This shows that there are 19 blocks with 75-100% free space. This table can now be reorganized using the *shrink* command; this will move the segmented data to the beginning of the segment and adjust the HWM.

```
alter table
   pkg.tab_dbms_space_usage
enable row movement;
```

```
Table altered
```

```
alter table
   pkg.tab_dbms_space_usage
shrink space;
```

```
Table altered
```

Lastly, the space can be checked again using the *space_usage* procedure of package *dbms_space*.

```
Unformatted Blocks = 0
Unformatted Bytes = 0
FS1 Bytes (at least 0 to 25% free space) = 8192
FS1 Blocks(at least 0 to 25% free space) = 1
FS2 Bytes (at least 25 to 50% free space)= 8192
FS2 Blocks(at least 25 to 50% free space)= 1
FS3 Bytes (at least 50 to 75% free space) = 0
FS3 Blocks(at least 50 to 75% free space) = 0
FS4 Bytes (at least 75 to 100% free space) = 0
FS4 Blocks(at least 75 to 100% free space)= 0
Full Blocks in segment = 994
Full Bytes in segment  = 8142848
```

Then, using the *space_usage* procedure, it becomes evident as to which objects are within spaces badly used in the database. From this information, use the *shrink*

---

command and reorganize these objects. This reduces loss of space and enhances performance as the reading of the object will be made in fewer blocks.

Procedure dbms_space unused_space

The *dbms_space unused_space* procedure is used to return information about space that is un-used by an object (where an object is a table, an index or a cluster). This procedure only works with objects that reside in a tablespace with an Automatic Segment Space Management (ASSM) storage option (bitmap freelists as opposed to one-way linked-list freelists).

The procedure *dbms_space unused_space* is also useful for locating objects that are wasting space. The example below demonstrates the complete operation for checking the space not used in a determined table.

In this example, a new table is created and its unused space is checked with the procedure *unused_space* of package *dbms_space*.

🖫 Code 2.18 – dbms_space_unused_space.sql

```
conn pkg/pkg#123
create table tab_dbms_unused_space
tablespace
    users
as
select
    *
from
    dba_objects;
--Checking the unused space
set serveroutput on
declare
    tt_blk              number;
    tt_bytes            number;
    unu_blk             number;
    unu_bytes           number;
    last_ext_file_id number;
    last_ext_blk_id  number;
    last_used_blk    number;

 begin
   dbms_space.unused_space(
       segment_owner            => 'pkg',
       segment_name             => 'tab_dbms_unused_space',
       segment_type             => 'table',
       total_blocks             => tt_blk,
       total_bytes              => tt_bytes,
       unused_blocks            => unu_blk,
       unused_bytes             => unu_bytes,
       last_used_extent_file_id => last_ext_file_id,
       last_used_extent_block_id => last_ext_blk_id,
```

```
         last_used_block                => last_used_blk);
   dbms_output.put_line('object_name = freelist_t');
   dbms_output.put_line('-----------------------------------');
   dbms_output.put_line('Total Number of blocks = ' || tt_blk);
   dbms_output.put_line('Total unused blocks    = ' || unu_blk);
 end;
/
OBJECT_NAME = FREELIST_T
-----------------------------------
Total Number of blocks = 1152
Total unused blocks    = 112
```

Now let's delete some rows from this table and then execute the *alter table xxx shrink space* command is executed. After this, some extents are freed to be used again and the unused space can be rechecked.

```
delete from
   tab_dbms_unused_space;

68936 rows deleted

/

0 rows deleted

commit
/

Commit complete

--Checking the number of extents
select
   count(*),
   bytes
from
   dba_extents
where
   segment_name = 'tab_dbms_unused_space'
and
   owner='pkg'
group by
   bytes;

   COUNT(*)      BYTES
---------- ----------
         8    1048576
        16      65536
--Freeing up extents that was deleted
alter table
   tab_dbms_unused_space
enable row movement;

Table altered

alter table
   tab_dbms_unused_space shrink space;
```

```
Table altered

--Check the number of extents again (now there is just one extent because
the table is empty after the delete command)
select
    count(*),
    bytes
from
    dba_extents
where
    segment_name = 'tab_dbms_unused_space
and
    owner='pkg'
group by bytes;

    COUNT(*)       BYTES
---------- ----------
         1       65536
--Checking the unused space again (now we can see just 4 unused and 4 used
blocks.
-- It depends of db_clock_size and the storage type of tablespace)


set serveroutput on
declare
    tt_blk              number;
    tt_bytes            number;
    unu_blk             number;
    unu_bytes           number;
    last_ext_file_id    number;
    last_ext_blk_id     number;
    last_used_blk       number;

begin
    dbms_space.unused_space(
        segment_owner            => 'pkg',
        segment_name             => 'tab_dbms_unused_space',
        segment_type             => 'table',
        total_blocks             => tt_blk,
        total_bytes              => tt_bytes,
        unused_blocks            => unu_blk,
        unused_bytes             => unu_bytes,
        last_used_extent_file_id => last_ext_file_id,
        last_used_extent_block_id => last_ext_blk_id,
        last_used_block          => last_used_blk);
    dbms_output.put_line('object_name = freelist_t');
    dbms_output.put_line('-----------------------------------');
    dbms_output.put_line('Total Number of blocks = ' || tt_blk);
    dbms_output.put_line('Total unused blocks    = ' || unu_blk);
end;/


OBJECT_NAME = FREELIST_T
-----------------------------------
Total Number of blocks = 8
Total unused blocks    = 4
```

As we have illustrated, the *unused_space* procedure shows the space that is not used below the HWM in any table or index segment.

The HWM represents the border between the blocks that are stored (lines still are in the blocks) or had previously stored rows (deleted lines) and the blocks that have never stored rows (a fresh empty data block acquired from the freelist).

The identified blocks have never been used usefully by the segments and therefore, can be set free for use when needed.

Package *dbms_space_admin*

The *dbms_space_admin* package supplies important functionality for locally managed tablespaces. In this package, the following sub-programs are found:

- *assm_segment_verify* (procedure)
- *assm_tablespace_verify* (procedure)
- *assm_segment_synchwm* (procedure)
- *segment_corrupt* (procedure)
- *segment_drop_sorrupt* (procedure)
- *segment_dump* (procedure)
- *segment_verify* (procedure)
- *tablespace_fix_bitmaps* (procedure)
- *tablespace_fix_segment_extblks* (procedure)
- *tablespace_fix_segment_states* (procedure)
- *tablespace_migrate_from_local* (procedure)
- *tablespace_migrate_to_local* (procedure)
- *tablespace_rebuild_bitmaps* (procedure)
- *tablespace_rebuild_quotas* (procedure)
- *tablespace_relocate_bitmaps* (procedure)
- *tablespace_verify* (procedure)

Procedure dbms_space_admin *assm_tablespace_verify*

The *assm_tablespace_verify* procedure is a corruption checking utility that verifies all the bitmap freelists against the tablespace extents. Thus, wrongly marked bits as used or error free will be identified. When executed, this procedure generates a dump file called *sid_ora_process_ID.trc* that is generated in a directory specified by the initialization parameter *user_dump_dest*.

Below is a simulated datafile corruption where this procedure is executed to check the results of this corruption.

> **Note**: *dd* is a UNIX command and will not work in a Windows environment.

🖫 **Code 2.19 – dbms_space_admin_assm_tbs_verify.sql**

```
--Let's simulate a block corruption
--Create a new tablespace
create tablespace
test_corrupt
datafile
   '/oracle/app/oradata/ora11g/tbs_corrupt.dbf' size 100M;
--Check the datafile of you tablespace
select
   file_name
from
   dba_data_files
where
   tablespace_name='test_corrupt';
--Create a table on new tablespace
create table tab_dbms_space_adm_corrupt
tablespace test_corrupt
as
select
   *
from
   dba_objects;
--Let's corrupt our datafile (at OS level)
[ora11g@dbms trace]$ dd if=/dev/urandom
of=/oracle/app/oradata/ora11g/tbs_corrupt.dbf bs=8192 seek=13 count=1
1+0 records in
1+0 records out

--Try to select all rows of table;
select
   count(*)
from
   tab_dbms_space_adm_corrupt;
select
   count(*)
from
   tab_dbms_space_adm_corrupt
```

```
ORA-01115: IO error reading block from file 12 (block # 17)
ORA-01110: data file 12: '/oracle/app/oradata/ora11g/tbs_corrupt.dbf'
ORA-27072: File I/O error
Additional information: 4
Additional information: 12
Additional information: 16384


--Run the procedure tablespace_verify and let this show the error about
corrupted blocks
exec dbms_space_admin.assm_tablespace_verify(
        tablespace_name     => 'test_corrupt',
        ts_option           => 20,
segment_option       => NULL);

begin dbms_space_admin.assm_tablespace_verify(
        tablespace_name     => 'test_corrupt',
        ts_option           => 20,
        segment_option      => NULL);
end;
/

ORA-01578: ORACLE data block corrupted (file # 12, block # 13)
ORA-01110: data file 12: '/oracle/app/oradata/ora11g/tbs_corrupt.dbf'
ORA-06512: at "sys.dbms_space_admin", line 362
ORA-06512: at line 1
```

As shown above, the *assm_tablespace_verify* procedure can verify the integrity of the segments within an ASSM tablespace. After finding an error in any tablespace segment, the DBA should implement the steps necessary to fix the problem as quickly as possible in order to minimize the end user layer impact.

Procedure *dbms_space_admin* *tablespace_migrate_to_local*

The *tablespace_migrate_to_local* procedure allows tablespaces to be migrated from dictionary managed to locally managed tablespaces. In this case, migrate all non-SYSTEM tablespaces to locally managed before migrating the SYSTEM tablespace if the intention is to migrate in READ WRITE mode. Also note that temporary tablespaces cannot be migrated.

We will touch briefly on what reasons there might be for migrating dictionary managed tablespaces to locally managed tablespaces. Locally managed tablespaces manage their own extents internally, keeping one bitmap in each datafile to create a mapping of the free blocks and the used blocks in a certain datafile.

Each bit in one bitmap corresponds to a block or set of blocks. When the extents are allocated or set free for use, Oracle updates the values of the bitmap to show the new status of the blocks. These updates do not generate rollback information nor do they cause any changes to tables in the data dictionary. An event which would occur in the case of a tablespace was managed by the dictionary.

Therefore, locally managed tablespaces do not require the data dictionary and do not generate rollback, nor need coalescing. Still, they bring an advantage in reducing fragmentation and avoiding problems commonly faced by dictionary managed tablespaces such as recursive updates.

When a table changes, a dictionary table changes also, thereby probably requiring another dictionary table change to reflect it and so on.

Block contention like freelists and dictionary objects are no longer necessary, so contention for them is eliminated with locally managed tablespaces as different blocks of the bitmap can be concurrently modified at any time. This greatly simplifies administration and enhances performance in most cases.

It is important to remember that the DBUA (Database Upgrade Assistant) utility does not make this migration automatically when it is used for an upgrade version of the database.

It is only possible to make a migration from dictionary managed tablespaces to local managed tablespaces using procedures existing in package *dbms_space_admin*.

Let's begin by comparing these two new methods of space management, LMT and ASSM:

Locally managed tablespace (LMT) vs Dictionary managed (DMT):

The LMT is implemented by adding the extent management local clause to the tablespace definition syntax. Unlike the older dictionary managed tablespaces (DMTs), LMTs automate extent management and keep the Oracle DBA from being able to specify the *next* storage parameter to govern extent sizes. The only exception to this rule is when *NEXT* is used with *minextents* at table creation time.

In a dictionary managed tablespace (DMT), the data dictionary stores the free space details. While the free blocks list is managed in the segment heard of each table, inside the tablespace), the Free space is recorded in the *sys.uet$* table, while used space in the sys.uet$ table.

But with high DML-rate busy tablespaces the data dictionary became a I/O bottleneck and the, ,movement of the space management out of the data dictionary

and into the tablespace have two benefits. First, the tablespace become independent and can be transportable (transportable tablespaces). Second, locally managed tablespaces remove the O/O contention away from the SYS tablespace.
Segment size management manual vs segment size management auto.

Here is how to migrate the SYSTEM tablespace from dictionary managed to local managed.

🖫 Code 2.20 – dbms_space_admin_mig_to_local.sql

```
conn pkg/pkg#123
--How to migrate SYSTEM tablespace from dictionary managed to locally
managed
--Check if you have temporary tablespace other than SYSTEM
col file_name for a40
select
   file_name,
   tablespace_name
from
   dba_temp_files;
col tablespace_name for a30
select
   tablespace_name,
   contents
from
   dba_tablespaces
 where
    contents = 'temporary';
--Check if undo tablespace is online (if you are using automatic undo
management)
select
 tablespace_name,contents
  from
 dba_tablespaces
 where
 contents = 'undo';
--Put all tablespace in read only mode (do not include temporary tablespace
or tablespaces that has rollback segments)
select
   'alter tablespace '||tablespace_name||' read only;'
from
   dba_tablespaces
where
   contents <> 'temporary'
and
   contents <> 'undo'
and
   tablespace_name not in ('SYSTEM','SYSAUX');


'ALTER TABLESPACE'||TABLESPACE_
----------------------------------------------------------
alter tablespace  users read only;
alter tablespace  example read only;
alter tablespace  apps_ts_tx_data read only;
```

```
alter tablespace   pkg_data read only;
alter tablespace   pkg_idx read only;
alter tablespace   pkg_data_32M read only;
alter tablespace   pkg_idx_32M read only;
alter tablespace   pkg_data_32M_manual read only;


--Put the database in restricted mode
alter system enable restricted session;

System altered

col host_name for a20
select
   instance_name,
   host_name,
   logins
from
   v$instance;

INSTANCE_NAME    HOST_NAME            LOGINS
---------------- -------------------- ----------
ora11g           dbms.f2c.com.br      restricted

--Change the SYSTEM tablespace
exec dbms_space_admin.tablespace_migrate_to_local('SYSTEM');



--Verify the tablespace extent management
select
   tablespace_name,
   extent_management
from
   dba_tablespaces
where
   tablespace_name = 'SYSTEM';

TABLESPACE_NAME               EXTENT_MANAGEMENT
----------------------------- -----------------
SYSTEM                        local

--Disable restricted mode
alter system disable restricted session;

System altered

--Put tablespaces in reead write mode
select
   'alter  tablespace ' || tablespace_name || ' read write;'
from
   dba_tablespaces
where
   contents <> 'temporary'
and
   contents <> 'undo'
and
   tablespace_name not in ('SYSTEM', 'SYSAUX');
```

```
'ALTERTABLESPACE'||TABLESPACE_
-----------------------------------------------------------
alter   tablespace users read write;
alter   tablespace example read write;
alter   tablespace apps_ts_tx_data read write;
alter   tablespace pkg_data read write;
alter   tablespace pkg_idx read write;
alter   tablespace pkg_data_32M read write;
alter   tablespace pkg_idx_32M read write;
alter   tablespace pkg_data_32M_manual read write;
```

Procedure *dbms_space_admin assm_segment_synchwm*

The *assm_segment_synchwm* procedure is used to detect and resolve HWM out-of-sync of an ASSM segment, to keep the HWM highs and lows closer together.

To use this procedure, it is necessary to apply the patch as described in BUG 6493013 in MOSC. MOSC note 4067168.8 shows a related bug, a problem of performance in table scan operations when using PQ (parallel query) where there are some blocks between HWM and LWM of the segment.

Below is an example using this procedure. If the value returned by this procedure is 1, then the segment requires HWM synchronization. A value will return 0 if the segment has already had HWM synchronized.

🖫 Code 2.21 – dbms_space_admin_assm_seg_sync.sql

```
conn pkg/pkg#123
--Procedure to detect and resolve HWM out-of-sync of an ASSM segment
set serveroutput on
declare
   result number;
   begin
   result := dbms_space_admin.assm_segment_synchwm(
               segment_owner => 'pkg',
               segment_name => 'tab_dbms_space_admin',
               segment_type => 'table',
            check_only => 0);
--Where 1 = check only and 0 = perform synchronization
    dbms_output.put_line('synchwm check result: ' || result);
  end;
 /

synchwm check result: 0
```

The procedure was used to detect and resolve HWM out-of-sync of an ASSM segment.

Procedure dbms_space_admin
tablespace_fix_segment_extblks

The *tablespace_fix_segment_extblks* procedure is used to fix an existing problem where in some segments have different values in the columns, bytes, blocks and extents between the *dba_segments* and *dba_extents* views.

This problem is caused by DML and DDL operations. For example, the creation of an index using parallelism or frequent operations like deletes and inserts in a given table can cause an internal inconsistency between views. To fix it, *tablespace_fix_segment_extblks* procedure is used.

In the example below, there is a demonstrated check for the existence of this problem in a database and its remedy.

⊟ Code 2.22 – dbms_space_admin_tbs_fix_seg_extblks.sql

```
conn pkg/pkg#123

select
   /*+ rule */
   s.tablespace_name,
   s.segment_name segment,
   s.partition_name,
   s.owner owner,
   s.segment_type,
   s.blocks sblocks,
   e.blocks eblocks,
   s.extents sextents,
   e.extents eextents,
   s.bytes sbytes,
   e.bytes ebytes from dba_segments s,
   (select count(*) extents,
           sum(blocks) blocks,
           sum(bytes) bytes,
           segment_name,
           partition_name,
           segment_type,
           owner
   from
      dba_extents
   group by
      segment_name,
      partition_name,
      segment_type,
      owner) e
   where
      s.segment_name = e.segment_name
   and
      s.owner = e.owner
   and
```

```
        (s.partition_name = e.partition_name or s.partition_name is null)
    and
        s.segment_type = e.segment_type
    and
        s.owner not like 'SYS%'
    and
        s.segment_name='tab_dbms_space_admin'
    and
        ((s.blocks <> e.blocks) or (s.extents <> e.extents) or
  (s.bytes <> e.bytes))
/
```

| TABLESPACE_NAME | | | SEGMENT | | | PARTITION_ | OWNER | SEGMENT_TYPE |
SBLOCKS	EBLOCKS	SEXTENTS	EEXTENTS	SBYTES	EBYTES			
users			tab_dbms_space_admin				pkg	table
2816	2915	41	37	23068672	23052288			

```
exec dbms_space_admin.tablespace_fix_segment_extblks('users');
```

```
select
   /*+ rule */
   s.tablespace_name,
   s.segment_name segment,
   s.partition_name,
   s.owner owner,
   s.segment_type,
   s.blocks sblocks,
   e.blocks eblocks,
   s.extents sextents,
   e.extents eextents,
   s.bytes sbytes,
   e.bytes ebytes from dba_segments s,
   (select
       count(*) extents,
       sum(blocks) blocks,
       sum(bytes) bytes,
       segment_name,
       partition_name,
       segment_type,
       owner
     from
       dba_extents
     group by
       segment_name,
       partition_name,
       segment_type,
       owner) e
   where
       s.segment_name = e.segment_name
   and
       s.owner = e.owner
   and
       (s.partition_name = e.partition_name or s.partition_name is null)
   and
```

```
        s.segment_type = e.segment_type
    and
        s.owner not like 'SYS%'
    and
        s.segment_name='tab_dbms_space_admin'
    and
      ((s.blocks <> e.blocks) or (s.extents <> e.extents) or
      (s.bytes <> e.bytes))
/
```

| TABLESPACE_NAME | | | SEGMENT | | | PARTITION_ | OWNER | SEGMENT_TYPE |
SBLOCKS	EBLOCKS	SEXTENTS	EEXTENTS	SBYTES	EBYTES			
pkg_data			tab_dbms_space_admin				pkg	table
4224	4224	48	48	34603008	34603008			

As displayed, the data between views has been synchronized. If executing this procedure in the SYSTEM tablespace before the execution of procedure *tablespace_fix_segment_extblks* is desired, then execute the following command:

```
alter session set events '10912 trace name context forever, level 1';
```

It is important to remember that this procedure does not function for the migrated object case in previous versions of database 9i, 8i or 7.

Procedures *tablespace_rebuild_quotas,* *tablespace_rebuild_bitmaps* and *tablespace_verify*

The procedures presented below serve to fix up quotas of the tablespace, rebuild bitmap blocks and verify that bitmaps are consistent. If the procedure *segment_drop_currupt* is used to drop a segment currently marked corrupt and the space for this segment was not released, then execute these procedures used in example below.

⊟ Code 2.23 – dbms_space_admin_tbs_rebuild_verfy.sql

```
conn pkg/pkg#123
exec dbms_space_admin.tablespace_rebuild_bitmaps(
    tablespace_name => 'users');
exec dbms_space_admin.tablespace_rebuild_quotas(
      tablespace_name => 'users');
exec dbms_space_admin.tablespace_verify(
--If the tablespace is corrupted, then the following error will be showed

exec dbms_space_admin.assm_tablespace_verify(
      tablespace_name => 'test_corrupt',
      ts_option => 20,
      segment_option => NULL);
```

```
begin dbms_space_admin.assm_tablespace_verify(tablespace_name =>
'test_corrupt',ts_option => 20,segment_option => NULL); end;
ORA-01578: ORACLE data block corrupted (file # 12, block # 13)
ORA-01110: data file 12: '/oracle/app/oradata/ora11g/tbs_corrupt.dbf'
ORA-06512: at "sys.dbms_space_admin", line 362
ORA-06512: at line 1
```

Another situation when these procedures could be used would be for fixing media corruption of bitmap blocks in which three procedures would be executed in this order.

1. If the tablespace contains corrupted blocks, the execution of procedure *tablespace_verify* shows the error and writes the following message in the alert file of the database:

```
[ora11g@dbms trace]$ tail -f alert_ora11g.log
Hex dump of (file 12, block 13) in trace file
/oracle/app/diag/rdbms/ora11g/ora11g/trace/ora11g_ora_17795.trc
Corrupt block relative dba: 0x0300000d (file 12, block 13)
Bad header found during buffer read
Data in bad block:
 type: 58 format: 3 rdba: 0xb746c3d2
 last change scn: 0xca9b.ca24f02b seq: 0xc flg: 0x77
 spare1: 0xf9 spare2: 0xde spare3: 0x9c7f
 consistency value in tail: 0xf0b7c97b
 check value in block header: 0x7f3d
 computed block checksum: 0x4f39
Reread of rdba: 0x0300000d (file 12, block 13) found same corrupted data
Fri May 15 00:43:29 2009
Corrupt Block Found
        TSN = 14, tsname = test_corrupt
        RFN = 12, BLK = 13, RDBA = 50331661
        OBJN = -1, OBJD = 71776, OBJECT = test_corrupt, subobject =
        segment owner = , segment type = Temporary Segment
Errors in file
/oracle/app/diag/rdbms/ora11g/ora11g/trace/ora11g_ora_17795.trc
(incident=17057):
ORA-01578: ORACLE data block corrupted (file # 12, block # 13)
ORA-01110: data file 12: '/oracle/app/oradata/ora11g/tbs_corrupt.dbf'
Incident details in:
/oracle/app/diag/rdbms/ora11g/ora11g/incident/incdir_17057/ora11g_ora_17795_
i17057.trc
Errors in file
/oracle/app/diag/rdbms/ora11g/ora11g/trace/ora11g_ora_17795.trc
(incident=17058):
ORA-01578: ORACLE data block corrupted (file # , block # )
ORA-01578: ORACLE data block corrupted (file # 12, block # 13)
ORA-01110: data file 12: '/oracle/app/oradata/ora11g/tbs_corrupt.dbf'
Fri May 15 00:43:34 2009
Trace dumping is performing id=[cdmp_20090515004334]
Incident details in:
/oracle/app/diag/rdbms/ora11g/ora11g/incident/incdir_17058/ora11g_ora_17795_
i17058.trc
Trace dumping is performing id=[cdmp_20090515004335]
Fri May 15 00:43:47 2009
Sweep Incident[17057]: completed
Fri May 15 00:43:48 2009
```

```
Hex dump of (file 12, block 13) in trace file
/oracle/app/diag/rdbms/ora11g/ora11g/incident/incdir_17057/ora11g_m000_17814
_i17057_a.trc
Corrupt block relative dba: 0x0300000d (file 12, block 13)
Bad header found during validation
Data in bad block:
 type: 58 format: 3 rdba: 0xb746c3d2
 last change scn: 0xca9b.ca24f02b seq: 0xc flg: 0x77
 spare1: 0xf9 spare2: 0xde spare3: 0x9c7f
 consistency value in tail: 0xf0b7c97b
 check value in block header: 0x7f3d
 computed block checksum: 0x4f39
Reread of blocknum=13, file=/oracle/app/oradata/ora11g/tbs_corrupt.dbf.
found same corrupt data
Reread of blocknum=13, file=/oracle/app/oradata/ora11g/tbs_corrupt.dbf.
found same corrupt data
Reread of blocknum=13, file=/oracle/app/oradata/ora11g/tbs_corrupt.dbf.
found same corrupt data
Reread of blocknum=13, file=/oracle/app/oradata/ora11g/tbs_corrupt.dbf.
found same corrupt data
Reread of blocknum=13, file=/oracle/app/oradata/ora11g/tbs_corrupt.dbf.
found same corrupt data
Hex dump of (file 12, block 14) in trace file
/oracle/app/diag/rdbms/ora11g/ora11g/incident/incdir_17057/ora11g_m000_17814
_i17057_a.trc
```

2. Then, for the solution to the problem of bitmap corrupted blocks, we are able to execute the three procedures described above.

Package *utl_compress*

The *utl_compress* package supplies a series of utilities for the compression of datatypes RAW, BLOB or BFILE. It is created through the script *utlcomp.sql*.

The *utl_compress* package was designed using C language with known algorithms of compression which are compatible with utilitarian Lempel-Ziv; for example, *zip* for Windows and *compress* for UNIX. The compression and decompression of the files are always made on the server side and not on the client sidem, and the data is sent without compression to the server where it is compressed.

A list of subprograms of this package follows:

- *isopen* (function)

- *lz_compress* (function and procedure)

- *lz_compress_add* (procedure)

- *lz_compress_close* (procedure)

- *lz_compress_open* (procedure)

- *lz_uncompress* (function and procedure)

- *lz_uncompress _extract* (procedure)

- *lz_uncompress _open* (function)

- *lz_uncompress _close* (procedure)

See how to compress data in a table with a column of type LOB in which .txt and .doc files are stored.

Procedure *lz_compress* and *lz_uncompress*

Procedure *lz_compress*, of package *utl_compress*, reduces the size of a BLOB record by more than 50%. In this in case, it has a .txt file type; however, it is possible to use any type of binary files, such as .doc, .jpg, .dmp or anything else.

For tables that have historical data and LOB columns, the compression is very useful because performance on queries that use these tables is improved and storage space is also freed. A trigger could be created using package *utl_compress* that compresses data while inserts are being executed on a historical table and thus, the process can be automated.

The example below demonstrates compressions that release a lot of free space on storage. This will make the CEO of the company very satisfied as he/she will perhaps spend less money on disks and more money buying CPUs.

⊞ Code 2.24 – utl_compress_uncompress.sql

```
conn pkg/pkg#123

Connected to Oracle 11g Enterprise Edition Release 11.1.0.6.0
Connected as pkg

--Using procedures lz_compress and lz_uncompress with LOB data type
--Creating a table with BLOB column
create table tab_utl_compress (
    col_id number,
    col_blob BLOB)
;

Table created

--Create a Directory to keep the binary files (pictures, .doc and others)
create or replace directory
    pictures
as
    '/oracle/pictures';

Directory created

select
    *
```

```
from
    dba_directories
where
    directory_name ='pictures';
```

OWNER	DIRECTORY_NAME	DIRECTORY_PATH
SYS	pictures	/oracle/pictures

```
--Now let's insert one row with BLOB uncompressed and compressed and then
see the size differences
set serveroutput on
declare
    compress_quality integer := 1; --An integer in the range 1 to 9, 1=fast
compression , 9=best compression, default is 6
    file_size integer;
    binary_file blob;
    source_file bfile := bfilename('pictures', 'tab_utl_compress.txt');
    amount integer;
    a_compressed_blob;

 cursor blob_cur is
 select
    *
 from
    tab_utl_compress;

 begin
    insert into
        tab_utl_compress
    values
        (1, empty_blob());
    select
        col_blob BLOB
    into
        binary_file
    from
        tab_utl_compress
    where
        col_id = 1;

    -- Get the BLOG file size
    dbms_lob.fileopen(
        file_loc => source_file);
    file_size := dbms_lob.getlength(
                    source_file);

    -- Insert the file into table and get the size
    dbms_lob.loadfromfile(
        binary_file,
        source_file,
        file_size);
    file_size := dbms_lob.getlength(
                    lob_loc => binary_file);
    dbms_output.put_line('Size of uncompressed file "bytes": ' ||
file_size);

    -- Compressing the table using utl_compress   5
    a_compressed_blob := utl_compress.lz_compress(
```

```
                        src => binary_file,
                        quality =>  compress_quality);

    -- Now insert the compresses row into table tab_utl_compress
    insert into
       tab_utl_compress
    values
       (2, a_compressed_blob);

    file_size := dbms_lob.getlength(
                    lob_loc => a_compressed_blob);
    dbms_output.put_line('Size of compressed file "bytes": ' || file_size);

  exception
    when others then
    dbms_output.put_line('A problem have been founded');
    dbms_output.put_line(sqlcode || sqlerrm);
  end;
/
```

```
Size of uncompressed file "bytes": 16777000
Size of compressed file "bytes": 7567982
```

```
commit;
```

```
Commit complete
```

Summary

This chapter demonstrated the most useful packages for DBAs to use for the maintenance and organization of tablespaces, tables and indexes.

The Packages presented in this chapter were: *dbms_errlog, dbms_iot, dbms_lob, dbms_pclxutil, dbms_redefinition, dbms_rowid, dbms_space, dbms_space_admin* and *utl_compress*.

In the next chapter, we will present packages that can be used in the security area of the Oracle database.

Oracle Security Packages

Database security management is one of the biggest challenges and highest priorities companies are facing today. The ever increasing speed of processes, coupled with the worldwide scope of the Internet, make external attacks a continuous threat that must be monitored and defended against.

Oracle, throughout its history, has always been on the forefront in their improvement of database protection tools, both against external and internal attacks. In this chapter, we will cover the main packages related to Oracle's database security.

Package *dbms_crypto*

Oracle *dbms_crypto* allows a user to encrypt and decrypt Oracle data. Oracle *dbms_crypto* supports the National Institute of Standards and Technology (NIST) approved Advanced Encryption Standard (AES) encryption algorithm. Oracle *dbms_crypto* also supports Data Encryption Standard (DES), Triple DES (3DES, 2-key and 3-key), MD5, MD4, and SHA-1 cryptographic hashes, and MD5 and SHA-1 Message Authentication Code (MAC). This package can encrypt most common Oracle datatypes including RAW and large objects (LOBs) as well as BLOBs and CLOBs.

The package *dbms_crypto* will eventually replace the package *dbms_obfuscation_toolkit* because it is easier to use and supports a larger amount of algorithms. For a complete list of the algorithms supported by the package *dbms_crypto*, access the *Oracle Database PL/SQL Packages and Types Reference* manual.

It is important to note that package *dbms_crypto* cannot be used with type *varchar2*. As a workaround, it is necessary to convert *varchar2* into the uniform database character set AL32UTF8 and then convert to a *raw* datatype. Only then can the user encrypt using the package *dbms_crypto*. Below are practical examples using procedures from the package *dbms_crypto*.

Checking for Modifications on Stored PL/SQL

This process stores the *checksum* results which auditors can access at any time when searching for alterations made to objects. Following are the procedures used in the example and a brief description:

- *hash*: This function takes a variable-length input string and converts it to a fixed length. This fixed length can be used to identify if data has been changed or not because of its distinct value.

- *hashmd5*: It generates a 128-bit hash more powerful than MD4

Below, the privilege below should be assigned to the user that will handle the *dbms_crypto* package.

🖫 Code 3.1 – dbms_crypto_audit_procedures.sql

```
conn sys@ora11g as sysdba
show user
grant all on dbms_crypto to pkg;
grant select on dba_source to pkg;

conn pkg@ora11g
show user
```

The function below is created to check whether or not an object was changed.

```
create or replace function vrfy_changes(
                    source_owner in varchar2,
                            source_name  in varchar2,
                            source_type  in varchar2)
    return varchar2 as
    code_source clob;
    md5hash        varchar2(32);
    cursor source_cursor is
        select
            text
        from
            dba_source
        where
            owner = upper(source_owner)
        and
            name = upper(source_name)
        and
            type in upper(source_type)
        order by
            line;
  begin
    code_source := '';
    for source_record in source_cursor loop
      code_source := code_source || source_record.text;
    end loop;
    md5hash := rawtohex(dbms_crypto.hash(src => code_source,
                                    typ => dbms_crypto.hash_md5));
```

```
    return md5hash;
  end;
  /
```

Function created

show errors

No errors for function pkg.vrfy_changes

Now a table that will store *checksum* information is created.

```
drop table audit_hash_source purge
/
Table dropped
```

```
create table audit_hash_source(
   owner varchar2(30),
   name varchar2(30),
   type varchar2(12),
   hash varchar(32),
   calculation_date date not null)
/
```

Table created

```
create unique index
   idx_audit_hash
on
   audit_hash_source(owner,name,type)
/
```

Index created

The procedure is created and it is used to test the *vrfy_changes* function.

```
create or replace procedure pkg.proc_test as
   begin
      null;
   end;
/
```

Procedure created

Here, the hash value is gathered before the procedure changes. This value is inserted in the *audit_hash_source* table.

```
select
   vrfy_changes('pkg','proc_test','procedure') hash
from
   dual;
```

```
HASH
--------------------------------
6A9AFF108D24F016C3F5C138763E0F59
```

```
--Insert hash values in the audit table
insert into
   audit_hash_source
select
   owner,
   object_name,
   object_type,
   vrfy_changes(owner, object_name, object_type),
   sysdate
from
   dba_objects
where
   object_type = 'procedure'
and
   owner = 'pkg'
 /

4 rows inserted

commit
 /

Commit complete
```

A change is made in the *proc_test* procedure. A different *hash* value is apparent after this step.

```
create or replace procedure pkg.proc_test as
   a varchar2(20);
   begin
      execute immediate ('select * from dual;');
   end;
/

Procedure created
```

Finally, the query below is used in conjunction with the function *vry_changes* to retrieve the changes that happened in the *proc_test* procedure and show the new hash value.

```
select
   owner,
   name,
   type,
   calculation_date,hash
from
  audit_hash_source
where
   type = 'procedure'
and
   vrfy_changes(owner, name, type) <> hash;

OWNER NAME       TYPE     CALCULATION_DATE   HASH
----- ---------  -------  ----------------   ------------------------------
pkg   proc_test  procedure 24-May-09 04:46   6A9AFF108D24F016C3F5C138763E0F59
```

Auditing companies may demand verification regarding objects that have been altered as shown in the example above and the DBA should proceed as shown above. A common practice used by DBAs is to create a procedure as shown in the example above and schedule it in a job using the package *dbms_sheduler*. This will be examined in Chapter 7, *Management and Monitoring*, in order to keep the information updated and sent via email automatically.

Storing Encrypted Data into a *varchar2* Column

If we choose to store encrypted *raw* datatype in a column type *varchar2* data, it is necessary to convert the data using the function *howtohex* or *utl_encode* so that the information can be stored to a *varchar2* field type. Below is an example of how to execute this procedure using *dbms_crypto*.

🖫 Code 3.2 – dbms_crypto _ecn_dec_data.sql

```
Connected to Oracle 11g Enterprise Edition Release 11.1.0.6.0
Connected as pkg
```

A table is created to record the data that will be encrypted. Then some example rows are inserted on it.

```
drop table tab_dbms_crypto purge
/

Table dropped

create table tab_dbms_crypto(
    account_name varchar2(60 byte),
    account_passwd varchar2(256 byte)
 )
/

Table created

--Inserting some rows into table
insert into
    tab_dbms_crypto
       (account_name,
        account_passwd)
values
    ('user1', '#123$')
/

1 row inserted

insert into
    tab_dbms_crypto
       (account_name,
        account_passwd)
values
    ('user2', '$456%')
```

```
/

1 row inserted

insert into
   tab_dbms_crypto
      (account_name,
       account_passwd)
values
   ('user3', '(876%')
/

1 row inserted

commit
/

Commit complete
```

The table below is created to store encrypted data.

```
drop table tab_dbms_crypto_secrets purge;

Table dropped

 create table tab_dbms_crypto_secrets(
    value1 varchar2(128 byte),
    value2 raw(128)
  )
 /

Table created
```

Now a package that will execute the process of encrypting and decrypting data is created using these functions:

- *encrypt_aes128*: Advanced encryption standard. Block cipher. Uses 128-bit key.

- *chain_cbc*: Cipher block chaining

- *pad_pkcs5*: Password-based cryptography standard

- *randombytes*: This function generates random key values

```
create or replace package pkg_encrypt_decrypt
   as
   function enc_account_passwd(
   p_account_passwd in varchar2,
   p_account_name in varchar2,
   p_unlock_code in varchar2 default null)
   return varchar2;

   function dec_account_passwd(
   p_account_passwd in varchar2,
   p_account_name in varchar2,
   p_unlock_code in varchar2 default null)
   return varchar2;
```

```
end;
/

Package created

create or replace package body pkg_encrypt_decrypt as
   main_password  varchar2(32) := 'ThisIsTheSuperSe';
   free_passsword varchar2(10) := 'OpenSesame';
   enc_mode       number := dbms_crypto.encrypt_aes128 +
                             dbms_crypto.chain_cbc    +
                             dbms_crypto.pad_pkcs5;

   function enc_account_passwd(
      p_account_passwd in varchar 2,
      p_account_name   in varchar 2,
      p_unlock_code    in varchar 2 default NULL)
      return varchar2 as
      swordfish           raw(256);
      swordfish_enccrypted raw(256);
   begin
      if (p_unlock_code is null or p_unlock_code != free_password)
      then
         return null;
      end if;
```

The *randombytes* function below returns a *raw* value containing an encrypted secure pseudo-random sequence of bytes which can be used to generate random material for encryption keys.

```
--We generate the swordfish, this "random" number will be needed to decrypt
the password

      swordfish := dbms_crypto.randombytes(16);

-- This function encrypts raw data using a stream or block cipher with a
user supplied key

      enccrypted swordfish:= dbms_crypto.encrypt(swordfish,
                                                 enc_mode,
                                                 utl_i18n.string_to_raw(
   main_password,
   'al32utf8')); --Notice how easy it is to perform the conversion to raw

swordfish_enccrypted := dbms_crypto.encrypt(swordfish,
                                            enc_mode,
                                            utl_i18n.string_to_raw(
   main_password,
   'al32utf8'));

      -- Inserting the account name, and swordfish, encrypted using the
main_password as key, in secrets table
      insert into
         tab_dbms_crypto_secrets
      values
         (p_account_name, enccrypted swordfish);
```

At this point, the password storage on column *account_passwd* is returned as an encrypted *account_passwd* random key.

```
      return
         utl_encode.base64_encode(
            dbms_crypto.encrypt(
               utl_i18n.string_to_raw(
                  p_account_passwd,
                  'al32utf8'),
               enc_mode,
               swordfish));
end;

   function dec_account_passwd(
      p_account_passwd in varchar2,
      p_account_name   in varchar2,
      p_unlock_code    in varchar2 default NULL)
   return varchar2 as
   swordfish raw(256);
   begin
      if (p_unlock_code is null or p_unlock_code != free_passssword)
      then
         return null;
      end if;

      select
         dbms_crypto.decrypt(
            value2,
            enc_mode,
            utl_i18n.string_to_raw(
               main_password,
               'al32utf8'))
      into
         swordfish
      from
         tab_dbms_crypto_secrets
      where
         value1 = p_account_name;
      return utl_i18n.raw_to_char(
         dbms_crypto.decrypt(
            utl_encode.base64_decode(
               p_account_passwd),
               enc_mode,
               swordfish),
            'al32utf8');
   end;
  end;
/
```

```
Package body created
```

Now the data without encryption is selected.

```
select
   *
from
   tab_dbms_crypto
```

```
/
```

```
ACCOUNT_NAME      ACCOUNT_PASSWD
------------      --------------
user1             #123$
user2             $456%
user3             (876%
```

Here, the data is encrypted using the package and function created in the first steps.

```
update
   tab_dbms_crypto
set
   account_passwd = pkg_encrypt_decrypt.enc_account_passwd(
                       account_passwd,
                       account_name,
                       'OpenSesame')
/
```

```
3 rows updated
```

```
commit
/
```

```
Commit complete
```

Finally, the encrypted data can be seen.

```
select
   *
from
   tab_dbms_crypto
/
```

```
ACCOUNT_NAME      ACCOUNT_PASSWD
------------      -----------------------------------------------
user1             6E42464477424C7145733576626F666F766D79344E773D3D
user2             7159616849675256554868D6B31736E2F4E4C747639513D3D
user3             4B5742784C6F3857783346454E58346A58396A5338673D3D
```

Just as with *encrypt*, *decrypt* can be done using the package and function created.

```
update
   tab_dbms_crypto
set
   account_passwd = pkg_encrypt_decrypt.dec_account_passwd(
                       account_passwd,
                       account_name,
                       'OpenSesame')
/
```

```
3 rows updated
```

```
commit
/
```

```
Commit complete

--Get the data without encryption again
select
   *
from
   tab_dbms_crypto
/

ACCOUNT_NAME    ACCOUNT_PASSWD
------------    ----------------
user1           #123$
user2           $456%
user3           (876%
```

This example uses the function *randombytes*. This function returns a *raw* value containing a cryptographically secure pseudo-random sequence of bytes which can be used to generate random material for encryption keys.

The *decrypt* and *encrypt* functions are also employed to encrypt and decrypt the *raw* data. Note that the following functions are called in order to find information related to cryptographic data in the database:

- *all_encrypted_columns*

- *dba_encrypted_columns*

- *user_encrypted_columns*

- *v$encrypted_tablespaces*

- *v$encryption_wallet*

- *v$rman_encryption_algorithms*

From Oracle 10g, a new feature named Transparent Data Encryption performs a similar functionality with some more flexibilities. More information about this can be found at http://www.dba-oracle.com/t_transparent_data_encryption_tde.htm.

Package *dbms_change_notification*

Imagine that the owner of an online bookstore chain wants to know when a new client was registered into their the system. Such a request can be met by several mechanisms:

1. **Insert Trigger:** A DML trigger could be used to send a nootification

2. **A CQN:** A Change Query Notification could create a register for all DML operations made in a specific table. In this case, if an insertion is made to a table of clients, a notification of this operation will be made.

This is only one example of what the *dbms_change_notification* package can do. It is also possible to receive notifications on DDL operations made to a table or index.

Here, the notifications are published for a DML event or a DDL operations

Applications that are running in the middle tier require rapid access to cached copies of database information while, at the same time, keeping the cache as current as possible in relation to the database.

Sadly, cached data becomes out of date or stale when a transaction modifies the data and commits, thereby putting the application at risk of accessing incorrect results. If the application uses Database Change Notification, then Oracle Database can publish a notification when a change occurs to registered objects with details on what changed. In response to the notification, the application can refresh cached data by fetching it from the back-end database.

Below is an illustration of an application with several queries in a table of clients called *pkg.clients*. If this table is accessed frequently, the performance of the queries is improved as long as the data is kept in the cache. However, if an update is made, the mid-tier cache must also be updated with that new information in order to avoid the user seeing outdated information in the system. We will now demonstrate how to create an Object Change Registration.

First, give the required privilege to the user that will execute the procedure.

🖫 Code 3.3 - dbms_change_notification.sql

```
Connected to Oracle 11g Enterprise Edition Release 11.1.0.6.0
Connected as pkg

conn sys / as sysdba

show user

grant change notification to pkg;
grant execute on dbms_cq_notification to pkg;
```

Change the parameter below to a value larger than 1 to receive notifications.

```
alter system set "job_queue_processes"=5 scope=both;
```

Three tables are created: one to record notifications about changes that will be made (*tab_notifications*), one to record the actual changes (*tab_changes*) and the last optional one to record *rowid* changes (*tab_rowid_changes*).

```
connect pkg/pkg;
REM Create the notification table
```

```
create table tab_notifications(
   id number,
   evt_type number);

REM  Create the changes record table
create table tab_changes(
   id number,
   tab_name varchar2(100),
   table_operation number);

REM Create the rowid table changes
create table tab_rowid_changes(
   id number,
   tab_name varchar2(100),
   row_id varchar2(30));
```

Create the procedure that will send notifications.

```
create or replace procedure proc_notifications_handler(sys_chnf_type in
sys.chnf$_desc) is
   id              number;
   tbname          varchar2(60);
   evt_type        number;
   numtables       number;
   operation_type  number;
   numrows         number;
   row_id          varchar2(20);
 begin
    id        := sys_chnf_type.registration_id;
    numtables := sys_chnf_type.numtables;
    evt_type := sys_chnf_type.event_type;

  insert into tab_notifications values(id, evt_type);

--Check if event is associated with notification
  if (evt_type = dbms_cq_notification.event_objchange) then
    for i in 1..numtables loop
      tbname          := sys_chnf_type.table_desc_array(i).table_name;
      operation_type  := sys_chnf_type.table_desc_array(I). Opflags;
      insert into tab_changes values(id, tbname, operation_type);

-- If row information is available for the operation
      If (bitand(operation_type, dbms_cq_notification.all_rows) = 0) then
-- Get the number of rows affected
        numrows := sys_chnf_type.table_desc_array(i).numrows;
      else
-- If there is no information about the rows
        numrows :=0;
      end if;

      for j IN 1..numrows loop
          Row_id :=
sys_chnf_type.table_desc_array(i).row_desc_array(j).row_id;
          insert into
 tab_rowid_changes values(id, tbname, Row_id);
        end loop;

    end loop;
```

```
  end if;
  commit;
end;
/
```

Now the table *pkg.clients* is added, so any changes regarding what is being monitored will be registered.

```
create table
 clients
as
select
   *
from
  scott.emp;

declare
  regds                         sys.chnf$_reg_info;
  id                            number;
  employee_num                  number;

begin
-- We set the flags we need (We'll use Reliable registration, ensuring the
notification is sent before the change is committed, plus, we need to track
rowid info) qosflags := dbms_cq_notification.qos_reliable +
        dbms_cq_notification.qos_rowids;
-- Now we'll create the registration
-- First step is to tell Oracle to define it with the notification_handler
we created before, and to use the flags we defined.
regds := sys.chnf$_reg_info ('proc_notifications_handler', qosflags, 0,0,0);

-- Last step, is to associate it with the tables we need (by selecting from
them after _notification.new_reg_start)
id := dbms_cq_notification.new_reg_start (regds);
select empno into employee_num from clients where empno = 7902;
dbms_cq_notification.reg_end;
end;
/
```

An update is executed on the *clients* table to generate a notification. After that, a query of *tab_notifications* is made to check these changes.

```
update
   clients
set
   sal=sal*1.05
where
   empno=7902;
commit;

--We can check all changes made that are been monitored on control tables
created bellow
select
   *
from
   tab_notifications
```

```
/
select
   *
from
   tab_changes
/
select
   *
from
   tab_rowid_changes
/
```

To check all notifications configured in the database, use the query shown below.

```
select
   *
from
   dba_change_notification_regs;
```

In conclusion, the package *dbms_change_notification* allows the database administrators to monitor the DML operations that are being executed in a specific table in a particular range of records.

Package *dbms_distributed_trust_admin*

The *dbms_distributed_trust_admin* package is used to manage a list of reliable servers that can access the local database via database links. In Oracle 11g and beyond, current user database links operate only within a single enterprise domain between trusted databases. The databases within the single enterprise domain must trust each other in order to authenticate users.

You specify an enterprise domain as being trusted by using the Oracle Enterprise Manager -- Enterprise Security Manager screen. If your current user database links are enabled for a domains by using Enterprise Security Manager, they will work for all databases within that domain by default.

If there are databases that should not be trusted within your domain, use the PL/SQL package *dbms_distributed_trust_admin* to indicate all databases which participate in a trusted enterprise domain, but cannot be trusted. For example, we may not want a training database to be considered a trusted database, even if it is in the same enterprise domain with production databases. You can use the *trusted_servers* view to obtain a list of trusted servers in your domain.

Prior to execution of the package *dbms_distributed_trust_admin*, it is necessary to have been granted *execute_catalog_role*. The view *trusted_servers* is used in order to identify which of the servers are reliable and which are not. In order to use *select* in the view *trusted_servers*, it is necessary to have the *select_catalog_role* privilege.

The value returned in the query view *trusted_servers* should look like the example below; therefore, allowing all of the servers that belong to the domain to have access to the database in which the query is being executed.

```
column name for a40
select
    *
from
    trusted_servers;

TRUST      NAME
---------  ----------------------------------------
Trusted    All
```

If the access of a specific server needs to be blocked, then the procedure *deny_server* is used, as shown below.

🖫 Code 3.4 – dbms_distributed_trust_admin_deny_server.sql

```
Connected to Oracle 11g Enterprise Edition Release 11.1.0.6.0
Connected as pkg

conn sys / as sysdba
show user

User is "pkg"

exec dbms_distributed_trust_admin.deny_server('bwfsdbsp01.b2winc.com');


column name for a40
select
    *
from
    trusted_servers;

TRUST      NAME
---------  ----------------------------------------
Trusted    All
Untrusted  bwfsdbsp01.b2winc.com
```

When no server is reliable, the procedure *deny_all* should be used as shown below.

🖫 Code 3.5 – dbms_distributed_trust_admin_deny_all.sql

```
Connected to Oracle 11g Enterprise Edition Release 11.1.0.6.0
Connected as pkg

conn sys / as sysdba
show user
```

```
User is "pkg"

exec dbms_distributed_trust_admin.deny_all;


select
  *
from
  trusted_servers;

TRUST     NAME
--------- -----------------------------------------
Untrusted All
```

Note that the default value of the configuration is *trusted all*. This allows all of the servers that are part of the same domain in an enterprise directory server to have free access. In order to force this option, the procedure *allow_all* is used as shown below:

🖫 Code 3.6 – dbms_distributed_trust_admin_allow_all.sql

```
Connected to Oracle 11g Enterprise Edition Release 11.1.0.6.0
Connected as pkg

conn sys / as sysdba
show user

User is "pkg"

exec dbms_distributed_trust_admin.allow_all;


select
  *
from
  trusted_servers;

TRUST     NAME
--------- -----------------------------------------
Trusted   All
```

In conclusion, by using the package *dbms_distributed_trust_admin*, it is possible to quickly block/allow the access of a database through the current user database links.

Package *dbms_fga*

Fine-Grained Auditing (FGA) is alkso called "row level security" and it was created in version 9i in order to allow auditing of specific rows. With this new form of auditing, you avoid the wasting of resources by auditing only the rows that are necessary. Oracle 9i only permitted the use of FGA through the *select* commands, but beginning with Oracle 10g, it became possible to configure FGA using the commands *insert*, *update*, *delete* and *merge*.

It is important to note that FGA is only supported with the cost-based optimizer. If the optimizer mode is not cost-based, or if the audited objects are not analyzed, there will be problems with the audit. Here is an example of when to use the *dbms_fga* package. Suppose a business wishes to find out which user is peeking into the system to find information on the salary bonuses placed in a table of the database. This can be done using the package *dbms_fga* where a policy audits and saves the information related to all users that have accessed certain records in a table.

In order to use this package, it is necessary to grant *execute* privileges on *dbms_fga* to the user who will be configuring the auditing policies. It is important to keep in mind that this "privileged" user will be able to remove policies of other users even though he has not created them.

Beginning with Oracle 10g r2, it became possible to set the parameter *audit_trail* = XML, allowing audit records to be written to XML files in the operating system. This increases the security in accessing the information because only those with permission on an operating system level can view these files. If, on the other hand, the parameter is set for DB, then people with a DBA role will be able to access the view containing the audit records. The following sections describe the procedures on how to configure FGA using the package *dbms_fga*.

Procedure *add_policy*

This procedure is used to create an auditing policy using a predicate as a condition of the audit. Note that the maximum number of FGA policies in a table or view is 256.

```
begin
    dbms_fga.add_policy(
        object_schema => 'pkg',
        object_name => 'tab_customer',
        policy_name => 'pkg_cust_policy',
        audit_condition => NULL,
        audit_column => 'card_no',
        handler_schema => 'pkg',
        handler_module => 'mod_alert',
        enable => TRUE,
        statement_types => 'insert,update',
        audit_trail => DB,
        audit_column_opts => NULL);
end;
```

Procedure *drop_policy*

This is used to drop a policy. Here is an example:

```
begin
dbms_fga.drop_policy(
    object_schema => 'pkg',
    object_name => 'tab_customer',
    policy_name => 'pkg_cust_policy');
end;
```

Procedure *enable_policy*

This procedure is used to enable a policy.

```
begin
dbms_fga.enable_policy(
    object_schema => 'pkg',
    object_name => 'tab_customer',
    policy_name => 'pkg_cust_policy',
    enable => TRUE);
end;
```

Procedure *disable_policy*

This procedure is used to disable a policy.

```
begin
dbms_fga.disable_policy(
    object_schema => 'pkg',
    object_name => 'tab_customer',
    policy_name => 'pkg_cust_policy',
    enable => TRUE);
end;
```

Using *dbms_fga* Package: Example

Below is a practical example of how to use the procedure package *dbms_fga*. In this example, a table *tab_customer* is created. It is audited by a created policy called *pkg_cust_policy*. The policy audits only *update* and *insert* commands that involve the column *cust_credit_limit*.

A table named *tab_violations* stores information about the user who executed the audited command. The procedure that is executed by the event handler is *proc_alert*. This inserts the records containing additional information in the *tab_violations* table regarding the user that is being audited. The event handler could also call a procedure to send an email alerting that a specific command was audited.

In this example, these procedures are in the same schema. However, for security reasons, it is better to store them in separate schemas from the data being audited.

🖫 Code 3.7– dbms_fga.sql

```
Connected to Oracle 11g Enterprise Edition Release 11.1.0.6.0
Connected as pkg

conn pkg/pkg123
show user

User is "pkg"
```

Primarily, two tables are created. The first, *tab_customer*, is the table that will be audited and the second, *tab_violations*, is the table that will record information about the user that triggered the audit record.

```
create table
    tab_customer
tablespace
    pkg_data
as
select
    *
from
    sh.customers ;

create table
    tab_violations(
        username varchar(20),
        userhost varchar(20),
        ip_addr  varchar(20),
        os_user varchar(20),
        time timestamp)
tablespace
    pkg_data;
```

Next, a procedure named *proc_alert* is created. This procedure adds valuable information to table *tab_violations* and is used as a parameter value for *handle_module*.

```
create or replace procedure
    proc_alert (
        schema_name varchar2,
        obj_name varchar2,
        policy_name varchar2)
as
begin
 insert into
    pkg.tab_violations(
        username,
        userhost,
        ip_addr,
        os_user,
        time)
 select
```

```
    user,
    sys_context('userenv','terminal'),
    sys_context('userenv','ip_address'),
    sys_context('userenv','os_user'),
    sysdate
 from
    dual;
end proc_alert;
/
```

Drop the policy if it already exists; otherwise, create the audit policy as follows:

```
begin
dbms_fga.drop_policy(
    object_schema => 'pkg',
    object_name => 'tab_customer',
    policy_name => 'pkg_cust_policy');
end;

--Create the policy that will audit update and insert statements done in
table tab_customer
begin
    dbms_fga.add_policy(
        object_schema => 'pkg',
        object_name => 'tab_customer',
        policy_name => 'pkg_cust_policy',
        audit_condition => '1=1',
        audit_column => 'cust_credit_limit',
        handler_schema => 'pkg',
        handler_module => 'proc_alert',
        enable => TRUE,
        statement_types => 'insert,update',
        audit_trail => dbms_fga.db+dbms_fga.extended,
        audit_column_opts => dbms_fga.any_columns);
end;
```

Finally, some changes are generated and audited. After that, query tables that have information about audited records.

```
--This row will be changes
select
    cust_id,
    cust_first_name,
    cust_credit_limit
from
    tab_customer
where
cust_id=17449;

CUST_ID CUST_FIRST_NAME      CUST_CREDIT_LIMIT
---------- -------------------- -----------------
    17449 Abigail                          15300

--Making some changes to be audited
update
    tab_customer
```

```
set
   cust_credit_limit = cust_credit_limit * 1.7
where
   cust_id=17449;

1 row updated

commit;

--Check the cust_credit_limit after changes
select
   cust_id,
   cust_first_name,
   cust_credit_limit
from
   tab_customer
where
cust_id=17449;

   CUST_ID CUST_FIRST_NAME       CUST_CREDIT_LIMIT
---------- -------------------- -----------------
     17449 Abigail                          26010

--Query to get information about changes
col db_user for a10
col schema for a10
col object_name for a15
col policy_name for a20

select
   db_user,
   object_schema "Schema",
   object_name,
   policy_name,
   to_char(timestamp,'YY-MM-DD HH24:MI:SS') "Time",
   sql_text
from
   dba_fga_audit_trail;

DB_USER Schema OBJECT_NAME  POLICY_NAME     Time             SQL_TEXT
---     ----   -----------  --------------- ----------------------- 
pkg     pkg    tab_customer pkg_cust_policy 09-07-20 22:37:21 update

tab_customer set cust_credit_limit = cust_credit_limit * 1.7 where cust_i

--Query to get violations already done generated by event handler
select
   *
from
   tab_violations;

USER  USERHOST   IP_ADDR   OS_USER   TIME
NAME
----  ---------  ---------  -------  ------------------------------
pkg   pportugal 10.10.10.1 Paulo    21-JUL-09 02.24.20.000000 AM
```

Any *update* or *insert* command made to the table *tab_customer* through the column *cust_credit_limit* is recorded in the audit table. Here are some useful views for getting information about FGA configurations:

- *fga_log$*: Table that records all audit information. This table is accessed through the *dba_fga_audit_trail* view. Data on this table can be purged. Make a backup before purging.

- *fga$*: This table stores information about audit policy object

- *dba_common_audit_trail*: Displays all audit trail entries

- *dba_fga_audit_trail*: Displays all audit records for FGA

- *dba_audit_exists*: This is an audit trail of the entries where the operation failed due to non-existing objects. This is actually filtered from the view *dba_audit_trail* where the return code is a value other than zero.

- *dba_audit_trail*: This is a view based on the *aud$* table which decodes most of the values inside the table to present it in a user friendly manner. For instance, the column *spare1* in *aud$* actually stores the operating system user name. The column *os_username* in this view gets its value from that column in the *aud$* table. Similarly, the column *action#* holds the user's action in a numeral form. For example, 108 indicates granting system privilege. The view decodes the numerical representation for the actions and presents the information in the column *action_name*. Therefore, this view is actually more useful for analysis than the *aud$* table itself.

Package *dbms_obfuscation_toolkit*

Another package used to encrypt and decrypt data is *dbms_obfuscation_toolkit*. This package allows the user to encrypt/decrypt data using algorithms Data Encryption Standard (DES) and Triple DES. The installation of this package is made using the scripts *dbmsobtk.sql* and *prvtobtk.plb* which must be executed through the user sys. Following the execution of these scripts, grant the *execute* privilege in the package to *public*. Although this package is being replaced by the package *dbms_crypto*, it is still being used for backward compatibility. The following is an example on how to use the package *dbms_obfsucation_toolkit* to encrypt a row's data.

First, let's create a table that stores credit card information, i.e., credit card numbers, numbers which must be encrypted because of their confidential nature. The encryption is done with two functions called *func_card_num_encrypt* and *func_card_num_encrypt_des3*, respectively. The first performs a regular encryption, whereas the second encrypts using the Triple DES algorithm.

⊞ Code 3.8 – dbms_obfuscation_toolkit.sql

```
Connected to Oracle 11g Enterprise Edition Release 11.1.0.6.0
Connected as pkg

conn sys / as sysdba
show user

User is "pkg"

create table
    tab_card_number (
        card_1_number       char(40),
        card_2_number       char(40),
        first_name          varchar2(20),
        last_name           varchar2(20));

create or replace function func_card_num_encrypt(input_val varchar2)
    return varchar2 is
    key_str      varchar2(40)  := 'ADFGHJHR&%JKJHJHSHJSJHS';
    return_val varchar2(40)  := NULL;
begin
    dbms_obfuscation_toolkit.DESEncrypt(input_string    => input_val,
                                        key_string       => key_str,
                                        encrypted_string => return_val);

    return return_val;

end;
/
show errors

create or replace function func_card_num_encrypt_des3(input_val varchar2)
    return varchar2 is
    key_str      varchar2(40)  := '4400002389774555RRHJHJWUYWY^%%^%';
    return_val varchar2(40)  := NULL;
begin

    dbms_obfuscation_toolkit.DES3Encrypt(input_string    => input_val,
                                         key_string       => key_str,
                                         encrypted_string => return_val,
                                         which            => 1);
    return return_val;
end;
/
show errors
```

Next, two triggers are created which make use of the functions created above. As soon as a user executes one of the commands of *insert* or *update* in the row *tab_card_number* in one of the credit card number columns, this information is encrypted.

For the first column *card_1_number*, the algorithm used for encryption is the DES and for the second column *card_2_number*, the algorithm is the Triple DES.

```
create or replace trigger trg_encrypt_card_1_number
    before insert or update of card_1_number on tab_card_number
```

```
   referencing old as old new as new
   for each row
begin
   :new.card_1_number := func_card_num_encrypt(:new.card_1_number);
end;
/
show errors

create or replace trigger trg_encrypt_card_2_number
   before insert or update of card_2_number on tab_card_number
   referencing old as old new as new
   for each row
begin
   :new.card_2_number := func_card_num_encrypt_des3(:new.card_2_number);
end;
/
show errors

select
   *
from
   tab_card_number;

insert into
   tab_card_number
values (
   '1111999922228888',
   '9006784523339988',
   'Paulo',
   'Portugal');

select
   *
from
   tab_card_number;
```

CARD_1_NUMBER	CARD_2_NUMBER	FIRST_NAME	LAST_NAME
¿¿ÒN ÉÔ<¿eÒì¾|?.|¿Y=K.ã¿.X ÷	.°w&Þ.DiF.y.«q¿)rJìð#A_G¶¿q`	Paulo	Portugal

As we see, the data is encrypted; thus, a query to the table containing the credit card numbers cannot be read without the code used for the encryption.

Package *dbms_rls*

A Virtual Private Database (VPD) security model uses the Oracle *dbms_rls* package (RLS stands for row-level security) to implement the security policies and application contexts. This requires a policy that is defined to control access to tables and rows. Virtual private databases have several other names within the Oracle documentation including RLS and fine-grained access control (FGAC).

Regardless of the name, VPD security provides a whole new way to control access to Oracle data. Most interesting is the dynamic nature of a VPD. At runtime, Oracle performs these near magical feats by dynamically modifying the SQL statement of the end user.

Oracle gathers application context information at user logon time and then calls the policy function, which returns a predicate. A predicate is a WHERE clause that qualifies a particular set of rows within the table.

Oracle dynamically rewrites the query by appending the predicate to users' SQL statements. Whenever a query is run against the target tables, Oracle invokes the policy and produces a transient view with a WHERE clause predicate pasted onto the end of the query, like so:

```
select * from book WHERE P1 …
```

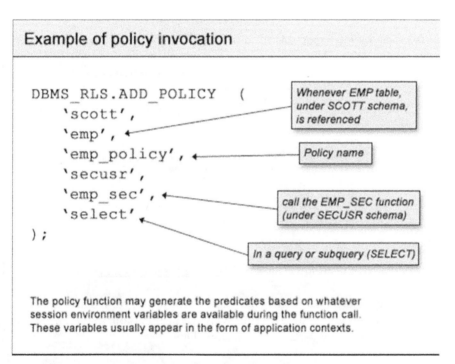

Figure 3.1: *Example of Policy Invocation*

VPDs are involved in the creation of a security policy and when users access a table or view that has a security policy. The security policy modifies the user's SQL, adding a *where* clause to restrict access to specific rows within the target tables. Take a close look at how this works.

VPD Usage with *set_context* Procedure

For the VPD to properly use the security policy to add the WHERE clause at the end user's SQL, Oracle must know details about the authority of the user. This is done at sign-on time using Oracle's *dbms_session* package. At sign-on, a database logon trigger executes, setting the application context for the user by calling *dbms_session.set_context*. The *set_context* procedure can be used to set any number of variables about the end user; for example, the application name, the user's name, and specific row restriction information. Once this data is collected, the security policy uses this information to build the run-time WHERE clause to append to the end user's SQL statement. The *set_context* procedure sets several parameters used by the VPD and requires three arguments:

```
dbms_session.set_context(namespace, attribute, value)
```

For example, assume there is a publication table and we want to restrict access based on the type of end user. Managers are able to view all books for their publishing company, while authors may only view their own books. So assume that user JSMITH is a manager and user MAULT is an author. At login time, the Oracle database logon trigger would generate the appropriate values and execute the statements shown below for each user:

```
dbms_session.set_context('publishing_application', 'role_name', 'manager');

dbms_session.set_context('publishing_application', 'user_name', 'jsmith');

dbms_session.set_context('publishing_application', 'company', 'rampant_techpress');

dbms_session.set_context('publishing_application', 'role_name', 'author');

dbms_session.set_context('publishing_application', 'user_name', 'mault');

dbms_session.set_context('publishing_application', 'company', 'rampant_techpress');
```

This example can be found at http://www.dba-oracle.com/ t_dbms_session.htm.

Once executed, view these values with the Oracle *session_context* view. This data will be used by the VPD at runtime to generate the WHERE clause. Note that each user has his or her own specific *session_context* values, shown here:

```
connect jsmith/manpass;

select
namespace, attribute, value
from
session_context;

NAMESPACE ATTRIBUTE VALUE
--------------- --------- ---------
publishing_application role_name manager
publishing_application user_name jsmith
```

```
publishing_application company rampant_techpress

connect mault/authpass;

select
namespace, attribute, value
from
session_context;

publishing_application role_name author
publishing_application user_name mault
publishing_application company rampant_techpress
```

Now see how this application context information is used by the VPD security policy. In Listing C, create a security policy function called *book_access_policy* that builds two types of WHERE clauses depending on the information in the *session_context* for each end user. Note that Oracle uses the *sys_context* function to gather the values.

```
create or replace function
   book_access_policy
   (obj_schema varchar2, obj_name varchar2) return varchar2

 is

 d_predicate varchar2(2000);

 begin

if sys_context('publishing_application','role_name')='manager' then

 d_predicate:=
 'upper(company)=sys_context(''publishing_application'',''company'')';

 else
   -- If the user_type session variable is set to anything else,

 -- display only this person's record --
   d_predicate:=

 'upper(author_name)=sys_context(''userenv'',''session_user'')';

end if;

return d_predicate;

 end;

end; /

 dbms_rls.add_policy (
   'pubs',
```

```
   'book',
   'access_policy',
   'pubs',
   'book_access_policy',
   'select'
);
```

Look at the code in this listing carefully. If the user was defined as a manager, their WHERE clause (*d_predicate*) would be:

```
where upper(company) = 'rampant_techpress';
```

For the author, they get a different WHERE clause:

```
where upper(author_name) = 'Mault';
```

VPDs in Action

It is now time to show the VPD in action. In Listing D, there are very different results from an identical SQL query depending on the application context of the specific end user.

```
connect jsmith/manpass;

select * from book;

Book                   Author
Title                  name          Publisher
-------------------    ------------  -------------------
Oracle9i RAC           mault         Rampant Techpress
Oracle job Interview   dburleson     Rampant Techpress
Oracle Utilities       dmmoore       Rampant Techpress
Oracle Troubleshooting rschumacher   Rampant Techpress
Oracle10i DBA Features mault         Rampant Techpress
connect mault/authpass;

select * from book;

Book                   Author
Title                  name          Publisher
-------------------    ------------  -------------------
Oracle9i RAC           mault         Rampant Techpress
Oracle10i DBA Features mault         Rampant Techpress
```

It should be obvious that VPD is a totally different way of managing Oracle access than grant-based security mechanisms. There are many benefits to VPDs:

- **Dynamic security:** No need to maintain complex roles and grants

- **Multiple security:** Able to place more than one policy on each object as well as stack them on other base policies. This makes VPD perfect for Web applications that are deployed for many companies.

- **No back doors:** Users no longer bypass security policies embedded in applications because the security policy is attached to the data.

- **Complex access rules may be defined:** With VPD, data values can be used to specify complex access rules that would be difficult to create with grant security. Access to rows can be easily restricted.

Of course, there are also some drawbacks to VPD security:

- **Difficult column level security:** Because access is controlled by adding a *where* clause, column-level access can only be maintained by defining multiple views for each class of end user.

- **In most cases, requires Oracle IDs for every user:** Unlike security that is managed externally, VPD requires that an Oracle user ID be defined for every role who connects to the database. This adds maintenance and overhead.

- **Hard to audit:** It is hard to write an audit script that defines the exact access for each specified user. This problem becomes even more acute for shops that mix security methods.

Problems with Mixing VPD and Grant Security

Now that we have established the areas of security and auditing, it should be clear that a method needs to be devised that ensures that security methods are not mixed in an inappropriate way. By themselves, each of these security mechanisms provides adequate access protection, but when these methods are mixed, it can often be difficult, if not impossible, to identify the access for individual users. It is up to the user to decide whether the security benefits of VPD are worth the extra administrative method.

Example: Hiding Source Code on *all_source* View

Some users have the *grant execute* privilege in system objects such as *packages* and *types*. With this privilege, they can make a query in the *all_sources* view allowing them to see an object's code. In order to block this access, use the package *dbms_rls* as shown in the example below. First, create a user that will have access to a package. Then modify the policy to prevent access of this procedure's source code.

⊞ Code 3.9 – dbms_rls_1.sql

```
Connected to Oracle 11g Enterprise Edition Release 11.1.0.6.0
Connected as pkg
```

```
conn sys / as sysdba
show user

User is "pkg"

create user no_access identified by no_access;
grant resource, connect to no_access;

create or replace package test_access as
   function hire (last_name varchar2, job_id varchar2,
      manager_id number, salary number,
      commission_pct number, department_id number)
      return number;
end test_access;
/


create or replace package body test_access as
   tot_emps number;
   tot_depts number;
function hire
   (last_name varchar2, job_id varchar2,
    manager_id number, salary number,
    commission_pct number, department_id number)
   return number is new_empno number;
begin
   select *
      into new_empno
      from dual;
      tot_emps := tot_emps + 1;
   return(new_empno);
end;
end test_access;
/

grant all on test_access to no_access;
```

Now the function which prevents users not listed in *pkg,sys* and *system* from accessing the function is created below.

```
create or replace function prevent_access_all_source(
   object_schema in varchar2,
   object_name varchar2)
return varchar2 is
begin
  if sys_context('userenv','session_user') not in
('pkg','sys','system') -if it's not one of those users
  then
-- Show only for their own procedures, functions and packages,.
    return 'not (sys_context(''userenv'',''session_user'') <>
           owner and type in (''package body'',''type
body'',''procedure'',''function''))';
  else
  return null;
  end if;
end;
/
show errors
```

```
--Drop policy if it already exists

begin
  sys.dbms_rls.drop_policy(
     object_schema => 'public',
     object_name => 'all_source',
     policy_name => 'policy_prevent_access');
end;
/
show errors

--Create policy

begin
  sys.dbms_rls.add_policy(
     object_schema => 'public',
     object_name => 'all_source',
     policy_name => 'policy_prevent_access',
     function_schema =>'pkg',
     policy_function => 'prevent_access_all_source',
     statement_types =>'select',
     enable => TRUE);
end;
/
show errors


--Check policy created
col "Obj owner" for a10
col "Obj Name" for a15
col "Function Owner" for a5
select
   object_owner "Obj owner",
   object_name "Obj Name",
   policy_name "Policy Name",
   pf_owner "Function Owner",
   function "Funct Name"
from
   dba_policies
where
   policy_name='policy_prevent_access';
```

```
Obj owner Obj Name  Policy Name            Function Owner Funct Name
------ ---------- -------------------- -------------- --------------------
public all_source policy_prevent_access pkg            prevent_access_all_source
```

After the policy is created, the user *no_access* tries to get the *source_code* of the package body *test_access* but nothing is returned by the query. This is because the policy has been implemented and is protecting the data. The user can see the *package* source code but not the *package body* as shown below:

```
show user

User is "no_access"
```

```
select
   text
from
   all_source
where
   name='test_access'
and
   owner='pkg'
and
   type = 'package';

TEXT
-------------------------------------------------------------------

package test_access AS
   function hire (last_name varchar2, job_id varchar2,
      manager_id number, salary number,
      commission_pct number, department_id number)
      return number;
end test_access;

6 rows selected

select
   text
from
   all_source
where
   name='test_access'
and
   owner='pkg'
and
   type = 'package body';

TEXT
-------------------------------------------------------------------
```

If we try, for example, to get the explain plan for this query, the error below occurs:

```
explain plan for
select
   text
from
   all_source
where
   name='test_access'
and
   owner='pkg'
and
   type = 'package body';

ORA-28113: policy predicate has error
```

A good view used to display all fine-grained security policies and predicates associated with the cursors in the library cache is *v$vpd_policy*.

Hiding Tables with dbms_rls

The following example demonstrates the prevention of a table's being exported by a specific user using the package *dbms_rls*. Initially, a function is created in which the condition is 1=2, i.e. no row is returned in the function. Then create the sample table and associated policy for preventing the table from being exported.

⊟ Code 3.10 – dbms_rls_2.sql

```
Connected to Oracle 11g Enterprise Edition Release 11.1.0.6.0
Connected as pkg

conn sys / as sysdba
show user

User is "pkg"

--Creating function
create or replace function hide_tab_exp
  (obj_schema varchar2, obj_name varchar2)
  return varchar2 is qualifier varchar2(500);
begin
  if sys_context ('userenv', 'session_user') = 'pkg' then
   qualifier := '1=2';
  else
   qualifier := '';
  end if;
  return qualifier;
end hide_tab_exp;

--Creating table
create table
   tab_dbms_rls
tablespace
   pkg_data
as
select
   *
from
   dba_objects;

--Creating policy
begin
    sys.dbms_rls.add_policy (
       object_schema => 'pkg',
       object_name => 'tab_dbms_rls',
       policy_name => 'hide_exp_tab',
       function_schema => 'pkg',
       policy_function => 'hide_tab_exp');
end
;

col "Obj owner" for a10
col "Obj Name" for a15
col "Function Owner" for a5
select
```

```
   object_owner "Obj owner",
   object_name "Obj Name",
   policy_name "Policy Name",
   pf_owner "Function Owner",
   function "Funct Name"
from
   dba_policies
where
   policy_name='hide_exp_tab';

Obj owner  Obj Name        Policy Name                      Funct  Funct Name
---------- --------------- -------------------------------- -----  -------
pkg        tab_dbms_rls    hide_exp_tab                     pkg    hide_tab_exp
```

If there is an attempt to export the table *tab_dbms_rls*, the following error will be displayed:

```
EXP-00079: Data in table "tab_dbms_rls" is protected. Conventional path may
only be exporting partial table.
. . exporting table          tab_dbms_rls           0 rows exported
```

VPDs have now been examined in detail in regards to the *dbms_rls* package.

Prevent Tool-based Access to the Database

Next, let;s look at blocking acccess to data via 3rd party tools auch as TOAD or Oracle's PL/SQL Developer. In this example, a function is created to identify the module that the user is using, and with this information, block access to a particular table.

🖫 Code 3.11 – dbms_rls_3.sql

```
Connected to Oracle 11g Enterprise Edition Release 11.1.0.6.0
Connected as pkg

conn sys / as sysdba
show user

User is "pkg"

create or replace function block_access_plsql_dev (
   schema in varchar2,
   object in varchar2)

return varchar2
   as
    begin
      return
         'upper(
            substr(
               sys_context(
               ''userenv'',
               ''module'')
            ,7
```

```
           ,16)
 )
<>''developer''';
    end;
/

--Create the policy
begin
    sys.dbms_rls.add_policy (
        object_schema => 'pkg',
        object_name => 'tab_dbms_rls',
        policy_name => 'block_tab_access_plsql_dev',
        function_schema => 'dyd',
        policy_function => 'block_access_plsql_dev',
        statement_types => 'select,insert,delete,update',
        update_check => TRUE);
end;
/

--Check the policy
col "Obj owner" for a10
col "Obj Name" for a15
col "Function Owner" for a5
select
    object_owner "Obj owner",
    object_name "Obj Name",
    policy_name "Policy Name",
    pf_owner "Function Owner",
    function "Funct Name"
from
    dba_policies
where
    policy_name='block_tab_access_plsql_dev';

Obj owner  Obj Name       Policy Name              Funct  Funct Name
--------   --------------  -----------------------  -----  ------------------
pkg        tab_dbms_rls   block_tab_access_plsql_dev sys    block_access_plsql_dev

--Try to access the table through PL SQL Developer
select
    *
from
    tab_dbms_rls;

ORA-28110: policy function or package sys.block_access_plsql_dev has error
```

This shows that when the user tries to query the table, an error is shown with the name of the function that is used in the policy created.

Below are some points about VPD/FGA:

1. To generate a trace in environments that use Fine Grained Access Control, use the command below:

```
alter session set events '10730 trace name context forever, level 1';
```

2. To bypass FGA and VPD policies, use the privilege *exempt access policy*. Be careful using this action and do not use the *with admin* option.

3. Use the function *sys_context (userenv, policy_invoker)* rather than *sys_context (userenv, session_user)* because the latter returns the user's logon, not the user that requested the RLS policy. This can cause security problems as shown in the MOSC 452322.1 note, "How to Implement RLS to Avoid Any Potential Issues".

Package *dbms_wms*

The *dbms_wms* package provides an interface to the Oracle Database Workspace Manager. Even though *dbms_wms* is not specifically designed for security of Oracle's database, it can be used for auditing as seen in the following example.

Oracle 9i first introduced the concept of a database "workspace manager". A workspace is an environment for a long-term transaction that allows versioning of table rows. A workspace can be shared among multiple users. The concept of workspace manager involves a series of short transactions and multiple data versions to implement a complete long-transaction event that maintains atomicity and concurrency. Oracle Workspace Manager workspaces are monitored using the Oracle Workspace Manager (*dbms_wm*) package with workspaces. Oracle also provides a Workspace Manager interface accessible from the database listing of OEM.

Features of Oracle Workspace Manager

Oracle lists the following features of Oracle Workspace Manager:

- Enables and disables versioning on one or more user tables as needed. The unit of versioning is a row.

- Captures changes to rows as new row versions and stores them in the version-enabled table alongside the original rows.

- Provides metadata information views to DBAs and developers to manage and report on all aspects of the Workspace Manager environment.

- Creates workspaces, shared by one or more users and organized in hierarchies, to group and isolate collections of row versions from one or more version-enabled tables.

- Tracks versions created in each workspace and automatically shows users the appropriate versions in the context of the entire database.

- Creates savepoints to group collections of versions within a workspace. Changes can be rolled back to a savepoint and users can go to a savepoint to see the state of the database as it existed as part of a particular milestone.

- Automatically detects data conflicts between workspaces and enables users to choose which version to keep: parent, child or original.

- Allows changes made in a workspace to be completely or partially merged (into parent), refreshed (from parent) or rolled back (deleted).

- Controls access to workspaces, workspace operations and data through access modes, privileges and locks, respectively.

- Compresses workspaces to reduce storage required and enhances performance by deleting savepoints and intermediate versions.

- Optionally, enables persistent history on a version-enabled table to timestamp all or just the latest change made to all row versions in that table. This enables users to "go to date" to see the state of the database as it existed at that time and see who made the changes.

- Integrated with Oracle 9i database including support for DDL on version-enabled tables, triggers, constraints, replication and import/export.

Assume that a financial manager wants to change the salary for all employees and he wants to simulate the costs incurred from these changes prior to seeking approval from the CEO. He has two plans in mind and wants to compare these and their impact on the company. The example below shows this simulation through the use of procedures in the package *dbms_wm*. First, grant the necessary privilege to the user that will manage the Workspace Manager.

💾 Code 3.12 – dbms_wm.sql

```
Connected to Oracle 11g Enterprise Edition Release 11.1.0.6.0
Connected as pkg

conn sys / as sysdba

grant
    connect,
    resource
to
    pkg;

grant
    create table
to
    pkg;

exec dbms_wm.grantsystempriv (
    priv_types => 'access_any_workspace,
merge_any_workspace, create_any_workspace, remove_any_workspace,
rollback_any_workspace',
    grantee => 'pkg',
    grant_option =>  'YES');
```

Next, we create an example table. This table needs to have a primary key to enable versioning.

```
conn pkg@ora11g

drop table
   tab_dbms_wm_sal
purge;

create table tab_dbms_wm_sal
(
   user_id               number(6) NOT NULL,
   user_name             varchar2(50) NOT NULL,
   sal                   number(10,2) NOT NULL)
tablespace pkg_data;

drop sequence
   seq_user_id;
create sequence
   seq_user_id
      minvalue 1
      maxvalue 9999999999999999999999999999
      start with 1
      increment by 1
      cache 20
      cycle;


alter table
   tab_dbms_wm_sal
add constraint
   pk_user_id
primary key (user_id);
```

Now we enable versioning on this table. The option *view_wo_overwrite* stores the complete history of information on the view *tab_dbms_wm_sal_hist*. Now insert some data in this table.

```
exec dbms_wm.enableversioning (
   table_name => 'tab_dbms_wm_sal',
   hist =>'view_wo_overwrite');

insert into
   tab_dbms_wm_sal
values
   (seq_user_id.nextval,'Paul',1000);

insert into
   tab_dbms_wm_sal
values
   (seq_user_id.nextval,'Robert',3000);

insert into
   tab_dbms_wm_sal
values
   (seq_user_id.nextval,'Michael',2500);
```

```
commit;
```

Now check the table values on both the original and history table.

```
col user_name for a10
select
   *
from
   tab_dbms_wm_sal;

USER_ID USER_NAME          SAL
------- ---------- ------------
      1 Paul           1000,00
      2 Robert         3000,00
      3 Michael        2500,00

col "ID" for a3
col "Workspace" for a9
col "Version" for a3
col "WM User" for a10
col "Salary" for a7
select
   user_id "ID",
   user_name,
   sal "Salary",
   wm_workspace "Workspace",
   wm_version "Version",
   wm_username "WM User",
   wm_optype "Op Type",
   to_char(wm_createtime,'dd-MON-yy hh24:mi') "Create Time"
from
   tab_dbms_wm_sal_hist;

USER_ID USER_NAME   Salary  Workspace Ver WM User    Op Type Create Time
------- ---------- ------- --------- --- ---------- ------- ---------------
      1 Paul       1000,00 live        0 pkg        I       26-JUL-09 21:53
      2 Robert     3000,00 live        0 pkg        I       26-JUL-09 21:53
      3 Michael    2500,00 live        0 pkg        I       26-JUL-09 21:53
```

At this point, two workspaces will be created named Change_Sal_Effect_1 and Change_Sal_Effect_2.

```
--Remove if they already exist
exec dbms_wm.removeworkspace(
   workspace => 'Change_Sal_Effect_1');

exec dbms_wm.removeworkspace(
   workspace => 'Change_Sal_Effect_2');

exec dbms_wm.createworkspace (
   workspace => 'Change_Sal_Effect_1',
   description => 'Salaries changes for first plan. Check company
impact.');

exec dbms_wm.createworkspace (
   workspace => 'Change_Sal_Effect_2',
```

```
     description => 'Salaries changes for second plan. Check company
impact.');
```

The manager can work on a first scenario, adjusting salaries and then testing the impact on his company.

```
execute dbms_wm.gotoworkspace(
    workspace => 'Change_Sal_Effect_1');

update
    tab_dbms_wm_sal
set
    sal = sal*1.3
where
    user_id=1;

update
    tab_dbms_wm_sal
set
    sal = sal*1.2
where
    user_id=2;

update
    tab_dbms_wm_sal
set
    sal = sal*1.5
where
    user_id=3;

commit;

col user_name for a10
select
    *
from
    tab_dbms_wm_sal;

USER_ID USER_NAME            SAL
------- ---------- ------------
      1 Paul              1300,00
      2 Robert            3600,00
      3 Michael           3750,00

col "ID" for a3
col "Workspace" for a20
col "Version" for a3
col "WM User" for a10
col "Salary" for a7
select
    user_id "ID",
    user_name,
    sal "Salary",
    wm_workspace "Workspace",
    wm_version "Version",
    wm_username "WM User",
    wm_optype "Op Type",
```

```
      to_char(wm_createtime,'dd-MON-yy hh24:mi') "Create Time"
from
     tab_dbms_wm_sal_hist;
```

```
ID USER_NAME  Salary Workspace             Ver WM User   Op Type Create Time
--- ---------- ------- -------------------- --- ---------- ------- ---------------
  1 Paul       1000,00 live                   0 pkg        I       26-JUL-09 21:53
  2 Robert     3000,00 live                   0 pkg        I       26-JUL-09 21:53
  3 Michael    2500,00 live                   0 pkg        I       26-JUL-09 21:53
  1 Paul       1300,00 Change_Sal_Effect_1   16 pkg        U       26-JUL-09 22:04
  2 Robert     3600,00 Change_Sal_Effect_1   16 pkg        U       26-JUL-09 22:04
  3 Michael    3750,00 Change_Sal_Effect_1   16 pkg        U       26-JUL-09 22:04
```

The steps below will freeze the workspace Change_Sal_Effect_1 so no changes can be made to this data. To do that, it is necessary to exit the workspace Change_Sal_Effect_1 because it cannot be frozen while users are in it.

```
execute dbms_wm.gotoworkspace(
    workspace => 'live'); --This is the live database Workspace. When users
connect to a database, they are placed in this workspace

execute dbms_wm.freezeworkspace(
    workspace => 'Change_Sal_Effect_1');
```

Here, the manager works on the second scenario of salary adjustments to decide which one is changes is the best.

```
execute dbms_wm.gotoworkspace (
    workspace => 'Change_Sal_Effect_2');

update
    tab_dbms_wm_sal
set
    sal = sal*1.1
where
    user_id=1;

update
    tab_dbms_wm_sal
set
    sal - sal*1.4
where
    user_id=2;

update
    tab_dbms_wm_sal
set
    sal = sal*1.3
where
    user_id=3;

commit;

col user_name for a10
select
    *
from
```

```
    tab_dbms_wm_sal;

col "ID" for a3
col "Workspace" for a20
col "Version" for a3
col "WM User" for a10
col "Salary" for a7
select
    user_id "ID",
    user_name,
    sal "Salary",
    wm_workspace "Workspace",
    wm_version "Version",
    wm_username "WM User",
    wm_optype "Op Type",
    to_char(wm_createtime,'dd-MON-yy hh24:mi') "Create Time"
from
    tab_dbms_wm_sal_hist;

ID USER_NAME  Salary Workspace          Ver WM User  Op Type Create Time
--- ---------- ------ ------------------- --- ---------- ------- --------------
  1 Paul       1000,00 live                 0 pkg       I       26-JUL-09 21:53
  2 Robert     3000,00 live                 0 pkg       I       26-JUL-09 21:53
  3 Michael    2500,00 live                 0 pkg       I       26-JUL-09 21:53
  1 Paul       1300,00 Change_Sal_Effect_1 16 pkg       U       26-JUL-09 22:04
  2 Robert     3600,00 Change_Sal_Effect_1 16 pkg       U       26-JUL-09 22:04
  3 Michael    3750,00 Change_Sal_Effect_1 16 pkg       U       26-JUL-09 22:04
  1 Paul       1100,00 Change_Sal_Effect_2 17 pkg       U       26-JUL-09 22:10
  2 Robert     4200,00 Change_Sal_Effect_2 17 pkg       U       26-JUL-09 22:10
  3 Michael    3250,00 Change_Sal_Effect_2 17 pkg       U       26-JUL-09 22:10
```

A savepoint is now created, enabling him to roll back to this point later. Then more changes are made on this workspace.

```
execute dbms_wm.createsavepoint (
    workspace => 'Change_Sal_Effect_2',
    savepoint_name =>  'Change_Sal_Effect_2_SP_1');

--Simulate more changes on Workspace Change_Sal_Effect_2

update
    tab_dbms_wm_sal
set
    sal = sal*1.1
where
    user_id=3;

commit;

col user_name for a10
select
    *
from
    tab_dbms_wm_sal;

USER_ID USER_NAME         SAL
------- ---------- ------------
      1 Paul          1100,00
      2 Robert        4200,00
      3 Michael       3575,00
```

```
col "ID" for a3
col "Workspace" for a20
col "Version" for a3
col "WM User" for a10
col "Salary" for a7
select
   user_id "ID",
   user_name,
   sal "Salary",
   wm_workspace "Workspace",
   wm_version "Version",
   wm_username "WM User",
   wm_optype "Op Type",
   to_char(wm_createtime,'dd-MON-yy hh24:mi') "Create Time"
from
   tab_dbms_wm_sal_hist;
```

ID	USER_NAME	Salary	Workspace	Ver	WM User	Op Type	Create Time
1	Paul	1000,00	live	0	pkg	I	26-JUL-09 21:53
2	Robert	3000,00	live	0	pkg	I	26-JUL-09 21:53
3	Michael	2500,00	live	0	pkg	I	26-JUL-09 21:53
1	Paul	1300,00	Change_Sal_Effect_1	16	pkg	U	26-JUL-09 22:04
2	Robert	3600,00	Change_Sal_Effect_1	16	pkg	U	26-JUL-09 22:04
3	Michael	3750,00	Change_Sal_Effect_1	16	pkg	U	26-JUL-09 22:04
1	Paul	1100,00	Change_Sal_Effect_2	17	pkg	U	26-JUL-09 22:10
2	Robert	4200,00	Change_Sal_Effect_2	17	pkg	U	26-JUL-09 22:10
3	Michael	3250,00	Change_Sal_Effect_2	17	pkg	U	26-JUL-09 22:10
3	Michael	3575,00	Change_Sal_Effect_2	18	pkg	U	26-JUL-09 22:10

Assume that this last change does not make sense and we want to roll back to the savepoint created before.

```
execute dbms_wm.gotoworkspace(
   workspace => 'live');

execute dbms_wm.rollbacktosp(
   workspace => 'Change_Sal_Effect_2',
   savepoint_name =>  'Change_Sal_Effect_2_SP_1');

col user_name for a10
select
   *
from
   tab_dbms_wm_sal;

col "ID" for a3
col "Workspace" for a20
col "Version" for a3
col "WM User" for a10
col "Salary" for a7
select
   user_id "ID",
   user_name,
   sal "Salary",
   wm_workspace "Workspace",
   wm_version "Version",
   wm_username "WM User",
   wm_optype "Op Type",
   to_char(wm_createtime,'dd-MON-yy hh24:mi') "Create Time"
```

```
from
   tab_dbms_wm_sal_hist;
```

```
ID USER_NAME  Salary Workspace            Ver WM User   Op Type Create Time
--- ---------- ------ -------------------- --- ---------- ------- ----------------
  1 Paul       1000,00 live                  0 pkg            I    26-JUL-09 21:53
  2 Robert     3000,00 live                  0 pkg            I    26-JUL-09 21:53
  3 Michael    2500,00 live                  0 pkg            I    26-JUL-09 21:53
  1 Paul       1300,00 Change_Sal_Effect_1  16 pkg            U    26-JUL-09 22:04
  2 Robert     3600,00 Change_Sal_Effect_1  16 pkg            U    26-JUL-09 22:04
  3 Michael    3750,00 Change_Sal_Effect_1  16 pkg            U    26-JUL-09 22:04
  1 Paul       1100,00 Change_Sal_Effect_2  17 pkg            U    26-JUL-09 22:10
  2 Robert     4200,00 Change_Sal_Effect_2  17 pkg            U    26-JUL-09 22:10
  3 Michael    3250,00 Change_Sal_Effect_2  17 pkg            U    26-JUL-09 22:10
```

Now gather the values of workspace Change_Sal_Effect_2 and Change_Sal_Effect_1.

```
execute dbms_wm.gotoworkspace(
   workspace => 'Change_Sal_Effect_2');

col user_name for a10
select
   *
from
   tab_dbms_wm_sal;

execute dbms_wm.unfreezeworkspace(
   workspace => 'Change_Sal_Effect_1');

execute dbms_wm.gotoworkspace(
   workspace => 'Change_Sal_Effect_1');

col user_name for a10
select
   *
from
   tab_dbms_wm_sal;
```

```
USER_ID USER_NAME          SAL
------- ---------- ------------
      1 Paul           1300,00
      2 Robert         3600,00
      3 Michael        3750,00
```

Assume that the manager has concluded that the first scenario is the best for the company and employees and will now discard the second scenario as below.

```
execute dbms_wm.gotoworkspace(
   workspace => 'live');

execute dbms_wm.unfreezeworkspace (
   workspace => 'Change_Sal_Effect_2');

execute dbms_wm.removeworkspace (
   workspace => 'Change_Sal_Effect_2');
```

Lastly, we will apply the changes from his first workspace to the live database. Before that, check the real values on the live database workspace.

```
execute dbms_wm.gotoworkspace(
    workspace => 'live');

col user_name for a10
select
    *
from
    tab_dbms_wm_sal;

execute dbms_wm.mergeworkspace(
    workspace => 'Change_Sal_Effect_1');

col user_name for a10
select
*
from
    tab_dbms_wm_sal;
```

```
USER_ID USER_NAME          SAL
------- ---------- ------------
      1 Paul           1300,00
      2 Robert         3600,00
      3 Michael        3750,00
```

```
col "ID" for a3
col "Workspace" for a20
col "Version" for a3
col "WM User" for a10
col "Salary" for a7
select
    user_id "ID",
    user_name,
    sal "Salary",
    wm_workspace "Workspace",
    wm_version "Version",
    wm_username "WM User",
    wm_optype "Op Type",
    to_char(wm_createtime,'dd-MON-yy hh24:mi') "Create Time"
from
    tab_dbms_wm_sal_hist;
```

ID	USER_NAME	Salary	Workspace	Ver	WM User	Op Type	Create Time
1	Paul	1000,00	live	0	pkg	I	26-JUL-09 21:53
2	Robert	3000,00	live	0	pkg	I	26-JUL-09 21:53
3	Michael	2500,00	live	0	pkg	I	26-JUL-09 21:53
1	Paul	1300,00	Change_Sal_Effect_1	16	pkg	U	26-JUL-09 22:04
2	Robert	3600,00	Change_Sal_Effect_1	16	pkg	U	26-JUL-09 22:04
3	Michael	3750,00	Change_Sal_Effect_1	16	pkg	U	26-JUL-09 22:04
1	Paul	1300,00	LIVE	15	pkg	U	26-JUL-09 22:13
2	Robert	3600,00	LIVE	15	pkg	U	26-JUL-09 22:13
3	Michael	3750,00	LIVE	15	pkg	U	26-JUL-09 22:13

All DML operations were recorded in a _hist_ table created when the procedure _enableversioning_ was run. This information is also useful for auditing and for that reason, was included in this chapter.

Summary

Oracle provides several methods for security and some of the most useful packages that deal with security were presented in this chapter with a real-world example of the use of these packages.

The next chapter will examine what, how and when to use _utl__ packages and will also give practical examples of using the _utl__ package procedures.

Oracle File Management and Network Packages

Oracle must be able to interface with the external OS environment and some Oracle packages were created specifically to manage operating system files. Part of the *utl_%* packages can be used to handle operating system files on Oracle Database and this chapter will show some of the most important of those packages and how to use each one of these powerful packages.

Package *utl_file*

This package was created with Oracle Database Version 7.3 and is intended to let DBAs and developers read and write operating system text files on the server side. It is created by default when the database is installed and the script that creates the *utl_file* package is *utlfile.sql* which is called by the *catproc.sql* script. A *public* synonym is created for this package, then the *execute* privilege is granted to *public*.

My Oracle Support (former MOSC) note 35378.1 shows an interesting method of outputting from Reports v2.5 and higher with *utl_file*. Even though an user has *read* and *write* access to a directory, he still cannot *open/read/write* access on subdirectories or parent directories. To do so, it is necessary to specify the full directory path directory, and the user also needs to have the required privileges on it.

The directories which are accessible by the *utl_file* package are only those that have a data directory object created for them, and those that are specified in the *utl_file_dir* initialization parameter. Theese *utl_file* directory objects can be created dynamically without needing to shut down the database and are therefore very easy to maintain.

The *utl_file* package provides a very easy way to work with operating system files. However, it has some important exceptions and subprograms and some of these exceptions and subprograms are demionstrated below.

The following example creates a procedure that could be used for generating UNIX-based *export* scripts using the *utl_file* package. It shows some of the most important procedures and functions of this package:

⊟ Code 4.1 – utl_file_create_exp_file.sql

```
conn sys@ora11g as sysdba

Connected to Oracle 11g Enterprise Edition Release 11.1.0.6.0
Connected as pkg

show user

User is "pkg"

--First create a directory
create directory test_dir as '/home/ora11g/dir_example';

create or replace procedure create_exp_file(user_login in varchar2,
                                            passwd     in varchar2,
                                            sid        in varchar2,
                                            file_name  in varchar2,
                                            directory  in varchar2) is

    buffer_size      integer := 100000;
    load_file        utl_file.file_type;
    file             varchar2(32) := 'expport.sh';
    add_date         varchar2(20) := to_char(sysdate,
                                        'ddmmrr' || '_' ||
'hh24:mi:ss');
    w_dir            varchar2(30) := directory;
    w_user           varchar2(30) := user_login;
    w_passwd         varchar2(30) := passwd;
    w_sid            varchar2(10) := sid;
    w_file_name      varchar2(30) := file_name;
    retrieved_buffer varchar2(200);

begin

    --Open file to write into
    load_file := utl_file.fopen(location  => w_dir,
                                filename  => file,
                                open_mode => 'w');
    --Write a line into the file opened
    utl_file.put_line(file => load_file,buffer =>
                    'exp ' || w_user || '/' || w_passwd || '@' || w_sid ||
                    ' full=y grants=y indexes=y rows=y file=' ||
                    w_file_name || '_' || add_date || '.dmp log=' || w_dir
|| '_' ||
                    add_date || '.log');

    --Now the file will be closed
    utl_file.fclose(file => load_file);

    --Open the file to read from it
    load_file := utl_file.fopen(location => w_dir,filename => file,open_mode
=> 'R');

    --Read the file
    utl_file.get_line(file => load_file, buffer => retrieved_buffer);

    --Print the information read
    dbms_output.put_line(a => retrieved_buffer);
```

```
  --Close the file
  utl_file.fclose(file => load_file);

exception
  when utl_file.invalid_path then
    raise_application_error(-20000, 'Invalid path or file name!');
    utl_file.fclose(file => load_file);
  when utl_file.invalid_mode then
    raise_application_error(-20001,
                            'The <open_mode> parameter in fopen is
invalid!');
    utl_file.fclose(file => load_file);
  when utl_file.read_error then
    raise_application_error(-20001, 'Read error!');
    utl_file.fclose(file => load_file);
  when utl_file.invalid_operation then
    raise_application_error(-20002,
                            'File could not be opened or operated on as
requested!');
    utl_file.fclose(file => load_file);
  when utl_file.write_error then
    raise_application_error(-20003,
                            'Operating system error occurred during the
write operation!');
    utl_file.fclose(file => load_file);
  when utl_file.invalid_filehandle then
    raise_application_error(-20004, 'Invalid file handle!');
    utl_file.fclose(file => load_file);
  when others then
    dbms_output.put_line('Other errors!');
    utl_file.fclose(file => load_file);
end create_exp_file;
```

Finally, use the procedure as follows to get the script generated according to parameters used:

```
SQL>
exec
create_exp_file(user_login => 'pkg',passwd => 'passwd_pkg',sid =>
'ora11g',file_name => 'file_teste',directory => 'test_dir');

exp pkg/passwd_pkg@ora11g full=y grants=y indexes=y rows=y
file=file_teste_280709_16:34:07.dmp log=test_dir_280709_16:34:07.log
```

The script containing this output was created on the OS directory specified by the database object directory created on the first step (*test_dir*):

```
[ora11g@dbms dir_example]$ cat export.sh
exp pkg/passwd_pkg@ora11g full=y grants=y indexes=y rows=y
file=file_teste_280709_16:34:07.dmp log=test_dir_280709_16:34:07.log
```

Another useful and simple example is the one below that allows creating a text file with rows from a table using the *utl_file* package.

Code 4.2 – utl_file_create_ext_table.sql

```
conn sys@ora11g as sysdba

Connected to Oracle 11g Enterprise Edition Release 11.1.0.6.0
Connected as pkg

show user

User is "pkg"

create or replace procedure create_ext_table is
   v_arq utl_file.file_type;

   cursor c_sales is
     select
        *
     from
        pkg.salgrade;

begin
   v_arq := utl_file.fopen(location  => 'test_dir',
                           filename  => 'ext_table_rows.txt',
                           open_mode => 'W');
   for r1 in c_sales loop
      utl_file.put_line(v_arq, 'Grade '||r1.grade||' Low Salary $'||r1.losal
|| ' High Salary $' || r1.hisal);
   end loop;
   utl_file.fclose(v_arq);
end;
```

Below is the last example on this package. It drafts information directly to a printer.
It was created for a printer named HP-Casa, and the database was running on a
computer named *pportugalcasa* on Windows.

Code 4.3 – utl_file_printing.sql

```
conn sys@ora11g as sysdba

Connected to Oracle 11g Enterprise Edition Release 11.1.0.6.0
Connected as pkg

show user

User is "pkg"

create or replace procedure utl_file_printing is
   u_file     utl_file.file_type;
   print_text varchar2(2000);
begin
   print_text := 'Testing your printer';
   u_file := utl_file.fopen(location => '\\pportugalcasa\HP-Casa',filename
=>  'file_test',open_mode =>  'W');
   dbms_output.put_line('Printing');

   utl_file.put_line(u_file, print_text);
```

```
    utl_file.fclose(u_file);
end;
```

These were just three examples showing some of what the *utl_file* package provides. Several other different and powerful scripts can be created with this package. For an additional useful example, look at My Oracle Support note: 779824, "Script to monitor and dump information from sessions holding database locks".

Package *utl_mail*

The *utl_mail* package was created in Oracle 10g as the successor to the combersome *utl_smtp* package for sending e-mail. It makes use of *utl_tcp* and *utl_smtp* internally. The main purpose of the *utl_mail* package is to do what *utl_smtp* does, but in a much easier way. These two packages will be covered now using as an example the task of sending email notifications of job errors.

The mechanism for sending email notifications can vary depending on the version of Oracle being used. Oracle 10g and higher allows the use of the simpler *utl_mail* package rather than the *utl_smtp* package available in previous versions.

Using *utl_smtp*

The obselete *utl_smtp* package was first introduced in Oracle 8i to give access to the SMTP protocol from PL/SQL. The package is dependent on the JServer option which can be loaded using the Database Configuration Assistant (DBCA) or by running the following scripts as the *sys* user if it is not already present.

```
conn sys/password as sysdba

@$ORACLE_HOME/javavm/install/initjvm.sql
@$ORACLE_HOME/rdbms/admin/initplsj.sql
```

Using the package to send an email requires some knowledge of the SMTP protocol, but for the purpose of this text, a simple *send_mail* procedure has been written that should be suitable for most error reporting.

🖫 Code 4.4 – utl_smtp_1.sql

```
conn sys@ora11g as sysdba

Connected to Oracle 11g Enterprise Edition Release 11.1.0.6.0
Connected as pkg

show user

User is "pkg"
```

```
* send_mail.sql
-- -- Parameters:
--     1) SMTP mail gateway.
--     2) From email address.
--     3) To email address.
--     4) Subject of email.
--     5) Text body of email.
-- *******************************************************************
create or replace procedure send_mail (
  p_mail_host  in  varchar2,
  p_from       in  varchar2,
  p_to         in  varchar2,
  p_subject    in  varchar2,
  p_message    in  varchar2)
as
   l_mail_conn    utl_smtp.connection;
begin
  l_mail_conn := utl_smtp.open_connection(p_mail_host, 25);
  utl_smtp.helo(l_mail_conn, p_mail_host);
  utl_smtp.mail(l_mail_conn, p_from);
  utl_smtp.rcpt(l_mail_conn, p_to);
  utl_smtp.open_data(l_mail_conn);
  utl_smtp.write_data(l_mail_conn, 'Date: ' || to_char(sysdate, 'DD-MON-YYYY
HH24:MI:SS') || Chr(13));
  utl_smtp.write_data(l_mail_conn, 'From: ' || p_from || Chr(13));
  utl_smtp.write_data(l_mail_conn, 'Subject: ' || p_subject || Chr(13));
  utl_smtp.write_data(l_mail_conn, 'To: ' || p_to || Chr(13));
  utl_smtp.write_data(l_mail_conn, '' || Chr(13));
  utl_smtp.write_data(l_mail_conn, p_message || Chr(13));
  utl_smtp.close_data(l_mail_conn);
  utl_smtp.quit(l_mail_conn);
end
  send_mail;
/
show errors
```

The following code shows how the *send_mail* procedure can be used to send an email.

```
begin
  send_mail(p_mail_host => 'smtp.mycompany.com',
            p_from      => 'me@mycompany.com',
            p_to        => 'you@mycompany.com',
            p_subject   => 'Test send_mail Procedure',
            p_message   => 'If you are reading this it worked!');
end;
/
```

The *p_mail_host* parameter specifies the SMTP gateway that actually sends the message.

Now that the email mechanism has been presented, how to capture errors and produce email notifications will be explained. The simplest way to achieve this is to place all the code related to the job into a database procedure or preferably, a packaged procedure. This allows the capture of errors using an exception handler and the generation of an appropriate email. As an example, assume there is a need for a procedure to gather database statistics for an Oracle instance. A procedure like the one below might be defined.

⊟ Code 4.5 – utl_smtp_2.sql

```
* automated_email_alert.sql
conn sys@ora11g as sysdba

Connected to Oracle 11g Enterprise Edition Release 11.1.0.6.0
Connected as pkg

show user

User is "pkg"

create or replace procedure automated_email_alert as
  l_mail_host  varchar2(50) := 'smtp.mycompany.com';
  l_from       varchar2(50) := 'jobs@mycompany.com';
  l_to         varchar2(50) := 'tim@mycompany.com';
begin
  dbms_stats.gather_database_stats(cascade => true,
                         options => 'gather auto');
  send_mail(p_mail_host => l_mail_host,
            p_from      => l_from,
            p_to        => l_to,
            p_subject   => 'automated_email_alert (mysid): Success',
            p_message   => 'automated_email_alert (mysid) completed
successfully!');
exception
  when others then
    send_mail(p_mail_host => l_mail_host,
              p_from      => l_from,
              p_to        => l_to,
              p_subject   => 'automated_email_alert (mysid): Error',
              p_message   => 'automated_email_alert'automated_email_alert RT
(mysid) failed with the following
error:' || sqlerrm);
end
 automated_email_alert;
/
show errors
```

If this procedure were run as part of a scheduled job, an email notification would be generated whether the job completed successfully or not. In the event of an error, the associated Oracle error would be captured and reported in the e-mail.

Another utilization for this is when there are several mission critical jobs; if for any reason the job fails, there is a need to inform the users first thing in the morning to prevent them from working with inaccurate data. Therefore, we created a very simple job that runs at 7 am, and checked *dba_jobs* to see if all other jobs completed okay. If they did not, it sends an e-mail to the senior analysts and DBA. Now, let's take a look at how *utl_mail* simplifies this process.

Using *utl_mail*

Oracle 10g first introduced the *utl_mail* package, which provides a simpler and more intuitive email API. The package is loaded by running the following scripts as the *sys* user.

```
conn sys/password as sysdba
@$ORACLE_HOME/rdbms/admin/utlmail.sql
@$ORACLE_HOME/rdbms/admin/prvtmail.plb
grant execute on utl_mail TO test_user;
```

Before the package can be used, the SMTP gateway must be specified by setting the *smtp_out_server* parameter. The parameter is dynamic, but the instance must be restarted before an email can be sent with *utl_mail*.

```
conn sys/password as sysdba
alter system set smtp_out_server='smtp.mycompany.com';
shutdown immediate
startup
```

With the configuration complete, it is now possible to send an email using the *send* procedure.

```
begin
  utl_mail.send(sender     => 'me@mycompany.com',
                recipients => 'you@mycompany.com',
                subject    => 'Test utl_mail.send procedure',
                message    => 'If you are reading this it worked!');
end;
/
```

As with the *utl_smtp* example, the code related to the job needs to be placed into a database procedure which captures errors using an exception handler and sends the appropriate email. The following procedure is the Oracle 11g equivalent of the one used in the *utl_smtp* example.

⊟ Code 4.6 – utl_mail_1.sql

```
* automated_email_alert_11g.sql

create OR replace procedure automated_email_alert_10g AS
  l_mail_host  varchar2(50) := 'smtp.mycompany.com';
  l_from       varchar2(50) := 'jobs@mycompany.com';
  l_to         varchar2(50) := 'tim@mycompany.com';
begin
  dbms_stats.gather_database_stats(cascade => true,
                                   options => 'gather auto');
  utl_mail.send(sender     => l_from,
                recipients => l_to,
                subject    => 'automated_email_alert_10g (mysid): Success',
                message    => 'automated_email_alert_10g (mysid) completed
```

```
successfully!');
exception
  when others then
    utl_mail.send(sender    => l_from,
                  recipients => l_to,
                  subject   => 'automated_email_alert__10g (mysid): Error',
                  message   => 'automated_email_alert__10g (mysid) failed
with the
following error:' || sqlerrm);
end
 automated_email_alert_10g;
/
show errors
```

Next, a mechanism for running operating system commands and scripts from within PL/SQL will be introduced.

If combining these techniques with the error logging method described previously, it may help to send additional information in the email (prefix, start and end timestamps) to help pinpoint the errors in the *error_logs* table.

How to Send Emails with Attachments

The following example shows how to send emails with attachment files. This file must already exist in the directory specified on the example.

This example opens an existing file in a directory specified by a directory object *test_dir*. It reads the file completely, then places the values in a variable named *attachment_text*. The *attachment_text* is used as a parameter for the *send_attach_varchar2* procedure, which forwards the text as an attachment.

🖫 Code 4.7 – utl_mail_2.sql

```
create or replace procedure p_send_email_with_attach(
                    directory  in varchar2,
                        recipients in varchar2,
                        subject   in varchar2,
                        message   in varchar2) is

    file_handle     utl_file.file_type;
    output          varchar2(4000);
    attachment_text varchar2(4000);
    add_date        varchar2(20) := to_char(sysdate,
                                     'ddmmrr' || '_' || 'hh24:mi:ss');
    v_dir           varchar2(30) := directory;
    v_recipients    varchar2(200) := recipients;
    v_sub           varchar2(30) := subject;
    v_message       varchar2(2000) := message;
begin
    file_handle := utl_file.fopen(location  => v_dir,
                            filename  => 'file_to_attach.txt',
```

```
                                    open_mode => 'R');

   loop
      begin
         utl_file.get_line(file_handle, output); -- we read the file, line
by line
         attachment_text := attachment_text||utl_tcp.crlf; --and store every
line in the attachment_text variable, separated by a "new line" character.
      exception
         when no_data_found then
            exit;
      end;
   end loop;

   utl_file.fclose(file_handle);

   utl_mail.send_attach_varchar2(sender      => 'rampant@rampant.cc',
                                 recipients => v_recipients,
                                 subject    => v_sub,
                                 message    => v_message,
                                 attachment => attachment_text);
exception
   when others then
      raise_application_error(-20001,
                              'Error: ' ||
                              sqlerrm);
end;
```

Note that in the script above, *crlf* stands for a new line character.

Those were some simple examples of what is possible to do with these powerful packages. There are a number of different functionalities for these packages, and developers always find them really useful for improving their programs through these.

Package *utl_raw*

This package is available since the release of Oracle version 8 and the purpose of *utl_raw* is to manipulate binary data. Prior to the introduction of the *utl_raw* package, the only way to work with binary data was through *hextoraw* and *rawtohex* functions. The scripts used to create this package are *utlraw.sql* and *prvtraw.plb* and they are automatically executed when the database is created.

The *long raw* datatype used in this example is provided for backward compatibility. Currently, the *blob* and *bfile* datatypes can be used to store larger amounts of binary data with additional flexibility and should be preferred over the *long raw* datatype when working with newer versions of Oracle.

Note that Oracle recommends converting *long raw* datatype to *lob* datatype. These datatypes *raw* and *long raw* are used to store binary data like documents, graphics and sound files. With more than twenty functions on this package, just some of the most important will be presented in the following examples.

This first example shows some of the main functions of package *utl_raw* that allow the manipulation of data by loading some values, applying several different binary functions provided, and showing the result.

🖬 Code 4.8 – utl_raw.sql

```
conn pkg@ora11g

Connected to Oracle 11g Enterprise Edition Release 11.1.0.6.0
Connected as pkg

create or replace procedure proc_utl_raw_functions(string_value in varchar2)
is
    v_string       varchar2(4000);
    v_string_raw long raw;
    v_string_raw1 long raw := utl_raw.cast_to_raw(c => 'any value');
begin
    v_string := string_value;

    dbms_output.put_line('This is the string ' || v_string);
    select utl_raw.cast_to_raw(c => v_string)
      into v_string_raw
      from dual;
    dbms_output.put_line('Using function cast_to_raw ' || v_string_raw);

    select utl_raw.cast_to_varchar2(r => v_string_raw) into v_string from
dual;
    dbms_output.put_line('Using function cast_to_varchar2 ' || v_string);

   select utl_raw.cast_to_number(r => v_string_raw) into v_string from dual;
    dbms_output.put_line('Using function cast_to_number ' || v_string);

   select utl_raw.length(r => v_string_raw) into v_string from dual;
    dbms_output.put_line('Using function length ' || v_string);


    select utl_raw.concat(r1 => v_string_raw,r2 => v_string_raw1) into
v_string from dual;
    dbms_output.put_line('Using function concat ' || v_string);

    select utl_raw.cast_to_varchar2(r => v_string) into v_string from dual;
    dbms_output.put_line('Show both values in varchar concatenated ' ||
v_string);

    select utl_raw.cast_to_varchar2(r => utl_raw.reverse(r => v_string_raw))
into v_string from dual;
    dbms_output.put_line('Using function reverse ' || v_string);

    select utl_raw.compare(r1 => v_string_raw,r2 => v_string_raw1) into
v_string from dual;
    dbms_output.put_line('Using function compare ' || v_string);
```

```
   select utl_raw.bit_and(r1 => v_string_raw,r2 => v_string_raw1) into
v_string from dual;
   dbms_output.put_line('Using function bit_and ' || v_string);

   select utl_raw.bit_or(r1 => v_string_raw,r2 => v_string_raw1) into
v_string from dual;
   dbms_output.put_line('Using function bit_or ' || v_string);

   select utl_raw.bit_xor(r1 => v_string_raw,r2 => v_string_raw1) into
v_string from dual;
   dbms_output.put_line('Using function bit_xor ' || v_string);

   select utl_raw.bit_complement(r => v_string_raw) into v_string from dual;
   dbms_output.put_line('Using function bit_complement ' || v_string);

end proc_utl_raw_functions;
```

Call the procedure and get results as below:

```
SQL>
 conn pkg/pkg

Connected.

SQL>
 show user

user is "pkg"

SQL>
set
serveroutput on

SQL>
call
proc_utl_raw_functions('paulo ');

This is the string Paulo
Using function cast_to_raw 5041554C4F20
Using function cast_to_varchar2 paulo
Using function cast_to_number -.00000000000000000000000000000000003616252269
Using function length 6
Using function concat 5041554C4F20414E592056414C5545
Show both values in varchar concatenated paulo any value
Using function reverse  oluap
Using function compare 1
Using function bit_and 4040510046004C5545
Using function bit_or 514F5D6C5F614C5545
Using function bit_xor 110F0C6C19614C5545
Using function bit_complement AFBEAAB3B0DF

Call completed.

SQL>
```

In this example, the main functions of package *utl_raw* have been used and they are briefly explained below:

- *cast_to_raw*: Converts *varchar2* into *raw*. The data is not modified and its only recast to *raw* datatype.

- *cast_to_varchar*: Converts *raw* into *varchar2*. It uses the current NLS character set.

- *cast_to_number*: Converts the binary representation of a number (in *raw)* into a number

- *length*: Returns the length in bytes of a *raw*

- *concat*: Concatenates a maximum of 12 raws into a single raw. The result cannot exceed the value of 32k; otherwise, it generates an error.

- *reverse*: Reverse a byte sequence in raw from end to end. Note: In the example, the input name (paulo) was reversed because the database was using a characterset with one byte per character. If the database has a different characterset, the results may vary because *utl_raw* does not deal with characters but with bytes instead.

- *compare*: Compare one raw with another and return 1 if they are identical or 0 if different

- *bit_and*: Perform a bitwise logical *and* of the values in raw1 and raw2 and return the *and* result in raw

- *bit_or*: Perform a bitwise logical *or* of the values in raw1 and raw2 and returns the *or* result in raw

- *bit_xor*: Perform bitwise logical *exclusive or* of the values in raw1 and raw2 and returns the *xor* result in raw

- *bit_complement:* Perform bitwise logical *complement* of the values in raw r and return the complement result raw

Package *utl_ref*

Since Oracle version 8, user-defined functions are supported and this package is used to write generic type methods without knowing the object table name. In sum, the *utl_ref* package allows for working with reference-based operations.

Each row of a table created using a type operator has an object ID. A reference is a pointer to an object ID and each row can have an identifier object.

It is important to note that the *ref* datatype is used to identify a unique row object. It is also used to assist in referencing based on other objects. The *ref* values are pointers to objects. To use this *utl_ref* package, the user must run two scripts: *utlrefld.sql* and *utl/ref.plb*, both of which are available in the *$ORACLE_HOME/rdbms/admin* directory.

The *utl_ref* package has four procedures:

1. *delete_object*: Deletes an object given a reference. The execution of this procedure has the same effect as the following command:

```
delete from
  object_table
where
  ref(t) = reference;
```

2. *lock_object*: Locks an object given a reference and permits only the object selection. The execution of this procedure has the same effect as the following command:

```
select
  value(t)
into
  object
from
  object_table t
where
  ref(t) = reference
for update;
```

3. *select_object*: Selects an object given a reference and its value into the PL/SQL variable object. The execution of this procedure has the same effect as the following command:

```
select
  value(t)
into
  object
from
  object_table t
where
  ref(t) = reference;
```

4. *update_object*: Updates an object given a reference with the value contained in the PL/SQL variable object. The execution of this procedure has the same effect as the following command:

```
update
  object_table t
set
  value(t) = object
where
  ref(t) = reference;
```

Below is an example of how to use the procedures of the *utl_ref* package:

📁 Code 4.9 – utl_ref.sql

```
conn pkg@ora11g

Connected to Oracle 11g Enterprise Edition Release 11.1.0.6.0
Connected as pkg

create or replace procedure proc_utl_ref is
    object_id cust_address_type := cust_address_type(
        street_address => 'Rua a',
        [psta;_code    => '8777',
        city           => 'City',
        state_province => 'RJ',
        country_id     => 'RJ');
    objref    ref cust_address_type;
begin
    select ref(x) into objref from tab_utl_ref x;

    --Selecting an object using the reference given

    utl_ref.select_object(
        ref => objref, object => object_id);
    dbms_output.put_line('Using select_object procedure: ');
    dbms_output.put_line(object_id.street_address || ',' ||
                        object_id.postal_code || ',' ||
                        object_id.city || ',' ||
                        object_id.state_province || ',' ||
                        object_id.country_id);

    --Change the value to use on update
    object_id := cust_address_type(street_address => 'Rua a',
                                   postal_code    => '8777',
                                   city           => 'City',
                                   state_province => 'RJ',
                                   country_id     => 'RJ');

    --Lock the object and execute the update
    utl_ref.lock_object(objref);
    utl_ref.update_object(objref, object_id);

    --Get the value updated
    utl_ref.select_object(objref, object_id);
    dbms_output.put_line('Show new value updated: ');
    dbms_output.put_line(object_id.street_address || ',' ||
                        object_id.postal_code || ',' ||
                        object_id.city || ',' ||
                        object_id.state_province || ',' ||
                        object_id.country_id);

    --Delete the object_id
    utl_ref.select_object(objref, object_id);
    utl_ref.delete_object(objref);
    commit;

    dbms_output.put_line('Delete the object(row) if you run this procedure
again the error "ORA-01403: no data found" will be showed.');
    dbms_output.put_line(object_id.street_address || ',' ||
                        object_id.postal_code || ',' ||
```

```
                    object_id.city || ',' ||
                    object_id.state_province || ',' ||
                    object_id.country_id);

end;
```

Executing the procedure two times will give the following results:

```
SQL>
set
  serveroutput on
SQL>
exec
  proc_utl_ref;
Using select_object procedure:

Street A,98876,San Francisco,CA,US
Show new value updated:
Rua a,8777,City,RJ,RJ
Delete the object(row) if you run this procedure again the error "ORA-01403:
no
data found" will be showed.
Rua a,8777,City,RJ,RJ


.

SQL>
exec
 proc_utl_ref;
begin
 proc_utl_ref;
end;
*

ERROR at line 1:
ORA-01403: no data found
ORA-06512: at "pkg.proc_utl_ref", line 9
ORA-06512: at line 1
```

It is evident that this procedure is working with just one object (row) on the example table. The second time, after the *delete_object* procedure is run, it generates an error. That is to show that, at this point, the data was actually deleted and it can no longer find data on the table.

Summary

File management is one of the day-to-day tasks of a database administrator and the packages presented on this chapter can always be used to increase the powerful packages that are available at Oracle Database.

The next chapter will cover some useful packages for Oracle tuning. So be prepared to practice some tuning!

Oracle Tuning

Most people would agree that the time spent with Oracle tuning is among the hardest tasks of any database administrator. Since its foundation, Oracle has launched a new database version approximately every three years. With each new release, the database includes many new functions and a large number of internal changes.

Even though these changes ultimately create a better database, many times, after migrating a database to the new version, performance issues may be discovered. The database administrator needs to tools to be able to pinpoint and fix problems as quickly as possible.

Every database is different, and there are few rules that apply to all systems. Each database has its own complexity and should be treated uniquely. Some common tasks that database administrators need to consider when dealing with tuning are reactive tuning, proactive tuning, hardware tuning, instance tuning, object tuning and SQL tuning.

Though the experience of a database administrator in resolving tuning issues is definitely a plus, Oracle offers some additional valuable packages that can be used to improve Oracle Database's overall performance and this chapter is dedicated to exploring these packages.

Package *dbms_advisor*

Before Oracle 10g, Oracle tuning was a very complex and time consuming task. The main tool database administrators had at their disposal was STATSPACK which collected a set of statistics about events that consume execution time. The DBA used this to find where the database was spending more time and investigate further on this event to try to find and solve the performance problem.

Since Oracle 10g, a new tool named the SQLAccess Advisor can be used to improve database performance by automatically recommending creation of certain suitable materialized views, indexes and partitions. This tool can be accessed from Oracle Enterprise Manager (OEM) or by directly invoking the *dbms_advisor* package. It also can show how to create a materialized view to ensure it is fast and refreshable and how to change a materialized view in order to enable its use with the query rewrite option.

The user needs to be granted a role named *advisor* and also needs to have the *select* privilege on the tables to be analyzed by the SQL Access Advisor; otherwise, the statement will be excluded from analysis. If all statements are excluded from analysis, the workload itself becomes invalid.

The example below shows some of the more important procedures, functions and constants of the *dbms_advisor* package. Now let's see it executed step by step. First of all, we grant the necessary privileges to the user of this example. In this case, it is *pkg* user.

Code 5.1 – dbms_advisor.sql

```
conn sys@ora11g as sysdba

Connected to Oracle 11g Enterprise Edition Release 11.1.0.6.0
Connected as sysdba

show user

User is "sys"

grant advisor to pkg;

conn pkg@ora11g

show user

User is "pkg"
```

Now the task is created using the *create_task* procedure, but first the *delete_task* procedure is executed just in case a task with the same name already exists.

```
exec dbms_advisor.delete_task(task_name => 'My Task Example');

declare
taskname varchar2(30) := 'My Task Example';
task_desc varchar2(256) := 'My Task - Description';
task_or_template varchar2(30) := 'My_Task_Template';
task_id number := 0;
wkld_name varchar2(30) := 'Workload_Test';
saved_rows number := 0;
failed_rows number := 0;
num_found number;

begin
--Create task
dbms_advisor.create_task(dbms_advisor.sqlaccess_advisor,task_id,taskname,tas
k_desc,dbms_advisor.sqlaccess_qltp);
--Reset task
dbms_advisor.reset_task(taskname);
```

The task is reset and all recommendations that belong to it will be removed. After resetting the task, it changes its status to *initial*.

The query below deletes previous workload task links and previous workloads if they already exist.

```
--Delete Previous Workload Task Link If it already exists
select
    count(*)
into
    num_found
from
    user_advisor_sqla_wk_map
where
    task_name = taskname
and
    workload_name = wkld_name;

if num_found > 0 then
    dbms_advisor.delete_sqlwkld_ref(taskname,wkld_name);
end if;

--Delete Previous Workload If it already exists
select
    count(*)
into
    num_found
from
    user_advisor_sqlw_sum
where
    workload_name = wkld_name;

if num_found > 0 then
    dbms_advisor.delete_sqlwkld(wkld_name);
end if;
```

Now the workload is created and associated to the task and then some workload parameters and task parameters are set. These will be explained below.

```
--Create the Workload
dbms_advisor.create_sqlwkld(workload_name => wkld_name);
--Link the Workload created to Task
dbms_advisor.add_sqlwkld_ref(
    task_name => taskname,
    workload_name => wkld_name);

--Set Workload Parameters --
dbms_advisor.set_sqlwkld_parameter(
    workload_name => wkld_name,
    parameter => 'valid_action_list',
    value => dbms_advisor.advisor_usused);

dbms_advisor.set_sqlwkld_parameter(
    workload_name => wkld_name,
    parameter => 'valid_module_list',
```

```
      value => dbms_advisor.advisor_usused);

dbms_advisor.set_sqlwkld_parameter(
    workload_name => wkld_name,
    parameter => 'sql_limit',
    value => '25');

dbms_advisor.set_sqlwkld_parameter(
    workload_name => wkld_name,
    parameter => 'valid_username_list',
    value => apps');

dbms_advisor.set_sqlwkld_parameter(
    workload_name => wkld_name,
    parameter => 'valid_table_list',
    value => dbms_advisor.advisor_usused);

dbms_advisor.set_sqlwkld_parameter(
    workload_name => wkld_name,
    parameter => 'invalid_table_list',
    value => dbms_advisor.advisor_usused);

dbms_advisor.set_sqlwkld_parameter(
    workload_name => wkld_name,
    parameter => 'order_list',
    value => 'priority,optimizer_cost');

dbms_advisor.set_sqlwkld_parameter(
    workload_name => wkld_name,
    parameter => 'invalid_action_list',
    value => dbms_advisor.advisor_usused);

dbms_advisor.set_sqlwkld_parameter(
    workload_name => wkld_name,
    parameter => 'invalid_username_list',
    value => dbms_advisor.advisor_usused);

dbms_advisor.set_sqlwkld_parameter(
    workload_name => wkld_name,
    parameter => 'invalid_module_list',
    value => dbms_advisor.advisor_usused);

dbms_advisor.set_sqlwkld_parameter(
    workload_name => wkld_name,
    parameter => 'valid_sqlstring_list',
    value => dbms_advisor.advisor_usused);

dbms_advisor.set_sqlwkld_parameter(
    workload_name => wkld_name,
    parameter => 'invalid_sqlstring_list',
    value => dbms_advisor.advisor_usused);

dbms_advisor.set_sqlwkld_parameter(
    workload_name => wkld_name,
    parameter => 'journaling',
    value => '4');

dbms_advisor.set_sqlwkld_parameter(
    workload_name => wkld_name,
```

```
    parameter => 'days_to_expire',
    value => '30');

dbms_advisor.import_sqlwkld_sqlcache(
    workload_name => wkld_name,
    import_mode => 'replace',
    priority => 2,
    saved_rows => saved_rows,
    failed_rows => failed_rows);

--Set Task Parameters
dbms_advisor.set_task_parameter(
    task_name => taskname,
    parameter => 'execution_type',
    value => 'full');

dbms_advisor.set_task_parameter(
    task_name => taskname,
    parameter => 'order_list',
    value => 'priority,disk_reads');

dbms_advisor.set_task_parameter(
    task_name => taskname,
    parameter => 'evaluation_only',
    value =>'FALSE');

dbms_advisor.set_task_parameter(
    task_name => taskname,
    parameter => 'mode',
    value =>'comprehensive');

dbms_advisor.set_task_parameter(
    task_name => taskname,
    parameter => 'storage_change',
    value =>dbms_advisor.advisor_uslimited);

dbms_advisor.set_task_parameter(
    task_name => taskname,
    parameter => 'dml_volatility',
    value =>'TRUE');

dbms_advisor.set_task_parameter(
    task_name => taskname,
    parameter => 'workload_scope',
    value =>'full');

dbms_advisor.set_task_parameter(
    task_name => taskname,
    parameter => 'def_index_tablespace',
    value =>dbms_advisor.advisor_usused);

dbms_advisor.set_task_parameter(
    task_name => taskname,
    parameter => 'def_index_owner',
    value =>dbms_advisor.advisor_usused);

dbms_advisor.set_task_parameter(
    task_name => taskname,
    parameter => 'def_mview_tablespace',
```

Advanced DBMS Packages

```
        value =>dbms_advisor.advisor_usused);

dbms_advisor.set_task_parameter(
    task_name => taskname,
    parameter => 'def_mview_owner',
    value =>dbms_advisor.advisor_usused);

dbms_advisor.set_task_parameter(
    task_name => taskname,
    parameter => 'def_mvlog_tablespace',
    value =>dbms_advisor.advisor_usused);

dbms_advisor.set_task_parameter(
    task_name => taskname,
    parameter => 'creation_cost',
    value =>'TRUE');

dbms_advisor.set_task_parameter(
    task_name => taskname,
    parameter => 'journaling',
    value =>'4');

dbms_advisor.set_task_parameter(
    task_name => taskname,
    parameter => 'days_to_expire',
    value =>'30');

end;
```

After using these two procedures, *set_sqlwkld_parameter* and *set_task_parameter,* we can now look at some of their parameters:

- **valid_action_list or invalid_action_list:** This contains a comma-delimited list of suitable actions, or unsuitable if using the *invalid* option, for analysis in a SQL Workload.

- **valid_module_list *or* invalid_module_list:* Contains a comma-delimited list of application modules that are suitable, or not in the case of using the *invalid* option, for analysis in a SQL Workload.

- **sql_limit:* Specifies the number of SQL statements to be analyzed

- **valid_username_list:** Specifies the username that will be used in SQL Workload

- **valid_table_list and invalid_table_list:** Specifies tables that are suitable for tuning analysis or not (supports wildcard %).

- **order_list:** In 11g, has been deprecated. Used to specify the primary natural order in which Access Advisor processes workload elements while doing analysis of SQL Workload.

- **valid_sqlstring_list *or* invalid_sqlstring_list:* Specifies a list of text strings that are suitable, or not in the case of using the *invalid* option, for processing in SQL Workload

---

- **journaling:** This option controls the logging level of messages to the journal that can be found in views *dba_advisor_journal* and *user_advisor_journal.* Some important values are:

  - *unused:* No journal messages

  - *fatal:* Explanation of fatal conditions

  - *error:* Explanations of errors

  - *warning:* Explanation of warnings

- *days_to_expire:* This is the value in days before the task will expire. It will then become a candidate for deletion on the next purge operation.

In this example, *we* have also used the *import_sqlwkld_sqlcache* procedure which creates a workload using the current data of the server's SQL cache.

To check if the task has been created, the view *dba_advisor_executions* (only available with 11g) or *dba_advisor_tasks* could be used as follows:

```
set linesize 200
col "Own" for a10
col "Adv_Name" for a20

select
    owner "Own",
    task_name "Tsk_Name",
    to_char(created, 'mm-dd-yy hh24:mi') "Created",
--    to_char(last_modified,'mm-dd-yy hh24:mi') "Modif",
    advisor_name "Adv_Name",
    status "Status"
from
    dba_advisor_tasks
where
    task_name='My Task Example'
--    execution_start > systimestamp - interval '1' hour ;

Own  Tsk_Name          Created         Adv_Name            Status
---- ----------------- --------------- ------------------- -----------
PKG  My Task Example   08-24-09 21:15  SQL Access Advisor  completed
```

After checking the task, just execute it so the advisor works using the workload generated and tries to gather the best recommendations for increasing the performance of the database. Note that if the task was already executed, the *ORA-13630* error will appear:

```
--Execute the task
exec dbms_advisor.execute_task(task_name => 'My Task Example');

begin dbms_advisor.execute_task(task_name => 'My Task Example'); end;

ORA-13630: The task My Task Example contains execution results and cannot be
executed.
```

Advanced DBMS Packages

```
ORA-06512: at "sys.dbms_advisor", line 201
ORA-06512: at line 1
```

After that, we reset the task and then execute the task again.

```
--If you want to execute this task again you can do the following:
--Reset the task using command as follows:
exec dbms_advisor.reset_task(task_name => 'My Task Example');

exec dbms_advisor.execute_task(task_name => 'My Task Example');

select * from dba_advisor_log where task_name='My Task Example'

set linesize 200
col "Own" for a10
col "Adv_Name" for a20
select
   owner "Own",
   task_name "Tsk_Name",
   to_char(created, 'mm-dd-yy hh24:mi') "Created",
   --   to_char(last_modified,'mm-dd-yy hh24:mi') "Modif",
   advisor_name "Adv_Name",
   status "Status"
from
   dba_advisor_tasks
where
  task_name='My Task Example'
  --   execution_start > systimestamp - interval '1' hour;

Own   Tsk_Name         Created          Adv_Name           Status
----  --------------   --------------   ------ -----------  --------
PKG   My Task Example  08-24-09 21:15   SQL Access Advisor  COMPLETED
```

After the execution of the task, all recommendations can be checked using the query below.

```
column owner   for a10
column command for a20
column attr1   for a10
column attr2   for a10
column attr3   for a10
column attr4   for a10

select
   owner,
   task_name,
   command,
   attr1,
   attr2,
   attr4,
   attr4,
   message
from
   dba_advisor_actions
where task_name='My Task Example';
```

The best solution to compile all recommendations of a workload is to create a procedure that will output them in an easily viewed format using the procedure below.

```
create or replace procedure advisor_recommendations (v_task_name in
varchar2) is
vv_task_name varchar2(30);
cursor adv_cur is

select
   owner,
   task_name,
   command,
   attr1,
   attr2,
   attr3,
   attr4,
   message
from
dba_advisor_actions
where task_name = v_task_name;
   v_owner        varchar2(20);
   v_command      varchar2(30);
   v_attr1        varchar2(2000);
   v_attr2        varchar2(2000);
   v_attr3        varchar2(2000);
   v_attr4        varchar2(2000);
   v_message      varchar2(500);
begin
vv_task_name := v_task_name;
   open adv_cur;
   loop
      fetch adv_cur into
        v_owner,vv_task_name,v_command, v_attr1, v_attr2, v_attr3,
v_attr4,v_message ;
      exit when adv_cur%notfound;
      dbms_output.put_line('Task_name = ' || v_task_name);
      dbms_output.put_line('Task Owner :              ' || v_command);
      dbms_output.put_line('Task Command :           ' || v_command);
      dbms_output.put_line('Atribute 1 - Name:       ' || v_attr1);
      dbms_output.put_line('Attribute 2 - tablespace: ' || v_attr2);
      dbms_output.put_line('Attribute 3:             ' || v_attr3);
      dbms_output.put_line('Attribute 4:             ' || v_attr4);
      dbms_output.put_line('Message:                 ' || v_message);
      dbms_output.put_line('#################################');
   end loop;
   close adv_cur;
   dbms_output.put_line('############ Advisor Recommendations
#############');
end advisor_recommendations;
/
```

When executing this procedure, the output will be seen as follows:

```
#################################
Task_name = sys_auto_sql_tuning_task
```

```
Task Owner :              gather table statistics
Task Command :            gather table statistics
Atribute 1 - Name    :    sys
Attribute 2 - tablespace : objauth$
Attribute 3              :
Attribute 4              :
Message                  : Consider collecting optimizer statistics for this
table.
###################################
Task_name = sys_auto_sql_tuning_task
Task Owner :              accept sql profile
Task Command :            accept sql profile
Atribute 1 - Name    :    sys_auto_sql_tuning_task
Attribute 2 - tablespace : 44
Attribute 3              :
Attribute 4              :
Message                  : Consider accepting the recommended SQL profile.
###################################
Task_name = sys_auto_sql_tuning_task
Task Owner :              rewrite query
Task Command :            rewrite query
Atribute 1 - Name    :
Attribute 2 - tablespace :
Attribute 3              :
Attribute 4              :
Message                  : Consider using "union all" instead of "union", if
duplicates are allowed or uniqueness is guaranteed.
```

Years ago, DBAs needed to tune all kinds of performance queries in a database. Now, Oracle Database comes with some very good packages to help with tuning the most frequent queries in the time it takes to finish a cup of coffee. Of course, tuning complex queries is still done the old fashioned way, but there is no need to waste time on the easy ones anymore. Next, let's look at the package *dbms_application_info*.

Package *dbms_application_info*

One of the most practical ways to find the bottleneck of SQL queries is to track and trace sessions being monitored. To do this, the *dbms_application_info* package can be used. It was created with Oracle Database version 7.2 with the script *dbmsapi.sql* called automatically by *catproc.sql*. In a nutshell, the *dbms_application_info* package registers modules or transactions executed on a database and the information can then be tracked using the *v$session*, *v$session_longops* and *v$session_longops* views.

Information registered within this package includes *v$session*, *v$session_longops* and *v$sqltext* views. The column *module* of the *v$session* view is usually the name of the program being executed. It is also possible to get values of *module* and *action* in the *v$sqlarea* view. These columns are usually set to easily identify the program being used, incorporating the *program* column and/or identifying what it is doing using the *action* column.

To identify sessions that are running Pro*C, use procedures *set_module*, *set_action* and *set_client_info* of the *dbms_application_info* package. It is also possible to identify JDBC connections using the *set_client_info* procedure. It is also very useful to record information about the long running queries on *v$session_longops* using the *dbms_application_info* package, thereby making possible tracking sessions that take a long time to finish.

There are six subprograms, procedures, in fact, that can be used inside the *dbms_application_info* package. Here are descriptions of each:

- **read_client_info:** This procedure reads the value of the *client_info* field of a current session

- **read_module:** This procedure reads the module and action fields of a current session

- **set_action:** This procedure sets the name of the current action within the current module

- **set_client_info:** This procedure sets the *client_info* field of the session

- **set_module:** This procedure sets the module that is running to a new module

- **set_session_longops:** This procedure sets a row in the *v$session_longops* table that can be used to identify modules and actions of long running queries like backups.

Below is an example of how to use *dbms_application_info* to register information about long running sessions in *v$session_longops*.

🖫 Code 5.2 – dbms_application_info_longops.sql

```
conn sys@ora11g as sysdba

Connected to Oracle 11g Enterprise Edition Release 11.1.0.6.0
Connected as sysdba

show user

User is "pkg"
--Create the example procedure
create or replace procedure dbms_app_info_longops_test
is
        v_rindex          binary_integer;
        v_slno            binary_integer;
        v_totalwork       number;
        v_sofar           number;
        v_obj_target   binary_integer;

    begin
        v_sofar := 0;
        v_totalwork := 10;
```

```
        while v_sofar < 10 loop

            --Execute your tasks here
            dbms_lock.sleep(5);

            v_sofar := v_sofar + 1;
            dbms_application_info.set_session_longops(
                rindex => v_rindex,
                slno => v_slno,
      op_name => '!!!pay -     load!!!'||
          to_char(systimestamp,'hh24:mi:ss'),
                target => v_obj_target,
                context =>  0,
                sofar => v_sofar,
                totalwork => v_totalwork,
                target_desc => 'pay tables',
                units => 'rows');
        end loop;
end;
/

--On another SQL prompt, query v$session_longops view

col SID for a5
col Serial for a8
col Target for a10
col Units for a8
col "Time Remaining" for a10

select
    sid "SID",
    serial# "Serial",
    to_char(start_time,'hh24:mi:ss') "Start Time",
    opname "Operation",
    target_desc "Target",
    units "Units",
    time_remaining "Time Remaining",
    elapsed_seconds "Elapsed Sec"
from
    v$session_longops;

SID  Serial Start Time  Op Name Target      Units    Time Remai Elapsed Sec
---  ------ ----------  ------- -----       -----    ---------- ----------
38   3848   27/10/2009  !!!Pay - LOAD!!!09/10/27 20:03:54  Pay Tables rows  20 5
```

This shows that it is easy to track long operation sessions using the *dbms_application_info* package together with the *v$session_longops* view.

Another interesting example shows how to identify Discoverer sessions for a specific workbook. More details can be found on MOSC Note: 279635.1. Basically, a function just needs to be created that uses *dbms_application_info*, and then register this function with the Oracle Discoverer Administrator GUI.

🖫 Code 5.3 – dbms_application_info_disco.sql

```
conn sys@ora11g as sysdba
```

```
Connected to Oracle 11g Enterprise Edition Release 11.1.0.6.0
Connected as sysdba

show user

User is "pkg"

--Create the function
create or replace function dbms_app_info_disc_client
    (workbook_name varchar2)
     return number is
begin
--Set client information that you need
dbms_application_info.set_client_info(
    fnd_global.user_id||'###'||
    fnd_global.resp_id||'###'||
    fnd_global.application_short_name||'###'||
    workbook_name);
return 1;
--
end dbms_app_info_disc_client;
```

Here are some brief examples on how to use the procedures *set_action*, *set_module* and *set_client_info*.

First, the *test_dbms_app_info* table is created to use with this example. Then a procedure that makes some inserts in this table is created setting information using *dbms_application_info* between *insert* commands. Lastly, check information generated by this session running a query on the v$session view.

🖫 Code 5.4 – dbms_application_info.sql

```
conn pkg@ora11g

Connected to Oracle 11g Enterprise Edition Release 11.1.0.6.0

show user

User is "pkg"

--Creating an example table
create table test_dbms_app_info (
    coltest varchar2(15)
    );

--Creating the procedure that will be used to do some inserts identified by
module, action and client info.

create or replace procedure proc_dbms_app_info
is
    t_time date;
begin
    dbms_application_info.set_module(
        module_name => 'add_phone',
        action_name => 'test_insert');
```

```
    t_time := systimestamp;

    insert into
       pkg.test_dbms_app_info
    values
       ('time'||t_time);

    sys.dbms_lock.sleep(5);

    insert into
       pkg.test_dbms_app_info
    values
       ('time'||t_time);

    dbms_application_info.set_client_info (
       client_info =>
          sys_contxt('userenv', 'ip_address'));

    sys.dbms_lock.sleep(5);

    insert into
       pkg.test_dbms_app_info
    values
       ('time'||t_time);

    dbms_application_info.set_module ('','');

end;
/

--Now we can query v$session view
col username for a10
col module for a10
col action for a15
col client_info for a15
select s.sid,
       s.username,
       s.command,
       s.status,
       s.module,
       s.action,
       s.client_info
  from v$session s
 where s.module ='add_phone';

SID USERNAME   COMMAND STATUS   MODULE    ACTION       CLIENT_INFO
---------- ------- ------   --------  -----------  -------------
38  pkg        47      active   add_phone test_insert 10.10.10.1
```

The client info will only appear when the second *insert* command is executed because the *set_client_info* procedure is used after the second *insert* command.

With these examples, it becomes easy to track sessions that are logged in the database, even if these come from different kinds of applications and connection types like *jdbc*, *Pro*C* programs and others. This is very helpful when finding who is causing performance problems in the environment is needed. This session can be traced and an educated assumption can be made with the information generated.

Package *dbms_aw_stats*

The *dbms_aw_stats* package is a new package created to allow the generation of statistics on dimensions and cubes used in OLAP databases. In Oracle 11g, a new form of materialized view named Cube Materialized View was created. The data is stored in an OLAP cube and not in a relational table. When joining this to other objects, or whenever there is a need to execute query rewrite on it, ensure that the statistics are up to date using the *dbms_aw_stats* package.

Oracle database needs this to create the corresponding execution plan for joins and query rewrites on these objects. Thus, one of the main reasons for keeping the statistics of dimensions and cubes updated is to ensure that Query Rewrite will be executed continuously.

This package has just one procedure named *analyze*. A good example of how and when to use this package is described here and is also on MOSC Note: 577293.1. To ensure that Query Rewrite is used on Cube Materialized Views, follow the example below:

🖫 Code 5.5 – dbms_aw_stats.sql

```
conn pkg@ora11g

Connected to Oracle 11g Enterprise Edition Release 11.1.0.6.0

show user

User is "pkg"

/*
1- Check that query rewrite is enabled in awm
2-Check constraints using dbms_cube_advise.mv_cube_advice
3-Check aggregation type because only sum, min and max can be leveraged by
rewrite cube
4-The status of MV should be 'usable'
5-The user who runs the query should have the global_query_rewrite privilege
6-Check statistics using package dbms_aw_stats as below:
*/

SQL>
exec
 dbms_aw_stats.analyze('dimension');
SQL>
exec
 dbms_aw_stats.analyze('cube');
```

This is a very easy package to use.

Package *dbms_connection_pool*

Created with Oracle 11g, the *dbms_connection_pool* package is used to create a database connection pool that is designed for short database activities when the environment has mid-tier applications. The name of this new feature is Database Resident Connection Pooling. It is designed for databases that receive thousands of connections from clients spread along application servers.

All servers and processes that are accessing the database through DRCP are pooled, and thus, are shared across connections coming from various application processes.

```
?/rdbms/admin/prvtkpps.plb
```

A default pool named *sys_default_connection_pool* is created when the Oracle 11g is created. The script *$ORACLE_HOME/rdbms/admin/prvtkpps.plb* is called by *catpdbms.sql,* which in turn is called by the *catproc.sql* script. Currently, only one pool is permitted; it is not possible to create a second pool.

This package has just five procedures:

- *alter_param*: Procedure used to alter a specific parameter. Other parameters remain unaffected.

- *configure_pool*: Procedure used to configure the pool using advanced configuration options

- *start_pool*: Procedure used to start the pool

- *stop_pool*: Procedure used to stop the pool

- *restore_defaults*: Procedure used to restore the default settings of a pool

Now we will show how to activate, change parameters, restore default settings and connect to the database using Database Resident Connection Pooling (DBRC).

The first step is to query *dba_cpool_info* to check the values of the default pool. Then some changes are made according to my needs using the *configure_pool* procedure which has the following parameters:

- **pool_name:** The name of the pool. Actually, there is just one that can be used, the default one.

- **minsize:** The minimum number of pool servers

- **maxsize:** Maximum number of pool servers acceptable

- **incrsize:** This is the incremented number of servers in case no server is available for application requests

- **session_cached_cursors:** Activate *session_cached_cursors* for all connections in the pool

- **inactivity_timeout:** Used to specify the time that a session can stay idle on this pool. If this time is reached, the session will be killed.

- **max_think_time:** Maximum idle time by the client. If exceeded, an *ORA-* will be shown.

- **max_use_session:** Maximum number of times a connection can be taken and released to the pool

- **max_lifetime_session:** Time to live for a session in the pool

Code 5.6 – dbms_connection_pool.sql

```
SQL>
 conn pkg@dbms

Connected to Oracle 11g Enterprise Edition Release 11.2.0.1.0
Connected as pkg

SQL>
show user

User is "pkg"

--Query dba_cpool_info view to check the status of the pool
col "Pool Name" for a30
col "Status" for a10
select
    connection_pool "Pool Name",
    status "Status"
from
    dba_cpool_info;

--Now, lest change some parameters of default pool
begin
dbms_connection_pool.configure_pool(
    pool_name => 'sys_default_connection_pool',
    minsize => 10,
    maxsize => 100,
    incrsize => 4,
    session_cached_cursors => 80,
    inactivity_timeout => 100,
    max_think_time => 50,
    max_use_session => 20000,
    max_lifetime_session => 50000);
end;
/
```

The *max_think_time* is 50 seconds. Simulate this idle time and see what happens. First start the pool using the *start_pool* procedure as below:

```
--Next, activate the pool using procedure start_pool
begin
dbms_connection_pool.start_pool(
    pool_name => 'sys_default_connection_pool');
end;
/

--Check the status of the pool. It is now active
col "Pool Name" for a30
col "Status" for a10
select
    connection_pool "Pool Name",
    status "Status"
from
    dba_cpool_info;
```

Now, easily connect to the database and wait 50 seconds to get this error as shown:

```
--Now using Easy Connect you can connect on database using this new pool
connect pkg/pkg123@dbms.f2c.com.br:1521/dbms:pooled

--Query the user connected in another session
col username for a10
select
    sid,
    serial#,
    username,
    server
from
    v$session
where
    server='pooled';

--Connect through this new service name and stay connect without executing
any command and watch the error
sqlplus pkg@dbms_pool

SQL>
set time on
13:48:45 SQL>
13:49:39 SQL>
select * from
 dual;
select * from
 dual

*
ERROR at line 1:
ORA-03113: end-of-file on communication channel
Process ID: 4127
Session ID: 27 Serial number: 196
It is also possible to create a new service using this activated pool.  The
service may then be used on client machines as needed.

-- And finally create a new service_name using pooled connection method
dbms_pool =
```

```
(descriptios =
  (address_list =
    (address = (protocol = tcp)(host = dbms.f2c.com.br)(port = 1521))
  )
  (connect_data =
    (server = pooled)
    (service_name = dbms)
  )
)
```

The best way to monitor DRCP activities to know if it is necessary to increase or change some parameters of the pool is through the views listed below:

- *v$cpool_conn_info*: Displays information about connections that are using DRCP

- *v$cpool_stats*: Displays statistical information about DRCP for that instance

These queries can be run during DRCP simulation:

```
--If you have reached the maximum capacity of your connection pool, you will
find waits on connection_status column of view below

col service for a10
select
   username,
   service,
   connection_status
from
   v$cpool_conn_info;

--Some useful statistics about your connection pool can be found on view
v$cpool_stats

col "Name" for a30
col "Open" for a5
col "Busy" for a5
col "Req" for a5
col "Misses" for a5
col "Waits" for a5
select
   pool_name "Name",
   num_open_servers "Open",
   num_busy_servers "Busy" ,
   num_requests "Req" ,
   num_misses "Misses",
   num_waits "Waits"
from
   v$cpool_stats;
```

To conclude, this new *dbms_connection_pool* feature will help significantly minimize the server resources used. The DRCP can manage connections much better than many current mid-tier applications do; for example, eliminating idle connections from the pool.

Package *dbms_libcache*

When using a tool like Real Application Cluster Guard where primary/second nodes have been configured, use *dbms_libcache* to transfer information from the library cache of the primary instance to the library cache of the secondary instance. This will save resources that will be needed by the new primary instance (old secondary) when loading the library cache.

The common name used for this process is "warming" the library cache. In cases of a server crash and a RAC failover, the new primary instance does not need to re-parse all SQL statements and re-compile all of the PL/SQL unit programs. The *dbms_libcache* package captures information about selected cursors that can be shared between RAC nodes and it then compiles the information and populates the secondary RAC instance with these SQL and PL/SQL executables.

The scripts used to create this package are *?/rdbms/admin/catlibc.sql* and *@?/rdbms/admin/dbmslibc.sql*. It is not created in database creation. Manually run this script as sys user:

```
SQL>
show
 user

USER is "sys"

SQL>
@?/rdbms/admin/catlibc.sql
```

For example, assume that the library cache of an instance named *dbms2* needs to be populated from an instance named *dbms1*. The command below will compile all cursors from user BPEL for SQL statements that were executed five or more times and have a minimum size of 800 bytes.

🖫 Code 5.7 – dbms_libcache.sql

```
SQL>
conn
 pkg@dbms

Connected to Oracle 11g Enterprise Edition Release 11.2.0.1.0
Connected as pkg

SQL>
show
 user

User is "pkg"
```

```
create public database link libc_link_dbms1
    connect to
        parser
    identified by
        manager
    using 'dbms1';

begin
dbms_libcache.compile_from_remote(
    p_db_link => 'libc_link_dbms1',
    p_username => 'pkg',
    p_threshold_executions => 10,
    p_threshold_sharable_mem => 800,
    p_parallel_degree => 4);
end;
/

Total SQL statements to compile=35
Total SQL statements compiled=35
```

In this example, the procedure *compile_from_remote* has compiled 35 programs inside the library cache of database instance *dbms2* using data from the library cache of database instance *dbms1*.

Package *dbms_monitor*

Tracing sessions are a common technique used by database administrators to track performance problems on SQL statements. Before Oracle 10g, different methods like *dbms_support* could be used to trace SQL sessions, alter session set events, and such. This is accomplished in Oracle 10g through the script *?/rdbms/admin/dbmsmntr.sql dbms_monitor*. The *dbms_monitor* package is used to monitor SQL sessions and enable statistics gathering using a client identifier or a combination of: service name, module and action.

The *dbms_monitor* package is created by default within the database. There is no need to run the script mentioned in the previous paragraph. Procedures included in this package can take several actions:

- Enable/disable statistics using client identifiers

- Enable/disable statistics using combinations of service name, module and action

- Enable/disable traces on session for a specific user identified by client identifier

- Enable/disable traces for all databases or a specific instance

- Enable/disable trace for a combination of service name, module and action

- Enable/disable trace in a specific session using session identifier SID of the local instance

Now see some practical examples of how and when to use the *dbms_monitor* package.

Easy SQL Analysis using the dbms_monitor *session_trace_enable* procedure

In the example below, a table is created without any index and without statistics collection. Then a trace is enabled in a session using the *dbms_monitor* package. After that, the *tkprof* utility will be used to analyze the gathered data, getting the execution plan the query executed. After analyzing and finding the query's full table scan, a proper index will be created and statistics collected. Finally, the query is executed again with a much faster response time. Once complete, the trace in session is disabled using the *dbms_monitor* package.

🖫 Code 5.8 – dbms_monitor.sql

```
SQL>
conn
 pkg@dbms

Connected to Oracle 11g Enterprise Edition Release 11.2.0.1.0
Connected as pkg

SQL>
show
 user

User is "pkg"

--Create a test table
create table
   test_dbms_monitor
as
select
   *
from
dba_objects;

--Make the table bigger (run this command some times to increase the table
size)
insert into
   test_dbms_monitor
select
   *
from
test_dbms_monitor;

commit;

--Enable trace in session using dbms_monitor
begin
dbms_monitor.session_trace_enable;
end;
/
```

```
begin

--Here, replace with your session_id and serial_num if disabling trace on
another session
dbms_monitor.session_trace_disable(session_id => 33,serial_num => 85);
end;

--Notice how you can specify the session where tracing will be enabled or
disabled, it's not necessarily limited to yours, thus, you don't need to
make any changes to your applications to be able to trace what they are
doing./
```

The trace generated on the directory can be found specified by *user_dump_dest*
parameters like the one below:

```
[ora11g@dbms trace]$ ls -la

/u01/app/oracle/diag/rdbms/dbms/dbms/trace/dbms_ora_3957.trc
-rw-r----- 1 ora11g oinstall 97126 Nov  9 14:46
/u01/app/oracle/diag/rdbms/dbms/dbms/trace/dbms_ora_3957.trc
```

Now let's run a query on the table created and check the generated trace. To check
the explain plan, use the *tkprof* utility. After that, analyze the explain plan of the query
executed.

```
--Run a query on table created
select
    count(*)
from
    test_dbms_monitor t
where
    t.object_id = 3289;

Executed in 32,766 seconds
```

Run the *tkprof* to generate the file that will be analyzed:

```
 [ora11g@dbms trace]$ tkprof dbms_ora_3957.trc dbms_ora_3957.txt
explain=pkg/pkg@dbms sort=exeela
```

Now locate the query and see a full table scan on this table; and then assume that we
conclude that an index is needed to improve query performance.

```
select
    count(*)
from
    test_dbms_monitor t
where
    t.object_id = 3289

call     count       cpu    elapsed       disk      query    current        rows
------- ------  -------- ---------- ---------- ---------- ----------  ----------
Parse        5      0.00       0.00          0          1          0           0
Execute      5      0.00       0.00          0          0          0           0
Fetch        5      6.59      34.12     128593     149249          1           5
```

```
-------  ------  --------- ---------- ---------- ---------- ----------  ----------
total      15     6.59        34.12      128593     149250          1          5
```

```
Misses in library cache during parse: 1
Optimizer mode: all_rows
Parsing user id: 46  (pkg)
```

```
Rows     Row Source Operation
-------  ---------------------------------------------------------
      1  sort aggregate (cr=21487 pr=21477 pw=0 time=0 us)
     64   table access full test_dbms_monitor (cr=21487 pr=21477 pw=0 time=11323557 us cost=5965
size=4537 card=349)
Rows     Execution Plan
-------  ---------------------------------------------------------
      0  select statement   node: all_rows
      1   sort (aggregate)
     64    table access (full) of 'test_dbms_monitor' (table)
```

```
Elapsed times include waiting on following events:
   Event waited on                             Times   Max. Wait  Total Waited
   --------------------------------------     Waited  ----------  ------------
   SQL*Net message to client                      10       0.00          0.00
   SQL*Net message from client                    10       0.01          0.05
   enq: KO - fast object checkpoint                2       1.01          1.05
   Disk file operations I/O                        1       0.00          0.00
   direct path read                             3849       0.35         26.82
   asynch descriptor resize                        5       0.00          0.00
   db file parallel read                           1       0.16          0.16
********************************************************************************
```

At this time, the index on column *object_id* is created and statistics for the table and index are gathered.

```
create index
   pkg.idx_obj_id
on
   pkg.test_dbms_monitor (object_id)
pctfree 10
initrans 2
maxtrans 255
logging
  storage(
  buffer_pool default
  flash_cache default
  cell_flash_cache default)
  tablespace "tbx_idx";

--Gather statistics for the table and indexe
begin
dbms_stats.gather_table_stats(
   ownname => 'pkg',
   tabname => 'test_dbms_monitor',
   estimate_percent => 30,
   degree => 4,
   granularity => 'ALL',
   cascade => TRUE,
   method_opt =>'for all indexed columns');
end;
/
```

Run the query again and look at the time and the plan at the trace file. Note that *tkprof* will need to be run again. It is also advised to clean up the buffer cache to make sure data is not cached, so the impact of the index that was just built for the query

---

performance should now be greatly improved thanks to the index and statistics collection that was done based on the findings with the *dbms_monitor* package.

```
alter system flush buffer_cache;
select
    count(*)
from
    test_dbms_monitor t
where
    t.object_id = 3289;

Executed in 0,031 seconds
```

Now the new explain plan that is using the index created can be seen and the new outstanding execution time.

```
select
    count(*)
from
    test_dbms_monitor t
where
    t.object_id = 3289
```

call	count	cpu	elapsed	disk	query	current	rows
Parse	1	0.00	0.00	0	0	0	0
Execute	1	0.00	0.00	0	0	0	0
Fetch	1	0.00	0.03	4	4	0	1
total	3	0.01	0.04	4	4	0	1

```
Misses in library cache during parse: 1
Optimizer mode: all_rows
Parsing user id: 46  (pkg)
```

Rows	Row Source Operation
1	sort aggregate (cr=4 pr=4 pw=0 time=0 us)
128	index range scan idx_obj_id (cr=4 pr=4 pw=0 time=508 us cost=3 size=640 card=128)(object id 26166)

Rows	Execution Plan
0	select statement mode: all_rows
1	sort (aggregate)
128	index mode: analyzed (range scan) of 'idx_obj_id' (index)

```
Elapsed times include waiting on following events:
  Event waited on                             Times  Max. Wait  Total Waited
  --------------------------------------      Waited ---------- ------------
  SQL*Net message to client                     2      0.00       0.00
  SQL*Net message from client                   2      0.00       0.00
  db file sequential read                       4      0.02       0.03
********************************************************************************
```

Lastly, use the *dbms_monitor* package again to disable the trace in session:

Advanced DBMS Packages

```
begin
dbms_monitor.session_trace_disable;
end;
/
```

How to Trace a Specific Client Session on a Multi-tier Environment

Suppose that we have a multi-tier environment and we need to trace a client session that could be connected to any of our available RAC nodes. Before Oracle 10g this was a complicated task, but it has improved with the creation of procedure *client_id_trace_enable*.

The case below shows how easy it is to identify a client session and trace it. First, the client session is identified. Execute the following command in a user session that will be traced or create a *logon_trigger* to identify all user sessions.

⊟ Code 5.9 – dbms_monitor_client_id_trace_enable.sql

```
SQL>
conn
 pkg@dbms

Connected to Oracle 11g Enterprise Edition Release 11.2.0.1.0
Connected as pkg

SQL>
show
 user

User is "pkg"

begin
dbms_session.set_identifier('pkg_client_id');
end;
/

--or create the logon trigger to identify all PKG user sessions (connect as
SYSDBA in another session and create this trigger)
create or replace trigger trg_pkg_logon
   after logon on pkg.schema
begin
     dbms_session.set_identifier('pkg_client_id');
end;
/
```

Use the following query to get the session information and check if the *client_identifier* column is identified correctly.

```
select
     sid,
```

```
    serial#,
    username,
    client_identifier
 from
    v$session
 where
    username='pkg';

      SID    SERIAL# USERNAME    CLIENT_IDENTIFI
---------- ---------- ---------- ---------------
       28        150 pkg         pkg_client_id
```

Now, from another session connected as *sys* or another user with appropriated privileges, execute the *client_id_trace_enable* procedure to enable trace when a session with *client_identifier =pkg_clinet_id* connects to the database.

```
begin
dbms_monitor.client_id_trace_enable(client_id => 'pkg_client_id',waits =>
TRUE,binds => TRUE,plan_stat => 'all_executions');
end;
/
```

The view *dba_enabled_traces* can be queried to check if the trace is already enabled:

```
col trace_type for a10
col primary_id for a22
col qualifier_id1 for a10

select
   trace_type,
   primary_id,
   qualifier_id1,
   waits,
   binds
from
   dba_enabled_traces;

TRACE_TYPE PRIMARY_ID             QUALIFIER_ WAITS BINDS
---------- ---------------------- ---------- ----- -----
client_id  pkg_client_id                     TRUE  TRUE
```

Next, let's generate some trace data; execute some SQL statements to generate trace data on a session of user *pkg*.

```
show user

user is "pkg"

select
   sys_context('userenv','client_identifier') client_id
from
   dual;

CLIENT_ID
--------------
pkg_client_id
```

```
select
   object_name
from
   test_dbms_monitor
where
   data_object_id=4400;

no rows selected
```

To quickly and easily find where and what the name of the trace file being generated is, use the next query enabling the SID of the session that needs to be monitored. It is important to mention that more than one trace can be generated; when using RAC or MTS, for instance. If this is the case, then use the *trcsess* utility to merge all these trace files into one.

```
show user

User is "sys"

select
   sid,
   serial#,
   username,
   sql_trace
from
   gv$session
where
   username='pkg';


    SID    SERIAL# USERNAME   SQL_TRACE
---------- ---------- ---------- ---------
       28        150 pkg        disabled
select
   distinct par.value
   || '/'
   || lower(instance_name)
   || '_ora_'
   || spid
   || '.trc' "Trace file name"
from
   v$instance i,
   v$process p,
   v$session m,
   v$session s,
   v$parameter par
where
   s.paddr = p.addr
and
   s.sid = m.sid
and
   par.name='user_dump_dest'
and
   m.SID=28;
```

```
Trace file name
------------------------------------------------------------
/u01/app/oracle/diag/rdbms/dbms/dbms/trace/dbms_ora_7310.trc
```

Finally, after the analysis of the trace and the solution of the performance problem within the query of user *pkg*, disable the trace of this client identifier and drop the trigger.

```
show user

User is "sys"

begin
dbms_monitor.client_id_trace_disable(
    client_id => 'pkg_client_id');
end;
/

drop trigger trg_pkg_logon;
```

If enabling SQL trace in all of the database sessions is desired, though this is not recommended for performance and space reasons, use the *database_trace_enable* procedure and then disable it by using the *database_trace_disable* procedure.

How to Enable Trace for All SQL*Plus Sessions

By using the *serv_mod_act_trace_enable* procedure, this has become an effortless task. Obviously, this can also be used to trace all sessions of other specific applications of particular interest. To enable the trace on all SQL Plus sessions, simply follow these steps:

🖫 Code 5.10 – dbms_monitor_srv_mod_act_trace_enable.sql

```
conn pkg@dbms

Connected to Oracle 11g Enterprise Edition Release 11.2.0.1.0
Connected as pkg

show user

User is "pkg"

--Check the session using SQL*Plus utility
col module for a15
col service_name for a15
select
    module,
    service_name
from
    v$session
where
    username = 'pkg';
```

```
MODULE           SERVICE_NAME
---------------  ---------------
SQL*Plus         sys$users

--Now just run the command below to enable the trace for all SQL Plus
sessions on service name sys$users

begin
   dbms_monitor.serv_mod_act_trace_enable(
      service_name => 'sys$users',
      module_name  =>  'SQL*Plus',
      waits => TRUE,
      binds => TRUE);
end;
/
```

```
--Check the enabled trace
  col trace_type for a15
  col primary_id for a22
  col qualifier_id1 for a10
  select
     trace_type,
     primary_id,
     qualifier_id1,
     waits,
     binds
  from
     dba_enabled_traces;
```

```
TRACE_TYPE       PRIMARY_ID              QUALIFIER_ WAITS BINDS
---------------  ----------------------  ---------- ----- -----
service_module   sys$users               SQL*Plus   TRUE  TRUE
```

That is all there is to it! All sessions connected to the database that are using SQL*Plus will have tracing enabled. Execute the *serv_mod_act_trace_disable* procedure to disable the trace. There is a parameter on this procedure named *instance_name* that could be used in a RAC environment where just one instance is specified or it can be left to NULL to enable it for all instances.

Package *dbms_odci*

Created by default or via the *?/rdbms/admin/catodci.sql* script, the *dbms_odci* package provides a function that calculates the approximate number of CPU instructions of a single CPU over a specified number of seconds, using the package function *dbms_odci. estimate_cpu_units*. The CPU usage values are returned in thousands of instructions, and in multi processor platforms, it measures a single CPU. The overhead of invoking the function is not included.

💾 Code 5.11 – dbms_odci.sql

```
conn pkg@dbms

Connected to Oracle 11g Enterprise Edition Release 11.2.0.1.0

Connected as pkg

show user

User is "pkg"
```

```
select
    dbms_odci.estimate_cpu_units(1) * 1000
from
    dual;
```

```
DBMS_ODCI.ESTIMATE_CPU_UNITS(1
------------------------------
              1128751983,24897
```

This package is used in Database Cartridges. A good example of this can be found on MOSC Note 763493.1, "Sample code on how to use *odcitable* Interface Approach with Pipelined Function". To learn more about Oracle Database Cartridges, go to *Oracle® Database Data Cartridge Developer's Guide 11g Release 2* (11.2), Doc Part Number E10765-01.

Package *dbms_outln*

First created with Oracle 8i (8.1.5), *dbms_outlln* is also known as the *?/rdnms/admin/dbmsol.sql* script and formerly known as *outln_pkg*. Stored outlines can be used to freeze the execution plan of certain SQL statements. When tuning a vendor application, you can use stored outlines to tune SQL when the source code cannot be changed. Once created, stored outlines may be swapped, allowing an improved query to be created with an outline, and swapped outside of the vendor application to use the improved execution plan.

The stored outlines feature will be eventually discontinued in favor of SQL plan management which uses SQL baselines, thereby providing better performance. Here is an example of how to create a stored outline that will be used to keep the same execution plan for the query used.

Suppose there is a query that is using an index properly, and a guarantee that it always works using the index created if required, even if the optimizer tries to change the execution plan based on new statistics or new indexes created. The query is executed, then the execution plan of this query that is inside the *shared_pool* will be fixed for future executions. The query uses a stored outline created by the *dbms_outln* package.

🖫 Code 5.12 – dbms_outln.sql

```
conn pkg@dbms

Connected to Oracle 11g Enterprise Edition Release 11.2.0.1.0
Connected as pkg

show user
User is "pkg"

select
   count(*)
from
   test_dbms_monitor t
where
   t.object_id=5443;

--Identify the sql_id of the query executed
select sql_text, sql_id, plan_hash_value, hash_value, child_number
    from v$sql
      where sql_text like '%test_dbms_monitor%';

SQL_TEXT               SQL_ID          PLAN_HASH_VALUE HASH_VALUE CHILD_NUMBER
---------------- --------------- ---------- -------------------------------------
select /*+ full(t)*/   count(*) from   test_dbms_monitor t where   t.object_i fb5856ddkf6k0
3536224278     1529289280    3

set echo on
set lines 300 pages 0
select t.*
    from v$sql s
       , table(dbms_xplan.display_cursor(s.sql_id, s.child_number, 'typical
allstats last')) t
    where s.sql_id = 'fb5856ddkf6k0' ;

Plan hash value: 3427986586
---------------------------------------------------------------------------
| Id  | Operation          | Name      | E-Rows |E-Bytes| Cost (%CPU)| E-Time
---------------------------------------------------------------------------
|   0 | select statement   |           |        |       |  3 (100)|
|   1 |  sort aggregate     |           |    1   |   5   |         |
|*  2 |   index range scan| idx_obj_id |  128   |  640  |  3   (0)| 00:00:01
---------------------------------------------------------------------------

--Create the stored outline
begin
dbms_outln.create_outline(
   hash_value => 3536224278,
   child_number => 0,
   category => 'pkg_cat');
end;
/

--Check if the stored outline was created successfully and if it has already
been used
col category for a10
col owner    for a10

select
   name,
   owner,
   category,
```

```
   used
from
   dba_outlines;
```

Note that the stored outline is created and will always be used by the optimizer when the *user_stored_outlines* session parameter is set. We will not go into much more detail as this package will be discontinued by SQL Plan Management in future releases. For reference, below is the list of procedures for this package:

- **drop_by_cat:** Drop an outline that belongs to a specific category

- **drop_unused:** Used to drop outlines that have never been used

- **exact_text_signatures:** Used to update outline signatures (only in Oracle version 8.1.6 or earlier)

- **update_by_cat:** Changes the category of all outlines in category *oldcat* to new category specified by *newcat* parameter.

- **update_signatures:** Used to update outline signatures to the current version of database. This is generally used when these outlines have been imported from an earlier database version.

One package that is not available anymore in Oracle 11gR2 is *dbms_outln_edit*. This being the case, it will not be covered in this book.

Package *dbms_profiler*

The *dbms_profiler* package is a built-in set of procedures used to capture performance information from PL/SQL. The *dbms_profiler* package has these procedures:

- *dbms_profiler.start_profiler*

- *dbms_profiler.flush_data*

- *dbms_profiler.stop_profiler*

The basic idea behind profiling with *dbms_profiler* is for the developers to understand where their code is spending the most time. They may then optimize and adjust accordingly. The *profiling* utility allows Oracle to collect data in memory structures and then dump it into tables as the application code is executed. In many ways, *dbms_profiler* is to PL/SQL what *tkprof* and Explain Plan are to SQL. Once the profiler is run, Oracle will place the results inside the *dbms_profiler* tables.

The *dbms_profiler* procedures are not part of the base installation of Oracle. Two tables need to be installed along with the Oracle supplied PL/SQL package. In the *$ORACLE_HOME/rdbms/admin* directory, two files exist that create the environment needed for the profiler to execute:

- *proftab.sql*: This creates three tables and a sequence and must be executed before the *profload.sql* file
- *profload.sql*: This creates the package header and package body for *dbms_profiler*. This script must be executed as the *sys* user.

Oracle: Starting a Profiling Session

The profiler does not begin capturing performance information until the call to *start_profiler* is executed.

```
SQL>
exec
 dbms_profiler.start_profiler ('Test of raise procedure by Scott');
```

Flushing Data During a Profiling Session

The *flush* command enables the developer to dump statistics during program execution without stopping the *profiling* utility. The only other time Oracle saves data to the underlying tables is when the profiling session is stopped, as shown here:

```
SQL>
exec
dbms_profiler.flush_data();
```

.

Stopping a Profiling Session

Stopping a profiler execution using the Oracle *dbms_profiler* package is done after an adequate period of time of gathering performance benchmarks determined by the developer. Once the developer stops the profiler, all the remaining (unflushed) data is loaded into the profiler tables.

```
SQL>
exec
 dbms_profiler.stop_profiler();
```

.

The Oracle *dbms_profiler* package also provides procedures that suspend and resume profiling such as *pause_profiler* and *resume_profiler*.

Analyzing *dbms_profiler* data

The table named *plsql_profiler_runs* contains information related to a profiling session. Things, such as when the run was started, who started it, and how long the run lasted are contained in this table. This table has the following important columns:

- *runid*: The unique run identifier given to each profiler execution

- *related_run*: *Run_id* of related run that can be called by the programmer

- *run_owner*: User who started the run

- *run_date*: Timestamp of the date of the run

- *run_comment*: User-provided text concerning anything about this run that they wish to specify. This is used mainly for documentation since *run_id* is hard to remember.

- *run_total_time:* Total elapsed time for this run

The *plsql_profiler_units* table defines each PL/SQL component (unit) that was executed during a profiler run. Benchmarks for each of the units are stored in this table in the following columns:

- *runid*: References *plsql_profiler_runs(runid)*

- *unit_number*: Internally generated library unit number

- *unit_type*: Library unit type, i.e. package, procedure and such

- *unit_owner*: Library unit owner name (the owner of the object)

- *unit_name*: Library unit name, e.g. the name of the object as defined in the *user_objects* view

- *unit_timestamp*: Time when the unit was created. The unit, being the procedural object (procedure, function, package). This column holds the same data as the created column in the *user_objects* view.

- *total_time*: Total time used by this unit for the given run

The *plsql_profiler_data* table is where the real performance benchmarks are stored from executing *dbms_profiler*. This table includes the execution statistics for each line of code contained in the PL/SQL unit. This table can be joined to the *user_source* view and can extract the actual line of code for each benchmark. The primary key includes *runid*, *unit_number*, and *line#*.

The following example shows how to use the *dbms_profiler* package to gather execution time information and locate the bottleneck in the overall process. First, the user *pkg* will run the *proftab.sql* script to create tables used to store profiling information.

📁 Code 5.13 – dbms_profiler.sql

```
conn pkg@dbms

Connected to Oracle 11g Enterprise Edition Release 11.2.0.1.0
Connected as pkg

show user

User is "pkg"

SQL>
show
 user

User is "pkg"

SQL>
@?/rdbms/admin/proftab.sql

Table dropped.

Table dropped.

Table dropped.

Sequence dropped.

Table created.

Comment created.
Table created.

Comment created.

Table created.

Comment created.

Sequence created.
```

Now, we create a package and analyze its performance with *dbms_profiler*. The package body has two queries. One that executes a full table scan and the other that uses an index scan much faster, so the *dbms_profiler* package will easily find in which query is the problem.

```
--Create a package that will call the test procedure
create or replace package test_dbms_profiler_pkg
as
procedure test_dbms_profiler_proc (n_obj in number);
end;
/

--Create the package body that will call an example procedure.
--This procedure will have a query that is doing a full tablescan and ---
another query using an index.
create or replace package body test_dbms_profiler_pkg as
```

```
   procedure test_dbms_profiler_proc (n_obj in number) is
      d_n_obj number;
      run_num_start number;
      run_num_stop number;
   begin
      --Start the profiling
      run_num_start:= dbms_profiler.start_profiler(
                     run_comment => 'Start pkg:
'||to_char(sysdate,'dd-Mon-RRRR hh:mi:ss'));

      select /*+ full(m) */
         count(*) into d_n_obj
      from
         test_dbms_monitor m
      where
         m.object_id=n_obj;
      dbms_output.put_line('First statement. Number os objects with
object_id='||n_obj||' is '||d_n_obj);

      select
         count(*) into d_n_obj
      from
         test_dbms_monitor m
      where m.object_id=n_obj;
      dbms_output.put_line('Second statement. Number os objects with
object_id='||n_obj||' is '||d_n_obj);

      run_num_stop:=dbms_profiler.stop_profiler;

      end test_dbms_profiler_proc;
end test_dbms_profiler_pkg;
/
```

Now run the following query to find the line that is consuming most of the execution time:

```
set linesize 200
column "Line" format 99999
column "Time spent/Line" format 999.999999
column "Type" format a12
column "Name" format a22
column "Occurrences" format 999999

select
   u.unit_type "Type",
   u.unit_name "Name",
   d.line# "Line",
   d.total_occur "Occurrences",
   d.total_time/1000000000 "Time spent/Line",
   d.min_time/1000000000 "Min Exec Time/Line",
   d.max_time/1000000000 "Max Exec Time/Line"
from
   plsql_profiler_units u,
   plsql_profiler_data d
where
   d.runid=u.runid
and
```

```
    d.unit_number = u.unit_number
and
    d.total_occur >0
and
    u.runid=2
order by u.unit_number, d.line#;
```

Type Name	Line	Occurrences	Time spent/Line	Min Exec Time/Line	Max Exec Time/Line
package_body_test_dbms_profiler_pkg 10.8385844	10	1	10.838584	10.8385844	
package_body_test_dbms_profiler_pkg .000483955	16	1	.000484	.000483955	
package_body_test_dbms_profiler_pkg .509954426	17	1	.509954	.509954426	
package_body_test_dbms_profiler_pkg .000020954	22	1	.000021	.000020954	
package_body_test_dbms_profiler_pkg .000006984	24	1	.000007	.000006984	

Now that the line that is spending more time to execute has been identified, use the query below to get the source code of this line:

```
--Get the source code of the line spending more time to execute
column "Line" format 99999
column "Total Time" format 999.999999
column "Type" format a12
column "Name" format a22
column "Occurrences" format 999999
column "Text Command" format a46

select  p.unit_name "Name",
        p."Occurrences" "Occurrences",
        p."Total Time" "Total Time",
        p.line# "Line",
        substr(s.text, 1, 75) "Text Command"
  from (select u.unit_name,
               d.total_occur "Occurrences",
               (d.total_time / 1000000000) "Total Time",
               d.line#
          from plsql_profiler_units u, plsql_profiler_data d
         where d.runid = u.runid
           and d.unit_number = u.unit_number
           and d.total_occur > 0
           and u.runid = 2) p,
       user_source s
 where p.unit_name = s.name(+)
   and p.line# = s.line(+)
   and p."Total Time" > 3
 order by p.unit_name, p.line#;
```

Name	Occurrences	Total Time	Line	Text Command
test_dbms_profiler_pkg	1	10.838584	10	select /*+ full(m) */

It is very easy to find the line responsible for using more than its share of resources. A little tuning to this statement will solve the performance problem.

Best Practices for Using *dbms_profiler*

1. **Wrap only for production:** Wrapping code is desired for production environments, but not for profiling. It is much easier to see the unencrypted form of the text in reports than it is to connect line numbers to source versions. Use *dbms_profiler* before wrapping code in a test environment, wrap it, and then put it in production.

2. **Eliminate system packages most of the time:** Knowing the performance data for internal Oracle processing does not buy much since nothing can be changed. However, knowing the performance problem is within the system packages will save some time with trying to tune the specific code when the problem is elsewhere.

When analyzing lines of code, it is best to concentrate on the following:

1. **Lines of code that are frequently executed:** For example, a loop that executes 5000 times is a great candidate for tuning. Guru Oracle tuners typically look for that "low hanging fruit" in which one line or a group of lines of code are executed much more than others. The benefits of tuning one line of code that is executed often far outweigh tuning those lines that may cost more yet are executed infrequently in comparison.

2. **Lines of code with a high value for average time executed:** The minimum and maximum values of execution time are interesting although not as useful as the average execution time. Min and max only tell how much the execution time varies depending on database activity. Line by line, a PL/SQL developer should focus on those lines that cost the most on an average execution basis. *dbms_profiler* does not provide the average, but it does provide enough data to allow it to be computed (Total Execution Time / # Times Executed).

3. **Lines of code that contain SQL syntax:** The main resource consumers are those lines that execute SQL. Once the data is sorted by average execution time, the statements that are the worst usually contain SQL. Optimize and tune the SQL through utilities such as Explain Plan, *tkprof*, and third party software.

Package *dbms_result_cache*

A new feature of Oracle 11g, the Result Cache, is a powerful tool that can be used to cache query and function results in memory. The cached information is stored in a dedicated area inside the shared pool where it can be shared by other PL/SQL programs that are performing similar calculations. If data stored in this cache changes, the values that are cached become invalid. This feature is useful for databases with statements that need to access a large number of rows and return only few of them.

> **Note:** The result cache does not help the vast majority of PL/SQL applications because they do not re-read the same information, and even if they do, the existing data buffers will have the information cached and ready for re-use.

The Result Cache is set up using the *result_cache_mode* initialization parameter with one of these three values:

1. *auto*: The results that need to be stored are settled by the Oracle optimizer

2. *manual*: Cache the results by hinting the statement using the result_cache|no_result_cache hint

3. *force*: All results will be cached

The *dbms_result_cache* package is used to yield the DBA management options of memory used by both SQL Result Cache and PL/SQL function Result Cache. Here are procedures and functions of the *dbms_result_cache* package:

- *bypass*: The procedure *bypass* turns the result cache functionality on and off. If set to true, the Result Cache is turned off and not used. The cache is not flushed by using this procedure. The example below turns off the result cache.

- *status*: This function returns the current status of the result cache functionality.

- *memory_report*: This procedure returns a report on the current memory used by the Result Cache. If the parameter *true* is passed, then a more detailed report is displayed.

- *flush*: The *flush* operation will remove all results from the cache. It has two Boolean parameters; the first determines if the memory is maintained in the cache or released to the system. The second parameter determines if the cache statistics are maintained or also flushed. The following example uses the defaults and will flush the cache, releasing the memory to the system and clearing the statistics.

- *invalidate*: The *invalidate* operation invalidates all results in the cache that are dependent on an object. These functions are overloaded, so the object can be identified by owner and name or by *object_id*.

- *invalidate_object*: The *invalidate_object* operation invalidates specific result objects. Result objects can be found from the *v$result_cache_objects* dynamic performance view.

A practical overview of how to use this procedures and function will be described below.

For this example, the SQL Result Cache is presented to the reader and how to clean up the Result Cache as well as how to use hints to fix the results of a query in Result Cache memory will be shown. First, take a look at the Result Cache initialization parameters. They are all set to their default values; therefore, it is necessary to use the *result_cache* hint to keep the results of queries in memory since the *result_cache_mode* initialization parameter is *manual*.

Code 5.14 – dbms_result_cache_sql.sql

```
conn pkg@dbms

Connected to Oracle 11g Enterprise Edition Release 11.2.0.1.0
Connected as pkg

show user

User is "pkg"

--Check result cache parameters
col name for a30
col value for a10
select
    name,
    value
from
    v$parameter
where
    name like '%result%';

NAME                           VALUE
------------------------------ ----------
result_cache_mode              manual
result_cache_max_size          1081344
result_cache_max_result        5
result_cache_remote_expiration 0
client_result_cache_size       0
client_result_cache_lag        3000

--Query the v$result_cache_objects to check if there is any cached object
select
    count(*)
from
    v$result_cache_objects;

COUNT(*)
----------
         0

--Use the result_cache hint because manual mode is being used for this
instance
select /*+ result_cache */
    count(*)
from
    employees
where
```

```
    employee_id=102;
```

Now queries Result Cache views that provide information like objects in memory, relationship dependencies and statistics of Result Cache.

```
--Checking the objects in Result Cache
col "Space Over" for a5
col "Space Unused" for a5
col "Obj_Name_Dep" for a26
select
    type "Type",
    name "Name",
    namespace "SQL|PL/SQL",
    creation_timestamp "Creation",
    space_overhead "Space Over",
    space_unused "Space Unused",
    cache_id "Obj_Name_Dep",
    invalidations "Invds"
from
    gv$result_cache_objects;

Type       Name                          SQL|PL/SQL Creation   Space Space Obj_Name_Dep nvds
-----      -----------  -----  -----  -------------------------- ----------
Dependency pkg.employees                            25/11/2009    0     0 pkg.employees
Result     select /*+ result_cache */   SQL         25/11/2009  269   751
5rcxpxpgrphzt3xdbnggrfnq99          0

--Check the Result Cache Setting and Statistics
select
    name "Name",
    value "Value"
from
v$result_cache_statistics;

Name                          Value
----------------------------- ----------
Block Size (Bytes)            1024
Block Count Maximum           1056
Block Count Current           32
Result Size Maximum (Blocks)  52
Create Count Success          3
Create Count Failure          0
Find Count                    40
Invalidation Count            0
Delete Count Invalid          0
Delete Count Valid            0
Hash Chain Length             1

--Check objects cached
select
    o.owner "Owner",
    o.object_id "ID",
    o.object_name "Name",
    r.object_no "Obj Number"
from
    dba_objects o,
    gv$result_cache_dependency r
```

```
where
   o.object_id = r.object_no;

Owner               ID Name       Obj Number
----------   ----------   ----------   ----------
pkg              26546 employees        26546

--Checking memory blocks and their status in Result Cache Memory
select
   *
from
   gv$result_cache_memory;
```

INST_ID	ID	CHUNK	OFFSET	FREE	OBJECT_ID	POSITION
1	0	0	0	NO	0	0
1	1	0	1	NO	1	0
1	2	0	2	YES		
1	3	0	3	YES		

```
.
.
.

--Check the relationship dependency between cached results and dependencies
col object_name for a10
select
   r.result_id,
   r.depend_id,
   o.owner,
   o.object_name,
   r.object_no
from
   v$result_cache_dependency r,
   dba_objects o
where
   r.object_no = o.object_id;

RESULT_ID  DEPEND_ID OWNER        OBJECT_NAM OBJECT_NO
----------   ----------   ----------   ----------   ----------
        1           0 pkg          employees        26546
```

Execute the *flush* operation to remove all objects from the memory Result Cache. There is the option to retain or release the memory and/or statistics as needed. Here all possibilities of flushing the Result Cache are found:

```
--Flush retaining statistics (default for both are FALSE)
begin
dbms_result_cache.flush (
   retainmem => FALSE,
   retainsta => TRUE);
end;
/

--Flush Retaining memory (default for both are FALSE)
begin
dbms_result_cache.flush (
   retainmem => TRUE,
   retainsta => FALSE);
end;
/
```

```
--Flush memory and statistics globally
begin
dbms_result_cache.flush(
    retainmem => TRUE,
    retainsta => FALSE,
    global => TRUE);
end;
/
```

It is very easy to keep the results of queries in memory, but pay attention to the *invalidations* column of the *v$result_cache_objects* table. This column shows when the results associated to an object in memory become invalid due to a data modification. To use Result Cache within a function, create the function passing the *result_cache* parameter as follows:

```
create or replace function fc_result_cache (obj_id IN number)
return boolean
result_cache relies_on (employees) is
….
```

The *result_cache* parameter is used so that the results returned by this function will be cached in memory until the data of *employees* table is modified, invalidating the results cached for this function.

Package *dbms_xplan*

Part of the tuning tasks that a database administrator needs to know is what plan a certain query is performing in the database. Since Oracle 9i Release 2, the *dbms_xplan* package is the tool used to accomplish this. It is necessary to first create the plan table that will be used to store information about the execution plan which will be displayed. The *catplan.sql* script must be executed to create the plan table; it can be found in the *$ORACLE_HOME/rdbms/admin* directory.

This package can also be used in conjunction with the Automatic Workload Repository (AWR). Poor plans are gathered in a report which shows its explain plan using the *dbms_xplan* package. Explain plans can be caught and shown via SQL Tuning Sets.

If the explain plan of a cursor that is running needs to be obtained, use the *dbms_xplan* package to read *v$sql_plan* and *v$sql_plan_statistics_all* views. Here are some examples on how to use this package to analyze and locate the performance problem of a query. The first demonstration will show how to view the explain plan for a SQL query using functions from the *dbms_xplan* package.

Code 5.15 – dbms_xplan_display.sql

```
conn sys@ora11g as sysdba

Connected to Oracle 11g Enterprise Edition Release 11.1.0.6.0
conn / as sysdba

--Create a test table
create table
   test_dbms_xplan
as
   select * from dba_objects;

--Explain plan for the query example below
explain plan for
select
   *
from
   test_dbms_xplan
where
   object_name = 'test';
select * from table(dbms_xplan.display);

PLAN_TABLE_OUTPUT
-------------------------------------------------------------------
Plan hash value: 3456749374


--------------------------------------------------------------------
| Id | Operation         | Name           | Rows | Bytes | Cost (%CPU)| Time      |
--------------------------------------------------------------------
|  0 | select statement  |                |  12  | 2484  | 285   (0)| 00:00:04 |
|* 1 |  table access full| test_dbms_xplan|  12  | 2484  | 285   (0)| 00:00:04 |
--------------------------------------------------------------------

Predicate Information (identified by operation id):
---------------------------------------------------

   1 - filter("object_name"='test')


Note
-----
   - dynamic sampling used for this statement (level=2)

17 rows selected.
```

The next example shows how to display a SQL plan in XML format by using the *build_plan_xml* function.

Code 5.16 – dbms_xplan_build_plan_xml.sql

```
conn sys@ora11g as sysdba

Connected to Oracle 11g Enterprise Edition Release 11.1.0.6.0
conn / as sysdba

explain plan
set statement_id = 'my_explain_test' for
select
```

```
      *
from
   test_dbms_xplan
where
   object_name = 'test';

set long 10000
set linesize 200
select
   dbms_xplan.build_plan_xml(
      statement_id => 'my_explain_test')
   as XML_Plan
from
   dual;
```

```
XML_PLAN
--------------------------------------------------------------------
<plan>
  <operation name="select statement" id="0" depth="0" pos="285">
    <card>12</card>
    <bytes>2484</bytes>
    <cost>285</cost>
    <io_cost>285</io_cost>
    <cpu_cost>21702581</cpu_cost>
    <time>00:00:04 </time>
  </operation>
  <operation name="table access" options="full" id="1" depth="1" pos="1">
    <object>test_dbms_xplan</object>
    <card>12</card>
    <bytes>2484</bytes>
    <cost>285</cost>
    <io_cost>285</io_cost>
    <cpu_cost>21702581</cpu_cost>
    <time>00:00:04 </time>
<project>&quot;test_dbms_xplan&quot;.&quot;owner&quot;[varchar2,30],
&quot;object_name&quot;[varchar2,128], &quot; test_dbms_xplan&quot;.
&quot;subobject_name&quot;[varcharR2,30], &quot;
test_dbms_xplan&quot;.&quot;object_id&quot;[number,22], &quot;
test_dbms_xplan&quot;.&quot;DAT
a_object_id&quot;[number,22], &quot;
test_dbms_xplan&quot;.&quot;object_type&quot;[varchar2,19], &quot;
test_dbms_xplan&quot;.&quot;created&qu
ot;[date,7], &quot; test_dbms_xplan&quot;.&quot;last_ddl_time&quot;[date,7],
&quot; test_dbms_xplan&quot;.&quot;timestamp&quot;[varchar2,19],
&quot; test_dbms_xplan&quot;.&quot;status&quot;[varchar2,7], &quot;
test_dbms_xplan&quot;.&quot;temporary&quot;[ varchar2,1], &quot;test_dbms_x
plan&quot;.&quot;generated&quot;[VARCHAR2,1], &quot;
test_dbms_xplan&quot;.&quot;secondary&quot;[ varchar2,1], &quot;
test_dbms_xplan&quot;.&qu
ot;namespace&quot;[number,22], &quot;
test_dbms_xplan&quot;.&quot;edition_name&quot;[varchar2,30]</project>
    <predicates
type="filter">&quot;object_name&quot;=&apos;test&apos;</predicates>
    <qblock>sel$1</qblock>
    <object_alias>test_dbms_xplan@sel$1</object_alias>
    <other_xml>
      <info type="db_version">11.2.0.1</info>
      <info type="parse_schema"><![cdata["pkg"]]></info>
      <info type="dynamic_sampling">2</info>
```

```
        <info type="plan_hash">3456749374</info>
        <info type="plan_hash_2">3594218905</info>
        <outline_data>
          <hint><![cdata[full(@"sel$1" "test_dbms_xplan"@"sel$1")]]></hint>
          <hint><![cdata[outline_leaf(@"sel$1")]]></hint>
          <hint><![cdata [all_rows]]></hint>
          <hint><![cdata [db_version('11.2.0.1')]]></hint>
          <hint><![cdata[optimizer_features_enable('11.2.0.1')]]></hint>
          <hint><![cdata [ignore_optim_embedded_hints]]></hint>
        </outline_data>
      </other_xml>
    </operation>
</plan>
```

Next, how to get the explain plan of a query that has gotten inside an AWR report will be examined. First of all, execute the query that will make a full-table scan.

🖫 Code 5.17 – dbms_xplan_display_awr.sql

```
conn sys@ora11g as sysdba

Connected to Oracle 11g Enterprise Edition Release 11.1.0.6.0

conn / as sysdba

exec dbms_workload_repository.create_snapshot;

select
   *
from
   test_dbms_xplan
where
   object_name = 'test';
```

Now run an AWR snapshot to gather information about the query just executed.

```
exec dbms_workload_repository.create_snapshot;
SQL>
@?/rdbms/admin/awrrpt
```

Open the AWR report and find the *sql_id* of the query executed. Use the command below to show the execution plan for the SQL query.

```
set linesize 140
set long 1000
select
   *
from
   table (dbms_xplan.display_awr(
           sql_id => 'g5r5yrz1rq9dy'));

PLAN_TABLE_OUTPUT
-----------------------------------------------------------------
SQL_ID g5r5yrz1rq9dy
--------------------
select    * from    test_dbms_xplan where    object_name = 'TEST'
```

```
Plan hash value: 3456749374

----------------------------------------------------------------------| Id  | Operation          |
Name           | Rows  | Bytes | Cost (%CPU)| Time     |----------------------------------------------------------------------| 0   | select statement   |
|        |       | 285 (100)|          |              |  0 | select statement  |
|  1 | table access full| test_dbms_xplan |   12 |  2484 |   285   (0)| 00:00:04 |
----------------------------------------------------------------------
Note
-----
   - dynamic sampling used for this statement (level=2)


17 rows selected.
```

This last example will show how to get the explain plan for a cursor that was just executed. To use *dbms_xplan* to display the cursor execution plan, first create and execute a PL/SQL block with an example cursor.

⊟ Code 5.18 – dbms_xplan_display_cursor.sql

```
conn sys@ora11g as sysdba

Connected to Oracle 11g Enterprise Edition Release 11.1.0.6.0
conn / as sysdba

set serveroutput on
declare
   v_obj_name varchar2(30);
   v_obj_type varchar2(30);

cursor c1 is
   select /* my_test_dbms_xplan */
      object_name,
      object_type
   from
      test_dbms_xplan;

begin
   open c1;
   fetch c1 into
      v_obj_name,
      v_obj_type ;
   while c1%found
      loop
         dbms_output.put_line(a => 'object name:'||v_obj_name);
         dbms_output.put_line(a => 'object type:'||v_obj_type);
      end loop;
   close c1;
end;
/
```

Now we locate the cursor by using the *v$sql_plan* view.

```
select
   sql_text,
   sql_id,
   child_number
from
```

```
    v$sql
where
    sql_text like '%select /* my_test_dbms_xplan%';
```

Get the explain plan of the cursor by using the *display_cursor* function in the *dbms_xplan* package.

```
select
    *
from
    table(dbms_xplan.display_cursor(
            sql_id => '2ckag8c758v6h',
            cursor_child_no => 0));
```

These are just some examples of the functionalities of this package. There are others that work in pretty much the same manner; for example, using *dbms_xplan* to explain an SQL execution plan in an SQL Tuning Set and more.

Package *dbms_spm*

A new feature of Oracle 11g is called SQL Plan Management which can be used to control the SQL plan evolution, guiding the optimizer to always choose a SQL plan that will not regress the performance.

Newly generated SQL plans will simply be included in SQL plan baselines only if it is found that the query performance will not become degraded, ideally optimizing performance. In other words, the SPM will test existing SQL and only generate improved plans for SQL statements which run faster than traditional SQL.
These SQL plans can be loaded from three different SQL sources:

1. SQL Tuning Sets (Captured manually)

2. AWR Snapshots

3. Cursor Cache (real-time SQL)

The *dbms_spm* package can be used to load SQL execution plans from the various sources mentioned above. Please note that the *administer sql management* grant privilege is needed to use the package *dbms_spm*.

Up until now, SQL plan baselines were shown which were not fixed. This means that the optimizer uses costing mechanisms to evaluate plans. With Manual SQL Management, plans can be fixed in baselines, thereby forcing the optimizer to consider only those plans from a plan baseline which have been manually marked as possible candidates.

There may be reasons why a guarantee may be desired for the execution plans of certain SQL not to change, i.e. plan stability. For example, a new application has been developed using Oracle which has been tested thoroughly and is now ready to be deployed to the customers.

Since it is unknown how the application will behave in the environment of the customer's site, the baselines could be fixed for the SQL and shipped together with the application. In this fashion, SQL can be pre-tuned, locked-down and deployed where they are fed into the customer's system, eliminating the possibility of performance regression.

If the *optimizer_capture_sql_plan_baselines* initialization parameter is set to TRUE (default is FALSE on 11g), then the SQL plan baselines will be loaded automatically for SQL plan history and *sql* statements. If this parameter is set to FALSE, then manually manage SQL plan baselines using the *dbms_spm* package.

The next example will show how to use the main procedures and functions of the *dbms_spm* package. This includes operations like changing attributes of SQL plans, configuring the SQL management base, creating a staging table to be used for transporting the SQL plan, dropping SQL baseline plans, loading plans from cursor and SQL Tuning Sets and more.

Suppose that we are running a query on a table that is doing a full table scan. We then decide to create an index on the referenced table, running the same query to get the new plan. If we guarantee plan stability by using SQL Plan Management, we will first have to evolve this new execution plan using the *dbms_spm* package in order to allow the database to use the new index as demonstrated next.

The first step will usually be to change the existing index to the invisible mode rather than dropping it. In the example, it will be dropped since this is just a test and the effect of dropping versus making invisible will give the same results. The query will then be made and the plan will be shown.

🖫 Code 5.19 – dbms_spm_1.sql

```
conn pkg@dbms

Connected to Oracle 11g Enterprise Edition Release 11.2.0.1.0
Connected as pkg

show user

User is "pkg"

--Let's drop the index so the optimizer will not use it
drop index emp_department_ix;
```

```
Index dropped.

select
   last_name
from
   employees
where
   department_id=100;

LAST_NAME
-------------------------
Greenberg
Faviet
Chen
Sciarra
Urman
Popp

6 rows selected.

--Get the plan for the query and note that it is doing a FTS on employee
table

explain plan for
select
   last_name
from
   employees
where
   department_id=100;
select
   *
from
   table(dbms_xplan.display);

PLAN_TABLE_OUTPUT
-------------------------------------------------------------------------------Plan hash value:
1445457117

---------------------------------------------------------------------
| Id | Operation          | Name      | Rows | Bytes | Cost (%CPU)| Time     |
---------------------------------------------------------------------
|  0 | SELECT STATEMENT   |           |    6 |   66 |    3   (0)| 00:00:01 |
|* 1 |  TABLE ACCESS FULL| EMPLOYEES |    6 |   66 |    3   (0)| 00:00:01 |
---------------------------------------------------------------------

Predicate Information (identified by operation id):
---------------------------------------------------

plan_table_output
```

Next, the procedure *load_plans_from_cursor_cache* will be used to load the execution plan into the SQL baseline. Note that the baseline is *accepted* and *enabled* by default when a manual load in the SQL baseline is done.

```
--Now import the explain used to the SQL Baseline
select
   sql_text,
   sql_id
from
   v$sql
```

```
where
   sql_text like '%employee%';
```

```
SQL_TEXT                                                SQL_ID
----------------------------------------------------------------------------------
select   last_name from   employees where   department_id=:"SYS_B_0"   0gh1gn1mv7u0u
```

```
--Load the sql_id into the SQL Basesile
declare
  v_sql_plan_id  pls_integer;
begin
  v_sql_plan_id := dbms_spm.load_plans_from_cursor_cache(
    sql_id => '0gh1gn1mv7u0u');
end;
/

.
```

```
--Check if the plan is being used and is accepted
select
   sql_handle,
   plan_name,
   enabled,
   accepted,
   fixed
from
   dba_sql_plan_baselines
where
   sql_text like '%employee%';
```

```
SQL_HANDLE                  PLAN_NAME                     ENA ACC FIX
-------------------------   ---------------------------   --- --- ---
sys_sql_1046c141c5de11a8    sql_plan_10jq1872xw4d8cf314e9e YES YES NO
```

Check the execution plan of the loaded baseline using the following statement:

```
--Check the execution plan if it is using the index
select
   *
from table(
   dbms_xplan.display_sql_plan_baseline(
      sql_handle=>'sys_sql_1046c141c5de11a8',
      format=>'basic'));
```

The output is as follows:

```
plan_table_output
----------------------------------------------------------------------------------
SQL handle: sys_sql_1046c141c5de11a8
SQL text: select   last_name from   employees where   department_id=100
----------------------------------------------------------------------------------
Plan name: sql_plan_10jq1872xw4d8cf314e9e      Plan id: 3476115102
Enabled: YES    Fixed: NO    Accepted: YES    Origin: manual-load
----------------------------------------------------------------------------------


plan_table_output
--------------------------------------------------------------------------Plan
hash value: 1445457117

---------------------------------------
```

```
| Id  | Operation        | Name      |
----------------------------------------
|   0 | select statement |           |
|   1 |  table access full| employees |
----------------------------------------
```

Now create the index on the *employee* table and then execute the query again. Note that the explain plan is still the same because only the first execution plan was loaded in the SQL baselines.

```
--Create the index so the optimizer will start to use it and check the plan
again
create index
    emp_department_ix
on
    employees (department_id)
tablespace
    tbs_idx;

Index created.

explain plan for
select
    last_name
from
    employees
where
    department_id=100;

Explained.

select
    *
from
    table(dbms_xplan.display);
```

```
plan_table_output
-----------------------------------------------------------------------------------------Plan hash
value: 1445457117

--------------------------------------------------------------------------------
| Id  | Operation        | Name      | Rows | Bytes | Cost (%CPU)| Time     |
--------------------------------------------------------------------------------
|   0 | select statement |           |    6 |    66 |    3   (0)| 00:00:01 |
|*  1 |  table access full| employees |    6 |    66 |    3   (0)| 00:00:01 |
--------------------------------------------------------------------------------

Predicate Information (identified by operation id):
---------------------------------------------------

plan_table_output
--------------------------------------------------------------------------------
   1 - filter("department_id"=100)

Note
-----
   - SQL plan baseline "sql_plan_10jq1872xw4d8cf314e9e" used for this statement

17 rows selected.
```

Run the query and check the *dba_sql_plan_baselines* again, revealing that the new plan generated for the same *sql_handler*. The last plan that is using an index was not accepted yet. To do so, it will need to be evolved.

```
select
    sql_handle,
    plan_name,
    enabled,
    accepted,
    fixed
from
    dba_sql_plan_baselines
where
    sql_text like '%employee%';
```

```
SQL_HANDLE                      PLAN_NAME                            ENA ACC FIX
------------------------------- ------------------------------------ --- --- ---
SYS_SQL_1046c141c5de11a8        sql_plan_10jq1872xw4d8c079fdff       YES NO  NO
SYS_SQL_1046c141c5de11a8        sql_plan_10jq1872xw4d8cf314e9e       YES YES NO
```

Now the evolved process will be used to accept the new *sql* execution plan that is utilizing the created index.

```
--Evolve the new sql plan
select
    dbms_spm.evolve_sql_plan_baseline(
        sql_handle => 'SYS_SQL_1046c141c5de11a8',
        plan_name => 'sql_plan_10jq1872xw4d8c079fdff')
from
    dual;
```

The output is as follows:

```
dbms_spm.evolve_sql_plan_baseline(sql_handle=>'sys_sql_1046C141C5DE11A8',plan_na
-------------------------------------------------------------------------------

-------------------------------------------------------------------------------
                        Evolve SQL Plan Baseline Report
-------------------------------------------------------------------------------

Inputs:
-------
  sql_handle = sys_sql_1046c141c5de11a8
  plan_name  = sql_plan_10jq1872xw4d8c079fdff
  time_limit = dbms_spm.auto_limit
  verify     = YES

dbms_spm.evolve_sql_plan_baseline(sql_handle=>'sys_sql_1046C141C5DE11A8',plan_na
-------------------------------------------------------------------------------
  commit     = YES

Plan: sql_plan_10jq1872xw4d8c079fdff
------------------------------------
  Plan was verified: Time used .09 seconds.
  Plan passed performance criterion: 3.42 times better than baseline plan.
  Plan was changed to an accepted plan.

                          Baseline Plan      Test Plan      Stats Ratio
                          -------------      ---------      -----------
  Execution Status:         complete         complete

dbms_spm.evolve_sql_plan_baseline(sql_handle=>'sys_sql_1046C141C5DE11A8',plan_na
-------------------------------------------------------------------------------
  Rows Processed:              6                6
```

```
Elapsed Time(ms):                        .64          .546              1.17
CPU Time(ms):                            .777         .666              1.17
Buffer Gets:                             7            2                 3.5
Physical Read Requests:                  0            0
Physical Write Requests:                 0            0
Physical Read Bytes:                     0            0
Physical Write Bytes:                    0            0
Executions:                              1            1


-------------------------------------------------------------------------------
dbms_spm.evolve_sql_plan_baseline(sql_handle=>'sys_sql_1046C141C5DE11A8',plan_na
-------------------------------------------------------------------------------
                          Report Summary
-------------------------------------------------------------------------------
Number of plans verified: 1
Number of plans accepted: 1
```

Lastly, check whether or not the execution plan being used is the new one. It must be
since it is the one that has the lowest cost to the Oracle optimizer.

```
--Check the plans again
select
    sql_handle,
    plan_name,
    enabled,
    accepted,
    fixed
from
    dba_sql_plan_baselines
where
    sql_text like '%employee%';


--Run the new explain plain and get the index being used
explain plan for
select
    last_name
from
    employees
where
    department_id=100;

select
    *
from
    table(dbms_xplan.display);
```

```
N_TABLE_OUTPUT
--------------------------
Plan hash value: 2056577954
```

Id	Operation	Name	Rows	Bytes	Cost (%CPU)	Time
0	select statement				6	66	2	(0)	00:00:01
1	table access by index rowid	employees			6	66	2	(0)	00:00:01
* 2	index range scan	emp_department_IX			6		1	(0)	00:00:01

```
Predicate Information (identified by operation id):

PLAN_TABLE_OUTPUT
-------------------------------------------------------------------------------

    2 - access("department_id"=100)
```

```
Note
-----
   - SQL plan baseline "sql_plan_10jq1872xw4d8c079fdff" used for this statement

18 rows selected.
```

The note at the end of the execution plan informs that the query is using a SQL Plan baseline.

Use the function *alter_sql_plan_baseline* to change attributes of a specific plan or all plans at once.

Here is an example that shows how to disable a specific SQL plan baseline and fixate the execution plan:

🖫 Code 5.20 – dbms_spm_2.sql

```
conn pkg@dbms
--Disable a specific sql baseline plan
set serveroutput on
declare
  v_sql_plan_id  pls_integer;
begin
  v_sql_plan_id := dbms_spm.alter_sql_plan_baseline(
    sql_handle      => 'sys_sql_1046c141c5de11a8',
    plan_name       => 'sql_plan_10jq1872xw4d8cf314e9e',
    attribute_name  => 'fixed',
    attribute_value => 'YES');
end;
/
```

Information about the SQL management base can be found in *dba_sql_management_config*. The configuration can be easily modified using the *configure* procedure as in the example below.

🖫 Code 5.21 – dbms_spm_3.sql

```
conn pkg@dbms
--SQL Management Base information
select
  decode(parameter_name ,
           'space_budget_percet','sysaux Percent',
           'plan_retention_weeks','Retention Weeks')
       "Par Name",
           parameter_value "Par Value"
from
dba_sql_management_config;

Par Name         Par Value
--------------- ----------
Sysaux Percent          10
Retention Weeks         53
```

```
--Change sysaux percent to 40% and retention weeks to 30 weeks (maximum
percent value is 50% and 10 years for retention time)
begin
dbms_spm.configure(parameter_name => 'space_budget_percent',parameter_value
=> 40);
dbms_spm.configure(parameter_name => 'plan_retention_weeks',parameter_value
=> 30);
end;
/

--SQL Management Base information
select
   decode(parameter_name ,
             'space_budget_percent',' sysaux Percent',
             'plan_retention_weeks','Retention Weeks')
          "Par Name",
          parameter_value "Par Value"
from
dba_sql_management_config;

Par Name         Par Value
---------------  ----------
SYSAUX Percent          40
Retention Weeks         30
```

To drop a single SQL plan or all plans associated with a SQL handle, you can use the *drop_sql_plan_baseline* procedure. Stored outlines from plan baselines can also be migrated into the SQL management base using the procedure *migrate_stored_outline*. Here is an example for each one of these procedures:

Code 5.22 – dbms_spm_4.sql

```
conn pkg@dbms
--Migrate all stored outlines to SQL Management Base (one plan baseline is
created for each stored outline)
--Create an stored outline
create outline emp_out for category pkg_outlines
on
select
   e.employee_id,
   e.last_name,
   d.department_name,
   d.department_id
from
   employees e,
   departments d
where
   e.department_id = d.department_id;

--Check the outline created
col name for a10
col owner for a5
col category for a20
select
  name,
  owner,
  category
```

```
from
   dba_outlines
where
 category='pkg_outlines';

--Migrate this outline and all others to SQL Management Base
set serveroutput on
declare
  my_report clob;
begin
  my_report := dbms_spm.migrate_stored_outline(
    attribute_name => 'all',
    fixed => 'yes' );
end;
/

select
   sql_text,
   origin
from
   dba_sql_plan_baselines
where
   sql_text like '%e.employee_id%';
```

To simply drop a SQL baseline, execute the command below:

```
--Dropping SQL Plan Baseline
declare
  v_sql_plan_id  pls_integer;
begin
  v_sql_plan_id := dbms_spm.drop_sql_plan_baseline(
    sql_handle => 'SYS_SQL_1046c141c5de11a8');
end;
/
```

Package *dbms_sql*

The *dbms_sql* package allows developers to write stored PL/SQL code that is capable of generating and executing data-specific DDL and DML statements without using hard-coded data values. The functionality of this package is very similar to that offered by the *execute immediate sentence* from Oracle 8i and on. Whenever possible, *execute immediate* should be preferred, mostly because it is far more readable and makes the code easier to maintain. However, there are times when *dbms_sql* could still be useful.

One of those scenarios where *dbms_sql* may still be used is when there is a need to retrieve a cursor handle and pass it to another procedure, or when it is not known how many columns need to be retrieved until runtime. It is also good to know that we can switch between both methods by using the *dbms_sql.to_refcursor* and *dbms_sql.to_cursor_number* functions. There are three different types of dynamic SQL that can be built:

- DDL commands

- DML statements (*delete, insert*, or *update* statement)

- DML queries (*select* statement)

Each of these operations has separate calls to procedures and functions contained in the *dbms_sql* package. In the end, the single steps can be broken down into a generic set of steps:

1. Build a command by concatenating strings together.

2. Open a cursor.

3. Parse the command.

4. Bind any input variables.

5. Execute the command.

6. Fetch the results (in the case of queries).

7. Close the cursor.

There are a number of procedures and functions contained within the *dbms_sql* package. The first of these to be examined are the *bind_variable* procedures.

The *bind_variable*() Procedures

The *bind_variable()* group of procedures is used to associate values with bind variables in the command that is being built. There are several implementations of this functionality:

```
procedure bind_variable (c        in       integer,
                         name  in       varchar2,
                         value in       number)

procedure bind_variable (c        in       integer,
                         name  in       varchar2,
                         value in       varchar2)

procedure bind_variable (c                   in       integer,
                         name                in       varchar2,
                         value               in       varchar2,
                         out_value_size in       integer)

procedure bind_variable (c        in       integer,
                         name  in       varchar2,
                         value in       date)

procedure bind_variable (c        in       integer,
                         name  in       varchar2,
                         value in       mlslabel)
```

There are several other implementations of the *bind_variable()* procedure with slightly different names such as *bind_variable_char()*, *bind_variable_raw()*, and *bind_variable_rowid*:

```
procedure bind_variable_char (c        in     integer,
                              name  in     varchar2,
                              value in     char)

procedure bind_variable_char (c               in     integer,
                              name            in     varchar2,
                              value           in     char,
                              out_value_size in     integer)

procedure bind_variable_raw (c     in     integer,
                             name  in     varchar2,
                             value in     raw)

procedure bind_variable_raw (c               in     integer,
                             name            in     varchar2,
                             value           in     raw,
                             out_value_size in     integer)

procedure bind_variable_rowid (c     in     integer,
                               name  in     varchar2,
                               value in     rowid)
```

While each of these procedures has a slightly different name, each of them accomplishes the same task; namely, storing a value in a bind variable.

The *close_cursor()* Procedure

The *close_cursor()* procedure is called to free up the resources used by a cursor. The procedure accepts a single parameter:

```
procedure close_cursor (c IN OUT integer)
```

The *c* parameter is a cursor ID number. The parameter returns from the procedure as NULL.

The *column_value()* Procedures

Like the *bind_variable()* procedure, there are several implementations of the *column_value()* procedure:

```
procedure column_value (c        in     integer,
                        position in     integer,
                        value          out number)

procedure column_value (c        in     integer,
                        position in     integer,
                        value          out varchar2)
```

```
procedure column_value (c          in     integer,
                        position in     integer,
                        value           out date)

procedure column_value (c          in     integer,
                        position in     integer,
                        value           out mlslabel)

procedure column_value (c             in      integer,
                        position      in      integer,
                        value              out number,
                        column_error       out number,
                        actual_length      out number)

procedure column_value (c             in      integer,
                        position      in      integer,
                        value              out varchar2,
                        column_error       out number,
                        actual_length      out number)

procedure column_value (c             in      integer,
                        position      in      integer,
                        value              out mlslabel,
                        column_error       out number,
                        actual_length      out number)

procedure column_value_char (c          in     integer,
                             position in     integer,
                             value           out char)

procedure column_value_char (c             in      integer,
                             position      in      integer,
                             value              out char,
                             column_error       out number,
                             actual_length      out number)

procedure column_value_raw (c          in     integer,
                            position in     integer,
                            value           out raw)

procedure column_value_raw (c             in      integer,
                            position      in      integer,
                            value              out raw,
                            column_error       out number,
                            actual_length      out number)

procedure column_value_rowid (c          in     integer,
                              position in     integer,
                              value           out rowid)

procedure column_value_rowid (c             in      integer,
                              position      in      integer,
                              value              out rowid,
                              column_error       out number,
                              actual_length      out number)
```

All of these procedures return the value of a column that was fetched using a call to the *fetch_rows()* function. The column's value is stored in the *value* parameter.

The example described below shows almost all procedures and functions of the *dbms_sql* package. It is used to dynamically create objects. So pass the DDL command to the procedure created, and then the procedure, when executed, will create the object using dynamic SQL through the *dbms_sql* package.

🖫 Code 5.23 – dbms_sql.sql

```
conn pkg@dbms

Connected to Oracle 11g Enterprise Edition Release 11.2.0.1.0
Connected as pkg

show user

User is "pkg"

grant all on dbms_sql to pkg;

create or replace procedure exec_command(p_sql_text_1 in clob,p_sql_text_2
in clob ) is
  compilation_error exception;
  pragma exception_init(compilation_error, -24344);
  v_sql_cursor_name   number := 0;
  v_sql_execute       number := 0;
  v_sql_errors_ocur   number := 0;
  v_select_error_code number := 0;
  v_select_error_mess varchar2(4000) := NULL;

begin
  --The open cursor will give an ID number to the cursor that will carry the
data structure
  v_sql_cursor_name := dbms_sql.open_cursor;
  --The parse check the sql statement syntax and associate the cursor to the
sql statement
  dbms_sql.parse(c                => v_sql_cursor_name,
              statement       => p_sql_text_1,
              language_flag => dbms_sql.native);
  --The execute will run the SQL statement
  v_sql_execute := dbms_sql.execute(v_sql_cursor_name);
  --The last_error_position function return the byte offset where the error
occured
  v_sql_errors_ocur := dbms_sql.last_error_position;
  --The close_cursor will just close the cursor
  dbms_sql.close_cursor(v_sql_cursor_name);
  dbms_output.put_line('Command executed ' ||p_sql_text_1);

  --Execute the second command
  v_sql_cursor_name := dbms_sql.open_cursor;
  --The parse check the sql statement syntax and associate the cursor to the
sql statement
  dbms_sql.parse(c                => v_sql_cursor_name,
              statement       => p_sql_text_2,
              language_flag => dbms_sql.native);
  --The execute will run the SQL statement
  v_sql_execute := dbms_sql.execute(v_sql_cursor_name);
  --The last_error_position funciton return the byte offset where the error
occurred
```

```
  v_sql_errors_occur := dbms_sql.last_error_position;
  --The close_cursor will just close the cursor
  dbms_sql.close_cursor(v_sql_cursor_name);
  dbms_output.put_line('Command executed ' ||p_sql_text_2);

exception
  when compilation_error then
    dbms_sql.close_cursor(v_sql_cursor_name);
  when others then
    begin
      dbms_sql.close_cursor(v_sql_cursor_name);
      raise_application_error(-20101,
                              sqlerrm || '  when executing ''' ||
                              p_sql_text_1||''||p_sql_text_2 || '''    ');
      v_select_error_code := sqlcode;
      v_select_error_mess := sqlerrm;
    end;
end exec_command;

--Create a table dynamically
exec exec_command(p_sql_text => 'create table test_dbms_sql (nome
varchar2(10))');



--Check the if table was created
desc test_dbms_sql

Name Type          Nullable Default Comments
---- ------------  -------- ------- --------
nome varchar2(10) Y

--Insert a row into the test_dbms_sql table using the second parameter as
commit
exec exec_command(p_sql_text_1 => 'insert into test_dbms_sql values
(''pportugal2'')',p_sql_text_2 => 'commit');



--Query the table and check the row inserted
select * from test_dbms_sql;

NOME
----------
pportugal2
```

A simple procedure was created, and it can be used to run any DDL or DML command through it. A table named *test_dbms_sql* was created and some rows inserted into it. Just be aware that Dynamic SQL is possibly the main cause of the worse cases of SQL injection in applications and one of the main security problems with dynamic SQL.

Newbies often write procedures that just receive part of a SQL sentence, concatenate it and run it, or even worse, just receive a sentence and run it as it appeared. Hackers could very easily use such a procedure to run whatever code they want with the privilege level of the owner's package, thus easily bypassing the security. So, do not create such a procedure on a production environment.

Package *dbms_sqltune*

SQL tuning work is one of the most time consuming and challenging tasks faced by Oracle DBAs and application developers. The Oracle 10g SQLTuning Advisor is intended to facilitate SQL tuning tasks and to help the DBA find the optimal SQL execution plan. The SQLTuning Advisor can search the SQL cache, the AWR, or user inputs to search for inefficient SQL statements. The SQL Tuning Advisor is available through the OEM console, or the *dbms_sqltune* package can be invoked manually.

The functionalities of the *dbms_sqltune* package include SQLTuning Advisor subprograms, SQL profile subprograms, SQL Tuning Set subprograms and real-time SQL Monitoring subprograms.The *advisor* privilege must be granted to the user in order to allow for executing tuning tasks activities.

The *dbms_sqltune* package provides a PL/SQL API for using the SQL Tuning Advisor tool. Running the SQL Tuning Advisor using PL/SQL API includes two steps:

1.   Create the SQL tuning task

2.   Execute the SQL tuning task

There are several options for the creation of an SQL tuning task. For example, the following process will examine the invocation of a single SQL statement. The *dbms_sqltune.create_task* function can be used to do the following:

```
declare
  my_sqltext clob;
  task_name varchar2(30);
begin
  my_sqltext := 'select object_type, count(*) from ';

  my_sqltext := my_sqltext || ' all_objects group by object_type';
  task_name := dbms_sqltune.create_tuning_task(
                    sql_text => my_sqltext,
                    bind_list => sql_binds(anydata.convertnumber(100)),
                    user_name => 'dabr',
                    scope => 'comprehensive',
                    time_limit => 60,
                    task_name => 'sql_tuning_task1');

end;
/
```

SQL tuning tasks can be created with SQL from the cursor cache, the AWR views, previously collected SQL Tuning Sets or from SQL trace files. The overloaded *dbms_sqltune.create_task* functions are provided to allow for changing the inputs.

After successfully creating a SQL tuning task, we can launch the SQL Tuning Optimizer to produce tuning recommendations. Use the *dbms_sqltune.execute_tuning_task* procedure to execute the specified task:

```
exec dbms_sqltune.execute_tuning_task ( 'sql_tuning_task1');
```

Now the DBA is ready to review recommendation details produced by the SQL Tuning Advisor. A query like the one below can be used to retrieve the SQL analysis results:

```
select dbms_sqltune.report_tuning_task('sql_tuning_task1') from dual;
```

The following is the resulting report.

```
DBMS_SQLTUNE.REPORT_TUNING_TASK('SQL_TUNING_TASK1')
-------------------------------------------------------------------
GENERAL INFORMATION SECTION
-------------------------------------------------------------------
Tuning Task Name    : sql_tuning_task1
Scope               : comprehensive
Time Limit(seconds): 1800
Completion Status   : completed
Started at          : 09/07/2004 16:24:41
Completed at        : 09/07/2004 16:24:41


-------------------------------------------------------------------
SQL ID  : g2wr3u7s1gtf3
SQL Text: 'select
 object_type, count(*)
from
 all_objects
group by
 object_type'

-------------------------------------------------------------------
FINDINGS SECTION (1 finding)
-------------------------------------------------------------------

1- Statistics Finding
---------------------
  Optimizer statistics for table "sys"."obj$" and its indices are stale.

  Recommendation
  --------------
    Consider collecting optimizer statistics for this table.
    execute dbms_stats.gather_table_stats(ownname => 'SYS',
```

The recommendation report contains problem findings and the corresponding recommendations for fixing the optimization problems.

This analysis process could consume significant processing times. Therefore, the *dbms_sqltune* package provides an API to manage tuning tasks such as:

- The *interrupt_tuning_task* procedure is used to stop the executing task. Any results that have already been produced will be preserved.

- The *cancel_tuning_task* procedure terminates the task that is executing without preserving its results.

- The *reset_tuning_task* procedure is used to stop the running task and reset it to the initial state.

- The *drop_tuning_task* procedure can be used to remove the task from the database.

During tuning analysis, the SQLTuning Advisor can recommend and automatically create SQL profiles. The SQL profile is a special object that is used by the optimizer. The SQL profile contains auxiliary statistics specific to a particular SQL statement.

The Oracle optimizer has just a few seconds to calculate a plan before beginning execution of the query. However, the Tuning Advisor can use more time, do some deeper calculations and find a better plan that can be stored in a *sql_profile* for the Oracle optimizer to use it automatically in all the subsequent times when the query is executed.

The SQL optimizer uses the information in the SQL profile to adjust the execution plan for the SQL statement that has the associated SQL profile. SQL profiles are great for SQL tuning because it is possible to tune SQL statements without any modification of the application source code or the text of SQL queries. The *dba_sql_profiles* view shows information about all existing SQL profiles.

The *dbms_sqltune* package can be used to manage SQL profiles. The SQL Tuning Advisor can recommend the use of a specific SQL profile. This SQL profile can be associated with SQL statements that are being analyzed by accepting it using *dbms_sqltune.accept_sql_profile*:

```
declare
  sqlprofile varchar2(30);
begin
  sqlprofile := dbms_sqltune.accept_sql_profile (
  task_name => 'sql_tuning_task1',
  name => 'sql_profile1');
end;
```

After the profile is defined, any stored SQL profile attributes such as *status, name, description,* and *category* can be altered using *dbms_sqltune.alter_sql_profile.* The *category* attribute is employed to limit user sessions that can use the particular SQL profile.

There is an initialization parameter called *sqltune_category* which allows for setting up the default SQL profile category for the database. The *dbms_sqltune.drop_sql_profile* procedure is used to remove the SQL profile from the database.

The *dbms_sqltune* package also provides a PL/SQL API to work with SQL Tuning Sets (STS). The STS is a database object that contains one or more SQL statements combined with their execution statistics and context such as particular schema, application module name, list of bind variables and more. The STS also includes a set of basic execution statistics such as CPU and elapsed times, disk reads and buffer gets, number of executions and such.

When creating a STS, the SQL statements can be filtered by different patterns such as application module name or execution statistics such as high disk reads. Once created, STS can be an input source for the SQL Tuning Advisor. Typically, the following steps are used to work with STS using the *dbms_sqltune* API. STS is created using the *dbms_sqltune.create_sqlset* procedure. For example, the following script can be used to create a STS called *sqlset1*:

```
exec dbms_sqltune.create_sqlset ( 'sqlset1');
```

STS is loaded from such sources as the AWR, another STS, the cursor cache or a SQL trace file. The following sample PL/SQL block loads STS from the current cursor cache:

```
declare
  cur dbms_sqltune.sqlset_cursor;
begin
   open cur for
   select
      value(p)
   from
      table (dbms_sqltune.select_cursor_cache) p;
dbms_sqltune.load_sqlset(
   sqlset_name => 'sqlset1',
   populate_cursor => cur);
end;
/
```

A SQL tuning task that uses STS as input can be created and executed like this:

```
exec dbms_sqltune.create_tuning_task (
        sqlset_name  => 'sqlset1',
        task_name => 'task1');
```

```
exec dbms_sqltune.execute_tuning_task ('task1');
```

The following syntax can be used to drop a SQL Tuning Set when finished:

```
exec dbms_sqltune.drop_sqlset ( 'sqlset1' );
```

All SQL Tuning Sets created in the database by querying the *dba_sqlset*, *dba_sqlset_binds*, *dba_sqlset_definitions*, and *dba_sqlset_statements* views are reviewed. For example, the *dbms_sqltune_show_sts.sql* query below shows the particular SQL statements associated with STS:

```
select
  s.sql_text,
  s.cpu_time
from
  dba_sqlset_statements s,
  dba_sqlset a
where
  a.name = 'sqlset1'
and
  s.sqlset_id =   a.id
and
  rownum <= 10
order by
  s.cpu_time desc
```

Clearly, Oracle 10g has introduced a rich set of powerful tools that can be used to identify and resolve possible performance problems. While these advisors cannot yet replicate the behavior of a senior DBA, they promise to get more intelligent with each new release of Oracle.

On the next practice example, ADDM will be used to identify the *sql_id* that is experiencing performance problems. The *dbms_sqltune* package will also be used to tune this SQL statement easily and quickly.

First, run a query on the *employee* table using in the WHERE clause a column that does not have an index, so a full table scan will be performed on it.

🖫 Code 5.24 – dbms_sqltune.sql

```
conn pkg@dbms

Connected to Oracle 11g Enterprise Edition Release 11.2.0.1.0
Connected as pkg

show user

User is "pkg"

--Drop the index if it already exists on employee table
drop index pkg.emp_department_ix;
```

```
--Execute the query that will perform a FTS
--Update statistics of table just to confirm the new plan
exec dbms_stats.gather_table_stats(
        ownname => 'pkg',
        tabname => 'employees',
        cascade => TRUE);

--The query is doing a FTS
select
   count(*)
from
   employees e
where
   e.department_id=100;

--Run a snapshot so the information will be caught by AWR
select
   dbms_workload_repository.create_snapshot
from
   dual;
```

Proceed by running the AWR report and the *sql_id* of the query having been executed. Extract the *sql_id* of the SQL statement, and then use this value on the next step.

Note that this value can also be obtained through other ways like querying the *v$sql* table.

```
@?/rdbms/admin/awrrpt.sql

SQL ordered by Elapsed Time                 DB/Inst: DBMS/dbms   Snaps: 156-
158
-> Resources reported for PL/SQL code includes the resources used by all SQL
     statements called by the code.
-> % Total DB Time is the Elapsed Time of the SQL statement divided
     into the Total Database Time multiplied by 100
-> %Total - Elapsed Time  as a percentage of Total DB time
-> %CPU    - CPU Time      as a percentage of Elapsed Time
-> %IO     - User I/O Time as a percentage of Elapsed Time
-> Captured SQL account for   68.1% of Total DB Time (s):          93
-> Captured PL/SQL account for   12.0% of Total DB Time (s):          93

      Elapsed               Elapsed Time
      Time (s)    Executions per Exec (s) %Total   %CPU    %IO   SQL Id
---------------- ------------- ------------- ------ ------ ------ ----
40.6                2         20.30   43.8   41.9   56.2 bzpq5u0yz7wy5
Module: PL/SQL Developer
select count(*) from employees e where e.department_id=100;
```

With the *sql_id* extracted from the AWR report, run *dbms_sqltune* and create the tuning task using the AWR information.

```
declare
 ttask varchar2(50);
begin
   ttask := dbms_sqltune.create_tuning_task(
```

Advanced DBMS Packages

```
      begin_snap => 157,
      end_snap => 158,
      sql_id => 'bzpq5u0yz7wy5',
      scope => dbms_sqltune.scope_comprehensive,
      time_limit => 30,
      task_name => 'Test DBMS Packages',
      description => 'Testing Tuning Tasks');
   dbms_output.put_line('Task Name: ' || ttask);
end;
/
```

Using *dbms_sqltune* to create the tuning tasks based on the cursor cache can be done as shown below:

```
declare
  l_sql_tune_task_id  varchar2(50);
begin
  l_sql_tune_task_id := dbms_sqltune.create_tuning_task (
                          sql_id      => 'bzpq5u0yz7wy5',
                          scope       => dbms_sqltune.scope_comprehensive,
                          time_limit  => 10,
                          task_name   => 'Test DBMS Packages Cursor',
                          description => 'testing cursor tuning!');
   dbms_output.put_line('Task Name: ' || l_sql_tune_task_id);
end;
/
```

An alternative is to create the tuning tasks using a SQL Tuning Set as follows:

```
--Create SQL Tuning Task base on a SQL Tuning Set
--First create the STS using the AWR taken above
begin
dbms_sqltune.create_sqlset(
   sqlset_name => 'STS Test DBMS Packages',
   description =>'Testing STS',
   sqlset_owner =>'pkg');
end;
/

--Then, load the tuning task using information of AWR
declare
sqlset_cur dbms_sqltune.sqlset_cursor;
begin
open sqlset_cur for
 select value(p)
   from table(dbms_sqltune.select_workload_repository(begin_snap=>157,
end_snap=>158)) p;
   dbms_sqltune.load_sqlset(
      sqlset_name=>'STS Test DBMS Packages',
      populate_cursor=>sqlset_cur,
      load_option => 'merge',
      update_option => 'accumulate',
      sqlset_owner=>'pkg');
end;
/
```

```
--Check the SQL Set created
select
   name
from
   dba_sqlset
where
   name like '%DBMS%';

--Check if the query was loaded in SQL Set
set linesize 200
col sqlset_name for a30
select
   sqlset_name,
   sql_text
from
   dba_sqlset_statements
where
   sqlset_name='STS Test DBMS Packages'
and
   sql_id='bzpq5u0yz7wy5';
```

Among other methods, it is also possible to include an SQL statement manually as on this example:

```
declare
   v_sql_query   varchar2(100);
   l_sql_task    varchar2(50);
begin
   v_sql_query := 'select count(*) from employess where department_id=100';

   l_sql_task := dbms_sqltune.create_tuning_task(
                        sql_text    => v_sql_query,
                        bind_list   =>
sql_binds(anydata.ConvertNumber(100)),
                        user_name   => 'pkg',
                        time_limit  => 60,
                        task_name   => 'Test Task DBMS Packages Manual',
                        description => 'Tuning task for an EMP to dept
join query.');
   dbms_output.put_line('Task Name: ' || l_sql_task);
end;
/
```

Proceed by executing the tuning task created. That will generate the report with the recommendation results.

```
--Check the task created
select
   task_id,
   task_name,
   created,
   advisor_name,
   status
from
   dba_advisor_tasks
```

```
where task_name like '%dbms%';


--Execute the task
begin
dbms_sqltune.execute_tuning_task(task_name => 'Test DBMS Packages');
end;
/

--Check the execution time of the task created
select
    owner,
    task_id,
    task_name,
    execution_start,
    execution_end,
    status
from
    dba_advisor_log
where
    task_name like '%dbms%';
```

Finally, the output report can be generated. It shows the recommendation of creating an index on the *employees* table to gain a large performance improvement.

```
--Get the report using report_tuning_task functions or using
dba_sqltune_plans view
set linesize 250
set long 200000
select
    dbms_sqltune.report_tuning_task(task_name => 'Test DBMS Packages')
from
    dual;
```

Here is found the output report and the index creation recommendation:

```
DBMS_SQLTUNE.REPORT_TUNING_TASK(TASK_NAME=>'TESTDBMSPACKAGES')
-----------------------------------------------------------------
GENERAL INFORMATION SECTION
-----------------------------------------------------------------
Tuning Task Name     : Test DBMS Packages
Tuning Task Owner    : pkg
Workload Type        : Single SQL Statement
Scope                : comprehensive
Time Limit(seconds): 60
Completion Status    : completed
Started at           : 12/02/2009 18:07:06
Completed at         : 12/02/2009 18:07:08
-----------------------------------------------------------------
Schema Name: PKG
SQL ID       : bzpq5u0yz7wy5
SQL Text     : select count(*) from employees e where e.department_id=100


-----------------------------------------------------------------
FINDINGS SECTION (1 finding)
-----------------------------------------------------------------
```

```
1- Index Finding (see explain plans section below)
---------------------------------------------------
   The execution plan of this statement can be improved by creating one or
more
   indices.

   Recommendation (estimated benefit: 95.83%)
   -----------------------------------------
   - Consider running the Access Advisor to improve the physical schema design
     or creating the recommended index.
     create index pkg.idx$$_01720001 on pkg.employees("department_id");

   Rationale
   ---------
     Creating the recommended indices significantly improves the execution plan
     of this statement. However, it might be preferable to run "Access Advisor"
     using a representative SQL workload as opposed to a single statement. This
     will allow to get comprehensive index recommendations which takes into
     account index maintenance overhead and additional space consumption.


-------------------------------------------------------------------------
EXPLAIN PLANS SECTION
-------------------------------------------------------------------------

1- Original
-----------
Plan hash value: 1756381138
-------------------------------------------------------------------------

| Id  | Operation          | Name      | Rows  | Bytes | Cost (%CPU)| Time     |

-------------------------------------------------------------------------

|   0 | select statement   |           |     1 |     3 | 19379   (1)| 00:03:53 |

|   1 |   sort aggregate   |           |     1 |     3 |            |          |

|*  2 |    table access full| employees |  394K| 1156K| 19379   (1)| 00:03:53 |

-------------------------------------------------------------------------

Predicate Information (identified by operation id):
---------------------------------------------------

   2 - filter("e"."department_id"=100)

2- Using New Indices
--------------------
Plan hash value: 1501025740


-------------------------------------------------------------------------
| Id  | Operation          | Name      | Rows  | Bytes | Cost (%CPU)| Time     |
|
-------------------------------------------------------------------------|   0 | select statement   |
|   1 |     3 |   808   (1)| 00:00:
10 |
|   1 |   sort aggregate   |           |     1 |     3 |            |
|
|*  2 |   index range scan| idx$$_01720001 |  394K| 1156K|   808   (1)| 00:00:
10 |
-------------------------------------------------------------------------
Predicate Information (identified by operation id):
---------------------------------------------------

   2 - access("e"."department_id"=100)
-------------------------------------------------------------------------
```

Specific examples of how to tune a query using the *dbms_sqltune* packages have now been presented. Following is a simple example of how to create a tuning task from a trace file.

Create a Tuning Task Using a Trace File

The *select_sql_trace* function allows the user to create an SQL tuning task using SQL statements gathered from a trace file. The following example shows how to proceed with this new 11g method.

🖫 Code 5.25 – dbms_sqltune_select_sql_trace.sql

```
conn pkg@dbms

Connected to Oracle 11g Enterprise Edition Release 11.2.0.1.0
Connected as pkg

show user

User is "pkg"

--First get you trace file name and location on 11g
set linesize 200
col name for a20
col value for a65
select
    name,
    value
from
    v$diag_info
where
    name ='Default Trace File';

NAME                VALUE
------------------- ----------------------------------------------------
Default Trace File  /u01/app/oracle/diag/rdbms/dbms/dbms/trace/dbms_ora_25896.trc

--Then enable the trace in your session and execute the query that will perform a full table scan
alter session set events '10046 trace name context forever, level 4';

--Run the query
select
    count(*)
from
    employees
where
    department_id=100;



--Disable the trace
alter session set events '10046 trace name context off';

--Create the mapping table that will record sql statements that was in trace
file
```

```
create table
   tab_map_dbms_sqltune
as
select
   object_id id,
   owner,
   substr(object_name, 1, 30) name
from
   dba_objects
where
   object_type
not in ( 'consumer group',
         'evaluation context',
         'function',
         'indextype',
         'java class',
         'java data',
         'java resource',
         'library',
         'LOB',
         'operator',
         'package',
         'package body',
         'procedure',
         'queue',
         'resource plan',
         'trigger',
         'type',
         'type body')
union all
select
   user_id id,
   username owner,
   null name
from
   dba_users;


-- create the directory object where the SQL traces are stored
create directory
   dbms_sqltune_dir
as
   '/u01/app/oracle/diag/rdbms/dbms/dbms/trace';

--Create the SQL Tuning Set
begin
dbms_sqltune.create_sqlset(sqlset_name => 'Test DBMS Packages Trace');
end;
/

-- Load SQL statements into SQL Tuning Set using the Trace File created
declare
  ref_cursor sys_refcursor;
begin
  open ref_cursor for
    select value(p)
      from table(dbms_sqltune.select_sql_trace(directory      =>
'dbms_sqltune_dir',
                                        file_name       =>
```

```
'dbms_ora_25896.trc',
                                          mapping_table_name =>
'tab_map_dbms_sqltune')) p;
  dbms_sqltune.load_sqlset(
    sqlset_name => 'Test dbms Packages Trace',
    populate_cursor => ref_cursor,
    sqlset_owner => 'pkg');
  close ref_cursor;
end;
/
```

After completing the SQL Tuning Set, the tuning task can now be created using such a SQL Set based on information that comes from a SQL trace file.

Package *dbms_stat_funcs*

This package provides statistical functions that can be used to provide analytical/descriptive data to the user. It is commonly used in data warehouse environments. Procedures of this package include:

- *exponential_dist_fit*: This procedure tests how well a sample of values fits an exponential

- *normal_dist_fit*: This procedure tests how well a sample of values fits a normal distribution

- *poisson_dist_fit*: This procedure tests how well a sample of values fits a Poisson distribution

- *summary:* This procedure summarizes a numerical column and returns as record of summary type

- *uniform_dist_fit*: This procedure tests how well a sample of values fits a uniform distribution

- *weibull_dist_fit*: This procedure tests how well a sample of values fits a Weibull distribution

In order to see how this package works, we will show an example of how to use the *summary* procedure of the *dbms_stat_funcs* package.

🖫 Code 5.26 – dbms_stat_funcs.sql

```
conn pkg@dbms

Connected to Oracle 11g Enterprise Edition Release 11.2.0.1.0
Connected as pkg

show user

User is "pkg"
```

```
--Create a table that will be used in test
create table test_dbms_stat_funcs (name varchar2(10), salary number(8,2));

--Insert some values on this table
insert into test_dbms_stat_funcs values ('John',5500);
insert into test_dbms_stat_funcs values ('Ellen',7000);
insert into test_dbms_stat_funcs values ('Michael',3000);
insert into test_dbms_stat_funcs values ('Steven',1500);
insert into test_dbms_stat_funcs values ('Samuel',1000);
insert into test_dbms_stat_funcs values ('Timothy',9500);
insert into test_dbms_stat_funcs values ('Paulo',8000);
insert into test_dbms_stat_funcs values ('Hermann',7700);
insert into test_dbms_stat_funcs values ('Nancy',8200);
insert into test_dbms_stat_funcs values ('Simone',9300);
commit;

--Gather statistics for table created
exec dbms_stats.gather_table_stats(ownname => 'pkg',tabname =>
'test_dbms_stat_funcs',cascade => TRUE);

--Summarize a numerical column. In this case will be the salary column:
set echo off
connect pkg/pkg
set serveroutput on
set echo on
declare
summary_type_out dbms_stat_funcs.SummaryType;
begin
dbms_stat_funcs.summary(p_ownername => 'pkg',p_tablename =>
'test_dbms_stat_funcs',p_columnname => 'salary',p_sigma_value => 3,s =>
summary_type_out);
dbms_output.put_line('Summary statistics of column Salary on Table
test_dbms_stat_funcs');
dbms_output.put_line('Count: '||summary_type_out.count);
dbms_output.put_line('Min: '||summary_type_out.min);
dbms_output.put_line('Max: '||summary_type_out.max);
dbms_output.put_line('Range: '||summary_type_out.range);
dbms_output.put_line('Mean:'||round(summary_type_out.mean));
dbms_output.put_line('Mode Count: '||summary_type_out.cmode.count);
dbms_output.put_line('Mode: '||summary_type_out.cmode(1));
dbms_output.put_line('Variance: '||round(summary_type_out.variance));
dbms_output.put_line('Stddev: '||round(summary_type_out.stddev));
dbms_output.put_line('Quantile 5 '||summary_type_out.quantile_5);
dbms_output.put_line('Quantile 25 '||summary_type_out.quantile_25);
dbms_output.put_line('Median '||summary_type_out.median);
dbms_output.put_line('Quantile 75 '||summary_type_out.quantile_75);
dbms_output.put_line('Quantile 95 '||summary_type_out.quantile_95);
dbms_output.put_line('Extreme Count:
'||summary_type_out.extreme_values.count);
dbms_output.put_line('Top 5: '||summary_type_out.top_5_values(1)||'-
'||summary_type_out.top_5_values(2)||'-
'||summary_type_out.top_5_values(3)||'-
'||summary_type_out.top_5_values(4)||'-'||summary_type_out.top_5_values(5));
dbms_output.put_line('Bottom 5:'||summary_type_out.bottom_5_values(5)||'-
'||summary_type_out.bottom_5_values(4)||'-
'||summary_type_out.bottom_5_values(3)||'-
'||summary_type_out.bottom_5_values(4)||'-
'||summary_type_out.bottom_5_values(5));
```

```
end;
/
```

The output of the *summary* procedure is as follows:

```
Summary statistics of column Salary on Table test_dbms_stat_funcs
Count: 11
Min: 1000
Max: 9500
Range: 8500
Mean:6018
Mode Count: 1
Mode: 5500
Variance: 9061636
Stddev: 3010
Quantile 5 1250
Quantile 25 4250
Median 7000
Quantile 75 8100
Quantile 95 9400
Extreme Count: 0
Top 5: 9500-9300-8200-8000-7700
Bottom 5:1000-1500-3000-1500-1000
```

```
--You can also use simple queries to get some of these statistical values as
stats_mode, median and others as below
select
    stats_mode(salary)
from
 test_dbms_stat_funcs;

select
   median(salary)
from
   test_dbms_stat_funcs;
```

Most of these functions used by the *summary* procedure can be used directly on a SQL query as shown on the last example.

Package *dbms_stats*

When a SQL statement is executed, the database must convert the query into an execution plan and choose the best way to retrieve the data. For Oracle, each SQL query has many choices for execution plans, including which index to use to retrieve a table row, what order in which to join multiple tables together, and which internal join methods to use since Oracle has nested loop joins, hash joins, star joins, and sort merge join methods. These execution plans are computed by the Oracle cost-based SQL optimizer commonly known as the CBO.

The choice of execution plans made by the Oracle SQL optimizer is only as good as the Oracle statistics. To choose the best execution plan, though not always true for a SQL query, Oracle relies on information about the tables and indexes in the query.

Starting with the introduction of the *dbms_stats* package, Oracle provides a simple way for the Oracle professional to collect statistics for the CBO. The old-fashioned *analyze* table and *dbms_utility* methods for generating CBO statistics are obsolete and somewhat dangerous to SQL performance because they do not always capture high-quality information about tables and indexes. The CBO uses object statistics to choose the best execution plan for all SQL statements.

The *dbms_stats* utility does a far better job in estimating statistics, especially for large partitioned tables, and the better stats result in faster SQL execution plans. The *dbms_stats* package offers a lot of statistics management tools such as:

- Gathering optimizer statistics
- Setting or getting statistics
- Deleting statistics
- Transferring statistics
- Locking or unlocking statistics
- Restoring and purging statistics
- User-defined statistics
- Pending statistics
- Comparing statistics
- Extended statistics

When changing statistics stored in the dictionary, the old versions are always saved automatically in case they are needed for future restore.

Procedures used to gather optimizer statistics are below:

1. *gather_database_stats*: Used to gather statistics for all objects in the database
2. *gather_dictionary_stats*: Used to gather statistics of dictionary schemes like SYS and SYSTEM or any other schema that has RDBMS components
3. *gather_fixed_objects_stats*: Used to gather statistics for all fixed tables; also called dynamic performance tables
4. *gather_index_stats*: Used to gather index statistics
5. *gather_schema_stats*: Used to gather all statistics for a specific schema

6. *gather_system_stats*: Used to gather system statistics

7. *gather_table_stats*: Used to gather table and index statistics

Procedures used to set and get optimizer statistics:

1. *prepare_column_values*: Used to convert specific values of minimum, maximum and histogram endpoints into Oracle internal representation for future storage

2. *set|get_column_stats*: Used to get|set all column information

3. *set|get_index_stats*: Used to get|set all index information

4. *set|get_system_stats*: Used to get|set system statistics from *stattab* or from dictionary

5. *set|get_table_stats*: Used to get|set table statistics

Procedures used to delete statistics from both used-defined or standard statistics:

1. *delete_column_stats*

2. *delete_database_stats*

3. *delete_dictionary_stats*

4. *delete_fixed_objects_stats*

5. *delete_index_stats*

6. *delete_schema_stats*

7. *delete_system_stats*

8. *delete_table_stats*

Procedures used to create and drop the *user statistics* table and transfer statistics from one database or table to another:

1. *create_stat_table*

2. *drop_stat_tabl*

3. *export|import_column_stats*: Used to export|import statistics from/to a particular column and store the values in a particular table specified by the *stattab* parameter

4. *export|import_database_stats*: Used to export|import statistics from/to all objects in the database and store these values in the user statistics table identified by *statown.stattab*

5. *export|import_dictionary_stats*: Used to export|import statistics from/to all dictionary schemas and store them in the user specified table defined by the *stattab* parameter

---

Package dbms_stats

6. *export|import_fixed_objects_stats*: Used to export|import statistics from/to fixed tables and store them in the user specified table defined by the *stattab* parameter

7. *export|import_index_stats*: Used to export|import statistics from/to a specific index and store them in the user specified table defined by the *stattab* parameter

8. *export|import_schema_stats*: Used to export|import statistics from/to all tables on a specific schema

9. *export|import_system_stats*: Used to export|import system statistics

10. *export_table_stats*: Used to export|import statistics from/to a specific table

The procedures below can be used to lock and unlock statistics on specified objects. The current statistics will then remain unchanged or they can be kept empty for a specific object.

1. *lock|unlock_schema_stats*: Lock|unlock statistics for all tables in a schema

2. *lock|unlock_table_stats*: Lock|unlock statistics for a specific table.

When statistics are gathered, Oracle stores old versions of statistics that can be used in case one experiences performance degradation after gathering these new statistics. Use the following procedures to restore and purge the statistics history:

1. *reset_global_pref_defaults*: Used to set global preferences to default values. These preferences include options like *cascade*, *estimate_percent* and *granularity*.

2. *restore_dictionary_stats*: Used to restore statistics for all dictionary tables

3. *restore_fixed_objects_stats*: Used to restore statistics for all fixed tables of a specified timestamp

4. *restore_schema_stats*: Used to restore statistics for all tables in a specific schema of a specified timestamp

5. *restore_system_stats*: Used to restore system statistics of a specified timestamp

6. *restore_table_stats*: Used to restore statistics of a specific table on a specified timestamp

Pending statistics can be collected to test if it will have success or not. So it can be published and can begin to be used or pending statistics can be deleted if it is found to not fit the specific environment properly. Procedures that can be used to execute these tasks are below:

1. *delete_pending_stats*: Used to delete pending statistics that have been collected but not published

2. *export_pending_stats*: Used to export statistics gathered and stored as pending stats

3. *publish_pending_stats*: Used to publish statistics gathered and stored as pending

The practical example below, including comments, illustrates all of the procedures shown above.

💾 Code 5.27 – dbms_stats.sql

```
conn pkg@dbms

Connected to Oracle 11g Enterprise Edition Release 11.2.0.1.0
Connected as pkg

show user

User is "pkg"

--First, use the pl/sql block below to get all default values being used
set echo off
set serveroutput on
declare
prefs varchar2(400);
begin
--Show cascade default value. If true index statistics is collected as part of gathering table
statistics
select dbms_stats.get_prefs(pname => 'cascade') into prefs from dual;
dbms_output.put_line('Cascade            = '||prefs);

--Show degree default value. Determine de degree of parallelism
select dbms_stats.get_prefs(pname => 'degree') into prefs from dual;
dbms_output.put_line('Degree             = '||prefs);

--Show estimate_percent default value. Percentage of rows to estimate.
select dbms_stats.get_prefs(pname => 'estimate_percent') into prefs from dual;
dbms_output.put_line('Estimate Percent    = '||prefs);

--Show method_opt default value. Control columns statistics collection and histograms
select dbms_stats.get_prefs(pname => 'method_opt') into prefs from dual;
dbms_output.put_line('Method_Opt          = '||prefs);

--Show no_invalidate default value. Control the invalidation of dependent cursors
select dbms_stats.get_prefs(pname => 'no_invalidate') into prefs from dual;
dbms_output.put_line('No Invalidate       = '||prefs);

--Show granularity default value. Determine the granularity of statistics on partitioned tables
select dbms_stats.get_prefs(pname => 'granularity') into prefs from dual;
dbms_output.put_line('Granularity         = '||prefs);

--Show publish default value. The statistics will be published as soon as it is finished or not
select dbms_stats.get_prefs(pname => ' publish ') into prefs from dual;
dbms_output.put_line('Publish             = '||prefs);

--Show incremental default value. Determine if global statistics of a partitioned table will be
maintained without the need of a full table scan
select dbms_stats.get_prefs(pname => 'incremental') into prefs from dual;
dbms_output.put_line('Incremental         = '||prefs);

--Show stale_percent default value. Determine the percentage of rows in a table needs to change
before the statistics becomes stale
select dbms_stats.get_prefs(pname => 'stale_percent') into prefs from dual;
dbms_output.put_line('Stale Percent       = '||prefs);

end;
/
```

```
--The output is below
Cascade             = dbms_stats.auto_cascade
Degree              = NULL
Estimate Percent    = dbms_stats.auto_sample_size
Method_Opt          = for all columns size auto
No Invalidate       = dbms_stats.auto_invalidate
Granularity         = auto
Publish             = TRUE
```

```
Incremental            = FALSE
Stale Percent          = 10

--Using set global preferences procedure
set serveroutput on
declare
prefs varchar2(40);
begin
--Set the degree value for all the database to 8
dbms_stats.set_global_prefs(
   pname => 'degree',
   pvalue => '8');
select
   dbms_stats.get_prefs(
      pname => 'degree')
   into
      prefs
from dual;
dbms_output.put_line('Default Value of degree for database now is =
'||prefs);
end;
/

--Using set table statistics for PKG user
set serveroutput on
declare
prefs varchar2(40);
begin
--Set publish statistics for employees table to false.  To  use next gathered
statistics you need to publish then using publish_pending_stats procedure
dbms_stats.set_table_prefs(
   ownname => 'pkg',
   tabname => 'employees',
   pname => 'publish',
   pvalue => 'false');

select
   dbms_stats.get_prefs(
      pname => ' publish ',
      ownname => 'pkg',
      tabname => 'employees')
   into
      prefs
from
   dual;

dbms_output.put_line('New default value of publish for pkg user is =
'||prefs);
end;
/
```

Gather table statistics example. On the example below, Oracle will automatically select the column from which it will collect histograms.

```
--Gather table statistics example. On this example Oracle will automatically
choose on which column it will collect histograms
begin
```

```
dbms_stats.gather_table_stats(
    ownname => 'pkg',
    tabname => 'employees',
    estimate_percent => 30,
    block_sample => TRUE,
    method_opt => 'for all columns size auto',
    degree => 4,
    cascade => TRUE);
end;
/
```

Check if the statistics collected are pending using the query on the *dba_tab_pending_stats* table.

```
select
    *
from
    dba_tab_pending_stats;
```

Suppose that we have tested the performance of these new statistics and we want to use it for everybody. Then publish these statistics using the *publish_pending_stats* procedure as follows:

```
begin
    dbms_stats.publish_pending_stats(
        ownname => 'pkg',
        tabname => 'employees',
        force => TRUE);
end;
/

--Check the table again and you will not find pending stats for this table
 select
     *
from
    dba_tab_pending_stats;
```

Now two new forms of gathering statistics are shown: multi-column and expression. They are part of a new statistics feature of Oracle 11g named Extended Statistics.

1. **Multi-column statistics:** Oracle 11g introduces multi-column statistics to give the CBO the ability to more accurately select rows when the WHERE clause contains multi-column conditions or joins.

2. **Expression statistics:** When using a function or a column in a WHERE clause, the CBO cannot accurately identify the selectivity of the column. Expression statistics is created to offer the CBO a wider selectivity to the explain plan.

The next example shows how to gather both multi-column and expression statistics using the *create_extended_stats* procedure.

🖫 Code 5.28 – create_extended_stats.sql

```
conn pkg@dbms

Connected to Oracle 11g Enterprise Edition Release 11.2.0.1.0
Connected as pkg

show user

User is "pkg"

--Gathering Extended Statistics with dbms_stats package
--Multi-Column Statistics
declare
v_result varchar2(100);
begin
v_result := dbms_stats.create_extended_stats(
   ownname => 'pkg',
   tabname => 'employees',
   extension => '(manager_id,department_id)');

dbms_output.put_line('Multi-column stats Name: 'a => v_result);
end;
/

--You could get the extended status name using the function
show_extended_stats_name function
select
   dbms_stats.show_extended_stats_name(
      ownname => 'pkg',
      tabname => 'employees',
      extension => '(manager_id,department_id)')
from
   dual;

--You can also use dba_stat_extensions view
select
   tbale_name,
   extension_name
from
   dba_stat_extensions
where
 table_name='employees';


--You can drop an extended stats group using the drop_extended_stats
procedure
begin
   dbms_stats.drop_extended_stats(
      ownname => 'pkg',
      tabname => 'employees',
      extension => '(manager_id,department_id)';
end;
/
```

Now, some examples of expression statistics:

```
--Expression statistics
declare
v_result varchar2(100);
begin
v_result := dbms_stats.create_extended_stats(ownname => 'pkg',tabname =>
'departments',extension => '(upper(department_name))');

dbms_output.put_line(a => 'Expression Stats Name: '||v_result);
end;
/

--You can also use the gather_table_stats procedure to create the expression
stats above as follows
begin
   dbms_stats.gather_table_stats(
      ownname => 'pkg',
      tabname => 'departments',
      method_opt => 'for all columns (upper(department_name))');
end;
/

--Check the statistics group created using the dba_stat_extensions
select
   table_name,
   extension_name
from
   dba_stat_extensions
where
   table_name in ('employees','departments');
```

Remember that the value *for all columns %* needs to be used on *method_opt* in order to gather statistics of grouped columns. Otherwise, specifying the column list using the command example *for columns (employee_id, department_id)* will need to be done. Next, let's explore the feature *create_extended_stats*.

Package *dbms_stats.create_extended_stats*

One of the most exciting new features of Oracle 11g in the *dbms_stats* package is specifically the ability to aid complex queries by providing extended statistics to the cost-based optimizer (CBO). The 11g extended statistics are intended to improve the optimizer's guesses for the cardinality of combined columns and columns that are modified by a built-in or user-defined function.

In Oracle 10g, dynamic sampling can be used to provide inter-table cardinality estimates, but dynamic sampling has important limitations. However, the 11g *create_extended_stats* in *dbms_stats* relieves much of the problem of sub-optimal table join orders, allowing for extended statistics on correlated columns.
In the absence of column histograms and extended statistics, the Oracle CBO must be able to guess the size of complex result sets information, and it sometimes gets it wrong. This is one reason why the *ordered* hint is one of the most popular SQL tuning

hints; using the *ordered* hint allows specifying that the tables be joined together in the same order that they appear in the *from* clause.

In this example, the four-way table join only returns 18 rows, but the query carries 9,000 rows in intermediate result sets, slowing down the SQL execution speed:

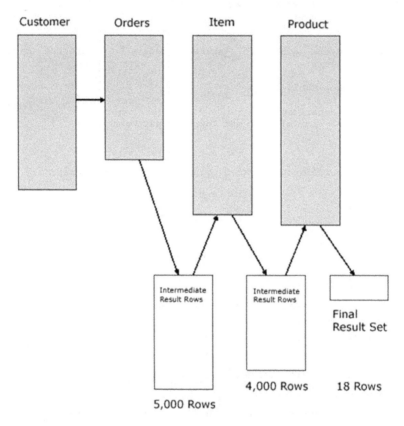

Figure 5.1: *A Suboptimal Table Join Order*

If the sizes of the intermediate results were able to be more accurately predicted by tipping off the optimizer with extended statistics, the table-join order can be resequenced to carry less intermediate baggage during the four-way table join; in this example, carrying only 3,000 intermediate rows between the table joins:

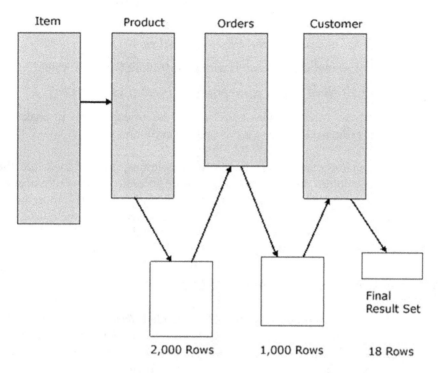

Item Product Orders Customer

2,000 Rows   1,000 Rows   18 Rows

Final
Result Set

Figure 5.2: *11g Extended Statistics Help the CBO Predict Inter-table Join Result Set Sizes*

The Oracle SQL optimizer has always been ignorant of the implied relationships between data columns within the same table. While the optimizer has traditionally analyzed the distribution of values within a column, it does not collect value-based relationships between columns.

For example, analyzing a table within *dbms_stats* will not tell the optimizer about implied data relationships:

- A specific *city_name* column correlates to specific *state_name* column values
- A *zip_code* column value is only NOT NULL when *country_code*=USA.
- A province name is NULL when *country_code*=USA.
- A *current_age* column is related to the *date_of_birth*
- The *senior_citizen_flag*='Y' correlates to rows where *sysdate-date_of_birth > 65*
- The *zodiac_sign* column directly relates to the value of *month_of_birth*

In addition, the specific application may have unique relationships between column values:

- A *credit_status* of *bad* indicates a *credit_rating* values below 400

- A *lawsuit_status* of *overturned* corresponds with an *appeal*=YES column value

- A *non_zero* value for *prison_sentence* corresponds to a verdict value of *guilty*

Without knowing these column value correlations, the optimizer might make an incorrect cardinality estimate, leading to a sub-optimal execution plan.

If Oracle knew about the relationships between the columns, it could look into the distribution of both columns and come up with a more accurate estimate of extended rows returned, leading to better execution plans. Obviously, the DBA must know about these unique data relationships. The more the DBA knows their data, the better they can help tip off the optimizer about these hidden correlations between column values.

Using *dbms_stats.create_extended_stats*

Take a closer look to understand how the 11g extended *dbms_stats* data helps the optimizer make better guesses of result set sizes. The new 11g *dbms_stats* package has several new procedures to aid in supplementing histogram data, and the state of these extended histograms can be seen in the *user_tab_col_statistics* view:

- *dbms_stats.create_extended_stats*

- *dbms_stats.show_extended_stats_name*

- *dbms_stats.drop_extended_stats*

The *dbms_stats.create_extended_stats* package can be used to tip off the optimizer about an implied relationship between columns in a table. To allow the DBA to tip off the optimizer and make it more intelligent, Oracle created extended statistics implemented via the *dbms_stats.create_extended_stats* procedure.

The *dbms_stats.create_extended_stats* procedure allows analyzing groups of columns instead of independent columns. Invoke *dbms_stats.create_extended_stats* like this:

```
dbms_stats.create_extended_stats (
   ownname    varchar2,
   tabname    varchar2,
   extension  varchar2)
 return varchar2;
```

The important argument is the extension because it specifies the relationship between the columns. The *dbms_stats.create_extended_stats* extension can be either an expression or a group of columns. For example, the extension can be specified as a set of column names like *prison_sentence* or *verdict* or an expression like *sale_price+sales_tax* can be used.

Creating Extended Statistics

Here are the steps to create extended statistics for related table columns with *dbms_stats.created_extended_stats*:

1. The first step is to create column histograms for the related columns.

2. Next, run *dbms_stats.create_extended_stats* to relate the columns together.

Unlike a traditional procedure that is invoked via an *execute (exec)* statement, Oracle extended statistics are created via a *select* statement. How to implement extended column statistics will now be shown.

The column histograms and column relationships might need to be created where the *total_price* column relates to the row expression where *total_price = product_price+sales_tax*:

```
-- ********************************
-- Create column histograms
-- ********************************
exec dbms_stats.gather_table_stats
   (null, 'sales' method_opt=> 'for all columns size skewonly);
-- ********************************
-- Verify existence of histograms
-- ********************************

select
   column_name,
   histogram
from
   user_tab_sol_statistics
where
   table_name = 'sales';


-- ******************************************
- Create the extended optimizer statistics
-- ******************************************
select
   dbms_stats.create_extended_stats
   (NULL, 'sales', '(product_price+sales_tax)')
from dual;
```

Package *dbms_storage_map*

This was first available within Oracle Database 9i Release 2 and, at that time, named IO Topology. Since Oracle 10g, it is now called Oracle Database File Mapping. This feature is very useful for tuning disk I/O when using Intelligent Storage Array (ISA) as it hides the path of datafiles.

The *dbms_storage_map* package can be used in conjunction with *file_mapping* initialization parameters and views named *v$map_%* for the mapping of files being used by Oracle Databases and are stored on RAID or LUNs. Here is a list of functions and procedures included in the *dbms_storage_map* package:

- *drop_all*: Used to drop all mapping information stored in the shared memory of an instance

- *drop_element*: Drops mapping information for a specified element

- *drop_file:* Drops mapping information for a specified file

- *lock_map:* Used to lock mapping information in shared memory

- *map_all:* Function used to build mapping information for all types of Oracle files (excluding archive logs)

- *map_element:* Function used to build mapping information for a specific element

- *map_file:* Function used to build mapping information for a specific file

- *map_object:* Function used to build mapping information for a specific object

- *restore:* Function used to load mapping information stored in the data dictionary to the shared memory of the instance

- *save:* Function used to save mapping information into data dictionary

- *unlock_map:* Used to unlock mapping information

The first thing that needs to be done in order to use the file mapping feature is set the *file_mapping* initialization parameter to TRUE. After that, configure the *filemap.ora* file and then use the *dbms_storage_map* package to map the files. Here is an example:

🖫 Code 5.29 – dbms_storage_map.sql

```
conn pkg@dbms

Connected to Oracle 11g Enterprise Edition Release 11.2.0.1.0
Connected as pkg

show user

User is "pkg"
```

```
--First alter the file_mapping initialization parameter
alter system set file_mapping=TRUE scope=both;

--Then, configure the filemap.ora file on your $ORACLE_HOME/rdbms/filemap.
Example:
######################################################################
#
# This is the configuration file that describes all the mapping libraries
#
# available.
#
#
#
# The following row needs to be created for each library:
#
# lib={vendor name}, {mapping library path}
#
#
#
# Note that the ordering of the libraries in this file is extremely
#
# important. The libraries are queried based on their order in the
#
# configuration file.
#
#
#
# Oracle provides a mapping library for EMC Symmetrix arrays. This library
#
# (LIBMAPSYM.SO) uses the SYMAPI and SYMLVM EMC libraries.
#
#
#
# UNCOMMENT THE ROW CORRESPONDING TO THAT LIBRARY ONLY IF THE SYM LIBRARIES
#
# ARE AVAILABLE.
#
######################################################################
#lib=Oracle: /opt/oracle/product/9.2.0/lib/libmapdummy.so

lib=Oracle: /dbebs/products/rdbms/lib/%s_mapdummy%


--Now tune the map_all procedure to start the mapping process
begin
   dbms_storage_map.map_all(dictionary_update => TRUE);
end;
/

--Save actual mapping information from shared memory to data dictionary
begin
   dbms_storage_map.save;
end;
/

--Restore mapping information stored on data dictionary into shared memory
begin
   dbms_storage_map.restore;
```

```
end;
/

--Unlock the mapping information in the shared memory of the instance
begin
    dbms_storage_map.unlock_map;
end;
/

--Mapping an object
begin
dbms_storage_map.map_object(objname => 'employees',owner => 'pkg',objtype =>
'table');
end;
/

--Check the where in the storage is the object
select
    mo..object_name Obj_Name,
    mf.file_name File_Name,
    me.elem_name, mo.depth,
    (sum(mo.cu_size * (mo.num_cu - decode
        (mo.parity_period, 0, 0, trunc(mo.num_cu / mo.parity_period)))) / 2)
o_size
from
    map_object mo,
    v$map_element me,
    v$map_file mf
where
    mo.object_name =  'employees'
and
    mo.object_owner = 'pkg'
and
    mo.object_type =  'table'
and
    me.elem_idx = mo.elem_idx
and
    mf.file_map_idx = mo.file_map_idx
group by
    mo.elem_idx,
    mo.file_map_idx,
    me.elem_name,
    mf.file_name,
    mo.depth,
    mo.object_name
order by
    mo.depth;
```

Obj_Name	File_Name	ELEM_NAME	DEPTH
employees	/u01/oracle/oradata/tbs_data.dbf	/dev/vx/dsk/ipfdg/ipf-vol1	0
employees	/u01/oracle/oradata/tbs_data.dbf	_sym_plex_/dev/vx/rdsk/ipf pdg/if-vol1_-1_-1	1
employees	/u01/oracle/oradata/tbs_data.dbf	_sym_subdisk_/dev/vx/rdsk/ ipfdg/ipf-vol1_0_1_0	2
employees	/u01/oracle/oradata/tbs_data.dbf	_sym_subdisk_/dev/vx/rdsk/ipf dg/ipf-vol1_0_2_0	2
employees	/u01/oracle/oradata/tbs_data.dbf	/dev/vx/rdmp/c2t1d1s2	3
employees	/u01/oracle/oradata/tbs_data.dbf	/dev/vx/rdmp/c2t1d2s2	3
employees	/u01/oracle/oradata/tbs_data.dbf	_sym_symdev_000183600407_00E	4
employees	/u01/oracle/oradata/tbs_data.dbf	_sym_hyper_000183600407_00D_0	5
employees	/u01/oracle/oradata/tbs_data.dbf	_sym_hyper_000183600407_00D_1	5

```
employees /u01/oracle/oradata/tbs_data.dbf   _sym_hyper_000183600407_00E_0    6
employees /u01/oracle/oradata/tbs_data.dbf   _sym_hyper_000183600407_00E_1    6
```

Next, we see some views that can be used to get information about the mapping feature.

```
--Information about objects mapped
select
    *
from
    map_object;
--Information abount mapping libraries loaded
select
    *
from
v$map_library;
--Information about file mapping structures in the shared memory
select
    *
from
    v$map_file;
--Information about element mapping structures
select
    *
from
    v$map_element;
--Information about all subelement mapping structures
select
    *
from
    v$map_subelement;
```

Package *dbms_trace*

Created with Oracle 8i (8.1.5), this package can be used to trace PL/SQL programs. It is installed by default when the database is created. All users can use it to generate traces but, by default, only *sys* user can view the trace output since trace tables are in the *sys* schema.

If a large volume of data needs to be kept from being generated, enable debug information to trace only a specified program unit as shown below by using this command before creating the program:

```
alter session set plsql_debug=true;
create or replace procedure|package|function …
```

Or by recompiling using the *debug* parameter:

```
alter procedure|function|package body compile debug;
```

In order to enable the *trace* utility, create tables that will hold the debug information by using the *tracetab.sql* script found in *$ORACLE_HOME/rdbms/admin*. The scripts that create the *dbms_trace* are *dbmspbt.sql* and *prvtpbt.sql*. They can also be found in *$ORACLE_HOME/rdbms/admin*. They are created under the *sys* schema and inside this script, a line that calls the *tracetab.sql* script can be uncommented if so desired.

It is possible to pause and resume the trace collection using the *trace_pause* and *trace_resume* constants. This will prevent a large volume of data from being created.

The number of events to be traced can also be limited by using the *trace_limit* constant. This constant tries to limit the number of trace events to 8192. This value can be modified by setting the 10940 event to *n* level where (trace events = 1024 * *n*). In the following example, how to use the *dbms_trace* and its procedures will be shown.

🖫 Code 5.30 – dbms_trace.sql

```
conn pkg@dbms

Connected to Oracle 11g Enterprise Edition Release 11.2.0.1.0

--Logon with sys user and create trace tabs
show user

user is "sys"

@?/rdbms/admin/tracetab.sql

--Create some procedures to test the dbms_trace utility
create or replace procedure test_dbms_trace(loop_count number,
                                            dep_id     number) is
  v_emp_cnt number;
begin
  for counter in 0 .. loop_count loop
    select
        count(*)
    into
        v_emp_cnt
    from
        employees e
    where
        e.department_id = dep_id;
  end loop;

  dbms_output.put_line('Number of employees in department id ' || dep_id ||'
is ' || v_emp_cnt);

exception
  when others then
    dbms_output.put_line('Error!!');
end;
/

--Execute the set_plsql_trace procedure with trace_all_lines constant
begin
```

```
      dbms_trace.set_plsql_trace(
         trace_level => dbms_trace.trace_all_lines);
--Run the procedure
      test_dbms_trace(loop_count => 2,dep_id => 100);
--Stop to generate trace data
      dbms_trace.clear_plsql_trace();
end;
/

--Get trace information generated
set linesize 200
col event_comment for a30
select
   event_seq as seq,
   stack_depth,
   event_kind as kind,
   substr(event_unit, 1, 10) as unit,
   event_line as line,
   event_comment
from
   plsql_trace_events;
```

The query result is:

```
 SEQ STACK_DEPTH      KIND UNIT          LINE EVENT_COMMENT
---------- -----------  ---------- ----------  ---------- ------------------------------
        1                     38                          PL/SQL Trace Tool started
        2                     40                          Trace flags changed
        3          4          51 dbms_trace      21 New line executed
        4          3          51 dbms_trace      75 New line executed
        5          3          51 dbms_trace      76 New line executed
        6          2          51 dbms_trace      81 New line executed
        7                     41                          PL/SQL Trace paused
        8                     42                          PL/SQL Trace resumed
        9          1          51 <anonymous       5 New line executed
       10                     41                          PL/SQL Trace paused
       11                     42                          PL/SQL Trace resumed

 SEQ STACK_DEPTH      KIND UNIT          LINE EVENT_COMMENT
---------- -----------  ---------- ----------  ---------- ------------------------------
       12          2          51 test_dbms_       1 New line executed
       13          2          51 test_dbms_       5 New line executed
       14          2          51 test_dbms_       6 New line executed
       15          2          51 test_dbms_       5 New line executed
       16          2          51 test_dbms_       6 New line executed
       17          2          51 test_dbms_       5 New line executed
       18          2          51 test_dbms_       6 New line executed
       19          2          51 test_dbms_       5 New line executed
       20          2          51 test_dbms_      16 New line executed
       21                     41                          PL/SQL Trace paused
       22                     42                          PL/SQL Trace resumed

 SEQ STACK_DEPTH      KIND UNIT          LINE EVENT_COMMENT
---------- -----------  ---------- ----------  ---------- ------------------------------
       23          3          51 dbms_outpu       5 New line executed
       24          3          51 dbms_outpu       7 New line executed
       25          3          51 dbms_outpu       8 New line executed
       26          3          51 dbms_outpu       9 New line executed
       27          3          51 dbms_outpu      10 New line executed
       28          3          51 dbms_outpu      13 New line executed
       29          3          51 dbms_outpu             213 New line executed
       30                     41                          PL/SQL Trace paused
       31                     42                          PL/SQL Trace resumed
       32          2          51 test_dbms_      16 New line executed
       33                     41                          PL/SQL Trace paused

 SEQ STACK_DEPTH      KIND UNIT          LINE EVENT_COMMENT
---------- -----------  ---------- ----------  ---------- ------------------------------
       34                     42                          PL/SQL Trace resumed
```

```
35            3        51 dbms_outpu      111 New line executed
36            3        51 dbms_outpu      115 New line executed
37                     41                     PL/SQL Trace paused
38                     42                     PL/SQL Trace resumed
39            2        51 test_dbms_       21 New line executed
40                     41                     PL/SQL Trace paused
41                     42                     PL/SQL Trace resumed
42            1        51 <anonymous        7 New line executed
43                     41                     PL/SQL Trace paused
44                     42                     PL/SQL Trace resumed

SEQ STACK_DEPTH     KIND UNIT            LINE EVENT_COMMENT
--------- ----------- ---------- ---------- ---------- ------------------------------
45            2        51 dbms_trace       94 New line executed
46            3        51 dbms_trace       72 New line executed
47            4        51 dbms_trace       66 New line executed
48            5        51 dbms_trace       12 New line executed
49            4        51 dbms_trace       66 New line executed
50            4        51 dbms_trace       67 New line executed
51            3        51 dbms_trace       75 New line executed
53            4        51 dbms_trace       21 New line executed
54                     39                     PL/SQL trace stopped

54 rows selected.
```

The trace level can be defined using *dbms_trace* constants, thereby minimizing the analysis time. An example is using the *trace_all_exceptions* constant to trace only exceptions or by using the *trace_limit* constant to limit the number of lines that the trace will generate in the trace table.

Notice that when the trace is stopped using the *clear_plsql_trace* procedure, a row will be inserted into trace table with a comment like "PL/SQL trace stopped".

Package *dbms_workload_repository*

Oracle 10g contains a new feature called Automatic Workload Repository that is basically used to maintain performance statistics and solve performance problems. More than twenty functions and procedures compose the *dbms_workload_repository* package. They are used to manage the AWR repository, display reports and create baselines and snapshots.

Here is an example showing some of the more useful functions and procedures.

🖫 Code 5.31 – dbms_workload_repository.sql

```
Connected to:
Oracle 11g Enterprise Edition Release 11.2.0.1.0 - Production
With the Partitioning, Oracle Label Security, OLAP, Data Mining,
Oracle Database Vault and Real Application Testing options

--Create and drop snapshots
--Create snapshot
begin
dbms_workload_repository.create_snapshot;
end;
/
```

```
--Drop snapshot
--Get information about stored snapshots using dba_hist_snapshot view
begin
--drop a range of snapshots
  dbms_workload_repository.drop_snapshot_range(
    low_snap_id => 110,
    high_snap_id => 203,
    dbid =>123661118 );
end;
/

--Mark an SQL ID to be captured on all snapshots independent of its level of
statistics
begin
   dbms_workload_repository.add_colored_sql(
     sql_id => 'gwj1f651t001a');  --Use the v$sqltext to find your sql_id
end;
/

--Create a baseline
begin
  dbms_workload_repository.create_baseline(
    start_snap_id => 100,
    end_snap_id => 200,
    baseline_name => 'Test Baseline',
    expiration => 60);
end;
/

--Display baseline metrics
begin
  dbms_workload_repository.select_baseline_metric(
    l_baseline_name => 'Test Baseline',
    l_dbid =>123661118,
    l_instance_num => 2);
end;
/

--Creating baseline template for a single time period
begin
  dbms_workload_repository.create_baseline_template (
    start_time  => to_date('21-jun-2008','dd-mon-yyyy'),
    end_time    => to_date('21-sep-2008','dd-mon-yyyy'),
    baseline_name  => 'Single_Mon_08',
    template_name  => 'Single_Mon_08',
    expiration     => null ) ;
end;
/

--Create a repeating baseline template
begin
dbms_workload_repository.create_baseline_template (
   day_of_week           => 'sunday',
      hour_in_day            => 4,
      duration               => 12,
      start_time => to_date('11-jun-2009','dd-mon-yyyy'),
      end_time   => to_date('11-jun-2009','dd-mon-yyyy'),
      baseline_name_prefix  => 'Sunday_Base_Maint'
      template_name          => 'Sunday_Base_Maint',
```

Package dbms_workload_repository

```
   expiration               => 120,
      dbid                   => 123661118 );
end;
/
```

When modifying snapshot settings, the *interval* and the *retention* are set to minutes.

The *topnsql* is used to specify the number of SQL to collect for each criteria like elapsed time, CPU time, parse calls, shareable memory, version count and such.

```
begin
dbms_workload_repository.modify_snapshot_settings(
   retention => 7200,
   interval =>60 ,
   topnsql =>10 ,
   dbid => 123661118);
end;
/

--Modify the baseline window size (number of days). Needs to be less than or
equal to the AWR retention time
begin
   dbms_workload_repository.modify_baseline_window_size(
      window_size => 7,
      dbid => 123661118);
end;
/
```

Useful views for AWR are:

- *dba_hist_snapshot*: View to find snaphot information

- *dba_hist_sql_plan*:   Contains time-series data about each object, table, index or view involved in the query

- *dba_hist_wr_control*: Controls information about the Workload Repository

- *dba_hist_baseline:* Information about baselines

- *v$metric, v$metric_history, v$metricname:* Views with metric information

There are more of them that start with *dba_hist*, and they are grouped by their type of performance statistics:

- Database waits

- Metric statistics

- Time model statistics

- System statistics

- SQL statistics

- OS statistics

- Datafile I/O statistics

- Segment statistics

There are many functions in the *dbms_workload_repository* package that can be used to generate reports containing information about Automated Session History and Automatic Workload Repository. Here are a few of the most important functions.

Code 5.32 – dbms_workload_repository_func_rep.sql

```
Connected to:
Oracle 11g Enterprise Edition Release 11.2.0.1.0 - Production
With the Partitioning, Oracle Label Security, OLAP, Data Mining,
Oracle Database Vault and Real Application Testing options

--Function reports
--Using awr_report_text function
select
   output
from
   table (dbms_workload_repository.awr_report_text(
            l_dbid =>123661118 ,
            l_inst_num => 1,
            l_bid =>191 ,
            l_eid =>192 ));
```

The output will look something like this:

```
OUTPUT
------------------------------------------------------------------------------
WORKLOAD REPOSITORY report for

DB Name       DB Id    Instance    Inst Num Startup Time    Release     RAC
-----------   --------- ----------- -------- -------------- ---------- ---
DBMS         123661118 dbms              1 09-Dec-09 21:00 11.2.0.1.0  NO

Host Name        Platform                      CPUs Cores Sockets Memory(GB)
---------------- ------------------------------ ---- ----- ------- ----------
dbms.f2c.com.br  Linux IA (32-bit)               1                      .99

              Snap Id      Snap Time     Sessions Curs/Sess
OUTPUT
------------------------------------------------------------------------------

            --------- ------------------- -------- ---------
Begin Snap:     191 10-Dec-09 02:00:32       38      4.1
  End Snap:     192 10-Dec-09 03:00:29       38      4.1
   Elapsed:           59.96 (mins)
   DB Time:            1.76 (mins)

Cache Sizes                     Begin        End
~~~~~~~~~~~                   ---------- ----------
         Buffer Cache:           92M         92M  Std Block Size:       8K
     Shared Pool Size:          152M        152M  Log Buffer:       5,952K

OUTPUT
------------------------------------------------------------------------------
Load Profile              Per Second   Per Transaction  Per Exec  Per Call
~~~~~~~~~~~~              ------------- --------------- ---------- ---------
        DB Time(s):           0.0             0.2        0.00       0.01
        DB CPU(s):            0.0             0.1        0.00       0.01
        Redo size:        1,173.9         5,923.4
     Logical reads:          58.2           293.6
     Block changes:           6.4            32.1
     Physical reads:          0.1             0.5
    Physical writes:          0.6             3.2
```

```
        User calls:           2.5              12.8
           Parses:            2.7              13.6

OUTPUT
-----------------------------------------------------------------------
       Hard parses:           0.0               0.2
  W/A MB processed:           0.0               0.1
            Logons:           0.1               0.3
          Executes:           7.2              36.3
         Rollbacks:           0.0               0.0
      Transactions:           0.2
```

Other functions that could be used are:

- *awr_sql_report_text|html*: AWR report in text or HTML format. Oracle recommends using *awrsqrpt.sql*.

- *awr_diff_report_text|html*: Compares AWR periods and the output could be in text or HTML format. Oracle recommends using *awrddrpt.sql*.

- *awr_global_diff_report_text|html*: Displays global AWR compare periods in text or HTML format.

- *awr_global_report_text|html*: Displays AWR global report in text or HTML format. Oracle recommends the use of *awrrpt.sql* or *awrrpti.sql* for RAC.

Summary

By now, the reader should have a clear idea of how, when and which packages will help in fixing performance problems in daily work such as packages that can advise indexes, materialized views and create profiles as well as packages that can trace sessions, collect statistics and much more.

In addition to Oracle Tuning, Database Backup is also one of the tasks that all DBAs must know in order to keep their jobs. In the next chapter, how to use the more important backup and recovery packages will be examined.

Oracle Backup and Recovery Packages

If we compare the human body to a technological environment, the database would represent the heart. Without a heart, one cannot survive, and neither can a company without a database. As with backup plans, recoveries should be planed and tested from time to time. This will guarantee that no error will happen when a backup needs to be restored.

This chapter will demonstrate the main packages that should be used to backup and recover a database. We will show examples of how, when and why to use them.

So now let's get started!

Package *dbms_datapump*

The *dbms_datapump* package is used to move data and metadata in and out of databases, this package provides an API that is used as the base for *expdp* and *impdp* utilities. The *dbms_datapump* package can be used to execute tasks such as copying datafiles to another database, using a direct path to load data, creating external tables and using a network link to import data. The subsequent examples will show, step-by-step, the important tasks that can be accomplished with *dbms_datapump*.

This package provides options for monitoring and controlling the job by simply attaching the job's session using the *attach* procedure. the roles *datapump_exp_full_database* and *datapump_imp_full_database* must be granted to the user who will be utilizing this package.

How to Export a Full Database

In this example, use the *dbms_datapump* package to export a full database. In a full export, schemas like *sys*, *xdb*, *ordsys*, *mdsys*, *ctxsys*, *ordplugins* and *lbacsys* are not exported.

🖫 Code 6.1 – dbms_datapump_exp_full.sql

```
conn sys@ora11g as sysdba

Connected to Oracle 11g Enterprise Edition Release 11.1.0.6.0
Connected as sysdba
```

```
show user

User is "pkg"

declare
handler          number;
v_job_status     varchar2(20);
v_get_status     ku$_Status;
v_pct_completed number;
v_job_status_out ku$_JobStatus;

begin
--Operation could be export, import or sqlfile
--Job_mode could be full, schema, table, tablespace or transportable
--Name of the job
--Version of database objects to be extracted. latest, compatible or a
specific value
handler := dbms_datapump.open(
            operation => 'export',
            job_mode => 'full',
            job_name => 'Exp full db_10',
            version => 'latest');

dbms_output.put_line(a => 'My handler number is :'||handler);

            --Here you set 4 parallel processes to the exp job
            dbms_datapump.set_parallel(
              handle => handler,
              degree => 4);

            --File name
            --Directory where the dump file will be created
            --Specify the file type
            dbms_datapump.add_file(
              handle => handler,
              filename => 'exp_full_19_dec_2009_5.dmp',
              directory => 'data_pump_dir',
              filetype =>dbms_datapump.ku$_file_type_dump_file);

            --Use set_parameter procedure to set compression
            dbms_datapump.set_parameter(
              handle => handler,
              name => 'compression',
              value => 'ALL');

            dbms_datapump.start_job(handle => handler,service_name =>
'dbms');

            v_pct_completed := 0;
            v_job_status := 'undefined';

        --Forcing the detach on session
        dbms_datapump.detach(handle => handler);

end;
/
```

The *dba_datapump_jobs* view can be queried to get information about the job created such as operation type, job mode, number of workers processing the job and so on.

```
col job_name for a15
col operation for a6
col job_mode for a10
col state for a10
col data_pump_sessions for a3

select
    j.job_name,
    j.operation,
    j.job_mode,
    j.state,
    j.degree,
    j.datapump_sessions
from
    dba_datapump_jobs j;
```

```
JOB_NAME          OPERAT JOB_MODE   STATE          DEGREE DATAPUMP_SESSIONS
----------------  ------ ---------- ---------- ---------- -----------------
Exp full db_10    export full       executing           4                 5
```

If more information about the sessions being executed needs to be found, use the following query that will join the view *v$session* with *dba_datapump_sessions*.

```
col sid for 990
col "User" for a10
col "Program" for a30
col "Job Name" for a15
col "Type" for a10

select
    s.sid,
    s.username "User",
    s.program "Program",
    s.action "Job Name",
    d.session_type "Type"
from
    gv$session s,
    dba_datapump_sessions d
 where
    s.saddr = d.saddr;
```

How to Create a Dump Procedure to Automate Dump Operations

Rather than creating an export/import *dump* command for each dump operation, simply create a procedure that will receive all parameters necessary to automatically generate the *export* command using the *dbms_datapump* package. The procedure in the sample code below can be used for operations such as exporting a full database or merely one table.

⊟ Code 6.2 – dbms_datapump_exp_proc.sql

```
conn sys@ora11g as sysdba

Connected to Oracle 11g Enterprise Edition Release 11.1.0.6.0
Connected as pkg

create or replace procedure exp_proc (
   v_job_name in varchar2,
   v_dump_file_name in varchar2,
   v_operation in varchar2 default 'export',
   v_job_mode in varchar2 default 'full',
   v_table in varchar2 default NULL,
   v_parallel in number default 1,
   v_directory in varchar2 default 'data_pump_dir',
   v_logfile in varchar2 default 'logfile%u.log')
is
  percent_done number;      -- Percentage of job complete
  job_state varchar2(30);   -- To keep track of job state
  js ku$_JobStatus;         -- The job status from get_status
  v_sts ku$_Status;         -- The status object returned by get_status
  v_handler        number;

begin

   v_handler := dbms_datapump.open(
      operation => v_operation,      --Oparation could be export, import
or sqlfile
      job_mode => v_job_mode,        --Could be full, schema, table,
tablespace or transportable
      job_name => v_job_name,        --Name of the job
      version => 'latest');

         --Specify only one table to be exported
   if v_job_mode = 'table' then
     dbms_datapump.metadata_filter(
        handle => v_handler,
        name => 'name_list',
        value => v_table);
    end if;

   dbms_output.put_line(a => 'My v_handler number is :'||v_handler);

   --Here you set 4 parallel processes to the exp job
   dbms_datapump.set_parallel(
      handle => v_handler,
      degree => v_parallel);

   --File name
   --Directory where the dump file will be created
   --Specify the file type
   dbms_datapump.add_file(
      handle => v_handler,
      filename => v_dump_file_name,
      directory => v_directory,
      filetype =>dbms_datapump.ku$_file_type_dump_file);

   --Add logfile
   dbms_datapump.add_file(
```

```
        handle => v_handler,
        filename => v_logfile,
        directory => v_directory,
        filetype => dbms_datapump.ku$_file_type_log_file);


--Use set_parameter procedure to set compression
    dbms_datapump.set_parameter(
        handle => v_handler,
        name => 'compression',
        value => 'ALL');

    dbms_datapump.start_job(
        handle => v_handler,
        service_name => 'dbms');

    percent_done := 0;
    job_state := 'undefined';
    while (job_state != 'completed') and (job_state != 'stopped') and
(job_state != 'not running') loop
        dbms_datapump.get_status(v_handler,
            dbms_datapump.ku$_status_job_error +
            dbms_datapump.ku$_status_job_status +
            dbms_datapump.ku$_status_wip,-1,job_state,v_sts);

        js := v_sts.job_status;

        if js.percent_done != percent_done
        then
            dbms_output.put_line('*** Job percent done = ' ||
                                 to_char(js.percent_done));
            percent_done := js.percent_done;
        end if;

    end loop;
    dbms_output.put_line('Job has completed');
    dbms_output.put_line('Final job state = ' || job_state);
    dbms_datapump.detach(v_handler);
end;
```

Execute this procedure once to see the results. Note that on this execution, only the employees table will be exported.

```
exec exp_proc(
    v_job_name => 'job_test1',
    v_dump_file_name => 'exp_dump_%U.dmp',
    v_operation => 'export',
    v_job_mode => 'table',
    v_table => 'employees',
    v_parallel => 1,
    v_directory => 'data_pump_dir',
    v_logfile => 'exp_log_file1.log');
```

A dump file containing the employees table data will be generated. This file is named *exp_dump_01.dmp* along with a log file named *exp_log_file1.log*. The output of the log file is shown below:

Package dbms_datapump

```
[ora11g@dbms dpdump]$ cat exp_log_file1.log
Starting "pkg"."job_Test1":
Estimate in progress using blocks method...
Processing object type table_export/table/table_data
Total estimation using blocks method: 560 MB
Processing object type table_export/table/table
Processing object type table_export/table /index/index
Processing object type table_export/table /constraint/ constraint
Processing object type table_export/table /index/statistics/index_statistics
Processing object type table_export/table /comment
Processing object type table_export/table / constraint /ref_ constraint
Processing object type table_export/table /trigger
Processing object type table_export/table /statistics/table_statistics
Processing object type table_export/table /statistics/user_pref_ statistics
. . exported "pkg"."employees"                    87.15 MB 7012352
rows
Master table "pkg"."job_Test1" successfully loaded/unloaded
*************************************************************************
**
Dump file set for pkg.job_Test1 is:
  /u01/app/oracle/admin/dbms/dpdump/exp_dump_01.dmp
Job "pkg"."job_test1" successfully completed at 09:23:10
```

In addition, this procedure checks the percentage of execution and shows it at the end with the handler number and the final job state. This monitoring block could be migrated to a new procedure that would be used just for monitoring jobs being executed.

Monitoring Dump Jobs Using Queries

Queries on views like *dba_datapump_sessions* and *dba_datapump_jobs* can be used to get the exp/imp dump job's information. The query below is used to show jobs created and their status, parallelism and sessions being used.

```
col job_name for a15
col operation for a6
col job_mode for a10
col state for a15
col data_pump_sessions for a3
select
   j.job_name,
   j.operation,
   j.job_mode,
   j.state,
   j.degree,
   j.datapump_sessions
from
   dba_datapump_jobs j;

JOB_NAME        OPERAT JOB_MODE   STATE           DEGREE DATAPUMP_SESSIONS
--------------- ------ ---------- --------------- ---------- ----------------
Job_full_test1  export full       executing           2                3
```

Here is another query that can be used for finding SIDs of dump jobs running on a database.

```
col sid for 990
col "User" for a10
col "Program" for a30
col "Job Name" for a15
col "Type" for a10

select
   s.sid,
   s.username "User",
   s.program "Program",
   s.action "Job Name",
   d.session_type "Type"
from
   gv$session s,
   dba_datapump_sessions d
 where
    s.saddr = d.saddr;
```

SID	User	Program	Job Name	Type
35	pkg	oracle@dbms.f2c.com.br (DM00)	Job_full_test1	master
50	pkg	oracle@dbms.f2c.com.br (DW00)	Job_full_test1	worker

Package *dbms_file_transfer*

The *dbms_file_transfer* package is used to transfer and copy binary files between or within databases. Binary files such as archive logs, RMAN backups, spfiles, datafiles, change tracking files, Data Guard configuration and Data Pump files can be used within this package. Some possible operations completed using the *dbms_file_transfer* package are:

- Create a file copy within the same database

- Copy files from a remote database

- Copy local files into a remote database

Procedures used for these tasks are:

- *copy_file*: Copies files from the source directory to a destination directory on the same database. Can be used to copy files between ASM and file system.

- *get_file*: Copies files from a remote database. Can be used to copy files between ASM and file system.

- *put_file*: Copies a local file to a remote database. Can be used to copy files between ASM and file system.

Review these commands one procedure at a time. First, a procedure called *proc_file_transfer* is created and all the procedures of the *dbms_file_transfer* package are demonstrated within it. Two databases will be needed to test *put* and *get* procedures. The second database in this example is named ORADB.

💾 Code 6.3 – dbms_file_transfer.sql

```
conn sys@ora11g as sysdba

Connected to Oracle 11g Enterprise Edition Release 11.1.0.6.0
Connected as pkg

--First create source and destination directories
conn / as sysdba
grant execute on dbms_file_transfer to pkg;
grant select on dba_directories to pkg;
grant alter database to pkg;
grant alter tablespace to pkg;

--Create this directory on source database to test copy procedure
create or replace directory dir_source as
'/u01/app/oracle/oradata/DBMS/datafile/';
create or replace directory dir_dest as
'/u01/app/oracle/oradata/DBMS/dir_dest/';

--Create this directory on remote database to test get procedure
create or replace directory dir_source as '/u01/app/oracle/oradata/ORADB/';

--Create one database link to test get and put procedures
create database link ORADB
  connect to pkg identified by pkg
  using 'ORADB';
```

Create the package that has all three procedures inside it to test a simple datafile copy.

```
--Create package
create or replace package pkg_file_transfer as
  procedure proc_file_transfer_copy (
    v_dir_source in varchar2,
    v_dir_dest in varchar2,
    v_file_name_orig in varchar2,
    v_file_name_dest in varchar2,
    v_file_type in varchar2);

  procedure proc_file_transfer_get (
    v_dir_source in varchar2,
    v_dir_dest in varchar2,
    v_source_database in varchar2,
    v_file_name_orig in varchar2,
    v_file_name_dest in varchar2,
    v_file_type in varchar2);

  procedure proc_file_transfer_put (
    v_dir_source in varchar2,
    v_dir_dest in varchar2,
    v_file_name_orig in varchar2,
    v_file_name_dest in varchar2,
    v_dest_database in varchar2,
    v_file_type in varchar2);
```

Advanced DBMS Packages

```
end pkg_file_transfer;
```

Now, create the package body. Notice the code of each procedure example.

The first procedure, *proc_file_transfer_copy*, is used to copy a datafile from one place to another and then make the database use the copy instead so the original file is not deleted automatically. Note the parameters used as they will be utilized with the *dbms_file_transfer* package in spite of which datafile will be used.

```
   --Create package body
create or replace package body pkg_file_transfer is

  procedure proc_file_transfer_copy (
     v_dir_source in varchar2,
     v_dir_dest in varchar2,
     v_file_name_orig in varchar2,
     v_file_name_dest in varchar2,
     v_file_type in varchar2) as

  v_tbs varchar2(30);
  v_old_path varchar2(100);
  v_new_path varchar2(100);

  begin

  if v_file_type = 'datafile' then

    select
       tablespace_name
       into v_tbs
    from
       dba_data_files
    where
       file_name like '%'||v_file_name_orig;

    execute immediate 'alter tablespace '||v_tbs||' offline normal';
  end if;

  dbms_file_transfer.copy_file(
     source_directory_object => v_dir_source,
     source_file_name => v_file_name_orig,
     destination_directory_object => v_dir_dest,
     destination_file_name => v_file_name_dest);
     dbms_output.put_line(a => 'File '||v_file_name_orig||' copied from
'||v_dir_source||' to directory '||v_dir_dest||';');

  select
     directory_path
     into v_old_path
  from
     dba_directories
  where
     directory_name=v_dir_source;

  select
```

```
                directory_path
                into v_new_path
        from
                dba_directories
        where
                directory_name=v_dir_dest;

        execute immediate
                'alter database rename file '''
                        ||v_old_path
                        ||v_file_name_orig
                        ||''' to '''
                        ||v_new_path
                        ||v_file_name_dest
                        ||''' ';

        execute immediate
                'alter tablespace '||v_tbs||' online';
        end;
```

The second procedure, *proc_file_transfer_get,* is used to copy a remote datafile from the ORADB database. Make sure that the correct directories are created to avoid a "file does not exist" error.

```
procedure proc_file_transfer_get (
        v_dir_source in varchar2,
        v_dir_dest in varchar2,
        v_source_database in varchar2,
        v_file_name_orig in varchar2,
        v_file_name_dest in varchar2,
        v_file_type in varchar2) as

v_tbs varchar2(30);
v_old_path varchar2(100);
v_new_path varchar2(100);

begin

        if v_file_type = 'datafile' then

                select
                        tablespace_name
                        into v_tbs
                from
                        dba_data_files
                where
                        file_name like '%'||v_file_name_orig;

                pkg.put_tbs_offline@oradb('||v_tbs||');
        end if;

        dbms_file_transfer.get_file(
                source_directory_object => v_dir_source,
                source_file_name => v_file_name_orig,
                source_database => v_source_database,
                destination_directory_object => v_dir_dest,
```

```
            destination_file_name => v_file_name_orig);

      dbms_output.put_line(a =>
         'File '
            ||v_file_name_orig
            ||' moved from '
            ||v_dir_source
            ||' to directory '
            ||v_dir_dest
            ||';');

   select
      directory_path
      into v_old_path
   from
      dba_directories
   where
      directory_name=v_dir_source;

   select
      directory_path
      into v_new_path
   from
      dba_directories
   where
      directory_name=v_dir_dest;


   execute immediate
      'alter database rename file '''
         ||v_old_path
         ||v_file_name_orig
         ||''' to '''
         ||v_new_path
         ||v_file_name_dest
         ||''' ';

   execute immediate 'alter tablespace '||v_tbs||' online';

   end;
```

The last procedure in this example, *proc_file_transfer_put*, is used to copy a local datafile to a remote database named ORADB.

```
procedure proc_file_transfer_put (
   v_dir_source in varchar2,
   v_dir_dest in varchar2,
   v_file_name_orig in varchar2,
   v_file_name_dest in varchar2,
   v_dest_database in varchar2,
   v_file_type in varchar2) as

v_tbs varchar2(30);
v_old_path varchar2(100);
v_new_path varchar2(100);

begin
```

```
if v_file_type = 'datafile' then

  select
    tablespace_name
    into v_tbs
  from
    dba_data_files
  where
    file_name like '%'||v_file_name_orig;

  execute immediate 'alter tablespace '||v_tbs||' offline normal';
end if;


dbms_file_transfer.put_file(
source_directory_object => v_dir_source,
source_file_name => v_file_name_orig,
destination_directory_object => v_dir_dest,
destination_file_name => v_file_name_dest,
destination_database => v_dest_database);

dbms_output.put_line(a =>
  'File '
  ||v_file_name_orig
  ||' moved from '
  ||v_dir_source
  ||' to directory '
  ||v_dir_dest
  ||';');

  select
  directory_path
  into v_old_path
from
  dba_directories
where
  directory_name=v_dir_source;

select
  directory_path
  into v_new_path
from
  dba_directories
where
  directory_name=v_dir_dest;


execute immediate
  'alter database rename file '''
    ||v_old_path
    ||v_file_name_orig
    ||''' to '''
    ||v_new_path
    ||v_file_name_dest
    ||''' ';

execute immediate 'alter tablespace '||v_tbs||' online';
```

```
    end;

end pkg_file_transfer;
```

The following two procedures must be created on a remote database; in this instance, the ORADB database will be used.

```
--Create this procedure on remote database to change status of tablespace
create or replace procedure put_tbs_offline(
   v_tbs_name in varchar2)
as
begin
    execute immediate
       'alter tablespace '||v_tbs_name||' offline normal';
end;
/

--Create this procedure on remote database to change status of tablespace
create or replace procedure put_tbs_online(
   v_tbs_name in varchar2)
as
begin
    execute immediate
       'alter tablespace '||v_tbs_name||' online';
end;
/
```

In the following example, the datafile named *o1_mf_users_5gfvv3fy_.dbf* will be renamed *users01.dbf* in a new directory specified by the *v_dir_dest* parameter.

```
exec pkg_file_transfer.proc_file_transfer_copy(
   v_dir_source => 'dir_source',
   v_dir_dest => 'dir_dest',
   v_file_name_orig => 'o1_mf_users_5gfvv3fy_.dbf',
   v_file_name_dest => 'userS01.dbf',
   v_file_type =>'datafile');
```

The next example will copy a remote datafile from the users tablespace to a local directory defined by the *v_dir_dest* parameter. The new file name will be *users_1_bkp.dbf.* The source file is identified by the remote database link used in the *v_source_database* parameter.

```
exec pkg_file_transfer.proc_file_transfer_get(
   v_dir_source => 'dir_source',
   v_dir_dest => 'dir_dest',
   v_source_database => 'ORADB',
   v_file_name_orig => 'users01.dbf',
   v_file_name_dest => 'users_1_bkp.dbf',
   v_file_type => 'datafile' );
```

The final example uses the *proc_file_transfer_put* procedure to copy a local file into a remote directory. The remote location is specified by the *v_destination_database* parameter. In this case, the ORADB database.

```
exec pkg_file_transfer.proc_file_transfer_put(
   v_dir_source => 'dir_source',
   v_dir_dest => 'dir_dest',
   v_file_name_orig => 'users01.dbf',
   v_file_name_dest => 'users01_remote.dbf',
   v_dest_database => 'ORADB',
   v_file_type => 'datafile');
```

Note that the *v_file_type* parameter was created to allow the user to break up specific types of files that can then be copied using *dbms_file_transfer* packages like ASM files, dump files, spfiles and others.
Feel free to increment this code to fit in specific requirements.

Package *dbms_transaction*

Commonly used SQL commands like *commit, rollback, set transaction read only,* and *alter session advise commit* can also be used inside procedures through the *dbms_transaction* package. Its purpose is to manage distributed transactions using procedures and functions of the package. The *dbms_transaction* package allows us to commit, rollback, purge or create *savepoints* to transactions. Created automatically since Oracle 7.3.4 by the *dbmstrns.sql* script, the *dbms_transaction* package is created under the *sys* schema and a public synonym is also created, granting the execute privilege to the public.

There are more than fifteen procedures and functions. Rather than describing each one, we will give examples utilizing some of the more important ones. An easy way to find the transaction ID and the current undo segment being used is by running the *local_transaction_id* function as shown here:

```
set serveroutput on
declare
v_local_tran_id varchar2(40);
begin
 --Start a read/write transaction
 dbms_transaction.read_write;
 select
    dbms_transaction.local_transaction_id
 into
    v_local_tran_id
 from
    dual;
 dbms_output.put_line('My local transaction id is: '||v_local_tran_id);
end;
/

My local transaction id is: 7.9.1470
```

```
SQL>
select
 name
from
 v$rollname
where
 usn=7;

NAME
------------------------------
_SYSSMU7_2224510368$
```

The undo segment can be identified by the numbers before the first ".". In the case above, the undo segment number is 7.

When and How to Use *purge_lost_db_entry* Procedure

During the *commit* process of a distributed transaction, if one of the nodes participating in the transaction process fails and the database is recreated after the recovery process is completed, then the transaction will be lost and recorded in the *dba_2pc_pending* view. The *purge_lost_db_entry* procedure is used to purge this kind of lost transaction from a local site. Any transaction that is in a state other than *prepared* can be purged.

If the transaction has a value of *yes* in the column *mixed*, then use the *purge_mixed* procedure. This could happen when using *commit force* or *rollback force* and one site will *commit* the transaction while the other site will *rollback* the transaction. Purge should only be used when the database is lost or has been recreated.

In this next example, how to find and purge lost transactions will be revealed.

🖫 Code 6.4 – dbms_transaction.sql

```
conn pkg@dbms

Connected to:
Oracle 11g Enterprise Edition Release 11.2.0.1.0 - Production
With the Partitioning, Oracle Label Security, OLAP, Data Mining,
Oracle Database Vault and Real Application Testing options

SQL>
show
 user

User is "pkg"
SQL>

--Using purge_lost_db_entry

--Query dba_2pc_pending to get transactions ids to be purged
select
```

```
   local_tran_id,
   global_tran_id,
   state,
   mixed
from
   dba_2pc_pending;

--Now try to purge the transaction using the purge_db_entry procedure
begin
dbms_transaction.purge_lost_db_entry(xid => 'local_tran_id');
end;
/

--If you find an error like this one below,
ORA-30019: Illegal rollback Segment operation in Automatic Undo mode

--then you need to follow these steps:
commit;

alter session set "_smu_debug_mode" = 4;

begin
dbms_transaction.purge_lost_db_entry('local_tran_id');
end;
/


--Or, if you got this another error below
ORA-06510: PL/SQL: unhandled user-defined exception
ORA-06512: at "sys.dbms_transaction", line 94
ORA-06512: at line 1


--then you need to follow these steps:
rollback force '7.12.102';

Commit;

alter system set "_smu_debug_mode" = 4;

begin
dbms_transaction.purge_lost_db_entry('local_tran_id');
end;
/

--Another useful queries that generate the purge to the command is below:

select
   'commit force '''||local_tran_id||''';'
from
   dba_2pc_pending;

select
   'exec dbms_transaction.purge_lost_db_entry('''||local_tran_id||''');'
from
   dba_2pc_pending
where
   state='forced commit';
```

If a transaction is found in a *prepared* state without an entry in the transaction table, it can be cleaned up manually by using these steps:

🖫 Code 6.5 – dbms_transaction_man_purge.sql

```
conn pkg@dbms
--Manually purge lost entries

--Find the prepared transaction
select
   local_tran_id,
   state
from
   dba_2pc_pending;

LOCAL_TRAN_ID            STATE
---------------------    ----------------
   7.12.102              prepared

--Find the transaction located on a rollback segment
select
   ktuxeusn,
   ktuxeslt,
   ktuxesqn, /* transaction id */
   ktuxesta status,
   ktuxecfl flags
from
   x$ktuxe
where
   ktuxesta!='inactive'
and
   ktuxeusn= 1; -- rollback segment number

--If you don't find any transaction, then you should delete it manually
set transaction use rollback segment SYSTEM;

delete from
   sys.pending_trans$
where
   local_tran_id = '7.12.102';

delete from
   sys.pending_sessions$
where
   local_tran_id = '7.12.102';

delete from
   sys.pending_sub_sessions$
where
   local_tran_id = '7.12.102';
commit;
```

All this information may be found in MOSC Note: 401302.1. If more information about how to resolve transaction problems is desired, take a time to read MOSC Note 126069.1. There, many sample scenarios will be found.

Package dbms_transaction

Package *dbms_flashback*

The first flashback functionalities came with the *dbms_flashback* packages within the release of Oracle 9i. Flashback functionalities enabled the DBA to specify a consistent point-in-time for the session and by using *dbms_flashback.enable_at_time(my_timestamp)*, a session could be put into a state which reads the consistent image of the database as it was at a point-in-time in the past. Flashback was enhanced in version 9.2 when Oracle introduced the *flashback query* functionality. The *flashback query* enabled users to query data as it appeared in the past using a normal SQL:

```
select …
  from…
    as of timestamp|scn
  where……;
```

Reading data by specifying a timestamp or a system change number (SCN) was also common at the time.

Internally, every *select* is a *select as of timestamp sysdate*. Only as of version 9.2 was the normal user able to specify a timestamp to read the consistent data. This concept was extended in Oracle's first 10g release on a row level. Consequently, the *flashback versions query* functionality could be used to view all versions of a given row between two timestamps and two SCNs.

Once the transactions had been identified, it was also possible to look at the *undo_sql* column of a view called *flashback_transaction_query*. The transaction's ID, using the pseudo column *versions_xid*, could also be found. Here, changes which were made by the same transaction could be found per the appropriate *select any transaction* system privilege.

```
select
 undo_sql
  from
 flashback_transaction_query
    where
 xid=hextoraw('my_transaction-id');
```

This gave the principal option to spool the undo SQL from the *flashback_transaction_query* view and execute it to undo changes. However, this was not practical because of dependencies in transactions and applications which made it difficult to undo things in the correct sequence. Luckily, this has been addressed in Oracle 11g of which a closer review of the new functionality will be given shortly.

All flashback functionalities covered so far have utilized information from the undo segments in order to read the consistent image of data in the past. These types of functionalities do not change anything in the database, but instead read data as it was in the past because undo data is the logical information needed to undo a change. This being the case, if the logical information needed to undo a change is overwritten in between, an error message appears explaining that it is not possible to reconstruct the consistent data in the past. However, 10gR1 introduced a number of other extensively new functionalities under the name *flashback*.

An example of the unique 10gR1 functionalities is the *flashback drop*. The *flashback drop* utilizes the so-called recycle bin which could be disabled with the *recyclebin* parameter in Oracle 10gR2. The *recyclebin* had been enabled by default in prior releases, and in 10gR1 this parameter is the hidden parameter *_recyclebin*. If a DBA drops a table in 10g, it is internally renamed and the segment stays where it is. These extents are available for reuse or review in *dba_free_space*, but the server tries not to use them as long as possible.

Oracle starts reusing these extents before auto extending a datafile. Once the server has reused the extents, it is not possible to flashback to before the drop. This enables the user to flashback the drop, and simply renames the object back to its original name. Indexes and triggers are also flashed back. Foreign key constraints are not flashed back with the table. They must be manually recreated!

Since the object remains the same as before the drop operation, it also becomes possible for the DBA to read from it using the new name. The *flashback query* also offers the ability to read the object as it was in the past by using the new name and *select*.

```
flashback table my_table
to timestamp|scn;
```

The DBA is limited in the inability to flashback to before *ddl* statements because if the definition of the table changed in between the flashback operation, it would error out.

How to Recover Deleted Rows From a Table

If a user has accidentally deleted rows from a table, the *dbms_flashback* package can be used to remedy this error. The number of retrievable rows will depend on the amount of available undo tablespace. Time will also be a factor since as undo space is filled with new entries, the rows that are needed may become lost forever.

First, we check to see if the database is in *archivelog* mode and whether or not the supplemental log has being enabled in this database.

📓 Code 6.6 – dbms_flashback_rec_del_rows.sql

```
conn sys@ora11g as sysdba

Connected to Oracle 11g Enterprise Edition Release 11.1.0.6.0
Connected as pkg

--First it is needed to enable archive log and add supplemental log data on
database
conn / as sysdba
shutdown immediate;
startup mount;
alter database archivelog;
alter database open;
alter system archive log current;
alter database add supplemental log data;
```

Next, we create the tables that will be used in this example. The *tab_dbms_flashback1*
table receives test data and *tab_rec_scn* records system change numbers before each
transaction.

```
--Table to record scn
create table
    tab_rec_scn (
    scn number,
    time_scn date);

--Test table
create table
    tab_dbms_flashback1 (
    col1 varchar2(6),
    col2 number);
```

Now, the PL/SQL block below inserts rows in the *tab_dbms_flashback1* table using
different transactions, and then these rows are deleted.

```
declare
rec_scn number;
begin
  rec_scn := dbms_flashback.get_system_change_number;
  insert into tab_rec_scn values (rec_scn,systimestamp);
  dbms_output.put_line(a => 'SCN at Part1 is '||rec_scn);
  insert into tab_dbms_flashback1 values ('Part11',rec_scn);
  insert into tab_dbms_flashback1 values ('Part12',rec_scn);
  commit;
  dbms_lock.sleep(5);
  rec_scn := dbms_flashback.get_system_change_number;
  insert into tab_rec_scn values (rec_scn,systimestamp);
  dbms_output.put_line(a => 'SCN at Part1 is '||rec_scn);
  insert into tab_dbms_flashback1 values ('Part21',rec_scn);
  insert into tab_dbms_flashback1 values ('Part22',rec_scn);
  commit;
  dbms_lock.sleep(5);
  rec_scn := dbms_flashback.get_system_change_number;
  insert into tab_rec_scn values (rec_scn,systimestamp);
  dbms_output.put_line(a => 'SCN at Part1 is '||rec_scn);
```

```
   insert into tab_dbms_flashback1 values ('Part31',rec_scn);
   insert into tab_dbms_flashback1 values ('Part32',rec_scn);
   commit;
   dbms_lock.sleep(5);
   delete from tab_dbms_flashback1;
   commit;
end;
/
```

Imagine that we need to rollback these rows because the delete was a mistake. We will use some queries to see what is going on with my table data right now.

```
--Query to return information about transactions id and start/end scn number
select
   versions_xid,
   versions_startscn,
   versions_endscn,
   versions_operation,
   col1,
   col2
from
   tab_dbms_flashback1
versions between scn minvalue and maxvalue;

--Query the main table and repair that all rows ware deleted
select
   *
from
   tab_dbms_flashback1
order by
   col1;

--Query scn table to get each scn created
select
   *
from
   tab_rec_scn
order by
   time_scn;
```

A procedure named *proc_flashback_tab_rows* is created that will retrieve the original rows of the *tab_dbms_flashback1* table using the *dbms_flashback* package. All deleted rows will roll back.

```
create or replace procedure proc_flashback_tab_rows (v_scn in number) is
v_col1 varchar2(6);
v_col2 number;
cursor cur1 is
   select
      col1,
      col2
   from
      tab_dbms_flashback1;
c1_rec cur1 % rowtype;
```

```
begin
dbms_flashback.enable_at_system_change_number(
   query_scn => v_scn);

open cur1;

loop
   fetch cur1 into v_col1,v_col2;
   exit when cur1%notfound;
   if (v_col1 is not null) then
      dbms_flashback.disable;
      insert into
         tab_dbms_flashback1
      values
         (v_col1,
          v_col2);

      commit;
   end if;
end loop;
exception
when others then
      raise_application_error(-20001,'An error was encountered -
'||sqlcode||' error  '||sqlerrm);
end;
```

Next, we obtain the system change number for the exact time prior to the accidental *delete* command. Then we roll back all rows deleted using the value of *versions_start_scn* in the query below. The value must be the exact time to which the rows should be rolled back.

```
select
   versions_xid,
   versions_startscn,
   versions_endscn,
   versions_operation,
   col1,
   col2
from
   tab_dbms_flashback1
versions between scn minvalue and maxvalue;
```

VERSIONS_XID	VERSIONS_STARTSCN	VERSIONS_ENDSCN	VERSIONS_OPERATION	COL1	COL2
07000B0046070000	2405181		D	Part32	2405176
07000B0046070000	2405181		D	Part31	2405176
07000B0046070000	2405181		D	Part22	2405174
07000B0046070000	2405181		D	Part21	2405174
07000B0046070000	2405181		D	Part12	2405167
07000B0046070000	2405181		D	Part11	2405167
0A0000003D070000	2405177	2405181	I	Part32	2405176
0A0000003D070000	2405177	2405181	I	Part31	2405176
03001F001D060000	2405175	2405181	I	Part22	2405174
03001F001D060000	2405175	2405181	I	Part21	2405174
02001A00FB070000	2405172	2405181	I	Part12	2405167
02001A00FB070000	2405172	2405181	I	Part11	2405167

```
12 rows selected
```

The value can be used from the procedure created to get all rows deleted in the table quickly and easily.

```
--Table has no rows
select * from tab_dbms_flashback1 order by col1;

COL1        COL2
------ ----------

--Execute the procedure that will recover rows deleted
exec test_flashback(v_scn => 2405177);


--Query the table again to see the rows deleted
select
    *
from
    tab_dbms_flashback1
order by
    col1;

COL1        COL2
------ ----------
Part11    2405167
Part12    2405167
Part21    2405174
Part22    2405174
Part31    2405176
Part32    2405176
```

In this example, the *enable_at_system_change_number*, *disable* and *get_system_change_number* procedures of the *dbms_flashback* package have been used. There are two additional procedures in the *dbms_flashback* package:

1. *enable_at_time*. This procedure is similar to the *enable_at_system_change* number procedure but instead of using the SCN, time is used.

2. *transaction_backout*: A method used to provide a backout of a transaction and its dependents based on the undo data.

How to Backout a Transaction and Its Dependents

This example will demonstrate how to roll back an entire transaction and its dependents using the *transaction_backout* procedure from the *dbms_flashback* package of Oracle 11g. Two tables will be used in this example so how to roll back one transaction that involves multiple tables can be viewed.

The first step is to create the test tables and their constraints. They are named *tab_dbms_flashback_2* and *tab_dbms_flashback_3*.

🖫 Code 6.7 – dbms_flashback_trans_backout.sql

```
conn sys@ora11g as sysdba

Connected to Oracle 11g Enterprise Edition Release 11.1.0.6.0
Connected as pkg

--Create the test tables
create table
   tab_dbms_flashback2 (
   col1 varchar2(6),
   col2 number);

alter table tab_dbms_flashback2
  add constraint pk_col1 primary key (col1);

alter table tab_dbms_flashback2
  add constraint fk_col1 foreign key (col1)
  references tab_dbms_flashback3 (col1) on delete cascade;

create table tab_dbms_flashback3 (
   col1 varchar2(6),
   col2 number);

alter table tab_dbms_flashback3
  add constraint pk_col1 primary key (col1);
```

Next, transactions are executed in order to insert some rows on both tables.

```
--Note that tables are empty
select
   *
from
   tab_dbms_flashback2;

select
   *
from
   tab_dbms_flashback3;

--Executing some transactions
begin
insert into tab_dbms_flashback3 values ('1A' ,1);
insert into tab_dbms_flashback3 values ('1B' ,2);
insert into tab_dbms_flashback2 values ('1A' ,1);
insert into tab_dbms_flashback2 values ('1B' ,2);
commit;
dbms_lock.sleep(5);
insert into tab_dbms_flashback3 values ('2A' ,3);
insert into tab_dbms_flashback3 values ('2B' ,4);
commit;
dbms_lock.sleep(5);
insert into tab_dbms_flashback3 values ('3A' ,5);
commit;
dbms_lock.sleep(5);
commit;
dbms_lock.sleep(5);
end;
```

```
--Query tables again
select
   *
from
   tab_dbms_flashback2;

select
   *
from
   tab_dbms_flashback3;
```

Now, find the *transaction_id* that should be rolled back using the *flashback_transaction_query* view as below:

```
--Query flashback_transaction_query to get the transaction id that you need
to rollback
col table_name for a20
col operation for a10
col start_timestamp for a30
  select
     xid,
     table_name,
     operation,
     start_timestamp
  from
     flashback_transaction_query
  where
     table_name in (
     'tab_dbms_flashback2',
     'tab_dbms_flashback3')
  and
     start_timestamp > systimestamp - interval '15' minute
  and
     operation='insert'
  order by
     start_timestamp;
```

```
XID                TABLE_NAME           OPERATION   START_TIMESTAMP
----------------   --------------------  ----------  -------------------
030006002B060000   tab_dbms_flashback3  insert      1/1/2010 17:06:10
030006002B060000   tab_dbms_flashback3  insert      1/1/2010 17:06:10
0A001F0047070000   tab_dbms_flashback2  insert      1/1/2010 17:06:10
0A001F0047070000   tab_dbms_flashback3  insert      1/1/2010 17:06:10
0A001F0047070000   tab_dbms_flashback2  insert      1/1/2010 17:06:10
0A001F0047070000   tab_dbms_flashback3  insert      1/1/2010 17:06:10
0500210004070000   tab_dbms_flashback3  insert      1/1/2010 17:06:19
```

Next, we execute the *transaction_backout* procedure using the *xid* of the transaction to be backed out and note the results.

```
--Rollback the first transaction. This will remove the  first 4 rows
inserted on both tables
select * from tab_dbms_flashback2;
```

```
select * from tab_dbms_flashback3;

set serveroutput on
declare
 xa sys.xid_array := sys.xid_array();
begin
xa := sys.xid_array('0A001F0047070000');
dbms_flashback.transaction_backout(numtxns => 1,xids =>  xa,options =>
dbms_flashback.cascade);
end;
/
```

The tables can now be queried again and the rows that were targeted are no longer there. Two rows from the *tab_dbms_flashback2* table were deleted as well as two rows from *tab_dbms_flashback3*.

```
select
    *
from
    tab_dbms_flashback2;

COL1          COL2
------ ----------
```

```
select
    *
from
    tab_dbms_flashback3;

COL1          COL2
------ ----------
2A              3
2B              4
3A              5
```

Programs *dbms_logmnr* and *dbms_logmnr_d*

Oracle LogMiner is an auditing tool that uses redo entries embedded in online redo log files or archived redo log files and data dictionary information to reconstitute the DML statements that produced those changes. Every change made to any table data including the data dictionary are recorded in the Oracle redo log files.

Together, the column *sql_redo* and the SCN of *v$logmnr_contents* can provide relevant information on the activity within the database at the time the analyzed files were produced. In addition, this view contains the segment name and owner which is useful in further identification of the objects being altered.

The *v$logmnr_contents* view contains log history information. When a *select* statement is executed against the *v$logmnr_contents* view, the archive redo log files are read sequentially. Translated records from the redo log files are returned as rows in the *v$logmnr_contents* view. This continues until either the filter criteria, such as *EndTime* or *endSCN* specified at startup, is met or the end of the archive log file is reached.

The Log Miner operations are conducted using the *dbms_logmnr* and *dbms_logmnr_d* PL/SQL package procedures. Data of interest is retrieved using the *v$logmnr_contents* view. The main steps are as follows:

1. Ensure that supplemental logging is on. Log Miner requires that supplemental logging be enabled prior to starting the Log Miner session.

2. Specify a Log Miner dictionary. Either use the *dbms_logmnr_d.build* procedure or specify the dictionary when the Log Miner process is started, depending on the type of dictionary that is to be used.

3. Specify a list of redo and archive log files for analysis. For this, use the *dbms_logmnr.add_logfiles* procedure, or direct Log Miner to create a list of log files for analysis automatically when Log Miner is started.

4. Then start the Log Miner session by using the *start_logmnr* procedure.

5. Request the redo data of interest. For this, query the *v$logmnr_contents* view.

6. End the Log Miner session by using the *end_logmnr* procedure of *dbms_logmnr_d*.

The next example demonstrates the method of using Log Miner to recover deleted historical data from the archived redo logs.

How to Recover Deleted Historical Data Using Log Miner

This example shows, step by step, the recovery strategy used in order to retrieve historical deleted rows. The first step is to enable the supplemental log of the database if it is not already on.

💾 Code 6.8 – dbms_logmnr.sql

```
conn sys@ora11g as sysdba

Connected to Oracle 11g Enterprise Edition Release 11.1.0.6.0
Connected as sysdba

conn / as sysdba

shutdown immediate;
startup mount;
alter database archivelog;
alter database open;
alter system archive log current;
alter database add supplemental log data;

select d.supplemental_log_data_min from v$database d;
```

```
SUPPLEMENTAL_LOG_DATA_MIN
------------------------
yes
```

Next, run the PL/SQL block shown below. It will get the SCN before and after an *insert* command is done in the *tab_logmnr* table.

```
--Simulate one transaction and get this SCN before and after it
truncate table tab_logmnr;
create table tab_logmnr (col1 varchar2(10), col2 number);
set serveroutput on
declare
v_scn number;
begin
v_scn := dbms_flashback.get_system_change_number;
dbms_output.put_line(a => 'SCN before the insert is : '||v_scn);
insert into tab_logmnr values ('TT1',21);
commit;
v_scn := dbms_flashback.get_system_change_number;
dbms_output.put_line(a => 'SCN before the insert is : '||v_scn);
end;
/
```

The next step is to specify the redo log files that will be processed by Log Miner and their paths by using the *add_logfile* procedure:

```
--This query mount the command to add redo log files that will be processed
by Log Miner
select
    'exec dbms_logmnr.add_logfile(LogFileName => '''||member||''', options =>
dbms_logmnr.new);'
from
    v$logfile
where
    is_recovery_dest_file='no';

--Commands generated. Copy the output, select the lines that contain the
logfile numbers interested in analyzing, and then run the resulting script.
alter system switch logfile;

begin
dbms_logmnr.add_logfile(
    logfilename =>
'/u01/app/oracle/oradata/DBMS/onlinelog/o1_mf_1_5gfvrzvt_.log', options =>
dbms_logmnr.new);

dbms_logmnr.add_logfile(
    logfilename =>
'/u01/app/oracle/oradata/DBMS/onlinelog/o1_mf_2_5gfvs0p8_.log', options =>
dbms_logmnr.new);

dbms_logmnr.add_logfile(
    logfilename =>
'/u01/app/oracle/oradata/dbms/onlinelog/o1_mf_3_5gfvs2m0_.log', options =>
dbms_logmnr.new);
```

```
end;
/
```

Start the Log Miner using the *start_logmnr* procedure:

```
exec dbms_logmnr.start_logmnr(
    Options => dbms_logmnr.dict_from_online_catalog
              +dbms_logmnr.committed_data_only);
```

Now use the *build* procedure of the *dbms_logmnr_d* package to build the dictionary. This information is extracted to a flat file or to the redo log file.

```
--Extract the dictionary to a flat file
begin
dbms_logmnr_d.build(
    dictionary_filename => 'dicti_flat_file.ora',
    dictionary_location => '/u01/app/oracle/logmnr',
    options => dbms_logmnr_d.store_in_flat_file);
end;
/

--Or Extract the dictionary to redo log files
begin
dbms_logmnr_d.build(options => dbms_logmnr_d.store_in_redo_logs);
end;
/
```

If using redo log files, query the *v$archived_log* table to see which log archives contain an extracted dictionary:

```
select
    name
from
    v$archived_log
where
    dictionary_begin='yes';

select
    name
from
    v$archived_log
where
    dictionary_end='yes';
```

Check if the executed command is in the generated dictionary file by using a *grep* command:

```
[ora11g@dbms logmnr]$ pwd
/u01/app/oracle/logmnr
[ora11g@dbms logmnr]$ ls -la
total 23908
drwxr-xr-x  2 ora11g oinstall      4096 Jan  1 23:43 .
drwxrwxr-x 11 ora11g oinstall      4096 Jan  1 22:50 ..
```

Programs dbms_logmnr and dbms_logmnr_d

```
-rw-r--r--  1 ora11g oinstall 24442513 Jan  5 08:21 dicti_flat_file.ora
[ora11g@dbms logmnr]$ grep tab_logmnr dicti_flat_file.ora
insert_into obj$_table values
(28076,28082,46,'tab_logmnr',1,'',2,to_date('01/01/2010 23:41:08',
'MM/DD/YYYY HH24:MI:SS'),to_date('01/05/2010 08:12:09', 'MM/DD/YYYY
HH24:MI:SS'),to_date('01/01/2010 23:41:08', 'MM/DD/YYYY
HH24:MI:SS'),1,'','',0,,6,1,46,'','', );
[ora11g@dbms logmnr]$
```

Alternately, a simple query with *v$logmnr_contents* can be used and the *sql_undo* command can be ready to use at anytime.

```
select
   sql_redo,sql_undo
from
   sys.v_$logmnr_contents c
where
   c.table_name='tab_logmnr';
```

```
SQL_REDO                                                              SQL_UNDO
-------------------------------------------------------------------- ----------
insert into "pkg"."tab_logmnr"("col1","col2") values ('tt1','21');   delete from
"pkg"."tab_logmnr" where "col1" = 'tt1' and "col2" = '21' and rowid
= 'AAAG24AAEAAAxGeAAA';
```

The *undo* command was discovered. An error can be rolled back using this command any time it is desired.

Programs *dbms_logmnr_cdc_publish* and *dbms_logmnr_cdc_subscribe*

These change data capture (CDC) packages were created in order to minimize drudgery in a Data Warehouse system where the change data capture feature identifies changed data on tables. Only changed data is stored and is available for further analysis without any need for re-analyzing all tables. These packages have been renamed in Oracle 11g, respectively, *dbms_cdc_publish* and *dbms_logmnr_cdc_subscribe*.

Prior to the development of *dbms_cdc_publish* and *dbms_logmnr_cdc_subscribe*, the user had to extract database information into flat files manually. They were then loaded into another database for analysis. Now the process is done automatically and can capture changes resulting from DML commands such as *insert*, *update* and *delete*. The following example will show how to create a simple change data capture configuration.

How to Configure Change Data Capture

The *tab_cdc* table is used in this example. Here all *insert*, *update* and *delete* commands are executed. DBMS is the source database as well as the staging or destination database because synchronous mode is being used. There are two types of change data capture: synchronous and asynchronous. The first type captures data in real time while they are been inserted via triggers.

The asynchronous method uses online redo log files to read and get data after they have been committed. The synchronous method is being used in this example. There are three modes for capturing changes with the asynchronous method. More information on theese methods can be found in the Oracle Database Data Warehousing Guide documentation.

First, create the change table dependent on the original table:

🖫 Code 6.9 – dbms_logmnr_cdc.sql

```
conn sys@ora11g as sysdba

Connected to Oracle 11g Enterprise Edition Release 11.1.0.6.0
Connected as sysdba

--Creating test table
drop table pkg.tab_cdc;
create table pkg.tab_cdc_1 (
   id number,
   first_name varchar2(20),
      last_name varchar2(20))
tablespace tbs_data;
```

Next, designate both the publisher user (they will own the change table) and the subscriber user (they will be the one that can see data on change table).

```
--Create the publisher user
create user user_publisher identified by dbms;
grant
   create sequence,
   execute_catalog_role,
   select_catalog_role,
   create table,
   create session
to
   user_publisher;

grant execute on dbms_cdc_publish to user_publisher;
begin
dbms_streams_auth.grant_admin_privilege(
   grantee => 'user_publisher');
end;
```

```
/
grant dba to user_publisher;
grant create tablespace to user_publisher;
grant unlimited tablespace to user_publisher;
grant all on pkg.tab_cdc to user_publisher;

--Create subscriber user
create user user_subscriber identified by dbms;
grant create session to user_subscriber;
```

In order to use the change data capture feature, some database initialization parameters should be modified. In this example, only one parameter needs to be changed: *java_pool_size* should have a minimum value of 50000000 bytes.

```
--Your database should have the following initialization parameter value
when using Synchronous
alter system set java_pool_size=50000000 scope=both;
```

Create the change set that will capture changes from *sync_source*. This is the default source when using the synchronous method.

```
--Create the change set that will capture change from sync_source source
that is the default source when using Synchronous method
begin
dbms_logmnr_cdc_publish.create_change_set(
change_set_name => 'dbms_set_cdc_sync',
description => 'Change set test.',
change_source_name => 'sync_source');
end;
/
```

Now, create the change table using the *create_change_table* procedure.

```
--Now, create the change table using create_change_table procedure
conn user_publisher/dbms@dbms
begin
dbms_logmnr_cdc_publish.create_change_table(
   owner => 'user_publisher',
--Schema owner of change table
   change_table_name => 'tab_cdc_change',
--Change table name
   change_set_name => 'dbms_set_cdc_sync',
--Change set name
   source_schema => 'pkg',
--Table owner
   source_table => 'tab_cdc',
--Table source name
   column_type_list => 'id number, first_name varchar2(20), last_name
varchar2(20)',    --Columns to be monitored
   capture_values => 'both',
--Both is used to capture original and changed data. One row is create for
old value and another row is created for a new value on an Update operation
   rs_id => 'Y',
--Storage an operation capture order number
```

```
   row_id => 'N',
--Rowid number
   user_id => 'Y',
--User id
   timestamp => 'Y',
--Timestamp of the execution command
   object_id => 'N',
--Object id altered
   source_colmap => 'Y',
--
   target_colmap => 'Y',
   ddl_markers => 'N',
   options_string => NULL);
end;
/
```

In a case where this table has already been created, execute the *drop_change_table* procedure to drop it:

```
--Use drop_change_table procedure to drop a change table
begin
   dbms_logmnr_cdc_publish.drop_change_table(
      owner => 'pkg',
      change_table_name => 'tab_change_1',
      force_flag => 'Y');
end;
/
```

Now grant the *select* privilege to the subscriber user; this is the person who will view the changed data. After that, simulate some transactions on the source table. The changes on the change table will then be seen.

```
--Grant the select on change table to the subscriber
grant select on user_publisher.tab_cdc_change to user_subscriber;


--Doing some changes on source table and getting these new values on change
table
conn pkg/pkg@dbms
insert into tab_cdc values (1,'Paulo','Portugal');
insert into tab_cdc values (2,'John','Wayne');
insert into tab_cdc values (3,'Mike','Morgan');
insert into tab_cdc values (4,'Elber','Portugal');
commit;

conn user_subscriber/dbms@dbms
col id for a5
col first_name for a15
col last_name for a15
col operation$ for a2
select
   operation$,
   commit_timestamp$,
   id,
```

```
   first_name,
   last_name
from user_publisher.tab_cdc_change;
```

The next step is to create a subscription that will receive changed data to a view used by the subscriber user.

```
--Create a subscription
conn user_subscriber/dbms@dbms
begin
   dbms_logmnr_cdc_subscribe.create_subscription(
      change_set_name => 'dbms_set_cdc_sync',
      description => 'Change set example',
      subscription_name => 'subscription_dbms_1');
end;
/
```

Use the *subscribe* procedure to specify which columns will be incorporated. In this example, just the *first_name* and *last_name* columns will be seen by the subscriber.

```
begin
   dbms_logmnr_cdc_subscribe.subscribe(
      subscription_name => 'subscription_dbms_1',
      source_schema => 'pkg',
      source_table => 'tab_cdc',
      column_list => 'first_name, last_name',
      subscriber_view => 'tab_cdc_sub_view');
end;
/
```

Now use the *active_subscription* procedure so the subscription will be ready to receive changed data. After that, check the view created on this subscriber and make some changes to the source table logging in as the owner of the source table.

```
begin
   dbms_logmnr_cdc_subscribe.activate_subscription(
      subscription_name => 'subscription_dbms_1');
end;
/

--Check subscribe view and get the results
select
   first_name,
   last_name
from
   tab_cdc_sub_view;

conn pkg/pkg@dbms
insert into tab_cdc values (5,'Fred','Arley');
commit;
```

Call the *extended_window* procedure in order to retrieve the next available change data.

```
--Call the extended_window procedure in order to get the next available
change data
conn user_subscriber/dbms@dbms
begin
dbms_logmnr_cdc_subscribe.extend_window(
subscription_name => 'subscription_dbms_1');
end;
/

select
   first_name,
   last_name
from
   tab_cdc_sub_view;
```

If the data of this subscriber needs to be purged, execute the *purge_window* procedure. After that, check the view again to confirm that the view is empty.

```
--If you need to purge the data of this subscriber just execute the
purge_window procedure
begin
dbms_logmnr_cdc_subscribe.purge_window(
subscription_name => 'subscription_dbms_1');
end;
/


--Check the view again and notice that after executing purge_window
procedure the values were gone
select
   first_name,
   last_name
from
   tab_cdc_sub_view;
```

To drop the subscription, use the *drop_subscription* procedure.

```
begin
dbms_logmnr_cdc_subscribe.drop_subscription(
subscription_name => 'subscription_dbms_1');
end;
/
```

Here are some useful views for finding information about the change data capture configuration:

```
--Views used to obtain information about Change Data Capture
select * from all_change_sources;            --Display all change sources
select * from all_change_propagations;       --Display all change propagations
select * from all_change_propagation_sets;   --Display all change propagations sets
select * from all_change_sets;               --Display all change sets
select * from all_change_tables;             --Display all change tables
select * from dba_source_tables;             --Display all source tables
select * from dba_subscriptions;             --Display all subscriptions
select * from dba_subscribed_tables;         --Display all subscribed tables
select * from dba_subscribed_columns;        --Display all source tables subscribed columns
```

This example shows just one of the change data capture methods that can be used. Other scripts can be created using other methods, such as asynchronous hotlog, asynchronous distributed hotlog and asynchronous autolog publishing. Pay close attention to each pre-requisite configuration because each one will have different advised values for their initialization parameters as well as their own parameter values for each procedure of the *dbms_logmnr_cdc_subscribe* and *dbms_logmnr_cdc_publish* packages.

Package *dbms_repair*

Another approach for finding and correcting corrupted data on tables and indexes is the *dbms_repair* package. It is unnecessary to drop and recreate objects with this method; in some instances, it is counter-productive or not even possible. With the *dbms_repair* package, not only is it unnecessary to drop the object, the corrupted object may continued to be used while the repair operation is done.

Some limitations do exist when using this package and they are:

- Clusters are not supported with the *check_object* procedure

- LOB indexes and IOT are not supported

- Bitmap indexes or function-based indexes are not supported with the *dump_orphan_keys* procedure

- Keys with more than 3950 bytes are not supported with the *dump_orphan_keys* procedure

There are other ways of finding corrupted data including the *db_verify* utility, the *analyze table* command and *db_block_checking*. The initialization parameters *db_block_checking* and *db_block_checksum* will need to have a value of TRUE to check corrupted blocks before they are marked as corrupt. Two tables must first be created under the SYS schema before the *dbms_repair* utility can be used. Fortunately, a procedure in the package itself (*admin_tables*) creates these tables and eliminates the need to hunt for a script in *$ORACLE_HOME/rdbms/admin*.

```
dbms_repair.admin_tables (
    table_name in varchar2,
    table_type in binary_integer,
    action in binary_integer,
    tablespace in varchar2 default NULL);
```

Where parameters of this procedure means:

- *table_name:* The name of the table to be processed, as determined by the action

- *table_type:* Either *orphan_table* or *repair_table*

- *action*: Either *create_action*, *purge_action* or *drop_action*. When *create_action* is specified, the table is created in the SYS schema. *purge_action* deletes all rows in the table that apply to objects that no longer exist. *drop_action* drops the table.

- *tablespace*: The tablespace in which the newly created table will reside. This tablespace must already exist.

The following command is used to create the two tables needed for our test. The command is executed twice with different parameters, once for the repair table and once for the orphan table.

```
begin
dbms_repair.admin_tables(
table_name => 'repair_test',
table_type => dbms_repair.repair_table,
action => dbms_repair.create_action,
tablespace => 'scottwork'
);
end;

begin
dbms_repair.admin_tables(
table_name => 'orphan_test',
table_type => dbms_repair.orphan_table,
action => dbms_repair.create_action,
tablespace => 'scottwork'
);
end;
```

The two tables are now created. A description of the two tables reveals the following:

```
SQL> desc repair_test;

Name Null? Type
------------------------------------- -------- ---------------
object_id NOT NULL number
tablespace_id NOT NULL number
relative_file_id NOT NULL number
block_id NOT NULL number
corrupt_type NOT NULL number
schema_name NOT NULL varchar2(30)
object_name NOT NULL varchar2(30)
baseobject_name varchar2(30)
partition_name varchar2(30)
corrupt_description varchar2(2000)
repair_description varchar2(200)
marked_corrupt NOT NULL varchar2(10)
check_timestamp NOT NULL date
fix_timestamp date
reformat_timestamp date

SQL> desc orphan_test
```

```
Name Null? Type
----------------------------------------- -------- ---------------
schema_name NOT NULL varchar2(30)
index_name NOT NULL varchar2(30)
ipart_name varchar2(30)
index_id NOT NULL number
table_name NOT NULL varchar2(30)
part_name varchar2(30)
table_id NOT NULL number
keyrowid NOT NULL rowid
key NOT NULL rowid
dump_timestamp NOT NULL date
```

Repair tables will contain those objects that have corrupted blocks. Orphan tables, on the other hand, are used to contain corrupted nodes of indexes with no predecessor on the three structure of the index, hence the name.

In the next example, see how to repair corrupted data using the *dbms_repair* package.

How to Repair Corrupt Data Using *dbms_repair* Package

This example shows how to repair corrupted data using the *dbms_repair* package, thereby permitting the execution of DML commands on the corrupted table. First of all, it is necessary to create admin tables using the *admin_tables* procedure. Then check for tables that have the corrupted blocks.

🖫 Code 6.10 – dbms_repair.sql

```
conn sys@ora11g as sysdba

Connected to Oracle 11g Enterprise Edition Release 11.1.0.6.0
Connected as sysdba

--Creating admin tables
--Create repair table in tablespace tbs_data. The name must start with
repair_ prefix.

conn / as sysdba
begin
   dbms_repair.admin_tables(
      table_name => 'repair_tab',
      table_type => dbms_repair.repair_table,
      action => dbms_repair.create_action,
      tablespace => 'tbs_data');
end;
/
--Create orphan table in tablespace tbs_data. The name must start with
orphan_ prefix.
begin
   dbms_repair.admin_tables(
      table_name => 'orphan_tab',
      table_type => dbms_repair.orphan_table,
      action => dbms_repair.create_action,
```

```
          tablespace => 'tab_data');
end;
/
```

Make a backup of the table that will be used for this test. For this example, the table name is *locations*.

```
create tablespace
   tbs_corrupt
   datafile '/u01/app/oracle/oradata/dbms/datafile/tbs_corrupt.dbf' size
100M;

--drop table pkg.bkp_jobs;
create table
   pkg.bkp_locations tablespace tbs_corrupt as select * from pkg.locations;

create unique index
   pkg.idx_uni_location_id
on
   pkg.bkp_locations (location_id);
```

Make a full backup of the database. At the end, how to recover the corrupted block will appear.

```
RMAN> backup database plus archivelog;

Let's corrupt some data in this table. First, create a file with some
characters on /tmp named bad_file.dd. Insert any characters in it and save
prior to running the command below.

set heading off
set lines 113
select 'dd if=/tmp/bad_file.dd of=' || f.file_name || ' bs=8192 conv=notrunc
seek=' ||
        to_number(s.header_block + 1) || ' << EOF'
  from dba_segments s, dba_data_files f, dba_tables t
 where f.tablespace_name = t.tablespace_name
   and s.segment_name = t.table_name
   and t.table_name = 'bkp_jobs'
   and s.owner = t.owner
   and t.owner = 'pkg';
set heading on
```

Use the *dd* command (in Unix OS) generated by the query above to damage the disk and, consequently, damage the table.

```
[ora11g@dbms tmp]$ dd if=/tmp/bad_file.dd
of=/u01/app/oracle/oradata/DBMS/datafile/tbs_corrupt.dbf bs=8192
conv=notrunc seek=131 << EOF
> EOF

0+1 records in
0+1 records out
55 bytes (55 B) copied, 0.0313551 seconds, 1.8 kB/s
```

After damaging the disk, check the corruption using the *analyze table ... validate structure* command.

```
analyze table
   pkg.bkp_jobs
   validate structure;

--Clean blocks in buffer cache
alter system flush buffer_cache;

analyze table pkg.bkp_jobs validate structure;

*
ERROR at line 1:
ORA-01578: ORACLE data block corrupted (file # 10, block # 131)
ORA-01110: data file 10:
'/u01/app/oracle/oradata/dbms/datafile/tbs_corrupt.dbf'
```

If the *bkp_locations* table is attempted to be queried, an error similar to this will appear:

```
ORA-01578: Oracle data block corrupted (file #4, block # 44043)
ORA-01110: datafile 4: '/u01/app/oracle/oradata/dbms/dir_dest/userS01.dbf'
```

Next, use the *check_object* procedure to find which blocks were corrupted on the *bkp_locations* table.

```
--Find the corrupted blocks in object
set serveroutput on
declare v_corrupt_blocks_num int;
begin
v_corrupt_blocks_num :=0;
   dbms_repair.check_object(
      schema_name => 'pkg',
      object_name => 'bkp_locations',
      repair_table_name => 'repair_tab',
      corrupt_count => v_corrupt_blocks_num);
   dbms_output.put_line(a => 'Number of corrupt blocks in table is '||
v_corrupt_blocks_num);
end;
/
```

Mark the corrupt blocks if they are not yet marked by using the *fix_corrupt_blocks* procedure.

```
--Mark blocks as corrupt if they are not marked yet
declare v_fix_count int;
begin
v_fix_count   := 0;
   dbms_repair.fix_corrupt_blocks(
      schema_name => 'pkg',
      object_name => 'bkp_locations',
      object_type => dbms_repair.table_object,
      repair_table_name => 'repair_tab',
      fix_count=> v_fix_count);
```

```
    dbms_output.put_line(a => 'Num Fixed blocks: ' || to_char(v_fix_count));
end;
/
```

Now inform the database to permit users so they can execute DML operations on the object that has corrupt blocks using the *skip_corrupt_blocks* procedure.

```
--Now you can tell the database to permit users execute DML operations on
this
--object that have corrupt blocks using the skip_corrupt_blocks procedure
begin
    dbms_repair.skip_corrupt_blocks(
        schema_name => 'pkg',
        object_name => 'bkp_locations',
        object_type => dbms_repair.table_object,
        flags => dbms_repair.skip_flag);
end;
/
```

Try to query the corrupted table again. DML operations are now permitted, but the corrupted blocks are not visible. Therefore, the rows belonging to these blocks are not being seen, as shown below.

```
--Try to query the corrupted table again. DML operations is permitted now
but the blocks
--corrupted are not able to be seen so the rows belonging to this block are
not seing as you see below
--Note that DML operations are alowed
insert into
    pkg.bkp_locations
    values('10','DBA',10000,100000);

commit;

--Here you can now, see just new data not the corrupted data
select
    *
from pkg.bkp_locations;
```

Here, the table indexes should be checked to make sure that no point exists for a corrupt block in the table.

```
set serveroutput on
declare
  v_key_count int;
begin
  v_key_count := 0;
  dbms_repair.dump_orphan_keys (
    schema_name        => 'pkg',
    object_name        => 'idx_ini_job_id',
    object_type        => dbms_repair.index_object,
    repair_table_name  => 'repair_tab',
    orphan_table_name  => 'orphan_tab',
    key_count          => v_key_count);
```

```
   dbms_output.put_line('The number of orphan key counts is: ' ||
to_char(v_key_count));
end;
/
```

To see if the table has *skip_corrupt* enabled, check on the *dba_tables* view.

```
select
   table_name,
   skip_corrupt
from
   dba_tables
where table_name='bkp_locations';
```

In order to recover the corrupted block, execute the RMAN command:

```
RMAN> blockrecover datafile 4 block 131;
```

Finally, analyze the table once again to check if there are still any corrupt blocks. This example has shown how to repair and recover a corrupt block, thereby allowing the user to access the table normally while permitting the user to execute DML commands on the table.

Package *dbms_streams_tablespace_adm*

Despite being an Oracle Streams package, *dbms_streams_tablespace_adm* is included in this chapter as its main purpose is copying and moving tablespaces between databases. Before delving into examples of this package, highlight some of its concepts. The *dbms_streams_tablespace_adm* package provides different procedures for working with two types of tablespaces.

1. Simple self-contained tablespaces: This is a tablespace whose objects do not have any relationships to other objects outside the tablespace. For example, there are no foreign keys referencing objects in other tablespaces, no indexes in the tablespace are for tables outside of it, and no parts of a partitioned table in the tablespace are stored in other tablespaces.

2. Self-contained tablespace set: Very similar to the above, but instead of a single tablespace, it is a group composed of several tablespaces. All objects in the group may reference only other objects in the group. To check whether or not a tablespace is self-contained, use the *transport_set_check* procedure of the *dbms_tts* package, shown in the next example.

Here are the main procedures of this package:

- *attach_simple_tablespace*: Makes use of Data Pump in order to import a simple tablespace or a set when using the *attach_tablespaces* procedure. Once exported using this package or other methods like RMAN, Transport Tablespace or Data Pump export, the user must have the *imp_full_database* role set in order to make use of this procedure.

- *clone_simple_tablespace.* Used to clone a simple tablespace or a set if using the *clone_tablespace* procedure. It is mandatory that the tablespace being cloned is online before starting the process.

- *detach_simple_tablespace.* Used to disassociate the tablespace, or the set of tablespaces if using the *detach_tablespace* procedure, from the database. The user must have the *exp_full_database,drop_tablespace* role set in order to make use of this procedure.

- *pull_simple_tablespace.* Procedure used to copy a tablespace, or a set of tablespaces if using the *pull_tablespace* procedure, from a remote database and place it in the current database. The user must have the *exp_full_database, manage tablespace* or *alter tablespace* roles set to use this procedure.

A single example will be used to show the overall process of transporting a tablespace from one database to another using the *dbms_streams_tablespace_adm* package and RMAN.

Transport Tablespaces Between Databases Using RMAN and dbms_streams_tablespace_adm Package

For this example, the source database is named DBMS and the destination database is ORADB. First, create two tablespaces that will be transported from the DBMS database to the ORADB database. One table will be created in each tablespace.

Code 6.11 – dbms_streams_tablespace_adm.sql

```
conn sys@ora11g as sysdba

Connected to Oracle 11g Enterprise Edition Release 11.1.0.6.0
conn / as sysdba

create tablespace transp_1 datafile
'/u01/app/oracle/oradata/dbms/datafile/transp_1.dbf' size 100M;

create tablespace transp_2 datafile
'/u01/app/oracle/oradata/dbms/datafile/transp_2.dbf' size 100M;

create table
   pkg.test1
tablespace
   transp_1 as
select
   *
from
   dba_objects;
```

```
create table
   pkg.test2
tablespace
   transp_2 as
select
   *
from
   dba_objects;
```

Note that we create the user *pkg* in the destination database if it does not already exist. We also create the directory object where the datafiles will be exported:

```
--Create the user pkg on destination database
create user pkg identified by pkg;
grant connect,resource to pkg;

--Create directory object where datafiles will be exported
--On DBMS database (Source database) and on ORADB database (destination
database)
create directory transp_tbs_dir as '/u01/app/oracle/transp_tbs_dir';
grant read,write on directory transp_tbs_dir to system
```

The next step is to use the RMAN command that will prepare the tablespace set to be transported. Make sure a backup is available before executing this step. In summary, RMAN performs the following steps:

1. The auxiliary instance is created. This is where the restore and recovery is done.

2. A backup of the controlfile of the source database is restored and the auxiliary instance is mounted.

3. A proper backup of the tablespace is restored in the auxiliary instance.

4. RMAN performs the recovery at the specified point chosen by the *until* parameter.

5. The auxiliary instance is opened.

RMAN changes the tablespace mode to read-only and calls the Data Pump Export utility, which then exports the structure of objects belonging to the tablespaces. This is much faster than a traditional export as the data itself remains in the datafiles that will be copied. Finally, RMAN will shut down, dropping the auxiliary instance and its files.

```
--From RMAN command line you will execute the following script to check the
current scn or use another value as you want
select current_scn from v$database;
--Or use until time
--until time
"to_date('02 NOV 2007 14:37:00','DD MON YYYY hh24:mi:ss')";

--Where:
```

```
--Auxiliary destination is the temporary directory used by rman to mount
transport scripts using a temporary clone database.
--Datafiles from sys,sysaux and undo tablespaces, redo log files,control
files will be placed on this directory.
--Tablespace destination is the destination of datafiles that will be
transported and scripts needed by Data Pump utility.
export ORACLE_SID=dbms
rman target /
run {
transport tablespace 'transp_1',' transp _2'
auxiliary destination '/u01/app/oracle/ transp _tbs_dir'
tablespace destination '/u01/app/oracle/ transp _tbs_dir'
Datapump directory transp _tbs_dir
dump file 'transp_tbs.dmp'
import script 'transp_tbs.imp'
export log 'transport_tbs.log'
until scn 3054645;
}
```

Here is the output of the above script:

```
/*
   The following command may be used to import the tablespaces.
   Substitute values for <logon> and <directory>.
   impdp <logon> directory=<directory> dumpfile= 'transp_tbs.dmp'
transport_datafiles= /u01/app/oracle/transp_tbs_dir_source/transp_1.dbf,
/u01/app/oracle/transp_tbs_dir_source/transp_2.dbf
*/

----------------------------------------------------------------
-- Start of sample PL/SQL script for importing the tablespaces
----------------------------------------------------------------
-- creating directory objects
create directory streams$dirobj$1 as
'/u01/app/oracle/transp_tbs_dir_source/';
/* PL/SQL Script to import the exported tablespaces */
declare
  -- the datafiles
  tbs_files       dbms_streams_tablespace_adm.file_set;
  cvt_files       dbms_streams_tablespace_adm.file_set;
  -- the dumpfile to import
  dump_file       dbms_streams_tablespace_adm.file;
  dp_job_name     varchar2(30) := NULL;
  -- names of tablespaces that were imported
  ts_names        dbms_streams_tablespace_adm.tablespace_set;
begin
  -- dump file name and location
  dump_file.file_name :=  transp_tbs.dmp';
  dump_file.directory_object := 'trans_tbs_source';
  -- forming list of datafiles for import
  tbs_files( 1).file_name :=  'transp_1.dbf';
  tbs_files( 1).directory_object :=  'streams$dirobj$1';
  tbs_files( 2).file_name :=  'transp_2.dbf';
  tbs_files( 2).directory_object :=  'streams$dirobj$1';
  -- import tablespaces
  dbms_streams_tablespace_adm.attach_tablespaces(
    datapump_job_name     => dp_job_name,
    dump_file             => dump_file,
```

```
        tablespace_files        => tbs_files,
        converted_files         => cvt_files,
        tablespace_names        => ts_names);
    -- output names of imported tablespaces
    if ts_names is not NULL and ts_names.first is not NULL then
        for i in ts_names.first .. ts_names.last loop
            dbms_output.put_line('imported tablespace '|| ts_names(i));
        end loop;
    end if;
end;
/
-- dropping directory objects
drop directory streams$dirobj$1;
-----------------------------------------------------------------
-- End of sample PL/SQL script
-----------------------------------------------------------------
```

Note that two options for attaching the tablespace set into the destination database will be found. Choose the second option which has the package exemplified on this topic. The PL/SQL block makes use of the *dbms_streams_tablespace_adm* package. The next step is simply copying and pasting it into a SQL session on the destination database.

```
-- creating directory objects
create directory streams$dirobj$1 AS  '/u01/app/oracle/transp_tbs_dir/';
/* PL/SQL Script to import the exported tablespaces */
declare
    -- the datafiles
    tbs_files       dbms_streams_tablespace_adm.file_set;
    cvt_files       dbms_streams_tablespace_adm.file_set;
    -- the dumpfile to import
    dump_file       dbms_streams_tablespace_adm.file;
    dp_job_name     varchar2(30) := NULL;
    -- names of tablespaces that were imported
    ts_names        dbms_streams_tablespace_adm.tablespace_set;
begin
    -- dump file name and location
    dump_file.file_name :=  'transp_tbs.dmp';
    dump_file.directory_object := 'transp_tbs_dir';
    -- forming list of datafiles for import
    tbs_files( 1).file_name :=  'transp_1.dbf';
    tbs_files( 1).directory_object :=  'streams$dirobj$1';
    tbs_files( 2).file_name :=  'transp_2.dbf';
    tbs_files( 2).directory_object :=  'streams$dirobj$1';
    -- import tablespaces
    dbms_streams_tablespace_adm.attach_tablespaces(
        datapump_job_name       => dp_job_name,
        dump_file               => dump_file,
        tablespace_files        => tbs_files,
        converted_files         => cvt_files,
        tablespace_names        => ts_names);
    -- output names of imported tablespaces
    if ts_names is NOT NULL and ts_names.first is NOT NULL then
        FOR i IN ts_names.first .. ts_names.last loop
            dbms_output.put_line('imported tablespace '|| ts_names(i));
        end loop;
```

```
   end if;
end;
/
-- dropping directory objects
drop directory streams$dirobj$1;
```

Lastly, we check the newly attached tablespace and its objects:

```
select * from v$tablespace;

      TS# NAME                             INC BIG FLA ENC
---------- ----------------------------    --- --- --- ---
        0 system                           YES NO  YES
        1 sysaux                           YES NO  YES
        2 undotbs1                         YES NO  YES
        3 temp                             NO  NO  YES
        4 users                            YES NO  YES
        5 transp_1                         YES NO  YES
        6 transp_2                         YES NO  YES

select count(*) from pkg.test1;

  COUNT(*)
----------
     67491

select count(*) from pkg.test2;

  COUNT(*)
----------
     67492
```

This example has shown how to transport a tablespace between databases using RMAN together with the *dbms_streams_tablespace_adm* package. All other procedures of this package are used to clone, attach, detach and pull tablespaces in or between databases. The approach used in this example demonstrates the steps that can also be used with these other procedures.

Package *dbms_tdb*

RMAN provides a method for transporting databases between different platforms of the same endian formats using the *convert database* command. This package verifies that the source database has the same endian formats as the destination database. It also checks the state of the current database and its suitability for transport. The DBA role must be granted to the user executing the *dbms_tdb* package.

Some constants that exist with this package are:

- *skip_none*: If used, it checks all datafiles of database

- *skip_offline*: Skips all offline datafiles

- *skip_readonly*: Skips all read-only datafiles

A view named *v$db_transportable_platform* shows all platforms to which this database can be transported with this method. Here are two functions of this package:

1. *check_db*: Checks if the source database is ready to be transported by inspecting the endian format of the source and destination databases. It also checks that the current state of the source database is in read-only mode.

2. *check_external*: This function checks if the database has any external tables or bfiles that may need special attention when transporting the databases between platforms.

Here are some examples on how to use these functions:

Remember to check the possible conversion values of the source and destination database by using the *v$db_transportable_platform* view.

🖫 Code 6.12 – dbms_tdb.sql

```
conn sys@ora11g as sysdba

Connected to Oracle 11g Enterprise Edition Release 11.1.0.6.0
conn / as sysdba

select
    *
from
    v$db_transportable_platform;

PLATFORM_ID PLATFORM_NAME                          ENDIAN_FORMAT
----------- -------------------------------------- -------------
          7 Microsoft Windows IA (32-bit)          Little
         10 Linux IA (32-bit)                      Little
          5 HP Tru64 UNIX                          Little
         11 Linux IA (64-bit)                      Little
         15 HP Open VMS                            Little
          8 Microsoft Windows IA (64-bit)          Little
         13 Linux x86 64-bit                       Little
         12 Microsoft Windows x86 64-bit           Little
         17 Solaris Operating System (x86)         Little
         19 HP IA Open VMS                         Little
         20 Solaris Operating System (x86-64)      Little
         21 Apple Mac OS (x86-64)                  Little
```

Now execute the *check_db* function to get the results:

```
--Execute the check_db function
set serveroutput on
declare
    v_db_is_ok boolean;
    v_db_is_ok_1 boolean := TRUE;
    begin
    v_db_is_ok := dbms_tdb.check_db(
```

```
                  target_platform_name => 'Solaris Operating System (x86-
64)',
                  skip_option => dbms_tdb.skip_none);

   if  v_db_is_ok = v_db_is_ok_1 then
     dbms_output.put_line('Database Ready to be transported!' );
   else
     dbms_output.put_line('Database not Ready to be transported!' );
   end if;
 end;
/
```

```
Database is not open in read-only mode. Open the database in read-only mode
and retry.
Database not ready to be transported!
```

Next, execute the *check_external* function in order to list external objects that may exist.

```
--Execute the check_external function
set serveroutput on
declare
v_ext_exists boolean;
v_ext_exists_1 boolean;
begin
   v_ext_exists := dbms_tdb.check_external;
  if  v_ext_exists = v_ext_exists_1 then
    dbms_output.put_line('Database without external objects!' );
  else
    dbms_output.put_line('Database have external objects!' );
  end if;

end;
/
```

```
The following directories exist in the database:
sys.transp_tbs_dir, sys.transp_tbs_source, sys.transp_tbs_dest,
sys.transp_tbs, sys.logmnr_dir, sys.dir_dest, sys.dir_source, sys.exp_dbms,
sys.dbms_sqltune_dir, sys.xmldir, sys.data_pump_dir
Database have external objects!
```

The functions of the *dbms_tdb* package are easily executed; not to mention, very helpful in letting it be known if the conversion process is viable.

Package *dbms_tts*

One step in transporting tablespaces between databases processes is checking whether or not the tablespace is self-contained. This is accomplished with the *dbms_tts* package. If the tablespace transport set is not self-contained, all of its violations are inserted into a temporary table accessed by the *transport_set_violations* view. The user must have the *execute_catalog_role* privilege set to use this package.

Be aware that disabled referential constraints do not prevent a tablespace from being transported. Only enabled constraints violate the tablespace, and then only if they reference a table outside of the tablespace set that is being checked. This package has four procedures that are described here:

1. *downgrade*: Used to downgrade transportable tablespace related data

2. *transport_set_check*: Used to check if a tablespace set is transportable or not

3. *checkTablespace*: Checks if the tablespace is temporary and if it has any external objects that prevent it from being transported

4. *transport_char_set_check_msg*: Used to check if the character set is compatible for transport

How to Check if a Tablespace is Transportable

An example of each procedure will be used in the following code. They will show possible errors that may arise if the tablespace is not compatible or ready to be transported.

🖫 Code 6.13 – dbms_tdb.sql

```
conn sys@ora11g as sysdba

Connected to Oracle 11g Enterprise Edition Release 11.1.0.6.0
conn / as sysdba

--Get the name of tablespaces to be checked
select * from v$tablespace;

--Procedure to check if a tablespace is transportable or not
--Get the tablespace name and number values
set serveroutput on
declare
v_tbs_num number;
v_tbs_name varchar2(30);
begin
  dbms_tts.checkTablespace(a_tsname => '&v_tbs_name',a_ts_num =>
v_tbs_num,upcase => TRUE);

  select
    name into v_tbs_name
  from
    v$tablespace
  where
    ts#=v_tbs_num;

  dbms_output.put_line('The tablespace name is :'||v_tbs_name||' and number
is:'||v_tbs_num||'.');
end;
/
```

```
--Procedure to check if a tablespace set is transportable or not
set serveroutput on size 1000000
declare
   v_violations varchar2(2000);
cursor v_violations_cur is
select * from transport_set_violations;
begin
   dbms_tts.transport_set_check(
      ts_list => 'users, tbs_data',
      incl_constraints => TRUE,
      full_check => TRUE);
open v_violations_cur;
   if v_violations_cur%isopen then
      loop
         fetch v_violations_cur into v_violations;
         exit when v_violations_cur%notfound;
         dbms_output.put_line(
            a => 'Violations found: '||v_violations);
      end loop;
   end if;
close v_violations_cur;
end;
/

--Function to check if the char set is compatible or not
declare
v_error_msg varchar2(100);
begin

 if dbms_tts.transport_char_set_check(
      ts_list => 'users, tbs_data',
      target_db_char_set_name => 'WE8ISO8859P15',
      target_db_nchar_set_name => 'AL16UTF16',err_msg => v_error_msg) then
      dbms_output.put_line(a => 'Tablespace char set are OK!');
   else
      dbms_output.put_line(a => 'Tablespace char set are incompatible!');
   end if;
end;
/

--Procedure to check if the char set is compatible or not
set serveroutput on
begin
dbms_tts.transport_char_set_check_msg(
      ts_list => 'users, tbs_data',
      target_db_char_set_name => 'WE8ISO8859P15',
      target_db_nchar_set_name => 'AL16UTF16');
end;
/

set serveroutput on
begin
dbms_tts.transport_char_set_check_msg(
      ts_list => 'users, tbs_data',
      target_db_char_set_name => 'ZHS16GBK',
      target_db_nchar_set_name => 'AL16UTF16');
end;
/
```

Package dbms_tts

```
--Procedure to downgrade tablespace data if the actual database release
didn't support the transportable tablespace operation
exec dbms_tts.downgrade;
```

Summary

This chapter showed how and when to use almost all packages designed for backup and recovery purposes. In the next chapter, Oracle management and monitoring packages will be explained and demonstrated.

Oracle Management and Monitoring Packages

Nowadays, database administrators have an assortment of GUI tools to help them administer and monitor their databases. Yet none of these tools lets anyone know which command is being executed by the tool and all that is happening behind the scenes. This chapter will explain some of the more important packages that are used by these GUI tools; even some that have not been explored or incorporated into a GUI.

Oracle Enterprise Manager (OEM) Database Control and Grid Control, for instance, are great tools offered by Oracle for monitoring Oracle databases. Some packages give the user the option to generate scripts before executing them so they will know which command will be executed. Since this is not a common feature, the user often does not have the chance to become familiar with all scripts that may be internally executed.

I will now show some of the main packages and give examples so the reader will know how, when and why to use these packages.

Package *dbms_alert*

The *dbms_alert* package is created by executing the *catproc.sql* file and is owned by *sys*. Once granted the execute privilege to *dbms_alert*, it can be executed by any software component that can call a stored procedure including SQL*Plus, Java and Pro*C.

The *dbms_alert* package provides a mechanism for the database to notify a client, i.e. anything listening, of an event asynchronously which means that the application does not need to periodically check for the occurrence of events. With *dbms_alert*, when an event occurs, a notification is sent. Prior to *dbms_alert*, *dbms_alert* developers created a polling process that checked the status of something on the database, like a completed job, by looking for a table value that the process had just updated. The *dbms_alert* package renders such techniques obsolete and is one of the most useful monitoring packages.

The *dbms_alert* package is even more helpful when dealing with three-tier web applications: client, web server, and database. Web applications are stateless by nature, meaning that the web server processes a request and it is done. This means that there is no tethered connection like a user is accustomed to with SQL*Plus, Oracle Applications, or SAP R/3. The Oracle *dbms_alert* provides a way for the database to initiate contact with the web server, who in turn can notify clients attached to it.

Here is a practical example of how and when to use the *dbms_alert* package. Say a manager wants me to create a method that could automatically let them know when a salary has changed. This can be implemented by using the *dbms_alert* package as described below:

⊞ Code 7.1 – dbms_alert.sql

```
conn sys@ora11g as sysdba

Connected to Oracle 11g Enterprise Edition Release 11.1.0.6.0
conn / as sysdba

--Create the salary table
create table tab_salary (
emp_id number,
sal    number(8,2));
```

Create a trigger that will use the *signal* procedure to create alert signals when a transaction commits.

```
--Create a trigger that will use the signal procedure to create alert
signals when a transaction commits.
create or replace trigger trg_tab_salary
after insert or update
on tab_salary
for each row
declare
 v_message varchar2(1800);
begin
  if inserting then
    v_message := 'New Salary is: ' || :new.sal;
  else
    v_message := 'updated salary: ' || :old.sal;
  end if;
  dbms_alert.signal(name => 'salary_update_alert',message =>  v_message);
end trg_tab_salary;
/
```

Next, create the procedure that will monitor the changes made to the *salary* table.

```
--Create the procedure that will monitor the changes made on salary table
create or replace procedure proc_dbms_alert_msg is
 v_message  varchar2(1800);
 v_status pls_integer;
 v_name  varchar2(30) := 'salary_update_alert';
begin
  dbms_alert.register(name => v_name);
  dbms_alert.waitone(name => v_name,message =>  v_message,status =>
v_status,timeout => 10);
```

```
  if v_status = 0 then
  --You could send an email to the manager here if desired
     dbms_output.put_line(a => 'Signal received! Name:'||v_name||' '  ||
v_message || ' Status: ' || to_char(v_status));
  else
     dbms_output.put_line(a => 'Timeout occurred!' );
  end if;

end proc_dbms_alert_msg;
/
```

In one session, execute the created procedure. In another session, execute any command that will start the trigger generating an alert signal.

```
--Execute the monitoring procedure on one session
set serveroutput on
exec proc_dbms_alert_msg;

--Execute a command that inserts or updates salary table on another session
and go back to the first session to check messages created.
insert into
   tab_salary
values (1,500000);

insert into
   tab_salary
values (2,100000);

update tab_salary
set sal=sal*0.5
where emp_id=2;

commit;
```

Here is the output from the session executing the *monitoring* procedure:

```
SQL>
exec
 proc_dbms_alert_msg;

Signal received! Name:salary_update_alert Updated Salary: 100000 Status: 0
```

Many different methods that could be used to monitor and act on specific operations that are happening within the database can be created.

Package *dbms_auto_task_admin*

Oracle 11g introduces a new feature called Automated Maintenance Tasks (AMR) and AMR starts with some of the more common duties of a database administrator. Information gathered from the AWR repository is analyzed by Autotask and it then

---

builds the correct tasks to be executed in next maintenance window. These tasks might include:

- Optimizer statistics gathering

- Automatic Segment Advisor

- SQL Tuning Advisor

One way of changing the Autotask configuration is through the *dbms_auto_task_admin* package. Alternately, the Oracle Enterprise Manager (OEM) can be used. Some important views used to collect information through the Autotask configuration are explained here:

- *dba_autotask_task*: This view shows information about task execution time, current status, priority and historical data like last and best times

- *dba_autotask_window_clients*: This view displays information about current windows available in the database belonging to *maintenance_window_group*

- *dba_autotask_client_history*: View used to show historical information for each job execution

- *dba_autotask_operation*: View used to display operation information for each client, such as attributes and status

- *dba_autotask_job_history*: This view provides information about job runs after each execution

- *dba_autotask_client*: View used to display statistical data for each task for the last seven days. It also shows an evaluation for the last 30 days.

- *dba_autotask_window_history*: Shows historical information for each maintenance task window

The next example shows how to change the Autotask configuration as well as disable it if desired. If the Autotask feature needs to be disabled from the database, execute the *disable* procedure as follows:

🖫 Code 7.2 – dbms_auto_task_admin.sql

```
conn sys@ora11g as sysdba

Connected to Oracle 11g Enterprise Edition Release 11.1.0.6.0
conn / as sysdba

--check the actual status of your task
select
    autotask_status
from
    dba_autotask_window_clients;
--disable Autotask
exec dbms_auto_task_admin.disable;
```

```
--check the status again
select
   autotask_status
from
   dba_autotask_window_clients;

--enable autotask
exec dbms_auto_task_admin.enable;


--disable all taks for a client
set serveroutput on
declare
v_status_before varchar2(10);
v_status_after varchar2(10);
begin
select
   status into v_status_before
from
   dba_autotask_client
where
   client_name='sql tuning advisor';
dbms_output.put_line(a => 'client status before command:
'||v_status_before);
dbms_auto_task_admin.disable('sql tuning advisor',NULL,NULL);

select
   status into v_status_after
from
   dba_autotask_client
where
   client_name='sql tuning advisor';
dbms_output.put_line(a => 'client status after command: '||v_status_after);
end;
/
```

Next, the *get_p1_resources* procedure is used to return the percentage of resources allocated to each Autotask included in the High Priority Group.

```
--Get information the percent of resources used by each Autotask that is in
high priority group
declare
v_stats_group_pct number;
v_seq_group_pct number;
v_tune_group_pct number;
v_health_group_pct number;
begin
dbms_auto_task_admin.get_p1_resources(v_stats_group_pct,v_seq_group_pct,v_tu
ne_group_pct,v_health_group_pct);
dbms_output.put_line(a =>
   'Percentage of resources for Statistics Gathering:
'||v_stats_group_pct||chr(10)||
   'Percentage of resources for Space Management:
'||v_seq_group_pct||chr(10)||
   'Percentage of resources for SQL Tuning: '||v_tune_group_pct||chr(10)||
   'Percentage of resources for Health Checks: '||v_health_group_pct);
```

```
end;
/
```

If it is necessary to change resource consumption utilization, this can be done through the *set_p1_resources* procedure.

```
--If it is necessary to change resource consumption utilization, then it can
be done through set_p1_resources procedure
set serveroutput on
declare
v_stats_group_pct number;
v_seq_group_pct number;
v_tune_group_pct number;
v_health_group_pct number;
begin
v_stats_group_pct := 15;
v_seq_group_pct := 30;
v_tune_group_pct := 30;
v_health_group_pct := 25;

    dbms_auto_task_admin.set_p1_resources(
        stats_group_pct => v_stats_group_pct,
        seg_group_pct => v_seq_group_pct,
        tune_group_pct => v_tune_group_pct,
        health_group_pct => v_health_group_pct);
end;
/
```

Now, assume that I have a Real Applications Cluster (RAC) environment with three nodes and we want to spread tasks between them. The service names are *dbms1*, *dbms2* and *dbms2*:

```
col client_name for a35
col service_name for a15
select
    client_name,
    service_name
from
    dba_autotask_client;
--Get the service name that will be assossiated with client_name
select
    name
from
    dba_services;
--Make the association
begin
    dbms_auto_task_admin.set_client_service(
        client_name => 'sql tuning advisor',
        service_name => 'dbms');
end;
/
```

In order to get the attribute values of a certain client, use the *get_client_attributes* procedure.

```
--In order to get the attribute values of a certain client you can use
get_client_attributes procedure
--Get the client name
select
   client_name
from
   dba_autotask_client;

declare
v_service_name varchar2(20);
v_service_name_1 varchar2(20);
v_window        varchar2(20);
v_client_name   varchar2(30);
begin
   v_client_name := 'auto space advisor';
   dbms_auto_task_admin.get_client_attributes(
      client_name => v_client_name,
      service_name => v_service_name,
      window_group => v_window);

   select decode(v_service_name,NULL,'NULL') into v_service_name_1 from
dual;

   dbms_output.put_line(a =>
      ' Attributes for client '||v_client_name||chr(10)||
      ' - Service_Name is: '||v_service_name_1||chr(10)||
      ' - Window Group is: '||v_window);
end;
/
```

Make the association. If the client attribute values need to be changed, use the
set_attribute procedure as follows:

```
--If you need to change client attribute values then use set_attribute
procedure as follows:
--Get the client name and current attributes
select
   client_name ,attributes
from
   dba_autotask_client;
--Change some attribute values
begin
   dbms_auto_task_admin.set_attribute(
      client_name =>'auto space advisor' ,
      attribute_name =>'safe_to_kill' ,
      attribute_value =>'FALSE');
end;
/

begin
   dbms_auto_task_admin.set_attribute(
      client_name =>'auto space advisor' ,
      attribute_name =>'volatile' ,
      attribute_value =>'FALSE');
end;
/
```

```
--Get the results
select
    client_name ,attributes
from
    dba_autotask_client;
```

If the intent is to change the task priority of any client, operation and/or individual task level, use the *override_priority* procedure.

```
--To override the priority of auto space advisor client you can execute this
command below:
--Get the current value
select
    client_name,
    priority_override
from
    dba_autotask_client;

--Change the priority to urgent
begin
    dbms_auto_task_admin.override_priority(
        client_name => 'auto space advisor',
        priority => dbms_auto_task_admin.priority_urgent);
end;
/

--Get the new value
select
    client_name,
    priority_override
from
    dba_autotask_client;
```

Package *dbms_comparison*

One of the many features included in Oracle 11g is the *dbms_comparison* package. This important package was created to compare objects, schemas or data between databases or schemas.

Database objects that may be compared include tables, single-table views and/or materialized views. A table can also be compared with a materialized view.

Some organizations have environments that share database objects between multiple databases. This kind of replicated object is commonly used in Oracle Stream configurations. The *dbms_comparison* package can be used to compare objects; if there is any discrepancy, they can be re-synchronized.

Some prerequisites exist in order to use this package:

1. The source database must be an Oracle 11g Release 1 or later.

2. The destination database must be an Oracle database.

3. The character set must be the same.

Assume that we want to compare two tables between *dbms* and *oradb* databases named *tab_comparison_orig* and *tab_comparison_dest*. If any divergence is found, synchronize them and then check the data that must be equalized at the end of the process.

The first step is to create the tables to be compared and synchronized, and then insert some data on the source table.

🖫 Code 7.3 – dbms_comparison.sql

```
conn sys@ora11g as sysdba

Connected to Oracle 11g Enterprise Edition Release 11.1.0.6.0

conn / as sysdba

--Create table example on both databases (dbms and oradb)
--On source database (dbms)
create table tab_comparison_orig
(id number,
first_name varchar2(10),
last_name  varchar2(10));

alter table tab_comparison_orig
  add constraint pk_id primary key (id);


--On destination database (oradb)
create table tab_comparison_dest
(id number,
first_name varchar2(10),
last_name  varchar2(10));

alter table tab_comparison_dest
  add constraint pk_id primary key (id);

--Insert some data on first database
insert into tab_comparison_orig values (1,'Paulo','Portugal');
insert into tab_comparison_orig values (2,'Elber','Portugal');
insert into tab_comparison_orig values (3,'Joao','Alfredo');
commit;
```

By checking the current values of tables, note that the destination table is empty. Next, create the database link in the source database so it will point to the destination database.

```
--Values from local table
select
   *
from
```

```
    pkg.tab_comparison_orig;

--Values from remote table
select
    *
from
    pkg.tab_comparison_dest@oradb;


--Create the database link pointing to destination database
create database link ORADB
    connect to SYSTEM identified by manager
    using 'ORADB';
```

Now it is time to create the comparison by using the *create_comparison* procedure, thereby designating the object to be compared and their owners.

```
--Create the comparison
begin
    dbms_comparison.create_comparison(
        comparison_name => 'comp_dbms_test',
        schema_name => 'pkg',
        object_name => 'tab_comparison_orig',
        index_schema_name => 'pkg',
        index_name => 'pk_id',
        dblink_name => 'ORADB',
        remote_schema_name => 'pkg',
        remote_object_name => 'tab_comparison_dest',
        column_list => '*',
        scan_mode => dbms_comparison.cmp_scan_mode_full);
end;
/

--Check the comparison created
select
    owner,
    comparison_name
from
    dba_comparison;
```

Execute the *compare* function. It will check for any data divergence between the objects being compared.

```
--Run the compare function
set serveroutput on
declare
    v_scan_info dbms_comparison.comparison_type;
    v_compare_result boolean;
begin
    v_compare_result:= dbms_comparison.compare(
                        comparison_name => 'comp_dbms_test',
                        scan_info => v_scan_info,
                        perform_row_dif => TRUE);

    if v_compare_result = TRUE then
        dbms_output.put_line(a => 'Tables are synchronized!');
```

```
    else
        dbms_output.put_line(a => 'Warning! Data divergence
found!'||chr(10)||
                               'Scan id differences: '||v_scan_info.scan_id);
    end if;
end;
/
```

Now that the results of the comparison are obtained and different data values from source table to destination table have been found, we use the *converge* procedure to synchronize the objects so they become equalized.

```
--Values from local table
select
    *
from
    pkg.tab_comparison_orig;

--Values from remote table
select
    *
from
    pkg.tab_comparison_dest@oradb;

set serveroutput on
declare
v_scan_out dbms_comparison.comparison_type;
begin
    dbms_comparison.converge(
        comparison_name => 'comp_dbms_test',
        scan_id => 4,
        scan_info => v_scan_out,
        converge_options => dbms_comparison.cmp_converge_local_wins,
        perform_commit => true);
    dbms_output.put_line(a => 'converge scand ID is:'||v_scan_out.scan_id);
    dbms_output.put_line(a => 'local rows
updated:'||v_scan_out.loc_rows_merged);
    dbms_output.put_line(a => 'remote rows
updated:'||v_scan_out.rmt_rows_merged);
    dbms_output.put_line(a => 'local rows
deleted:'||v_scan_out.loc_rows_deleted);
    dbms_output.put_line(a => 'remote rows
deleted:'||v_scan_out.rmt_rows_deleted);
end;
/

------------------------------------------------------------------
Converge Scand ID is:4
Local rows updated:0
Remote rows updated:3
Local rows deleted:0
Remote rows deleted:0
```

Note that the *cmp_converge_local_wins* constant value is used to specify whether the column values of the local database replace the column values of the remote database, or vice versa.

Checking the values again will show identical results from both of the synchronized tables.

```
--Values from local table
select
   *
from
   pkg.tab_comparison_orig;

--Values from remote table
select
   *
from
   pkg.tab_comparison_dest@oradb;
```

In sum, the most useful views pertaining to comparisons include:

- *dba_comparison*: Displays information about all comparisons created in a database

- *dba_comparison_columns*: Displays information about table columns that belong to a comparison

- *dba_comparison_scan*: Each time the *compare* function is executed, a new scan id is created. This view displays information about all executed scans.

- *dba_comparison_scan_values*: Displays value details for all comparisons

- *dba_comparison_row_dif*: This view displays information about different data values for all comparisons

As we mentioned before, this package can be used with different objects and schemas. By using the above example, other comparisons can be created as needed.

Package *dbms_db_version*

One of the improvements that began with the Oracle 10g PL/SQL new compiler was Conditional Compilation. This feature allows the compiler to precisely choose which code needs to be compiled without wasting time with unnecessary compilations. One of the functions this feature provides is the ability to enable self-tracing code while in a development environment and to disable it when it goes to a production environment.

Despite the fact that this feature was introduced with Oracle 10g Release 2, it was first available in the earlier releases of Oracle Database 10.1.0.4 and Oracle 9.2.0.6 as a patchset. In Oracle 10g Release 2, it is active by default and cannot be disabled.

Rather than becoming a reference manual for the Conditional Compilation feature, we will turn attention to the focus of this topic: explaining how and when to use the *dbms_db_version* package introduced in this feature. This next example will show how simple it is to use the *dbms_db_version* to separate different codes to be executed on different database versions and releases. First, we check the existence of constants in the database version to make sure that the procedure used in this example will not reference an inexistent constant.

🖫 Code 7.4 – dbms_db_version.sql

```
conn sys@ora11g as sysdba

Connected to Oracle 11g Enterprise Edition Release 11.1.0.6.0
conn / as sysdba

--First, check the existence of constants in your database version first
select
    text
from
    dba_source
where
    name = 'dbms_db_version'
order by line;
```

The output from the query above should look like this:

```
TEXT
--------------------------------------------------------------------
      This code structure will protect any reference to the code
      for version 12. It also prevents the controlling package
      constant dbms_db_version.ver_le_11 from being referenced
      when the program is compiled under version 10. A similar
      observation applies to version 11. This scheme works even
      though the static constant ver_le_11 is not defined in
      version 10 database because conditional compilation protects
      the $elsif from evaluation if the dbms_db_version.ver_le_10 is
      TRUE.
  */
  ver_le_9_1     constant boolean := FALSE;
  ver_le_9_2     constant boolean := FALSE;
  ver_le_9       constant boolean := FALSE;
  ver_le_10_1    constant boolean := FALSE;
  ver_le_10_2    constant boolean := FALSE;
  ver_le_10      constant boolean := FALSE;
  ver_le_11_1    constant boolean := FALSE;
  ver_le_11_2    constant boolean := TRUE;
  ver_le_11      constant boolean := TRUE;

TEXT
--------------------------------------------------------------------
```

This procedure is used to check the database version and release. It lets the user know which code would be executed in each case.

```
--This procedure is used to check the database version and release and
indicate the user which code would be executed in each one
create or replace procedure test_dbms_version is
    v_constant
    $if $$XXX_DB = 0 $then
        number;
    $elsif $$xxx_db = 1 $then
        binary_float;
    $else
        $error 'Value of plsql_ccflags is not correct. Must be xxx_db: ' ||
$$xxx_db
        $end
    $end

  begin

  $if $$xxx_db = 0 $then
        dbms_output.put_line('Parameter plsql_ccflags set to ' || $$xxx_db);
        $if dbms_db_version.ver_le_9 $then
            dbms_output.put_line(
                a => 'Version older than 9i!');
        $elsif dbms_db_version.ver_le_9_1 $then
            dbms_output.put_line(
                a => 'Version older than 9i Release 1!');
        $elsif dbms_db_version.ver_le_9_2 $then
            dbms_output.put_line(
                a => 'Version older than 9i Release 2!');
        $elsif dbms_db_version.ver_le_10 $then
            dbms_output.put_line(
                a => 'Version older than 10g!');
        $elsif dbms_db_version.ver_le_10_1 $then
            dbms_output.put_line(
                a => 'Version older than 10g Release 1!');
        $elsif dbms_db_version.ver_le_10_2 $then
            dbms_output.put_line(
                a => 'Version older than 10g Release 2!');
        $elsif dbms_db_version.ver_le_11 $then
            dbms_output.put_line(
                a => 'Version older than 11g!');
        $elsif dbms_db_version.ver_le_11_1 $then
            dbms_output.put_line(
                a => 'Version older than 11g Release 1!');
        $else
            dbms_output.put_line(
                a => 'Version older than 11g Release 2!');
        $end
  $else
      dbms_output.put_line(
        a => 'Parameter plsql_ccflags not set to the correct value! ' ||
$$XXX_DB);
  $end

end test_dbms_version;
/
```

Now set the *plsql_ccflags* initialization parameter to the value 0, enabling the procedure to go through the right code block. Next, execute the procedure and check the results.

```
alter procedure test_dbms_version compile plsql_ccflags = 'xxx_db:0' reuse
settings
/

begin
   test_dbms_version();
end;
/

Parameter plsql_ccflags set to 0
Version older than 11g!
```

Finally, we change the value of the flag to one that will not fit the correct information for testing the procedure; note the different output.

```
alter procedure test_dbms_version compile plsql_ccflags = 'xxx_db:1' reuse
settings
/

begin
   test_dbms_version();
end;
/

Parameter plsql_ccflags not set to the correct value! 1
```

This example could have included some code with newer features that work only with newer database versions and releases and an older code. Without this feature, this may generate an error, a common occurrence in an environment with many databases of different versions and releases.

Package *dbms_ddl*

This package first became available with Oracle Database 7.3.4 and provides the execution of some DDL commands through PL/SQL statements. Some of these DDL commands can be executed directly in the database while others cannot. Given the varying range of these procedures and functions, we will briefly describe them here so the reader will know when and how to use them.

- *alter_compile*: Compiles the PL/SQL object specified.

- *alter_table_not_referenceable*: Similar to executing the command *alter table <owner>.<table_name> not referenceable for <affected_schema>*. This command will prevent an object table from being the default *referenceable* table for the affected schema.

- *alter_table_referenceable*: The inverse to the procedure above. This command will make an object table the default *referenceable* table for the affected schema.

- *create_wrapped*: This procedure does what the *wrap* utility does, but with higher efficiency. It gets the *create* or *replace* command of an object, creates the *wrap* command and executes it automatically.

- *is_trigger_fire_once*: Function returns a TRUE value if the trigger being analyzed is a fire once trigger. A fire once trigger is a trigger that fires at a user session in all but the following instances:

  - Changes made by the Streams *apply* process

  - Changes made by the Streams procedures *execute_error* and *execute_all_errors of dbms_apply_adm* package

  - Changes made by a Logical Standby apply process

- *set_trigger_firing_property*: Procedure used to set trigger properties such as *fire_once* being TRUE or FALSE and *apply_server_only* which makes the trigger fire only in a Streams *apply* process.

- *wrap*: Functions used to create wrapped objects. This is a more manual approach than using the *create_wrapper* procedure.

I will now demonstrate how each of these *dbms_ddl* objects are used.

Procedures used to compile objects have the same effect as using the command *alter object_type <owner>.<object_type> compile*.

Although deprecated in Oracle 10g Release 2, this procedure is still available although Oracle recommends using the DDL command instead.

These types include packages, functions and procedures.

⊟ Code 7.5 – dbms_ddl.sql

```
conn sys@ora11g as sysdba

Connected to Oracle 11g Enterprise Edition Release 11.1.0.6.0
conn / as sysdba

begin
dbms_ddl.alter_compile(type => 'procedure',schema => 'pkg',name =>
'test_proc',reuse_settings => FALSE);
end;
/
```

This shows how to make an *object-relational* table with and without a reference. For further information on referenced objects, look at Oracle Database Object-Relational Developer's Guide 11g Release 2.

```
--Get an OID number
select
    sys_op_guid()
from
    dual;

--Create the type
create type
    mytype_new oid '804E80234A068536E0400A0A710A0F84'
    as object (first_name varchar2(30));

--Create one main table
create table
    tab_ref_ref_new of
    mytype_new;

--Create the referenced table
create table
    tab_ref_new of
    mytype_new oid
    as tab_ref_ref_new;

--Insert some values
insert into
    tab_ref_new values ('Paulo Portugal');

commit;

insert into
    tab_ref_new
select
    first_name
from
    tab_ref_ref_new;

commit;

select
    *
from
    tab_ref_new;

select
    *
from
    tab_ref_ref_new;

--Set or unset the referenceable table
begin
dbms_ddl.alter_table_referenceable(table_name => 'tab_ref');
end;
/
```

```
begin
dbms_ddl.alter_table_not_referenceable(table_name => 'tab_ref');
end;
/
```

When using Oracle Streams, it is possible to not have a trigger fire if the table is being modified by an *apply* process.

```
--Create a test trigger
create or replace trigger trg_tab_test
  before insert on tab_streams_dest
  for each row
begin
  insert into tab_streams_dest (id,first_name) values (:new.id,
:new.first_name);

end trg_tab_test;

--Change the trigger to fire_once
begin
   dbms_ddl.set_trigger_firing_property(
      trig_owner => 'pkg',
      trig_name => 'trg_tab_test',
      fire_once => TRUE );
end;
/

--Check if trigger is fire_once or not using is_trigger_fire_once procedure
set serveroutput on
begin
  if (dbms_ddl.is_trigger_fire_once(
         trig_owner => 'pkg',
         trig_name =>  'trg_tab_test')) then
    dbms_output.put_line(a => 'Trigger is fire_once!');
  else
    dbms_output.put_line(a => 'Trigger is not fire_once');
  end if;
end;
/

--Change the trigger to not be fire_once
begin
   dbms_ddl.set_trigger_firing_property(
      trig_owner => 'pkg',
      trig_name => 'trg_tab_test',
      fire_once => FALSE );
end;
/
```

If there is a procedure that involves codes that must be hidden from prying eyes, the *wrap* utility is used. The next example will show how simple it is to implement.

```
wrap iname=input_file_name.sql oname=output_file_name.plb
```

Created with Oracle 10g, the *wrap* procedure acts like the *wrap* utility by reading the PL/SQL code and encoding it, showing only the wrapped code. In addition, a package named *create_wrapped* was also developed. The main difference with this function is that it creates the wrapped object after generating it.

Here are some examples of how to generate wrapped code using these functions and procedures. First, a package already created in an earlier example is wrapped using wrap function.

Code 7.6 – dbms_wrap.sql

```
conn sys@ora11g as sysdba

Connected to Oracle 11g Enterprise Edition Release 11.1.0.6.0
conn / as sysdba

set serveroutput on
declare
   v_pkg_spec   varchar2(32767);
   v_pkg_body   varchar2(32767);
   v_wrap_code  varchar2(32767);

begin
   v_pkg_spec := 'create or replace package test_wrap_dbms
           as
           procedure test_dbms_profiler_proc (n_obj in number);
           end test_wrap_dbms ;';

   v_pkg_body := 'create package body test_wrap_dbms as
        procedure test_dbms_profiler_proc (n_obj in number) is
        d_n_obj number;
        run_num_start number;
        run_num_stop number;
        begin
        --Start the profiling
        run_num_start:= dbms_profiler.start_profiler(run_comment => ''Start
pkg: ''||to_char(sysdate,''dd-Mon-RRRR hh:mi:ss''));
           select /*+ full(m) */
              count(*) into d_n_obj
           from
              test_dbms_monitor m
           where
              m.object_id=n_obj;
           dbms_output.put_line(''First statement. Number of objects with
object_id=''||n_obj||'' is ''||d_n_obj);
           select
              count(*) into d_n_obj
           from
              test_dbms_monitor m
           where m.object_id=n_obj;
           dbms_output.put_line(''Second statement. Number of objects with
object_id=''||n_obj||'' is ''||d_n_obj);
        run_num_stop:=dbms_profiler.stop_profiler;
        end test_dbms_profiler_proc;
        end test_wrap_dbms;';
```

```
  --Generate the package specification
    v_wrap_code := dbms_ddl.wrap(ddl => v_pkg_spec);
  --Show the wrapped code
    dbms_output.put_line(a => v_wrap_code);

  --Generate package body
    v_wrap_code := dbms_ddl.wrap(ddl => v_pkg_body);
   --Show the wrapped code
    dbms_output.put_line(a => v_wrap_code);

end;
/
```

The wrapped code is generated as follows:

```
create or replace package test_wrap_dbms wrapped
a000000
2e
abcd
abcd
abcd
abcd
abcd
abcd
abcd
abcd
abcd
abcd
abcd
abcd
abcd
abcd
9
88 a6
+Vu313EjOfwewXfVs+DLKyL90oUwg5m49TOf9b9cFqFi0fSWlvJW466hl2KLCWfhSq8WaKnK
qhfqnFDK6gIvsY/IMB9Jmo8wDnUTsND2L+Pu2A7uH7u7XWOPKbCPH/weXasa3vDgqQpPmaL2
MMgLplSdrCodpnv4qEY=

create package body test_wrap_dbms wrapped
a000000
2e
abcd
abcd
abcd
abcd
abcd
abcd
abcd
abcd
abcd
abcd
abcd
abcd
abcd
abcd
b
```

3da 213
JFYTocxLnaOJ84gOHT7Tbl7JaDwwg+23miCsfC/G/jSdBhmmeIGkatM/wwHmDIPThl6M5mYM
UAKfCAIkP0Sky8EzS1aYGqG7uRKxHkl5BpKZv0Dd76+ew9GNVyse6vd58r3RmAcDbInOFlo+
4UoEHzcfgmsL63zmoDHOcOA1NBfnf48hMy8NyjSJWwaJAGMbTG7oVH11cGhj5AdWobwUACGZ
UsFVuRHaUBP1d2DasX7bIvQLRq1XrnB8DeKOFG1YsmBMx2bkvgwuYeA32bOM9wFqzkssCXlL
BTEBOAzeVDwB6NQEGMhyOHowqd6r6cner3BoXhFOoRi+rVBffEks9SNRPmwIMj1EEFm4hb0C
vJGtgI5MH5XvVaOuFBXd3tAp0AVh7z6uCSIlDKKoYOh/YsUmZ+UN19nPZGCpmpcuh681FThO
8SCNRgtrnxeAjliMQg1VHoOp5t/O/8RF9MEsQuTLptnEBxAzwTYinREFvj8TFCk0DL0Vr7+q
uUARoVUaXNy5GfvGpjp2

SQL>

This shows that the wrapped code was generated, but the package was not created. The code is there to be executed when needed.

The difference between the *wrap* function and the *create_wrapped* procedure is that the latter executes the wrapped code to create the object, as shown in the next example.

```
set serveroutput on
declare
    v_pkg_spec   varchar2(32767);
    v_pkg_body   varchar2(32767);
    v_wrap_code  varchar2(32767);

begin
    v_pkg_spec := 'create or replace package pkg.test_wrap_dbms
            as
            procedure test_dbms_profiler_proc (n_obj in number);
            end test_wrap_dbms ;';

    v_pkg_body := 'create package body pkg.test_wrap_dbms as
        procedure test_dbms_profiler_proc (n_obj in number) is
        d_n_obj number;
        run_num_start number;
        run_num_stop number;
        begin
        --Start the profiling
        run_num_start:= dbms_profiler.start_profiler(run_comment => ''Start
pkg: ''||to_char(sysdate,''dd-Mon-RRRR hh:mi:ss''));
            select /*+ full(m) */
                count(*) into d_n_obj
            from
                test_dbms_monitor m
            where
                m.object_id=n_obj;
            dbms_output.put_line(''First statement. Number of objects with
object_id=''||n_obj||'' is ''||d_n_obj);
            select
                count(*) into d_n_obj
            from
                test_dbms_monitor m
            where m.object_id=n_obj;
            dbms_output.put_line(''Second statement. Number of objects with
object_id=''||n_obj||'' is ''||d_n_obj);
        run_num_stop:=dbms_profiler.stop_profiler;
        end test_dbms_profiler_proc;
```

```
        end test_wrap_dbms;';

   --Generate the package specification
     v_wrap_code := dbms_ddl.wrap(ddl => v_pkg_spec);
   --Show the wrapped code
     dbms_output.put_line(a => v_wrap_code);
   --Execute the package specification
     dbms_ddl.create_wrapped(v_pkg_spec);

   --Generate package body
     v_wrap_code := dbms_ddl.wrap(ddl => v_pkg_body);
   --Show the wrapped code
     dbms_output.put_line(a => v_wrap_code);
   --Execute the package body
    dbms_ddl.create_wrapped(v_pkg_body);

end;
/
```

If an attempt to view the code of this procedure is made, something like this will appear:

```
--Try to get the code and repair that it is wrapped
select
    s.text
from
    dba_source s
where
    s.owner='pkg'
and
    s.name='test_wrap_dbms';

TEXT
-------------------------------------------------------------------
package      test_wrap_dbms wrapped
a000000
2e
abcd
abcd
abcd
9
88 a6
+Vu313EjOfwewXfVs+DLKyL90oUwg5m49TOf9b9cFqFi0fSWlvJW466hl2KLCWfhSq8WaKnK
qhfqnFDK6gIvsY/IMB9Jmo8wDnUTsND2L+Pu2A7uH7u7XWOPKbCPH/weXasa3vDgqQpPmaL2
MMgLplSdrCodpnv4qEY=

package body     test_wrap_dbms wrapped
a000000
2e
abcd
abcd
b
3da 213
JFYTocxLna0J84gOHT7Tbl7JaDwwg+23miCsfC/G/jSdBhmmeIGkatM/wwHmDIPThl6M5mYM
UAKfCAIkP0Sky8EzS1aYGqG7uRKxHkl5BpKZv0Dd76+ew9GNVyse6vd58r3RmAcDbInOFlo+
4UoEHzcfgmsL63zmoDHOcOA1NBfnf48hMy8NyjSJWwaJAGMbTG7oVH11cGhj5AdWobwUACGZ
UsFVuRHaUBP1d2DasX7bIvQLRq1XrnB8DeKOFG1YsmBMx2bkvgwuYeA32bOM9wFqzkssCX1L
BTEBOAzeVDwB6NQEGMhyOHowqd6r6cner3BoXhFOoRi+rVBffEks9SNRPmwIMj1EEFm4hb0C
vJGtgI5MH5XvVaOuFBXd3tAp0AVh7z6uCSI1DKKoYOh/YsUmZ+UNl9nPZGCpmpcuh681FThO
8SCNRgtrnxeAjliMQg1VHoOp5t/O/8RF9MEsQuTLptnEBxAzwTYinREFvj8TFCk0DL0Vr7+q
uUARoVUaXNy5GfvGpjp2
```

Package *dbms_debug*

Debugging is an essential skill for all application developers including those who use SQL and PL/SQL. Oracle 10g ships with the *dbms_debug* package (first available on the 8.1.6. version). Its main purpose is to provide the debug functionality for developers and database administrators who need to track problems in a PL/SQL object.

There are many tools on the market designed to debug PL/SQL objects. All of them utilize this package when debugging. The *debug* process is accomplished with two database sessions; the first will run the PL/SQL code and the second will monitor the session which receives the *dbms_debug* commands.

We will now simulate a process that will debug a session while it is running and test some procedures of the *dbms_debug* package. Oracle usually calls the first session the target session and the monitoring session is the debug session. There are two ways to enable the debug package. By session:

```
alter session set plsql_debug = TRUE;
```

Or simply with a target object through the following command:

```
alter  [object_type] [object_name] compile debug |debug body;
```

Here, object types include procedures, functions, types, triggers and packages. This example can be found in MOSC Note: 221346.1

In the first session, create a table to be used with this example. Then enable the debug in this session by setting the *plsql_debug* session parameters to TRUE. Next, initialize the debug using the *initialize* function and the *debug_on* procedure.

🖫 Code 7.7 – dbms_debug.sql

```
conn sys@ora11g as sysdba

Connected to Oracle 11g Enterprise Edition Release 11.1.0.6.0
conn / as sysdba

--On first session create the example table and enable debug on this session
drop table tab_test_debug;
create table
   tab_test_debug as
select
   *
from
   pkg.departments;
```

```
alter session set plsql_debug=TRUE;

var x varchar2(50)
begin
   :v_ssid := dbms_debug.initialize();
   dbms_debug.debug_on();
end;
/
print v_ssid

begin
   update
      tab_test_debug
   set
      manager_id=manager_id+100;

   dbms_output.put_line(
      a => 'Number of rows updated: '||sql%rowcount);
end;
/
```

In the second session, execute the PL/SQL block below using the SSID shown in the first session. Watch the line comments in order to be aware of what is happening in each code segment.

```
--On second session execute the PL/SQL block below using the SSID showed on
first session
set serveroutput on
exec dbms_debug.attach_session('&ssid');

declare
    v_program_info dbms_debug.program_info;
    v_pieces binary_integer;
    v_runtime_info dbms_debug.runtime_info;
    v_bin_int binary_integer;
    v_ret binary_integer;
    v_source varchar2(2000);
    v_mask pls_integer := dbms_debug.info_getstackdepth +
    dbms_debug.info_getbreakpoint +
    dbms_debug.info_getlineinfo +
    dbms_debug.info_getoerinfo;
    v_break_next_line pls_integer := dbms_debug.break_next_line;

begin
   v_ret := dbms_debug.synchronize(run_info => v_runtime_info,info_requested
=> 0);

   if v_ret != dbms_debug.success then
      dbms_output.put_line(a => 'Failed to syncronize!');
   end if;

   if v_runtime_info.reason = dbms_debug.reason_interpreter_starting then
      dbms_output.put_line(a => 'Interpreter is starting!');
   end if;

   --Check if target session is running a procedure or not
   if dbms_debug.target_program_running then
```

```
        dbms_output.put_line(a => 'A procedure is running!');
    else
        dbms_output.put_line(a => 'No running procedure!');
    end if;
```

To set a break line, use the block below, passing the line that will be the break. In this example, the breakpoint will be pointing to line 1.

```
v_program_info.namespace := NULL;
    v_program_info.name := NULL;
    v_program_info.owner := NULL;
    v_program_info.dblink := NULL;
    v_ret := dbms_debug.set_breakpoint(
                program => v_program_info,
                line# => 1,
                breakpoint# => v_bin_int);

    if v_ret != dbms_debug.success then
        dbms_output.put_line(a => 'Setting breakpoint failed. Breakpoint on
('||v_ret||')');
    end if;

    v_ret := dbms_debug.continue(run_info => v_runtime_info,breakflags =>
0,info_requested => v_mask);

    if v_ret != dbms_debug.success then
        dbms_output.put_line(a => 'Failed!');
    end if;

    dbms_output.put_line(a => 'Line number is :'||v_runtime_info.line#);
```

Check to see if the program is still running or has been terminated.

```
--Check if the program has terminated
    if v_runtime_info.terminated = 1 then
        dbms_output.put_line(a => 'Program has terminated');
    end if;

    if v_runtime_info.reason != 3 then
        dbms_output.put_line(a => 'Program interrupted!!');
    end if;

    --Get the program name
    dbms_output.put_line(a => 'Program name is
'||v_runtime_info.program.name);

    --Find the indexed table where OER is
    if v_runtime_info.oer != 0 then
        dbms_output.put_line(a => 'Exception is
'||sqlerrm(v_runtime_info.oer));
    end if;

    -- Print the next line info
    v_ret := dbms_debug.continue(
                run_info => v_runtime_info,
                breakflags => v_break_next_line,
```

```
                      info_requested => v_mask);

        if v_ret != dbms_debug.success then
            dbms_output.put_line(a => 'Failed!');
        end if;
        --Line failed
        dbms_output.put_line(a => 'Failed line is :'||v_runtime_info.line#);

        -- Find the line of code we're now on

dbms_debug.show_source(v_runtime_info.line#,v_runtime_info.line#,1,0,v_sourc
e,4000,v_pieces);
        dbms_output.put_line(a => 'Source code is '||chr(10)||v_source);

        --Go to the end
        v_ret := dbms_debug.continue(run_info => v_runtime_info,breakflags =>
0,info_requested => 0);

        if v_ret != dbms_debug.success then
            dbms_output.put_line(a => 'Failed!');
        end if;
end;
/
```

Now the debug session can be turned off using the *debug_off* procedure as follows:

```
--Turn off the debug on second session

exec dbms_debug.debug_off;
```

Go to the second session and run the PL/SQL block below. This will use the *synchronize* function to wait for the next signaled event to be sent. Finally, use the *detach_session* procedure to stop debugging in the target session.

```
declare
    v_runtime_info dbms_debug.runtime_info;
    v_ret binary_integer;
begin
    v_ret := dbms_debug.synchronize(
                run_info => v_runtime_info,
                info_requested => 0);

    v_ret := dbms_debug.continue(
                run_info => v_runtime_info,
                breakflags => 0,
                info_requested => 0);
end;
/

exec dbms_debug.detach_session;
```

The procedures and functions of this package can be modified to accommodate a user's own debug packages or even code their own debugger.

Package *dbms_describe*

The most common use for the *dbms_describe* package is to allow the user to gather information about a PL/SQL object. The *dbms_describe* package contains a single procedure named *describe_procedure*.

Traditionally, prtofesisonals use GUI tools to gather information on PL/SQL objects but occasionally the tool will not be available, thereby requiring the use of the *dbms_describe* package to accomplish this task. An example of this is when an application is being coded that needs to access this information.

In the next example, see how to gather information on a PL/SQL object by using the *dbms_describe* package. First, create the procedure to be analyzed by the *dbms_describe* package. This procedure should contain a lot of data types in order to be a good example.

Code 7.8 – dbms_describe.sql

```
conn sys@ora11g as sysdba

Connected to Oracle 11g Enterprise Edition Release 11.1.0.6.0
conn / as sysdba

--First, create the procedure that will be analyzed with dbms_describe
package.
--This procedure should have a lot of data types to make a good example.

create or replace procedure test_dbms_describe (
            v_long              in      long,
            v_rowid             out     rowid,
            v_character         in      character,
            v_char              in      char,
            v_raw               out     raw,
            v_long_raw          in      long raw,
            v_varchar2          in      varchar2,
            v_varchar           out     varchar,
            v_binary_integer    in      binary_integer,
            v_pls_integer       in      pls_integer,
            v_real              in      real,
            v_boolean           in      boolean,
            v_natural           out     natural,
            v_number            in      number,
            v_integer           in      integer,
            v_int               in      int,
            v_string            in out  string,
            v_smallint          in      smallint,
            v_decimal           in      decimal,
            v_floa              in      float,
            v_numeric           in out  numeric) as

begin
dbms_output.put_line(a => 'Test dbms_describe package!');
```

```
end;
/
```

Now we create the package used to describe the procedure above. This package will collect all information from each parameter of the procedure being described.

```
--Now you can create the package that will be used to describe the procedure
created above.
--This package will get all information about each parameter of procedure
being described.

create or replace package test_describe_plsql as
    procedure describe_plsql_obj (name varchar2);
end test_describe_plsql;
/

create or replace package body test_describe_plsql as

  procedure v_print_value(v_value varchar2, v_int_size integer) is
    n integer;
  begin
    n := v_int_size - lengthb(v_value);
    if n < 0 then
      n := 0;
    end if;
    dbms_output.put(v_value);
    for i in 1..n loop
      dbms_output.put(' ');
    end loop;
  end v_print_value;

  procedure describe_plsql_obj (name varchar2) is

      v_overload      dbms_describe.number_table;
      v_position      dbms_describe.number_table;
      v_level         dbms_describe.number_table;
      v_argument_name      dbms_describe.varchar2_table;
      v_datatype           dbms_describe.number_table;
      v_default_value      dbms_describe.number_table;
      v_mode_type        dbms_describe.number_table;
      v_length        dbms_describe.number_table;
      v_precision     dbms_describe.number_table;
      v_scale         dbms_describe.number_table;
      v_radix         dbms_describe.number_table;
      v_spare         dbms_describe.number_table;
      v_index             integer := 0;

  begin
      dbms_describe.describe_procedure(
          object_name => name,
          reserved1 => NULL,
          reserved2 => NULL,
          overload => v_overload,
          position => v_position,
          level => v_level,
          argument_name => v_argument_name,
```

```
            datatype =>  v_datatype,
            default_value => v_default_value,
            in_out => v_mode_type,
            length => v_length,
            precision => v_precision,
            scale => v_scale,
            radix => v_radix,
            spare => v_spare,
            include_string_constraints => TRUE);

        dbms_output.put_line(a => '##############    ##########
#########  #####');
        dbms_output.put_line(a => 'Column Position    Column Name       Data
Type   Mode');
        dbms_output.put_line(a => '##############    ##########
#########  #####');

        loop
            v_index := v_index + 1;
            v_print_value(to_char(v_position(v_index)), 20);
            v_print_value(v_argument_name(v_index), 19);
            v_print_value(to_char(v_datatype(v_index)), 11);
            v_print_value(to_char(v_mode_type(v_index)), 5);
            dbms_output.new_line;
        end loop;
    exception
        when no_data_found then
            dbms_output.new_line;
            dbms_output.put_line('##################');
            dbms_output.put_line('No more data found!');
            dbms_output.put_line('##################');

    end describe_plsql_obj;
end test_describe_plsql;
/
```

Finally, execute the procedure *describe_plsql_obj*, setting the object name as the parameter to be described.

```
exec test_describe_plsql.describe_plsql_obj(
        name => 'test_dbms_describe');
```

Column Position	Column Name	Data Type	Mode
1	v_long	8	0
2	v_rowid	11	1
3	v_character	96	0
4	v_char	96	0
5	v_raw	23	1
6	v_long_raw	24	0
7	v_varchar2	1	0
8	v_varchar	1	1
9	v_binary_integer	3	0
10	v_pls_integer	3	0
11	v_real	2	0
12	v_boolean	252	0
13	v_natural	3	1
14	v_number	2	0

```
15                v_integer          2        0
16                v_int              2        0
17                v_string           1        2
18                v_smallint         2        0
19                v_decimal          2        0
20                v_floa             2        0
21                v_numeric          2        2
###################
No more data found!
###################
```

Each parameter of *test_dbms_procedure* will be described with their positions, names, data types and mode, i.e. *in* or *out* or *in out*.

Package *dbms_hm*

Oracle health checks are an integral task for the Oracle DBA and Oracle 11g has introduced a new service and software to assist in performing health checks. As of 11g, Oracle is offering two new health check offerings:

- A premium health check service

- A free health monitor using *dbms_hm*

I will now examine the free health monitor by using the *dbms_hm* package.

Health monitor runs the following checks:

- **DB structure integrity check:** This check verifies the integrity of database files and reports failures if these files are inaccessible, corrupt or inconsistent. If the database is in mount or open mode, this check examines the log files and data files listed in the control file. If the database is in nomount mode, only the control file is checked.

- **Data block integrity check:** This check detects disk image block corruptions such as checksum failures, head/tail mismatch, and logical inconsistencies within the block. Most corruptions can be repaired using block media recovery. Corrupted block information is also captured in the *v$database_block_corruption* view. This check does not detect inter-block or inter-segment corruption.

- **Redo integrity check:** This check scans the contents of the redo log for accessibility and corruption as well as the archive logs, if available. The redo integrity check reports failures such as archive log or redo corruption.

- **Undo segment integrity check:** This check finds logical undo corruptions. After locating an undo corruption, this check uses PMON and SMON to try to recover the corrupted transaction. If this recovery fails, then Health Monitor stores information about the corruption in *v$corrupt_xid_list*. Most undo corruptions can be resolved by forcing a commit.

- **Transaction integrity check:** This check is identical to the undo segment integrity check except that it checks only one specific transaction.

- **Dictionary integrity check:** This check examines the integrity of core dictionary objects, such as *tab$* and *col$*. It performs the following operations:

  - Verifies the contents of dictionary entries for each dictionary object.

  - Performs a cross-row level check which verifies that logical constraints on rows in the dictionary are enforced.

  - Performs an object relationship check which verifies that parent-child relationships between dictionary objects are enforced.

Next, we will show how to use the *dbms_hm* package to gather information about database health.

First, query *v$hm_check* to find out what kind of checks can be done when using the *run_check* procedure. Keep in mind that checks that are internal cannot be run manually; use the clause *where internal_check='N'*.

Code 7.9 – dbms_hm_check_datafiles.sql

```
conn sys@ora11g as sysdba

Connected to Oracle 11g Enterprise Edition Release 11.1.0.6.0
conn / as sysdba

set linesize 100
set pagesize 50
col name for a30
col description for a50
select
   name,
   description
from
   v$hm_check
--Use the clause below to get just checks that can be run manually
--where internal_check='N';
```

The query above will show the following output:

```
NAME                         DESCRIPTION
---------------------------- --------------------------------------------
DB Structure Integrity Check Checks integrity of all database files
CF Block Integrity Check     Checks integrity of a control file block
Data Block Integrity Check   Checks integrity of a data file block
Redo Integrity Check         Checks integrity of redo log content
Transaction Integrity Check  Checks a transaction for corruptions
Undo Segment Integrity Check Checks integrity of an undo segment
Dictionary Integrity Check   Checks dictionary integrity
ASM Allocation Check         Diagnose allocation failure
```

These are the available options that can be run on the database check. In this example, perform a check for corrupted blocks using DB structure integrity check.

Package dbms_hm

335

```
--Check the integrity of all datafiles
begin
   dbms_hm.run_check(
      check_name => 'DB Structure Integrity Check',
      run_name => 'Check_Datafiles_Integrity',timeout => 3600);
end;

--Find your run check  using v$hm_run table
select
   run_id,
   name,
   run_mode,
   status
from
   v$hm_run
where
   name='Check_Datafiles_Integrity';

--Get the run report using get_run_report function
select
   dbms_hm.get_run_report(
      run_name => 'Check_Datafiles_Integrity',
      report_type => 'text',
      report_level => 'detail')
from
   dual;
```

As can be seen from the report output, one datafile is offline and could not be checked.

```
DBMS_HM.GET_RUN_REPORT(RUN_NAME)
------------------------------------------------------------------
Basic Run Information
 Run Name                 : Check_Datafiles_Integrity
 Run Id                   : 1681
 Check Name               : DB Structure Integrity Check
 Mode                     : manual
 Status                   : completed
 Start Time               : 2010-03-07 10:14:57.322729 -03:00
 End Time                 : 2010-03-07 10:14:57.635814 -03:00
 Error Encountered        : 0
 Source Incident Id       : 0
 Number of Incidents Created  : 0

Input Paramters for the Run
Run Findings And Recommendations
 Finding
 Finding     : Offline Datafile
 Name
 Finding ID  : 1685
 Type        : failure
 Status      : open
 Priority    : high
 Message     : Datafile 9:

'/u01/app/oracle/oradata/dbms/datafile/o1_mf_tbs1_5j241oph_.dbf'
             is offline
```

```
Message      : Some objects in tablespace TBS1 might be unavailable
Finding
Finding Name  : Tablespace Offline
Finding ID    : 1688
Type          : failure
Status        : open
Priority      : high
Message       : Tablespace 9: 'TBS1' is offline
Message       : Some objects in tablespace TBS1 might be unavailable
```

Another useful reason for running the Health Check is to find information about a specific corrupted block. Run the data block integrity check to accomplish this. To find which parameters can be used within this check, run the following query:

🖫 Code 7.10 – dbms_hm_check_block.sql

```
conn sys@ora11g as sysdba

Connected to Oracle 11g Enterprise Edition Release 11.1.0.6.0
conn / as sysdba

--Get list of checks and their possible parameters
col parameter for a15
col description for a20
col "check name" for a30
select
   p.name "parameter",
   p.description "description",
   c.name "check name"
from
   v$hm_check_param p,
   v$hm_check c
where
   p.check_id = c.id
and
   c.name = 'data block integrity check';

Parameter        Description           Check Name
---------------  --------------------  ------------------------------
blc_df_num       file number           data bock integrity check
blc_bl_num       block number          data bock integrity check
```

Next, execute the *run_check* procedure using the data block integrity check, specifying a specific data block that is suspected to be corrupt.

```
--Check the data block integrity
begin
   dbms_hm.run_check(
      check_name => 'data block integrity check',
      run_name => 'check_data_block_44043',
      timeout => 3600,
      input_params =>'blc_df_num=4;blc_bl_num=44043' ); --where 4 is the
datafile number and 44043 is the block number
end;
/
```

Finally, run the query below using *get_run_report* to see the results.

```
--Get the report
select
   dbms_hm.get_run_report(
      run_name => 'check_data_block_44043',
      report_type => 'text',
      report_level => 'detail')
from
   dual;
```

The output is shown here:

```
DBMS_HM.GET_RUN_REPORT(RUN_NAME)
--------------------------------------------------------------------
Basic Run Information
 Run Name                   : check_data_block_44043
 Run Id                     : 1721
 Check Name                 : data block integrity check
 Mode                       : manual
 Status                     : completed
 Start Time                 : 2010-03-07 10:40:52.503527 -03:00
 End Time                   : 2010-03-07 10:40:53.316608 -03:00
 Error Encountered          : 0
 Source Incident Id         : 0
 Number of Incidents Created : 0

Input Paramters for the Run
 blc_df_num=4
 blc_bl_num=44043

Run Findings And Recommendations
 Finding
 Finding Name  : media block corruption
 Finding ID    : 1725
 Type          : failure
 Status        : open
 Priority      : high
 Message       : block 44043 in datafile 4:
                 '/u01/app/oracle/oradata/DBMS/dir_dest/userS01.dbf' is media
                 corrupt
 Message       : Object locations owned by pkg might be unavailable
```

Assume that an *ORA-00600* is being experienced in the database and need to check, among other things, the data dictionary integrity. The following commands will need to be run:

Code 7.11 – dbms_hm_data_dict_check.sql

```
conn sys@ora11g as sysdba

Connected to Oracle 11g Enterprise Edition Release 11.1.0.6.0
conn / as sysdba
```

```
--Check the data dictionary integrity
begin
   dbms_hm.run_check(
      check_name => 'dictionary integrity check',
      run_name => 'dictionary_check',timeout => 3600);
end;
/

--Get the report
select
   dbms_hm.get_run_report(
      run_name => 'dictionary_check',
      report_type => 'text',
      report_level => 'detail')
from
   dual;
```

The output shows that there is a problem with inconsistency in the database dictionary.

```
DBMS_HM.GET_RUN_REPORT(RUN_NAME)
-------------------------------------------------------------------
Basic Run Information
 Run Name                    : dictionary_check
 Run Id                      : 1741
 Check Name                  : dictionary integrity check
 Mode                        : manual
 Status                      : completed
 Start Time                  : 2010-03-07 10:48:13.605103 -03:00
 End Time                    : 2010-03-07 10:48:20.389336 -03:00
 Error Encountered           : 0
 Source Incident Id          : 0
 Number of Incidents Created : 0

Input Parameters for the Run
 table_name=all_core_tables
 check_mask=all

Run Findings And Recommendations
 Finding
 Finding Name  : dictionary inconsistency
 Finding ID    : 1742
 Type          : failure
 Status        : open
 Priority      : critical
 Message       : SQL dictionary health check: obj$.namespace 47 on object
OBJ$
                 failed
 Message       : Damaged rowid is AAAAASAABAAATP3AAD - description: Object
                 Name aq_job$_586 is referenced
```

Note that the problem is at *all_core_tables* . To fix this problem, open a Service Request with Oracle Support. There are other checks that can be performed with the *dbms_hm* package in which the previous example can be used as a reference point.

Package *dbms_java*

Java has been in existence for more than a decade and is one of the more powerful development languages. Oracle, for instance, has developed many tools utilizing Java.

Oracle 11g comes with a lot of improvements in the Java language such as having the best native Java compiles, supporting Content Repository API for Java, having scalable Java with the automatic creation of 100% native Java code and more.

The *dbms_java* package is available when Oracle JVM is installed, which has been supported since Oracle 8i. This package lets developers use Java to create, store and deploy code within Oracle databases. we will highlight some of the more common uses of the *dbms_java* package. Functions and procedures will be demonstrated, and a brief description will be noted about each command.

The first example grants *execute* privileges to all files located in the */bin* directory to the pkg user.

🖫 Code 7.12 – dbms_java.sql

```
conn sys@ora11g as sysdba

Connected to Oracle 11g Enterprise Edition Release 11.1.0.6.0
conn / as sysdba

--Grant permission to execute any command on /bin directory to pkg user
begin
    dbms_java.grant_permission(
        grantee => 'pkg',
        permission_type => 'java.io.FilePermission',
        permission_name => '/bin/*',
        permission_action => 'execute');
end;
/

--Check the permission granted by consulting dba_java_policy view
col "kind" for a8
col "grantee"  for a10
col "type" for a25
col "name" for a10
col "action" for a10
select
    kind "kind",
    grantee "grantee",
    type_name "type",
    name "name" ,
    action "action"
from
    dba_java_policy
where
    grantee='pkg';
```

```
Kind     Grantee    Type                            Name        Action
-------- ---------- ------------------------- ---------- ----------
grant    pkg        java.io.FilePermission    /bin/*      execute
```

To change any native compiler option for a user session, use the *set_native_compile_option* procedure followed by the *native_compile_options* function to get the results.

```
--Change a native compile option for user session
begin
   dbms_java.set_native_compiler_option(
      optionName => 'optimizerLoopPagedConversion',
      value => 'false');
end;
/

--Get current native compile options
select
   dbms_java.native_compiler_options
from
   dual;


--Compile a java class
--Find the java to be compiled
select
   owner,
   name,
   source
from
   dba_java_classes
where
   name like 'java/io/FilePermissionCollection';

--Compile it using compile_class function!
select
   dbms_java.compile_class(
      classname => 'java/io/FilePermissionCollection')
from
   dual;
```

In order to get the full name of a Java object, use the *longname* function as shown in the next example:

```
--Long object name
select
   dbms_java.longname (object_name)
from
   user_objects
where
   object_type ='java class'
and
   status = 'valid'
and object_name like '%DelegateInvocationH%';
```

With more than 100 procedures and functions, the *dbms_java* package cannot be fully covered in this book. Most of the procedures and functions are executed by GUI or other programs and the user usually will not need to run them manually. This being said, it is wise to have at least a basic understanding of it and be familiar with how they are working within the database.

Package *dbms_job*

Starting with Oracle 10g, the Oracle scheduler was greatly improved with the *dbms_scheduler* package. Replacing the *dbms_job* with *dbms_scheduler* offers additional features by adding the ability to tie jobs with specific user-type privileges and roles. Although *dbms_scheduler* is the recommended package for jobs after Oracle 10g, we will give an example using the *dbms_job* package here.

Jobs are created to execute a task at a specific time. These tasks may be scheduled to run periodically at a future time if preferred. The *dbms_job* package supports Oracle Real Applications Clusters, thereby allowing the user to choose in which instance the job will run. One example is sufficient to show the more important procedures of this package. This example will show how to create a job that will run a procedure for gathering statistics for a specified schema.

First, create a procedure called *dbms_job*. This procedure is used to gather statistics for a specified schema; in this case, *pkg* schema.

🖫 Code 7.13 – dbms_job.sql

```
conn sys@ora11g as sysdba

Connected to Oracle 11g Enterprise Edition Release 11.1.0.6.0
conn / as sysdba

create or replace procedure proc_analyze_schema (v_schema in varchar2)
is
begin
   dbms_stats.gather_schema_stats(
       ownname => v_schema,
       estimate_percent => 30,
       method_opt => 'for all columns size 1',
       degree => 4,
       cascade => TRUE,
       force => TRUE);
end;
/
```

Next, create the job using the *submit* procedure, informing which procedure to be executed, the interval between run times and the next time it will start to run. This job is scheduled to run on the 7th day of each month at 6:00 pm.

```
declare
   v_jobnum number;
begin
   dbms_job.submit(
      job => v_jobnum,
      what => 'proc_analyze_schema(''pkg'');',
      next_date =>to_date('07-03-2010 18:00','dd-mm-yyyy hh24:mi') ,
      interval => 'sysdate+to_char(last_day(sysdate),''DD'' )',
      no_parse => TRUE,
      instance => 1 ,
      force => TRUE);
   commit;
end;
/
```

Check to see if it is running by using the *dba_jobs_running* view. Also, check the job details with the *dba_jobs* view.

```
--Check if the job is running
select * from dba_jobs_running;

SID JOB   FAILURES LAST_DATE  LAST_SEC THIS_DATE  THIS_SEC  INSTANCE
--- ---   -------- ---------  -------- ---------  --------  --------

57  22                                 07/03/2010 18:03:31      1
--Check job details
col what for a40
select
   job "job number",
   next_date "first run",
   total_time "Last exec time",
   what "what"
from
   dba_jobs
where
   schema_user='pkg';

JOB Number First Run    Last exec time What
---------- -----------  -------------- -----------------------------
        22 07/03/2010               149 proc_analyze_schema('PKG');
```

To remove a job, simply get the job number from the *dba_jobs* view and execute the *remove* procedure as follows.

```
begin
   dbms_job.remove(job => 22);
   commit;
end;
/
```

To change any parameter of a job, use the *change* procedure. In this example, the interval date of job 23 is changed.

```
begin
dbms_job.change(
```

```
      job => 23,
      what => 'proc_analyze_schema(''pkg'');',
      next_date =>to_date('07-03-2010 18:00','dd-mm-yyyy hh24:mi') ,
      interval => 'sysdate+to_char( (sysdate),''DD'' )');
end;
/
```

If what the job is executing needs to be changed, use the *what* procedure. In this example, change the schema that will have statistics gathered.

```
begin
   dbms_job.what(
      job => 23,
      what => 'proc_analyze_schema(''scott'');');
   commit;
end;
/

select
   what
from
   dba_jobs
where
   job=23;

WHAT
-----------------------------------------
proc_analyze_schema('scott');
```

To change the next time that the job will run, use the *next_time* procedure.

```
begin
   dbms_job.next_date(
      job => 23,
      next_date => to_date('07-03-2010 19:00','dd-mm-yyyy hh24:mi'));
   commit;
end;
/
```

If there is a RAC environment and a job needs to be fixed so it always runs on the same instance, use the *instance* procedure shown below.

```
begin
   dbms_job.instance(job => 23,instance => 1,force => TRUE);
   commit;
end;
/
```

To change the interval time that the job is executed, use the *interval* procedure.

```
begin
   dbms_job.interval(job => 23,interval => 'sysdate+1+to_char(
(sysdate),''DD'' )');
   commit;
```

```
end;
/
```

It is not uncommon to visit a new client and find a huge number of jobs with nobody knowing what they are doing and if their execution is really necessary. For those jobs that might be unnecessary, change their status to that of a broken job to prevent them from running, and do the checks before dropping them. Once it is sure that they are not needed, they can be deleted. To do this, use the *broken* procedure:

```
--Broken the job begin
    dbms_job.broken(
        job => 23,
        broken => TRUE,
        next_date => sysdate+1);
    commit;
end;
/

--Check if the job is broken
select
    job,
    broken
from
    dba_jobs
where job=23;
```

If the job should be run immediately, just execute the *run* procedure. Use the force option to run a job, even if the *affinity* option is set for this job and the user is connected to another instance.

```
begin
    dbms_job.run(
        job => 23,
        force => TRUE); --Run even if the instance that the user is connected
is not the affinity
end;
/
```

This last procedure can be used if a job needs to be recreated. It shows the *execute* command for the specified job and the command to set the affinity instance for that job.

```
set serveroutput on
declare
    v_mycall varchar2(2000);
begin
    dbms_job.user_export(job => 23,mycall => v_mycall );
    dbms_output.put_line(a => v_mycall);
end;
/
```

```
dbms_job.isubmit(job=>23,what=>'proc_analyze_schema(''pkg'');',next_date=>to
_date('2010-03-08:18:51:43','YYYY-MM-
DD:HH24:MI:SS'),interval=>'sysdate+1+to_char(least(sysdate),''DD''
)',no_parse=>TRUE);
```

```
--Shows both options (execution and instance)
set serveroutput on
declare
   v_mycall varchar2(2000);
   v_myinst varchar2(2000);
begin
   dbms_job.user_export(job => 23,mycall => v_mycall,myinst => v_myinst );
   dbms_output.put_line(a => 'job execution command :'||v_mycall);
   dbms_output.put_line(a => 'set instance command  :'||v_myinst);
   commit;
end;
/

job execution command :
dbms_job.isubmit(
   job=>23,
   what=>'proc_analyze_schema(''pkg'');',
   next_date=>to_date('2010-03-08:18:51:43','YYYY-MM-DD:HH24:MI:SS'),
   interval=>'sysdate+1+to_char(least(sysdate),''DD'' )',
   no_parse=>TRUE);

set instance command  :
dbms_job.instance(
   job=>23,
   instance=>1,
   force=>TRUE);
```

This shows that the *dbms_job* package is very simple to use. Remember, it is not the recommended approach since *dbms_scheduler* was added in Oracle 10g.

Package *dbms_ldap*

A continuous feature throughout Oracle's history has been the Lightweight Directory Access Protocol (LDAP). LDAP is a powerful tool that is central to Oracle Platform Security. The *dbms_ldap* package used to manage LDAP using PL/SQL language can perform many operations in a directory server. The examples that follow will demonstrate some of the more common tasks.

If the *dbms_ldap* package cannot be located, execute the command below logged in as a *sys* user in order to create it.

Code 7.14 – dbms_ldap.sql

```
conn sys@ora11g as sysdba
```

```
Connected to Oracle 11g Enterprise Edition Release 11.1.0.6.0
conn / as sysdba

--Create dbms_ldap package
@?/rdbms/admin/catldap.sql
```

This will show how to perform a search that will return all entries within a specific LDAP base directory.

```
set serveroutput on size 10000

declare
  v_ldap_message      dbms_ldap.message;
  v_ldap_entry        dbms_ldap.message;
  v_returnval              pls_integer;
  v_session           dbms_ldap.session;
  v_str_collection    dbms_ldap.string_collection;
  v_entry_index       pls_integer;
  v_ber_element       dbms_ldap.ber_element;
  v_attr_index        pls_integer;
  v_dn                varchar2(256);
  v_attrib_name       varchar2(256);
  i                   pls_integer;
  v_info              dbms_ldap.string_collection ;
  v_ldap_base         varchar2(256);
  v_ldap_port         varchar2(256);
  v_ldap_host         varchar2(256);
  v_ldap_user         varchar2(256);
  v_ldap_passwd       varchar2(256);

begin

--Here you can set your LDAP Server information
  v_ldap_host  := 'dbms.f2c.com.br' ;
  v_ldap_port  := '389';
  v_ldap_user  := 'cn=orcladmin';
  v_ldap_passwd:= 'welcome';
  v_ldap_base  := 'dc=demo_entries';

  v_returnval          := -1;
  dbms_output.put(a => 'DBMS_LDAP Search Example ');
  dbms_output.put_line(a => 'to directory .. ');
  dbms_output.put_line(a => rpad('LDAP Host ',25,' ') || ': ' ||
v_ldap_host);
  dbms_output.put_line(a => rpad('LDAP Port ',25,' ') || ': ' ||
v_ldap_port);

  dbms_ldap.use_exception := TRUE;
```

First, the *init* function is used to establish a connection with the LDAP server. The information about this connection is then displayed.

```
  v_session := dbms_ldap.init(
                  hostname => v_ldap_host,
                  portnum => v_ldap_port);
```

```
--Displaying information about the connection
dbms_output.put_line(a => rpad('Ldap session ',25,' ')  || ': ' ||
rawtohex(substr(v_session,1,8)) ||'(returned from init)');

--Now, the simple_bind_s function will achieve the user authentication to
LDAP directory server.

v_returnval := dbms_ldap.simple_bind_s(
                ld => v_session,
                dn => v_ldap_user,
                passwd => v_ldap_passwd);

dbms_output.put_line(rpad('simple_bind_s Returns ',25,' ') || ': '||
to_char(v_returnval));
```

Here, the *search_s* function begins searching in a synchronized way for a value placed in the filter parameters.

```
v_str_collection(1) := '*'; -- retrieve all attributes
v_returnval := dbms_ldap.search_s(
            ld => v_session,
            base =>  v_ldap_base,
            scope =>
            dbms_ldap.scope_subtree,
            filter => 'sn~=PAULO',
            attrs => v_str_collection,
            attronly =>  0,
            res => v_ldap_message);


 dbms_output.put_line(rpad('Search returns: ',25,' ') || ': ' ||
to_char(v_returnval));
 dbms_output.put_line (rpad('LDAP message: ',25,' ')  || ': ' ||
rawtohex(substr(v_ldap_message,1,8))
                                                    ||' "value
returned from your search!" ');
```

Next, the *count_entries* function is used to count the number of entries in a result set. After this, the *first_entry* function is used to get the first entry of that set.

```
 v_returnval := dbms_ldap.count_entries(
                ld => v_session,
                msg => v_ldap_message);

dbms_output.put_line(rpad('Number of Entries ',25,' ') || ': '||
to_char(v_returnval));
 dbms_output.put_line('###########################################');

--Use first_entry function to return the first entry in a result set
v_ldap_entry := dbms_ldap.first_entry(ld => v_session,msg =>
v_ldap_message);
v_entry_index := 1;

-- Get attributes of each entry found
while v_ldap_entry is NOT NULL loop
   -- print the current entry
```

```
    v_dn := dbms_ldap.get_dn(
            ld => v_session,
            ldapentry => v_ldap_entry);

    dbms_output.put_line (a => '            dn: ' || v_dn);
    v_attrib_name := dbms_ldap.first_attribute(
                        ld => v_session,
                        ldapentry => v_ldap_entry,
                        ber_elem => v_ber_element);

    v_attr_index := 1;
    while v_attrib_name is NOT NULL loop
```

The *get_values* function is used to get all values associated with a given attribute. After that, the *next_attribute* function is used to return the next attribute of a given entry in the result set.

```
    v_info := dbms_ldap.get_values(
                ld => v_session,
                ldapentry => v_ldap_entry,
                attr => v_attrib_name);

    if v_info.count > 0 then
      for i in v_info.first..v_info.last loop
        dbms_output.put_line(a => '            ' || v_attrib_name || ' : '
||substr(v_info(i),1,200));
      end loop;
    end if;

--Function next_attribute return the next attribute of a given entry in the
result set
    v_attrib_name := dbms_ldap.next_attribute(
                        ld => v_session,
                        ldapentry => v_ldap_entry,
                        ber_elem => v_ber_element);
    v_attr_index := v_attr_index+1;
  end loop;
```

Functions like *ber_free* and *msgfree* are used to free memory allocated to the *ber_element* structure. This frees up the chain of messages returned by synchronous search functions.

```
  dbms_ldap.ber_free(
    ber => v_ber_element,
    freebuf =>  0);

  v_ldap_entry := dbms_ldap.next_entry(
                    ld => v_session,
                    msg => v_ldap_entry);

  dbms_output.put_line('=========================================');
  v_entry_index := v_entry_index+1;
end loop;
```

```
-- Use msgfree function to free up the chain of messages associated with
the message handle returned by synchronous search functions

v_returnval := dbms_ldap.msgfree(
                    lm => v_ldap_message);
```

Lastly, the *unbind_s* function is used to close an active LDAP session and finish this example.

```
v_returnval := dbms_ldap.unbind_s(
                    ld => v_session);

dbms_output.put_line(a => rpad('unbind_res Returns ',25,' ') || ': '
||to_char(v_returnval));

dbms_output.put_line(a => 'Session Closed. Operation terminated!');

exception
  when others then
    dbms_output.put_line(' Error code    : ' || to_char(sqlcode));
    dbms_output.put_line(' Error Message : ' || sqlerrm);
    dbms_output.put_line(' Exception encountered .. exiting');
end;
/
```

Many tasks that the *dbms_ldap* package uses to manage an LDAP Directory Server were touched upon in this chapter. Other tasks and their examples can be found in the *Application Developer's Guide for Oracle Identity Management 11g Release 1 (11.1.1) E10186-01* and *Oracle Internet Directory Application Developer's Guide Release 2.1.1 A86082-01*.

Package *dbms_metadata*

Once a table or index definition has been accepted into the Oracle data dictionary, it can be difficult to reconstruct the DDL syntax from the dictionary without the help of specialized packages. Oracle provides the *dbms_metadata* package to extract table and index DDL, and this section will explore how to use *dbms_metadata* to extract the DDL for any table or index. This capability is very useful when a table definition needs to be migrated into a new Oracle database.

Traditionally, the extraction of DDL is called punching the DDL. The term punching dates back to the days when the code would be punched onto Hollerith cards.

The *dbms_metadata* package has 11 procedures, each tailored to a specific function. This theme will focus on the use of the *get_ddl* procedure. Here are a few examples of useful procedures which with the reader should be well acquainted.

This first example shows how to generate DDL for all tables belonging to a *pkg* user whose name does not begin with *sys%*.

🖫 Code 7.15 – dbms_metadata.sql

```
conn sys@ora11g as sysdba

Connected to Oracle 11g Enterprise Edition Release 11.1.0.6.0
conn / as sysdba

--Generate DDL for all tables of pkg user except tables that have their name
initialized by 'sys%'.
set pagesize 0
set long 90000
set feedback off
set echo off

select
   dbms_metadata.get_ddl(object_type => 'table',name => u.table_name,)
from
   user_tables u
where
   table_name not like 'sys%';
```

Next, see how to generate DDL for all *pkg* user indexes except those whose table name start with *sys%*.

```
--Generate DDL for all indexes of pkg user except for those with a table
name beginning by 'sys%'
set pagesize 0
set long 90000
set feedback off
set echo off
select
   dbms_metadata.get_ddl(object_type => 'index',name => u.index_name)
from
user_indexes u where table_name not like 'sys%';
```

The next script shows the user a new and practical method to gather information about index size.

🖫 Code 7.16 – dbms_metadata_idx size.sql

```
conn sys@ora11g as sysdba

Connected to Oracle 11g Enterprise Edition Release 11.1.0.6.0
conn / as sysdba

create or replace procedure get_index_size(schema_name in varchar2,
                                           index_name  in varchar2) as
   v_schema    varchar2(30);
   v_index     varchar2(30);
   v_owner     varchar2(30);
   v_obj       varchar2(30);
   v_idx_size  varchar2(30);

begin
 v_schema := schema_name;
 v_index := index_name;
```

Package dbms_metadata

```
   for r in (select index_name
               from dba_indexes
             where index_name like v_index
               and owner = v_schema) loop
     execute immediate 'explain plan set statement_id=''' || r.index_name ||
                       ''' for ' ||
                       dbms_metadata.get_ddl('index', r.index_name);
   end loop;
   for s in (select object_owner,
                     object_name,
                     cast(extractvalue(xmltype(other_xml),
                                       '/other_xml/info[@type="index_size"]')
as
                          number) idx_size
               from plan_table p
             where id = 1) loop
     v_owner := s.object_owner;
     v_obj    := s.object_name;
     v_idx_size := s.idx_size;
     dbms_output.put_line(a => 'Index Owner :' || v_owner);
     dbms_output.put_line(a => 'Index Name :' || v_obj);
     dbms_output.put_line(a => 'Index Size :' || v_idx_size);
   end loop;

end;
```

When the procedure is executed, the following results are seen:

```
set serveroutput on
exec get_index_size(schema_name => 'pkg',index_name => 'D%');

Index Owner :pkg
Index Name :dept_id_pk
Index Size :1048576
Index Owner :pkg
Index Name :dept_location_ix
Index Size :1048576
Index Owner :pkg
Index Name :dt_column_prompts_tl_pk
Index Size :16777216
Index Owner :pkg
Index Name :dt_date_prompts_tl_pk
Index Size :2097152
Index Owner :pkg
Index Name :dt_title_prompts_tl_pk
Index Size :2097152
```

Some improvements have being added to the *dbms_metadata* package: *set_transform_param*, *set_remap_param*, *set_count* and *set_filter* as well as others that can be referenced through Oracle documentation. The next example will show how to delete, change and filter parameter options from the DDL generated with the *dbms_metadata* package.

🖫 Code 7.17 – dbms_metadata_set_options.sql

```
conn sys@ora11g as sysdba

Connected to Oracle 11g Enterprise Edition Release 11.1.0.6.0
conn / as sysdba

set long 1000000
set pagesize 0

--Generate normal DDL
select
  dbms_metadata.get_ddl(
      object_type => 'table',
      name => 'ame_help',
      schema => 'pkg') from dual;

--Generate XML DDL
select
   dbms_metadata.get_xml(
   object_type => 'table',
   name => 'ame_help',
   schema => 'pkg')
from
   dual;

--Here the set_transform_param function is used to omit the storage clause
from DDL being generated.
exec dbms_metadata.set_transform_param(
     transform_handle => dbms_metadata.session_transform,
     name => 'storage',
     value => FALSE);

--Execute the get_ddl again and observe that storage clause was dropped.
select
   dbms_metadata.get_ddl(
      object_type => 'table',
      name => 'ame_help')
from
   dual;

--To change the session to default mode execute the command below
exec dbms_metadata.set_transform_param(
       transform_handle => dbms_metadata.session_transform,
       name => 'default');

--Use function get_query to return queries used internally by fetch function
which returns metadata for object meeting the criteria of functions like
open, set_count and others.
set serveroutput on
set pagesize 0

declare
 v_handle number;
 v_query varchar2(20000);
begin
  select
    dbms_metadata.open(object_type => 'table')
    into v_handle
```

Package dbms_metadata

```
from
    dual;

select dbms_metadata.get_query(handle => v_handle)
into v_query
from dual;

dbms_output.put_line(v_query);
dbms_metadata.close(v_handle);
end;
/
```

As these examples have shown, DDL scripts can be easily created using the *dbms_metadata* package. There are other procedures and functions not demonstrated here that are available in order to create customized DDL scripts.

Package *dbms_output*

The *dbms_output* package was introduced in Oracle 7 to allow PL/SQL output from the SQL buffer in SQL*Plus to be written as standard output. The *dbms_output* package was intended primarily as a debugging tool and is now being replaced by Oracle's step-through debuggers and several third-party tools. Its functionality is similar to the *printf()* function in C.

The *dbms_output* package is often used to handle runtime errors. It can be used to isolate the location of an error so that a developer can correct the problem. It is a handy debugging tool when used properly to "salt" PL/SQL with display statements showing the contents of variables.

In order to use the *dbms_output* package for debugging, issue the *set serveroutput on* command at the beginning of the session. It is this command that enables information to be buffered. At the end of the program execution, a *dbms_output* procedure named *get_lines* will read the buffer and print its results. If a public synonym needs to be created and the *execute* privilege granted to public, run the *dbmsotpt.sql* script.

The *put* and *put_lines* procedures fill the buffer with information and the *get_line* and *get_lines* procedure read this information. Examples of *dbms_output* utilization are shown next. The *disable* procedure is used to disable calls to any other procedure on *dbms_output* package and clean up the buffer.

```
exec dbms_output.disable;
```

The *enable* procedure is used to enable calls to any procedure like *put_line*, *new_line* and *get_line(s)*. The buffer size is specified in bytes. To specify an unlimited value, use

NULL. Remember that this procedure is not necessary if the *set serveroutput* command has already been called.

```
exec dbms_output.enable(buffer_size => NULL);
```

The *get_line* procedure is used to redeem what is in the buffer and show it in one line. The status shows 0 if it completed successfully and 1 if no rows are returned. Here is an example:

🖫 Code 7.18 – dbms_output.sql

```
conn sys@ora11g as sysdba

Connected to Oracle 11g Enterprise Edition Release 11.1.0.6.0
conn / as sysdba

declare
    v_get_line varchar2(32767);
    v_test_lines dbms_output.chararr;
    v_status integer;
    v_numlines integer := 2;
begin
    v_test_lines(1) := 'Line number 1!';
    v_test_lines(2) := 'Line number 2!';
    v_test_lines(3) := 'Line number 3!';
    v_test_lines(4) := 'Line number 4!';
    v_test_lines(5) := 'Line number 5!';
    dbms_output.put_line(a => 'L1: '||v_test_lines(1));
    dbms_output.put_line(a => 'L2: '||v_test_lines(2));
    dbms_output.put_line(a => 'L3: '||v_test_lines(3));
    dbms_output.put_line(a => 'L4: '||v_test_lines(4));
    dbms_output.put_line(a => 'L5: '||v_test_lines(5));

    --Show 3 lines using get_lines procedure
--    dbms_output.get_lines(lines => v_test_lines,numlines => v_numlines);
    --Show 1 line using get_line procedure
    dbms_output.get_line(line => v_get_line,status => v_status);
    dbms_output.put_line(a => 'Buffer data is:'||v_get_line);
    dbms_output.put_line(a => 'Status is 0 if one or more lines is returned
and 1 if no more lines exists in buffer. Status is: '||v_status);
end;
/
```

The *get_lines* procedure is used to return multiple lines at the same time. This next example will see how the *put_line* procedure is used to put a line in the buffer.

```
declare
    v_get_line varchar2(32767);
    v_test_lines dbms_output.chararr;
    v_status integer;
    v_numlines integer := 10;
begin
    v_test_lines(1) := 'Line number 1!';
    v_test_lines(2) := 'Line number 2!';
    v_test_lines(3) := 'Line number 3!';
```

```
      v_test_lines(4) := 'Line number 4!';
      v_test_lines(5) := 'Line number 5!';
      --Here you put lines on buffer
      dbms_output.put_line(a => 'L1: '||v_test_lines(1));
      dbms_output.put_line(a => 'L2: '||v_test_lines(2));
      dbms_output.put_line(a => 'L3: '||v_test_lines(3));
      dbms_output.put_line(a => 'L4: '||v_test_lines(4));
      dbms_output.put_line(a => 'L5: '||v_test_lines(5));

    --Get all lines that are in buffer
    dbms_output.get_lines(lines => v_test_lines,numlines => v_numlines);
    --Show the number of lines founded in buffer
    dbms_output.put_line(a => 'Number of lines founded in buffer is:
'||v_numlines);

    --Show all lines
    for i in 1 .. v_numlines loop
       dbms_output.put_line(a => 'All lines founded in buffer:'|| '"
'||v_test_lines(i)||' "' );
    end loop;

end;
/
```

The *new_line* procedure is used to insert an end-of-line marker. This procedure will be used in the next example to display a list of all usernames in the database, separated by new lines.

```
set serveroutput on
declare
v_users dba_users.username%type;
cursor c_users is
select username from dba_users order by username;

begin
open c_users;
loop
fetch c_users into v_users;
exit when c_users%notfound;

  dbms_output.enable(9999999);
  dbms_output.new_line();
  dbms_output.put_line(a => 'username:'||v_users);
  dbms_output.new_line();
end loop;
end;
/
```

These were just some examples showing what the *dbms_output* package can do. In summary, it is used mostly as a handy basic tool to help database administrators and developers debug their programs. Beware that there are more advanced debugging tools available that offer more advanced functionality and can usually be a better choice for all debugging needs, but only the simpler ones.

Package *dbms_pipe*

To explain the purpose of the *dbms_pipe* package, take into account the use of pipe in UNIX, represented by the "|" symbol, which allows the communication between one command and another. In other words, *dbms_pipe* allows inter-session communication on the same database.

Alone, this is not a very reliable way of message exchange as all information generated by *dbms_pipe* is stored in the System Global Area (SGA). As with any information inside SGA, it will be lost if the database goes down. Thus, applications that use it often combine it with Streams, proprietary methods to store the data sent, or rely on it only for non-critical data exchange.

To increase the security of this communication, two pipes can be used; private pipes and public pipes. Public pipes are dropped when there is no more data in it. They may be created implicitly, i.e. created automatically when first referenced, or explicitly, i.e. using the *create_pipe* procedure. The script used for creating the *dbms_pipe* package is *dbms_pipe.sql* and can be found at *$ORACLE_HOME/rdbms/admin*.

The next example works as an alert to inform an application that data has changed and needs to have its cache refreshed in order to show the new information. Suppose that there is an *employees* table and wewant to know each time the salary field is updated. To accomplish this, create a trigger that sends updated information to a session that is waiting for these changes.

First of all, create the *employees* table that will be used in this example.

🖫 Code 7.19 – dbms_pipe.sql

```
conn sys@ora11g as sysdba

Connected to Oracle 11g Enterprise Edition Release 11.1.0.6.0
conn / as sysdba

--First, create employees example table.
create table
   employees(
      name varchar2(30),
      sal number);
```

Next, create the package that will contain procedures for sending and receiving information via the *dbms_pipe* package.

```
create or replace package test_dbms_pipe as
 procedure send_message_pipe (v_name in varchar2, v_sal in number, v_date in
date default sysdate);
 procedure receive_message_pipe;
 procedure log_message (v_name in out varchar2, v_sal in out number, v_date
```

```
in out date);
end test_dbms_pipe;
/

create or replace package body test_dbms_pipe as

  procedure send_message_pipe(v_name in varchar2,
                              v_sal  in number,
                              v_date in date) as
    v_status number;
  begin
    dbms_pipe.pack_message(v_name);
    dbms_pipe.pack_message(v_sal);
    dbms_pipe.pack_message(v_date);

    v_status := dbms_pipe.send_message('message from pipe!');
    if v_status != 0 then
      raise_application_error(-20001, '!! message pipe error !!');
    end if;
  end send_message_pipe;

  --Create the procedure that will receive the message pipe
  procedure receive_message_pipe as
    v_result integer;
    v_name_r varchar2(3000);
    v_sal_r  number;

  begin
    v_result := dbms_pipe.receive_message(
                   pipename => 'message from pipe!',
                   timeout  => 10);

    if v_result = 0 then
      while v_result = 0 loop
        v_result := dbms_pipe.receive_message(
                       pipename => 'message from pipe!',
                       timeout  => 10);
        dbms_pipe.unpack_message(v_name_r);
        dbms_pipe.unpack_message(v_sal_r);
        dbms_output.put_line('Full Name: ' || v_name_r);
        dbms_output.put_line('Salary: ' || v_sal_r);

      end loop;
    else
      if v_result = 1 then
        dbms_output.put_line('Timeout limit exceeded!');
      else
        raise_application_error(-20002,
                             'error receiving message pipe: ' ||
                             v_result);
      end if;
    end if;

  exception
    when others then
      null;


  end receive_message_pipe;
```

```
end test_dbms_pipe;
/
```

Create the trigger on the *employees* table that will use the *send_message_pipe* procedure to send information to the pipe. This information will be read with the *receive_message_pipe* procedure.

```
--Create the trigger on employee table using the send procedure
create or replace trigger employees_upd_sal
    after insert on employees
    for each row
declare
    v_date_1 date;
begin
    v_date_1 := sysdate;
    test_dbms_pipe.send_message_pipe(v_name => :new.name, v_sal => :new.sal);
exception
    when others then
      raise_application_error(num => -20002,
                              msg => 'error message on trigger!');
end employees_upd_sal;
/
```

Finally, we open two sessions. In one, we execute the *receive_message_pipe* procedure that has a timeout configured for 15 seconds. This session will wait for 15 seconds if no inserts are being made to the *employees* table. After the 15 seconds, the timeout finishes and shows the values that were inserted in the table.

```
--On the first session, execute the procedure receive_message that will
output values being inserted in employees table.
set serveroutput on
exec test_dbms_pipe.receive_message_pipe;


--On the second session execute some insert commands on employees table.
insert into employees (name,sal) values ('John Paul',300000);
insert into employees (name,sal) values ('Mike',350000);
insert into employees (name,sal) values ('Brad',400000);
commit;
```

After we wait for fifteen seconds; the results of the first session will then be displayed.

To check pipes created on the database, use the *v$db_pipes* view as shown:

```
col name for a30
select
    *
from
    v$db_pipes;


OWNERID    NAME                              TYPE     PIPE_SIZE
```

```
---------- ----------------------------- ------- ----------
      message from pipe!              public      4480
```

To recap, one session has communicated with the other via *send_message_pipe* and *receive_message_pipe* procedures which are inside the *dbms_pipe* package. This is commonly known as inter-session communication.

Package *dbms_preprocessor*

The beginning of this chapter examined how and when to use the *dbms_db_version* package. Now the *dbms_preprocessor* package will be covered, which can be used in conjunction with the *dbms_db_version* package when the user is evaluating the conditional compilation PL/SQL feature.

The sole purpose of the *dbms_preprocessor* package is to provide an interface for displaying the source text of a PL/SQL program unit after conditional compilation directives have been applied. This package has only one procedure and one function.

The *print_post_processed_source* is responsible for printing post-processed source text; the *get_post_processed_source* function is used to return post-processed source text.

In the example below, the *get_post_processed_source* function is used to show the post-processed source text from a procedure created earlier in this chapter.

🖫 Code 7.20 – dbms_preprocessor.sql

```
conn sys@ora11g as sysdba

Connected to Oracle 11g Enterprise Edition Release 11.1.0.6.0
conn / as sysdba

set serveroutput on
declare
 v_source_lines dbms_preprocessor.source_lines_t;
 v_line_num number;
begin
  v_source_lines := dbms_preprocessor.get_post_processed_source(object_type
=> 'procedure',schema_name => 'pkg',object_name => 'test_dbms_version');
  v_line_num := 0;
  for i in 1..v_source_lines.last
  loop
    dbms_output.enable(100000);
    dbms_output.put_line('Line number: '||v_line_num||' Post-processed
source text lines: '||v_source_lines(i));
    v_line_num := v_line_num + 1;
  end loop;
end;
/
```

The next example shows the *print_post_processed_source* procedure being used to get post-processed source text of a PL/SQL program unit informed as a parameter.

```
--First, change the plsql flag and check the results
alter procedure test_dbms_version compile plsql_ccflags = 'xxx_db:0' reuse
settings;
--Check the results
set serveroutput on
begin
  dbms_preprocessor.print_post_processed_source(
    object_type => 'procedure',
    schema_name =>  'sys',
    object_name => 'test_dbms_version');
end;
/
```

The output from above will be different from the output shown after the *plsql_ccflags* parameter is changed. This is because the conditional compilation feature is being used and has changed the process of the program unit by using different steps.

```
--Change the plsql flag again and note the changes
alter procedure test_dbms_version compile plsql_ccflags = 'xxx_db:1' reuse
settings;

set serveroutput on
begin
  dbms_preprocessor.print_post_processed_source(
    object_type => 'procedure',
    schema_name =>  'sys',
    object_name => 'test_dbms_version');
end;
/
```

Results before changing the *plsql_ccflags* are:

```
....

....
dbms_output.put_line(
         a => 'Parameter plsql_ccflags not set to the correct value! ' ||  ⊥
);
....

....
```

After the changes, these are the new lines:

```
.....

.....

.....
dbms_output.put_line('Parameter plsql_ccflags set to ' ||  0      );
.....

.....
```

In this example, the values were able to be changed and viewed by using the *dbms_preprocessor* package without the need of executing or opening all the code. This is an useful package, and it is frequently used when developing commercial applications that need to be easily customizable for different environments.

Package *dbms_resconfig*

Oracle Database 9i Release 2 first introduced the Oracle XML DB repository. XML-DB lets XML developers store their XML data in a database; thus, providing more security, high availability, scalability and manageability for XML-tagged data.

Unlike Oracle Databases, XML repositories store data in a hierarchical mechanism. Files are stored as if in a common file system architecture. This makes it possible to store different file types, both structured and unstructured. Each file included in the repository is stored in a table just like any other information in an Oracle database: XML files, Microsoft Office documents, HTML files, image files, and such.

Now that the Oracle XML repository has been covered, let's examine how *dbms_resconfig* will help. A resource name is given to each object created in an XML repository. Then the *dbms_resconfig* package is used to configure resources in an Oracle XML repository and associate it with a resource configuration file. The resource configuration file, e.g. an XML file, is where the parameters are defined.

A single resource configuration file may be applied to its own resource or can be applied to all resources in the repository. This is accomplished with the *addresconfig* and *addrepositoryresconfig* procedures in the *dbms_resconfig* package. The next example will highlight some of the main procedures of the *dbms_resconfig* package.

💾 Code 7.21 – dbms_resconfig.sql

```
conn sys@ora11g as sysdba

Connected to Oracle 11g Enterprise Edition Release 11.1.0.6.0
conn / as sysdba

--Use getRepositoryResConfigPaths to get the actual values configured on
database
set serveroutput on
declare
   v_repconfig_vals xdb$string_list_t :=
dbms_resconfig.getRepositoryResConfigPaths();
begin
    for i in 1..v_repconfig_vals.count loop
      dbms_output.put_line(v_repconfig_vals(i));
    end loop;
end;
/


--Use deleteResConfig procedure to delete a configuration at a given
position in the target resource's configuration list
```

```
begin
   dbms_resconfig.deleteResConfig(
      respath => '/sys/xs/scrc.xml',
      pos => 1);
end;
/

--Use appendResConfig procedure to append the resource configuration
specified to the target resource configuration list
begin
   dbms_resconfig.appendResConfig(
      respath => '/sys/xs/',
      rcpath => '/sys/xs/scrc.xml',
      appendOption => dbms_resconfig.append_recursive);
end;
/


--Use the addResConfig to add the resource configuration to the resource
configuration list. If the position is not specified it is added to the end
of the list
begin
   dbms_resconfig.addResConfig(
      respath => '/sys/xs/',
      rcpath => '/sys/xs/scrc.xml');
end;
/

--Using getRepositoryResConfig to show the resource configuration of
repository list based on position specified
set long 10000
select
   dbms_resconfig.getRepositoryResConfig(pos => 5)
from
   dual;

--Using getResConfig to get information about a particular resource. You can
also use resource_view view.
select
   dbms_resconfig.getResConfig(
      respath => '/sys/xs/',
      pos => 4)
from
   dual;
```

These were just some procedures and functions of *dbms_resconfig* and their utilization. To learn more about Oracle XML Repository, go to http://tahiti.oracle.com. Here, nearly all Oracle Documentation can be found, including the *Oracle XML Developer's Guide 11g Release 2 (11.2)*.

Package *dbms_resource_manager* and *dbms_resource manager_privs*

The *dbms_resource_manager* package is used to administer the new resource plan and consumer group options in Oracle. The package contains several procedures that are used to create, modify, drop and grant access to resource plans, groups, directives and pending areas. The invoker must have the *administer_resource_manager* system privilege to execute these procedures. The procedures to grant and revoke this privilege are in the package *dbms_resource_manager_privs*. The calling syntax for all of the *dbms_resource_manager* packages is as follows:

```
dbms_resource_manager.create_plan (
    plan                      in varchar2,
    comment                   in varchar2,
    cpu_mth                   in varchar2 default 'emphasis',
    max_active_sess_target_mth in varchar2 default
                                'max_active_sess_absolute',
    parallel_degree_limit_mth  in varchar2 default
                              'parallel_degree_limit_absolute');
```

Where:

- *plan*: The plan name

- *comment*: Any text comment that should be associated with the plan name

- *cpu_mth*: One of *emphasis* or *round-robin*

- *max_active_sess_target_mth*: Allocation method for max. active sessions

- *parallel_degree_limit_mth*: Allocation method for degree of parallelism

There is a new procedure called *set_group_mapping* within the Oracle *dbms_resource_manager* that helps to map the session attributes to a consumer group. These attributes are of two types: login attributes and runtime attributes. Here are some examples using the Oracle *dbms_resource_manager*.

Assume that my company has just bought new servers and storage devices for my production environment. weneed to make certain that the new I/O is large enough to hold my production database. Consider using the Oracle I/O calibration feature to gauge how the new environment will behave.

Though Oracle provides a tool named ORION (Oracle I/O Calibration Tool), the focus is on the new Oracle 11g Feature I/O Calibration for the next example. It is configured through the *dbms_resource_manager* package. The first step is to check that the database has *asynch* enabled. This is done by checking the *filesystemio_options* and *disk_asunch_io* initialization parameters as follows:

```
conn sys@ora11g as sysdba

Connected to Oracle 11g Enterprise Edition Release 11.1.0.6.0
conn / as sysdba

--Check if the database is async I/O enable
select
   name,
   value
from
   v$parameter
where
   name in ('filesystemio_options','disk_asynch_io');


select
   distinct(asynch_io)
from
   v$iostat_file
where
   filetype_name in('data file','temp file');

--Enable asynch if it is disable using commands below
alter system set disk_asynch_io=true scope=both;
alter system set filesystemio_options=setall scope=both;
```

Next, execute the *calibrate_io* procedure, entering the number of disks that are there and the maximum latency desired. Check the calibration status by querying the *v$io_calibration_status* view.

```
set serveroutput on
declare
v_io    binary_integer;
v_mbps binary_integer;
v_latency binary_integer;
begin
   dbms_resource_manager.calibrate_io(
      num_physical_disks => 12,
      max_latency => 20,
      max_iops => v_io,
      max_mbps => v_mbps,
      actual_latency => v_latency);

   dbms_output.put_line(a => 'I/Os per second: '||v_io);
   dbms_output.put_line(a => 'MBs per second: '||v_mbps);
   dbms_output.put_line(a => 'Latency: '||v_latency);
end;
/

I/Os per second: 30
MBs per second: 26
Latency: 32
```

Now we query *dba_rsrc_io_calibrate* to get results indicating the maximum number of data block read requests that can be sustained per second (*max_iops*), maximum megabytes per second of maximum-sized read requests that can be sustained (*max_mbps*), maximum megabytes per second of large I/O requests that can be sustained by a single process (*max_pmbps*) and finally, latency for data-block read requests (*latency*).

```
select
   max_iops,
   max_mbps,
   max_pmbps,
   latency
from
   dba_rsrc_io_calibrate;

  MAX_IOPS   MAX_MBPS  MAX_PMBPS    LATENCY
---------- ---------- ---------- ----------
        67         24         24         28
```

Here are some rules and tips concerning Oracle Calibration:

- Only one calibration session can be executed at a time.

- The user needs to have *sysdba* privilege.

- If this procedure is being executed in a RAC environment, the workload is executed simultaneously for all instances.

- In order to check the latency, the *timed_statistics* initialization parameter must be set as TRUE.

Here are some useful I/O views:

- *v$iostat_function*: Components that use I/O are grouped by their functionality

- *v$iostat_consumer_group*: When Resource Manager is enabled, I/O statistics are gathered for all consumer groups which make up the current resource plan

- *v$iostat_file*: I/O statistics are gathered for individual files

- *v$iostat_network*: Gathers network statistics that may have something in common with I/O accessing files on a remote database

Here is a practical example that can be used to manage the resources of a database. We will specify certain limits at the user level, such as idle connection time, CPU utilization, parallel utilization, active sessions, query execution time limit (based on the optimization values), undo utilization and even I/O utilization for Oracle 11g.

In this simulation, assume that a resource plan named *dbms_plan* needs to be created. *dbms_plan* will have three groups named *grp_normal*, *grp_medium* and *grp_high*. These groups will have to follow these rules:

```
grp_normal:
CPU: 20%
active sessions: 10
parallelism: 4
idle time: 60 seconds
I/O (MB): 1GB
Undo space: 500MB
Query Execution Time: 10 min
grp_medium
CPU: 30%
active sessions: 20
parallelism: 8
idle time: 300 seconds
I/O (MB): 5GB
Undo space: 1GB
Query Execution Time: 120 min
grp_high
CPU: 45%
active sessions: 30
parallelism: 16
idle time: 600 seconds
I/O (MB): 10GB
Undo space: 5GB
Query Execution Time: 600 min
```

Now that the rules needed are given, let's begin the example. First of all, let's grant the *administer_resource_manager* privilege to the user that will be using the resource manager.

🖫 Code 7.23 – dbms_rerource_manager_plan.sql

```
conn sys@ora11g as sysdba

Connected to Oracle 11g Enterprise Edition Release 11.1.0.6.0
conn / as sysdba

exec dbms_resource_manager_privs.grant_system_privilege(
        grantee_name => 'pkg',
        privilege_name => 'administer_resource_manager',
        admin_option => TRUE);


--Now connect using pkg user
conn pkg@dbms

--Create some test users
create user user_1 identified by 123 default tablespace users;
create user user_2 identified by 123 default tablespace users;
create user user_3 identified by 123 default tablespace users;
```

The *create_pending_area* procedure must be executed at the beginning of the process because it is responsible for creating the pending area where changes will be made. First clear, and then create the pending area. Next, create the consumer groups with their comments.

```
begin
   dbms_resource_manager.clear_pending_area();
   dbms_resource_manager.create_pending_area();
   dbms_resource_manager.create_consumer_group(
      consumer_group => 'grp_normal',
      comment => 'Consumer with normal priority.',
      cpu_mth => 'round-robin');

   dbms_resource_manager.create_consumer_group(
      consumer_group => 'grp_medium',
      comment => 'Consumer with medium priority.',
      cpu_mth => 'round-robin');

   dbms_resource_manager.create_consumer_group(
      consumer_group => 'grp_high',
      comment => 'Consumer with high priority.',
      cpu_mth => 'round-robin');

   dbms_resource_manager.submit_pending_area;

end;
/
```

Confirm that the consumer groups were created by using the *dba_rsrc_consumer_groups*
view.

```
select
   consumer_group
from
   dba_rsrc_consumer_groups
where
   consumer_group like 'grp%';
```

Now create the plans that will limit the resource types for each group created. Note
that each group will have their limit values set according to the plan specified at the
beginning of this example.

```
declare
   spfilevalue varchar2(1000);
   scopeValue  varchar2(10) := 'memory';
   planName    varchar2(100) := 'dbms_plan';
begin
   dbms_resource_manager.clear_pending_area();
   dbms_resource_manager.create_pending_area();
   dbms_resource_manager.create_plan(plan    => 'dbms_plan',
                                     comment => 'Oracle dbms book');
   dbms_resource_manager.create_plan_directive(
      plan                   => 'dbms_plan',
      group_or_subplan       => 'grp_high',
      comment                => '',
      mgmt_p1                => 45,
      mgmt_p2                => NULL,
      mgmt_p3                => NULL,
      mgmt_p4                => NULL,
      mgmt_p5                => NULL,
```

```
        mgmt_p6                 => NULL,
        mgmt_p7                 => NULL,
        mgmt_p8                 => NULL,
        parallel_degree_limit_p1 => 16,
        switch_io_reqs          => NULL,
        switch_io_megabytes     => 10000,
        active_sess_pool_p1     => 30,
        queueing_p1             => NULL,
        switch_group            => 'grp_medium',
        switch_time             => NULL,
        switch_estimate         => TRUE,
        max_est_exec_time       => 36000,
        undo_pool               => 5242880,
        max_idle_time           => 600,
        max_idle_blocker_time   => NULL,
        switch_for_call         => TRUE);

   dbms_resource_manager.create_plan_directive(
        plan                    => 'dbms_plan',
        group_or_subplan        => 'grp_medium',
        comment                 => '',
        mgmt_p1                 => 30,
        mgmt_p2                 => NULL,
        mgmt_p3                 => NULL,
        mgmt_p4                 => NULL,
        mgmt_p5                 => NULL,
        mgmt_p6                 => NULL,
        mgmt_p7                 => NULL,
        mgmt_p8                 => NULL,
        parallel_degree_limit_p1 => 8,
        switch_io_reqs          => NULL,
        switch_io_megabytes     => 5000,
        active_sess_pool_p1     => 20,
        queueing_p1             => NULL,
        switch_group            => 'cancel_sql',
        switch_time             => NULL,
        switch_estimate         => TRUE,
        max_est_exec_time       => 7200,
        undo_pool               => 1048576,
        max_idle_time           => 300,
        max_idle_blocker_time   => NULL,
        switch_for_call         => TRUE);

   dbms_resource_manager.create_plan_directive(
        plan                    => 'dbms_plan',
        group_or_subplan        => 'grp_normal',
        comment                 => '',
        mgmt_p1                 => 20,
        mgmt_p2                 => NULL,
        mgmt_p3                 => NULL,
        mgmt_p4                 => NULL,
        mgmt_p5                 => NULL,
        mgmt_p6                 => NULL,
        mgmt_p7                 => NULL,
        mgmt_p8                 => NULL,
        parallel_degree_limit_p1 => 4,
        switch_io_reqs          => NULL,
        switch_io_megabytes     => 1000,
```

Package dbms_resource_manager and dbms_resource
manager_privs

```
        active_sess_pool_p1       => 10,
        queueing_p1               => NULL,
        switch_group              => 'kill_session',
        switch_time               => NULL,
        switch_estimate           => TRUE,
        max_est_exec_time         => 600,
        undo_pool                 => 524288,
        max_idle_time             => 60,
        max_idle_blocker_time     => NULL,
        switch_for_call           => TRUE);

    dbms_resource_manager.create_plan_directive(
        plan                      => 'dbms_plan',
        group_or_subplan          => 'other_groups',
        comment                   => '',
        mgmt_p1                   => 5,
        mgmt_p2                   => NULL,
        mgmt_p3                   => NULL,
        mgmt_p4                   => NULL,
        mgmt_p5                   => NULL,
        mgmt_p6                   => NULL,
        mgmt_p7                   => NULL,
        mgmt_p8                   => NULL,
        parallel_degree_limit_p1  => 2,
        switch_io_reqs            => NULL,
        switch_io_megabytes       => 100,
        active_sess_pool_p1       => 5,
        queueing_p1               => NULL,
        switch_group              => 'kill_session',
        switch_time               => NULL,
        switch_estimate           => TRUE,
        max_est_exec_time         => 100,
        undo_pool                 => 104857,
        max_idle_time             => 30,
        max_idle_blocker_time     => NULL,
        switch_for_call           => TRUE);

    dbms_resource_manager.submit_pending_area();
    select value into spfileValue from v$parameter where name = 'spfile';
    if spfilevalue is not null then
        execute immediate 'alter system set resource_manager_plan = ' ||
                        planName || ' scope=both';
    end if;
    dbms_resource_manager.switch_plan(plan_name => 'dbms_plan',
                                sid        => 'dbms');
end;
```

To confirm that the plan and its directives were created, use the *dba_rsrc_plans* and *dba_rsrc_plan_directives* views.

```
select
    plan
from
    dba_rsrc_plans
where plan ='dbms_plan';

select
```

```
      *
from
   dba_rsrc_plan_directives
where
   plan='dbms_plan';
```

It is now necessary to associate the users with the consumer groups by specifying the login names as shown below:

```
begin
   dbms_resource_manager.clear_pending_area();

   dbms_resource_manager.create_pending_area();

   dbms_resource_manager.set_consumer_group_mapping(
      dbms_resource_manager.oracle_user,
      'user_3',
      'grp_normal'
   );

   dbms_resource_manager.set_consumer_group_mapping(
      dbms_resource_manager.oracle_user,
      'user_2',
      'grp_medium'
   );

   dbms_resource_manager.set_consumer_group_mapping(
      dbms_resource_manager.oracle_user,
      'user_1',
      'grp_high'
   );

   dbms_resource_manager.submit_pending_area();
end;
/
```

Check that they are pointed to the right target by using the *dba_rsrc_group_mappings* view:

```
col value for a15 heading "User"
col attribute for a15 heading "Attribute"
col consumer_group for a 15 heading "Consumer Group"

select
   attribute,
   value,
   consumer_group
from
   dba_rsrc_group_mappings
order by value;

ATTRIBUTE        VALUE            CONSUMER_GROUP
---------------  ---------------  --------------------------------
ORACLE_FUNCTION  backup           batch_group
ORACLE_FUNCTION  copy             batch_group
```

```
ORACLE_FUNCTION  dataload         etl_group
ORACLE_USER      SYS              sys_group
ORACLE_USER      SYSTEM           sys_group
ORACLE_USER      user_1           grp_high
ORACLE_USER      user_2           grp_medium
ORACLE_USER      user_3           grp_normal

8 rows selected
```

If it is necessary to force a user to be in a specific group when he/she logs into the database, use the procedure below. It will make the user (*user_1*) belong to the *grp_medium* group when the user is logged in on the database.

```
begin
   dbms_resource_manager.clear_pending_area();

   dbms_resource_manager.create_pending_area();

   dbms_resource_manager.set_consumer_group_mapping(
      attribute => dbms_resource_manager.oracle_user,
      value => 'user_1',
      consumer_group => 'grp_high');

   dbms_resource_manager.submit_pending_area();
end;
/
```

Resource groups can also be defined by specifying the module name of a user that is using this module. The statement below maps the user with the module name PL/SQL to the resource group *normal* whenever the module activates:

```
begin
   dbms_resource_manager.clear_pending_area();

   dbms_resource_manager.create_pending_area();

   dbms_resource_manager.set_consumer_group_mapping(
      attribute => dbms_resource_manager.module_name,
      value => 'PL/SQL%',
      consumer_group => 'grp_normal');

   dbms_resource_manager.submit_pending_area();
end;
/
```

The *dbms_resource_manager* package is a powerful tool that lets database administrators take control of how users are utilizing server resources; thereby, allocating these resources to main users who need it at that time.

Package *dbms_resumable*

Resumable space allocation, introduced in Oracle 9i, is for all tablespaces at the session level. With *dbms_resumable* database operations are suspended when an out-of-space condition is encountered and the suspended operations automatically resumes when the error condition disappears. In Oracle 10g, *dbms_resumable* can be enabled at the instance level. Besides this improvement, automatic alert notification is sent when an operation is suspended.

This feature can be enabled by the SQL command.

```
alter system set resumable_timeout = <value in seconds>;
```

Setting the *resumable_timeout* initialization parameter, enable resumable space allocation system and specify a timeout interval by setting the *resumable_timeout* initialization parameter. For example, the following setting of the *resumable_timeout* parameter in the initialization parameter file causes all sessions to initially be enabled for resumable space allocation and sets the timeout period to one hour:

```
resumable_timeout=3600
```

If this parameter is set to 0, then resumable space allocation is disabled initially for all sessions. This is the default.

Use the *alter system set* statement to change the value of this parameter at the system level. For example, the following statement will disable resumable space allocation for all sessions:

```
alter system set resumable_timeout=0;
```

Within a session, a user can issue the *alter session set* statement to set the *resumable_timeout* initialization parameter and enable resumable space allocation, change a timeout value, or disable resumable mode.

Using *alter session* to enable and disable resumable space allocation, a user can enable resumable mode for a session. The *alter session enable resumable* statement is used to activate resumable space allocation for a given session. Developers are able to embed the *alter session* statement in programs to activate resumable space allocation. A new parameter, called *resumable*, is used to enable resumable space allocation for export, import and load utilities.

Statements do not suspend for an unlimited amount of time. A timed interval can be specified in the *alter session* statement to designate the amount of time that passes

---

before the statement wakes up and returns a hard return code to the user and rolls back the unit of work. If no time interval is specified, the default time interval of two hours is used.

When a resumable statement suspends because of an out-of-space condition, the following actions occur:

1. A system event that can be triggered is initiated. Developers are able to code triggers that fire when a statement suspends.

2. Entries are placed into system data dictionary tables. The data dictionary views *dba_resumable* and *user_resumable* can be accessed to retrieve the paused statement's identifier, text, status and error message.

3. Messages are written to the alert log identifying the statement and the error that caused the statement to suspend.

Oracle resumable space allocation is governed by the *dbms_resumable* package. To use resumable space management, also enable it on a session-by-session basis using the *alter session enable resumable* command. If the space condition is not corrected before the timeout is reached, the transaction will fail. A larger or smaller value can be configured if that is what is needed.

Once enabled, Oracle automatically detects the space condition and suspend the session. Oracle writes an entry to the alert log that the session has been suspended. Additionally, the *dba_resumable* view maintains a record of all currently suspended sessions. Once the DBA has corrected the space problem, the suspended session will automatically resume its operation at the point of suspension.

Oracle also provides an after suspend system trigger event that allows the response to be automated to a session suspend condition. Further, the *dbms_resumable* package is provided to allow for the handling of resumable space management from within SQL or PL/SQL.

With just three functions and three procedures, this package will now be exemplified. In this simulation, a table is created and values are inserted until the table space size has reached its limit. Then the *dbms_resumable* package is used to fix this issue without the need of starting the process from the beginning.

First, create the tablespace and table that is to be used for this example, and name it *tab_dbms_resumable*. In order to simulate an error quickly, the tablespace size will be 10M.

🖫 Code 7.24 – dbms_resumable.sql

```
conn sys@ora11g as sysdba
```

```
Connected to Oracle 11g Enterprise Edition Release 11.1.0.6.0
conn / as sysdba

create tablespace
   tbs_resum datafile size 10M;

create table
   tab_dbms_resumable (
      col1 varchar2(100),
      col2 varchar2(100))
tablespace
   tbs_resum;
```

Configure the resumable space allocation feature with a value of 30 minutes using the procedure below:

```
begin
   dbms_resumable.set_timeout(timeout => 600);   --30 minutes
end;
/
```

Create a trigger to enable the resumable space allocation feature in a user session every time the user *pkg* logs into the database.

```
create or replace trigger trg_resumable_pkg_user
 after logon
 on pkg.schema
 begin
 execute immediate 'alter session enable resumable timeout 600';
 end;
/
```

Create another trigger that will send an email every time the user *pkg* finds a resumable space problem in its session. This email will be sent to the DBA, informing them about the problem. It will contain information about which table and tablespace is experiencing the issue so it may be easily fixed by increasing the datafile pertaining to that tablespace.

```
create or replace trigger resumable_default
after suspend
on database
declare
   v_ret_value boolean;
   v_error_type varchar2(30);
   v_obj_type varchar2(30);
   v_obj_owner varchar2(30);
   v_tbs_name varchar2(30);
   v_obj_name varchar2(30);
   v_sub_obj_name varchar2(30);

begin
   --Get all error variables
   v_ret_value := dbms_resumable.space_error_info(
```

```
                    error_type => v_error_type,
                    object_type => v_obj_type,
                    object_owner => v_obj_owner,
                    table_space_name => v_tbs_name,
                    object_name => v_obj_name,
                    sub_object_name => v_sub_obj_name);

--Set timeout to 2 hours.This is the time that DBAs have to fix space
problem
    dbms_resumable.set_timeout(7200);

--Send notification email to DBAs
    execute immediate 'alter session set smtp_out_server = ''187.48.247.20''';
    utl_mail.send(sender => 'oradbms@f2c.com.br',
              recipients => 'paulo.portugal@f2c.com.br',
                  subject => 'Resumable Space problem!',
                  message => 'Check database for space problems!'||chr(10)||
                             'Error type:' ||v_error_type||chr(10)||
                             'Obj Name:' ||v_obj_name||chr(10)||
                             'Obj Type:' ||v_obj_type||chr(10)||
                             'Obj Owner:' ||v_obj_owner||chr(10)||
                             'Tablespace Name:' ||v_tbs_name||chr(10)||
                             'Sub object name:' ||v_sub_obj_name||chr(10),
                  mime_type => 'text; charset=us-ascii');

end;
/
```

Now execute some inserts in *tab_dbms_resumable* by the user *pkg*. Once the tablespace becomes full, the DBA is warned with an email informing on the resumable space problems.

```
--Login as pkg user
declare
v_count integer;
begin
    v_count :=0;
    while v_count < 10000000 loop
        insert into
            tab_dbms_resumable
        values
            ('testing data. dbms_resumable','this is a test using resumable
space allocation in oracle database');
        commit;
        v_count := v_count +1;
    end loop;
end;
/
```

In another session, logged in as system or another user with *dba* privilege, check the *dba_resumable* view for information pertaining to the session that hangs due to space problems.

```
col sql_text for a30
col error_msg for a30
```

```
select
   user_id,
   session_id,
   status,
   start_time,
   suspend_time,
   sql_text,
   error_number,
   error_msg
from
   dba_resumable;

--or
col error_msg for a30
select
   session_id,
   status,
   error_msg
from
   dba_resumable;

SESSION_ID STATUS    ERROR_MSG
---------- --------- ------------------------------
        56 suspended ORA-01653: unable to extend ta
                     ble pkg.tab_dbms_resumable by
                     128 in tablespace tbs_resum
```

The *alert.log* file can also be checked to find information on resumable space allocation problems that are occurring in the database. Lines like these will be shown:

```
Thu Apr 29 17:15:21 2010
statement in resumable session 'user pkg(46), Session 55, Instance 1' was
suspended due to
   ORA-01653: unable to extend table pkg.tab_dbms_resumable by 128 in
tablespace tbs_resum
```

Finally, fix the problem by increasing the datafile size of the tablespace experiencing the space problem and check the insert process again. Make sure that the time limit of resumable space timeout that was set for two hours is not exceeded.

```
select
   'alter database datafile '''||file_name||''' resize xx M|G;'
from
   dba_data_files
where
   tablespace_name='tbs_resum';

alter database datafile
'/u01/app/oracle/oradata/DBMS/datafile/tbs_resum.dbf' resize 70M;
```

As the old adage goes, "time is money". The *dbms_resumable* package can help save both by providing the ability to continue a process from the point that a space error happens rather than restarting the process from the beginning.

Package dbms_resumable

Package *dbms_scheduler*

The new *dbms_scheduler* package, available in 10g and later, is a monumental improvement over the older *dbms_jobs* facility. In fact, not only is it more capable in Oracle functionality and integration terms, but it also incorporates numerous real world job scheduler concepts such that, in some cases, it even competes with actual real world job scheduling solutions outside the database world. Not that this is necessarily an alternative, but it is believed that Oracle took a flawed and overly simple implementation and built the best scheduler inside the database one could hope for. Three areas where they have greatly improved the capabilities are:

1.   Easier specification of start and interval values

2.   Ability to schedule executables as well as PL/SQL

3.   Tight integration with Oracle's resource manager

Some companies are ideally suited for scheduled job execution and will benefit greatly from the new functionalities that come with the *jobs* package in Oracle 11g.

One in particular, named "lightweight" jobs, has the main purpose of reducing the overhead originated when many small jobs need to run in a short time period. These small jobs can generate redo overhead and hurt performance due to excessive metadata in the creation of these jobs since every job execution needs to modify a schema object (the scheduler object) as well as every job run takes some time to open and close the related session.

Lightweight jobs are not schema objects and are also optimized to open and close sessions faster; thus, they offer improved performance under these conditions. For larger jobs, or less frequent intervals, that time tends to be irrelevant, and regular jobs are still preferred over lightweight jobs. With more than sixty procedures and functions, this package is one of the more robust in the Oracle Database. Rather than spending time explaining each one, now focus on examples of the newer and most commonly used functionalities.

Say we just started working with a company and, when running my traditional database health check, we found too much CPU overhead. While tracking down which process is causing the overhead, we discover that jobs creation is the culprit. So we decide to use the new 11g feature, lightweight jobs, in order to tune up this process.

Lightweight jobs are invoked using the *create_job* procedure. we just need to specify the new *job_style* parameter as will be seen in the first example. The first step is to create the procedure that will be called by the program used in this example.

💾 Code 7.25 – dbms_scheduler_light.sql

```
conn sys@ora11g as sysdba

Connected to Oracle 11g Enterprise Edition Release 11.1.0.6.0
conn / as sysdba

create or replace procedure jobs_failed is
  cursor c1 is
    select
      log_id,
      job_name,
      log_date
    from
      dba_scheduler_job_log
    where
      status = 'failed'
    and
      log_date > sysdate - 1
    and
      job_name = 'job_monitor';
  l_message varchar2(1000);

begin
  for reg in c1 loop

    l_message := reg.log_id || reg.job_name;
    pkg.send_mail_new(sender     => 'paulo.portugal@rampant.cc',
                      recipients => 'dba@dbms.cc',
                      subject    => 'Failed Jobs',
                      message    => 'Failed Jobs ->' ||
                      reg.job_name ||  '---- Fail time ->' || reg.log_date);
  end loop;
end;
```

Next, create the program using the procedure *jobs_failed* that has just been created above.

```
--Lightweight jobs
--First create the program
begin
  /*--Drop if already exists
  dbms_scheduler.drop_program(
      program_name => 'my_test_print_program',
      force => TRUE);
  */
  dbms_scheduler.create_program(
      program_name => 'my_test_print_program',
      program_type => 'stored_procedure',
      program_action => '"pkg"."jobs_failed"',
      enabled => TRUE);
end;
/
```

Create the schedule for the job, specifying when it will start and the repeat interval. In this case, the interval will be one minute.

```
--Now create the schedule that you want to use in this job

begin
   /* --Drop if already exists
   dbms_scheduler.drop_schedule(
      schedule_name => 'my_schedule_1',
      force => TRUE);
   */
   dbms_scheduler.create_schedule(
      schedule_name => 'my_schedule_1',
      start_date => '25-JUN-10 09.00.00 PM Europe/Warsaw',
      repeat_interval => 'freq=daily;byminute=1',
      comments => 'my test schedule.');
end;
/
```

Finally, create the lightweight job using the *create_job* procedure as follows.

```
--Next create the lightweight job using the program created
begin

/*--Drop if already exists
   dbms_scheduler.drop_job(
         job_name => 'light_job_print',
         force => TRUE);
*/
   dbms_scheduler.create_job (
   job_name          =>  'light_job_print',
   program_name      =>  'my_test_print_program',
   repeat_interval   =>  'freq=secondly;interval=10',
   end_date          =>  '30-APR-09 04.00.00 AM Australia/Sydney',
   job_style         =>  'lightweight',
   comments          =>  'My lightweight job based on a program.');
end;
/
```

The next example will show how to create an array of jobs. This approach is a quicker alternative when the database administrator needs to create a set of jobs in a short period of time.

⊟   Code 7.26 – dbms_scheduler_array.sql

```
conn sys@ora11g as sysdba

Connected to Oracle 11g Enterprise Edition Release 11.1.0.6.0
conn / as sysdba

declare
  v_job              sys.job;
  v_job_array        sys.job_array;
begin
  v_job_array := sys.job_array();
v_job_array.extend(100);
for i in 1..100 loop
   v_job := sys.job(job_name => 'my_job_number_'||to_char(i),
                    job_style => 'lightweight',
```

```
                       job_template => 'my_test_print_program',
                                enabled => TRUE );
      v_job_array(i) := v_job;

end loop;
   dbms_scheduler.create_jobs(v_job_array,'stop_on_first_error');

end;
/

select job_name from dba_scheduler_jobs;

JOB_NAME
------------------------------
my_job_number_1
my_job_number_2
my_job_number_3
.
.
.

my_job_number_98
my_job_number_99
```

Information about jobs can be displayed using the *dba_scheduler_jobs* view. The following script uses this view to display information about currently defined jobs.

```
-- Parameters:
--    1) Specific username or all which doesn't limit output.
-- ****************************************************************
set verify off

select
   owner,
   job_name,
   job_class,
   enabled,
   next_run_date,
   repeat_interval
from
   dba_scheduler_jobs
where
   owner = decode(upper('&1'), 'ALL', owner, upper('&1'))
;
```

Information about job arguments can be displayed using the *dba_scheduler_job_args* view. The following script uses this view to display argument information about a specified job.

```
-- Parameters:
--    1) Specific username or all which doesn't limit output.
--    2) Job name.
-- ****************************************************************
set verify off
column argument_name format a20
column value format a30
```

```
select
   argument_position,
   argument_name,
   value
from
   dba_scheduler_job_args
where
   owner = decode(upper('&1'), 'all', owner, upper('&1'))
and
   job_name = upper('&2')
;
```

There are other views used to monitor: jobs, programs, schedules, logs and more. They all start with *dba_scheduler_%* . Now another useful feature in this package will be reviewed.

There are many times when an Oracle DBA needs to start a database process when an external event happens:

1. Upon arrival of a redo log from another instance

2. Upon arrival of an external file to a TEL feed. Note that more on the TEL feed can be found at http://www.dba-oracle.com/t_file_watcher.htm.

3. Upon arrival of a new file for becoming an external table

4. Upon arrival of a new object for BFILE inclusion

Before the Oracle file watcher utility, the DBA would have to write UNIX/Linux shell scripts to watch directories for new files, nohupping a daemon process to sleep for a few seconds, and check for a condition, ad infinitum, until the condition is met.

Starting in Oracle 11g, a new procedure is introduced in the *dbms_scheduler* package called *dbms_scheduler.create_file_watcher* that allows for stepping outside of the database and executing code when a specific external event occurs.

Note: The Oracle file watcher is not yet very sophisticated and it will only trigger code to execute upon the arrival of a new data file into the target directory.

Also note that there are limitations when the code execution time exceeds the arrival time for new files. By default, the arrival of new files will be ignored if the triggered job is already running. If the job needs to be fired for each new arrival, regardless of whether the job is already running or not, set *parallel_instances*=TRUE.

Oracle says that creating a file watcher involves these five steps. Creating a file watcher is not immediately obvious and the steps are a tad convoluted:

1. Create a credential

2. Create a file watcher

3. Create a program object with a metadata argument

4. Create an event-based job that references the file watcher

5. Enable all objects

Here are code samples for each of the five steps, per the Oracle documents:

1. Create a credential:

```
begin
  dbms_scheduler.create_credential('watch_credential', 'salesapps',
'sa324w1');
end;
/
```

2. Create a file watcher:

```
begin
  dbms_scheduler.create_file_watcher(
    file_watcher_name => 'eod_file_watcher',
    directory_path    => '?/eod_reports',
    file_name         => 'eod*.txt',
    credential_name   => 'watch_credential',
    destination       => NULL,
    enabled           => FALSE);
end;
/
```

3. Create a program object:

```
begin
  dbms_scheduler.create_program(
    program_name        => 'dssuser.eod_program',
    program_type        => 'stored_procedure',
    program_action      => 'eod_processor',
    number_of_arguments => 1,
    enabled             => FALSE);
end;
/
```

4. Define the metadata argument using the *event_message* attribute.

```
begin
  dbms_scheduler.define_metadata_argument(
    program_name       => 'dssuser.eod_program',
    metadata_attribute => 'event_message',
    argument_position  => 1);
end;
/
```

5. Prepare an event-based job:

```
begin
  dbms_scheduler.create_job(
    job_name            => 'dssuser.eod_job',
```

```
   program_name    => 'dssuser.eod_program',
   event_condition => null,
   queue_spec      => 'eod_file_watcher',
   auto_drop       => FALSE,
   enabled         => FALSE);
end;
/
```

6. Enable objects:

```
begin
dbms_scheduler.enable('dssuser.eod_program,dssuser.eod_job,eod_file_watcher'
);
end;
/
```

Information about file watchers can be viewed by querying *dba_scheduler_file_watchers*:

```
set linesize 100

column file_watcher_name format a20
column destination       format a15
column directory_path    format a15
column file_name         format a10
column credential_name   format a20
select
   file_watcher_name,
   destination,
   directory_path,
   file_name,
   credential_name
from
   dba_scheduler_file_watchers;
```

The *dbms_scheduler* has many more functionalities not covered in this book. Refer to the Oracle Documentation to learn more about the *dbms_scheduler* package.

Package *dbms_server_alert*

In the older days of Oracle management, the DBA had to write their own DBA alerts, and many Oracle professionals had extremely sophisticated alert scripts, like those listed below:

- **Server-side alerts**: UNIX/Linux shell scripts can be written to check for alert log messages, dump and trace files and such. For working scripts, see the Oracle script collection where working scripts are available for instant download.

- **Internal Oracle alerts**: Dozens of customized alerts have been created for every possible exception condition within Oracle, which is a valuable approach to alert the user before the database crashes. For examples of such scripts, see Jon Emmon's book, *Oracle Shell Scripting*. For a description of Oracle Linux commands, see the Oracle Linux command reference poster.

Starting in Oracle 10g, there is the ability to set alerts within OEM, specify the alert threshold and notification methods such as e-mail, pager and more. Oracle also created a procedural interface to the alert mechanism using the new *dbms_server_alert* package. The *dbms_server_alert* package contains procedures to set and get threshold values. When the space usage exceeds either of the two thresholds, an appropriate alert is issued. If the thresholds are not specified, the defaults are 85% for warning and 97% for critical thresholds.

The *dbms_server_alert* package has these procedures: *set_threshold*, *get_threshold*, *expand_threshold* and *view_threshold*. The *get_threshold* procedure can be called to check an existing threshold value. The *set_threshold* procedure can be called to change an existing threshold value. One simple *set_threshold* is showed below:

```
begin
    dbms_server_alert.set_threshold(
        metrics_id => dbms_server_alert.tablespace_pct_full,
        warning_operator => dbms_server_alert.operator_ge,
        warning_value => '10',
        critical_operator => dbms_server_alert.operator_ge,
        critical_value => '20',
        observation_period => 1,
        consecutive_occurrences => 3,
        instance_name => 'zmydb',
        object_type => dbms_server_alert.object_type_tablespace,
        object_name => 'cust'
    );
end;
/
```

The amount that thresholds are to be higher or lower than the baseline values can be specified by percentage DB Control that sets the thresholds using the derived values for each metric using the Oracle *dbms_server_alert.set_threshold* procedure for the *dbms_server_alert* package. All thresholds except for space related alerts should be explicitly defined. To enable the *dbms_server_alert* package functionality, set the *statistics_level* initialization parameter to TYPICAL or ALL.

The *dbms_server_alert* package has the corresponding DBA views to see the status of all scheduled alerts:

- *dba_outstanding_alerts*: This view shows all existing alerts

- *dba_alert_history*: This shows a history of all preexisting alerts that were set by *dbms_server_alert*

- *dba_alert_arguments*: This view shows the arguments to *dbms_server_alert*

- *dba_thresholds*: This new view shows the threshold values for all alerts

Here are some examples of the *dbms_server_alert* package.

Assume we need to configure some thresholds for *buffer cache hit*, *library cache hit*, *redo allocation hit*, *cursor cache hit* and *pga cache hit* that need to bypass their specified values chosen by the database administrator.

🖫 Code 7.27 – dbms_server_alert.sql

```
conn sys@ora11g as sysdba

Connected to Oracle 11g Enterprise Edition Release 11.1.0.6.0
conn / as sysdba

--Setting buffer cache hit threshold values
begin

   dbms_server_alert.set_threshold(
      metrics_id => dbms_server_alert. buffer_cache_hit,
      warning_operator => dbms_server_alert.operator_lt,
      warning_value => 99,
      critical_operator => dbms_server_alert.operator_lt,
      critical_value => 98,
      observation_period => 30,
      consecutive_occurrences => 1,
      instance_name => NULL,
      object_type => dbms_server_alert.object_type_system,
      object_name => NULL);

end;
/
```

Use the *get_threshold* procedure to return metric values of a specified threshold.

```
--Getting threshold values
set serveroutput on

declare
 v_war_operator  number(20);
 v_war_value varchar2(100);
 v_crit_oper  number(10);
 v_crit_val varchar2(100);
 v_obs_period number(10);
 v_cons_occurr number(10);
 v_metric_num number(10);
 v_metric_name varchar2(30);
begin
  dbms_server_alert.get_threshold(
     metrics_id => dbms_server_alert.buffer_cache_hit,
     warning_operator => v_war_operator,
     warning_value => v_war_value,
     critical_operator => v_crit_oper,
     critical_value => v_crit_val,
     observation_period => v_obs_period,
     consecutive_occurrences => v_cons_occurr,
     instance_name => NULL,
     object_type => dbms_server_alert.object_type_system ,
     object_name => NULL );
```

```
v_metric_num := to_number(dbms_server_alert.buffer_cache_hit);

    select
        metric_name
    into
        v_metric_name
    from
        v$metric
    where
        metric_id = v_metric_num and rownum =1;

    dbms_output.put_line(a => 'metric name:  ' || v_metric_name);
    dbms_output.put_line(a => 'warning operator:  ' ||
to_char(v_war_operator));
    dbms_output.put_line(a => 'warning value:      ' || v_war_value);
    dbms_output.put_line(a => 'critical operator: ' || to_char(v_crit_oper));
    dbms_output.put_line(a => 'critical value:     ' || v_crit_val);
    dbms_output.put_line(a => 'observation period:    ' || v_obs_period);
    dbms_output.put_line(a => 'consecutive occurrencies:     ' ||
v_cons_occurr);
end;
/
```

The example above shows how to set threshold values for a specific metric. It can be repeated to set the other hit metrics by changing the *metrics_id* parameter and setting the desired threshold values. The *view_thresholds* function shows which metrics are being used in the database, as shown here:

```
select
    distinct m.metric_name,
    v.object_type,
    v.metrics_id,
    v.instance_name,
    v.flags,
    v.warning_operator,
    v.warning_value,
    v.critical_operator,
    v.critical_value,
    v.observation_period,
    v.consecutive_occurrences,
    v.object_id,
    v.object_name
from
    table(dbms_server_alert.view_thresholds) v,
    v$metric m
where
    v.metrics_id = m.metric_id;
```

Oracle 11g's data dictionary displays the *dba_outstanding_alerts* view using the following source query:

```
select sequence_id,
       reason_id,
       owner,
       object_name,
```

```
             subobject_name,
       typnam_keltosd AS object_type,
       dbms_server_alert.expand_message(userenv('language'),
                                    mid_keltsd,
                                    reason_argument_1,
                                    reason_argument_2,
                                    reason_argument_3,
                                    reason_argument_4,
                                    reason_argument_5) AS reason,
       time_suggested,
       creation_time,
       dbms_server_alert.expand_message(userenv('language'),
                                    amid_keltsd,
                                    action_argument_1,
                                    action_argument_2,
                                    action_argument_3,
                                    action_argument_4,
                                    action_argument_5) AS
suggested_action,
       advisor_name,
       metric_value,
       decode(message_level, 32, 'notification', 'warning') as message_type,
       nam_keltgsd as message_group,
       message_level,
       hosting_client_id,
       mdid_keltsd AS module_id,
       process_id,
       host_id,
       host_nw_addr,
       instance_name,
       instance_number,
       user_id,
       execution_context_id,
       error_instance_id
  from wri$_alert_outstanding,
       x$keltsd,
       x$keltosd,
       x$keltgsd,
       dba_advisor_definitions
 where reason_id = rid_keltsd
   and otyp_keltsd = typid_keltosd
   and grp_keltsd = id_keltgsd
   and aid_keltsd = advisor_id(+)
/
```

From this last example on the *dbms_server_alert* package, the user should now understand what happens in the background when configuring thresholds using a GUI tool like Oracle Grid Control or Oracle Database Control.

Package *dbms_session*

The *dbms_session* package has many different functionalities. Most of them can be run through a SQL command line, and are used to/for:

- Work with context information

- Close database links

- Release and get information about memory

- Role information

- Disable and enable trace

- Consumer group user change

- Session ID identification

The next example will touch on some of the main procedures of this package and how they can be used.

The first example will focus on the *set_context* procedure for increasing Oracle database security using Virtual Private Database (VPD). For the VPD to properly use the security policy to add the WHERE clause to the end user's SQL, Oracle must know details about the authority of the user. This is done at sign-on time using Oracle's *dbms_session* package.

At sign-on, a database logon trigger executes, setting the application context for the user by calling *dbms_session.set_context*. The *set_context* procedure can be used to set any number of variables about the end user, including the application name, the user's name, and specific row restriction information. Once this data is collected, the security policy uses this information to build the runtime WHERE clause to append to the end user's SQL statement. The *set_context* procedure sets several parameters that are used by the VPD and accepts three arguments:

```
dbms_session.set_context(namespace, attribute, value)
```

For example, assume that there is a publication table and we want to restrict access based on the type of end user. Managers will be able to view all books for their publishing company, while authors may only view their own books. Stating that user jsmith is a manager and user mault is an author, at login time, the Oracle database logon trigger generates the appropriate values and execute the statements shown next. Create the package, which will have three procedures: one to set the context, one to clear a specific context and the last one that will clear all information pertaining to a specific context.

🖫 Code 7.28 – dbms_session_context.sql

```
conn sys@ora11g as sysdba

Connected to Oracle 11g Enterprise Edition Release 11.1.0.6.0
conn / as sysdba
```

```
create or replace package pkg_context as
   procedure proc_set_name_attr;
   procedure proc_clear_context;
   procedure proc_clear_all_context;
end pkg_context;
/

create or replace package body pkg_context as
procedure proc_set_name_attr is
v_current_user varchar2(30);
begin

select
   sys_context('userenv','current_user')
into
   v_current_user
from
   dual;   .

if v_current_user = 'jsmith'  then
    dbms_session.set_context(
         namespace => 'publishing_application',
         attribute => 'role_name',
         value => 'manager');

      dbms_session.set_context(
         namespace => 'publishing_application',
         attribute => 'user_name',
         value => 'jsmith');

      dbms_session.set_context(
         namespace => 'publishing_application',
         attribute => 'company',
         value => 'rampant_techpress');
else if v_current_user = 'pkguser'  then

      dbms_session.set_context(
         namespace => 'publishing_application',
         attribute => 'role_name',
         value => 'author');

      dbms_session.set_context(
         namespace => 'publishing_application',
         attribute => 'user_name',
         value => 'mault');

      dbms_session.set_context(
         namespace => 'publishing_application',
         attribute => 'company',
         value => 'rampant_techpress');
end if;

end;
procedure proc_clear_context is
   begin
      dbms_session.clear_context(namespace => 'publishing_application');
   end;

procedure proc_clear_all_context is
```

```
   begin
      dbms_session.clear_all_context(namespace => 'publishing_application');
   end;

end pkg_context;
/
```

Now we need to log in as *sys* user and create the context which will point to the procedure just created.

```
create or replace context
   publishing_application using pkg.pkg_context;
```

Log in as mault user and execute the procedure *proc_set_name_attr* to test that it is working. After executing the procedure, use the *sys_context* function to get the current user context values.

```
--Execute the procedure and check the context
execute pkg.pkg_context.proc_set_name_attr;

-- check if attribute was set
select
   sys_context('publishing_application','user_name' )
from
   dual;

select
   sys_context('publishing_application','role_name' )
from
   dual;

select
   sys_context('publishing_application','company' )
from
   dual;
```

Application Context is a security feature that can be used in conjunction with fine-grained access control for many things including improving application performance. It can also be used to cache attribute data for use in PL/SQL conditional statements.

Another functionality of *dbms_session* is the *set_identifier* procedure, which can be used to help identify a user session. Here is a simple example. An identifier can be set by executing the command below at the session level.

Code 7.29 – dbms_session_set_identifier.sql

```
conn sys@ora11g as sysdba

Connected to Oracle 11g Enterprise Edition Release 11.1.0.6.0
conn / as sysdba

exec dbms_session.set_identifier(client_id => 'dbms_session_app_dbms');
```

Or create a logon trigger specifying the identifier like this:

```
create or replace trigger trg_set_identifier
   after logon on database
begin
   if upper(user) ='pkg' then
   dbms_session.set_identifier(client_id => 'pkg_app_user');
   else
   dbms_session.set_identifier(client_id => 'not_app_user');
   end if;
end;
/
```

Query the *v$session* table to find out if there are any *pkg* users logged in:

```
select
   client_identifier
from
   v$session
where
   client_identifier is NOT NULL;

CLIENT_IDENTIFIER
-------------------------------------------------------------
not_app_user
dbms_session_app_dbms
```

The last functionality example for the *dbms_session* package will pertain to enabling and disabling a trace in a SQL session. The *set_sql_trace* procedure is used to enable SQL trace in a user session. It runs as the SQL command *alter session set sql_trace true*. If needed, for example, to trace all sessions by a specific user, create the trigger below:

Code 7.30 – dbms_session_trace.sql

```
conn sys@ora11g as sysdba

Connected to Oracle 11g Enterprise Edition Release 11.1.0.6.0
conn / as sysdba

create or replace trigger trg_pkg_trace
   after logon on database
begin
   if upper(user) ='pkg' then
      dbms_session.set_sql_trace(sql_trace => TRUE);
      commit;
   end if;
end;
/
```

Only DBA users are able to use the *dbms_monitor* package to enable a trace in any database session. Any database user can enable an SQL trace in their own session using the *session_trace_enable* procedure in the *dbms_session* package, as demonstrated in these next lines.

```
--Use this command below to enable trace in your session. Row source
statistics will be dumped for all executions defined by plan_stat new
parameter.
begin
dbms_session.session_trace_enable(waits =>TRUE ,binds => TRUE,plan_stat
=>'all_executions' );
end;
/
--Disable trace in your session
begin
dbms_session.session_trace_disable;
end;
/
```

There are other procedures and functions in *dbms_session* such as *set_role*, *close_database_link*, *reinitialize*, *is_role_enable*, *is_session_alive* and others. They will not be described here due to their ease of use.

Package *dbms_shared_pool*

Oracle shared pool is a shared memory area where PL/SQL and cursor objects are stored. The *dbms_shared_pool* package allows access to this area, offering procedures that help performance improvement by keeping objects most frequently accessed in this memory area. Package pinning has become a very important part of Oracle tuning, and with the introduction of system-level triggers in Oracle 8i, there is now an easy tool to ensure that frequently-executed PL/SQL remains cached inside the shared pool.

Just like using the KEEP pool with the data buffer caches, the pinning of packages ensures that the specified package always remains in the Most-Recently-Used (MRU) end of the data buffer. This prevents the PL/SQL from being paged-out and then reparsed upon reload. The Oracle DBA controls the size of this RAM region by setting the *shared_pool_size* parameter to a value large enough to hold all of the required PL/SQL code.

Pinning of packages involves two areas:

1. **Pinning frequently executed packages:** Oracle performance can be greatly enhanced by pinning frequently executed packages inside the SGA, or if there are some especially large mission-critical packages that are prone to be pushed outside of it and may take a very long time to load back when needed.

2. **Pinning the standard Oracle packages:** These are shown in the code listing below and should always be pinned to prevent reparsing by the Oracle SGA.

The *v$db_object_cache* view can be interrogated to see the most frequently used packages; for example, if they should be automatically pinned at database start-up time with an *on database startup* trigger using *dbms_shared_pool.keep*.

The Oracle shared pool contains Oracle's library cache, which is responsible for collecting, parsing, interpreting, and executing all of the SQL statements that go against the Oracle database. Hence, the shared pool is a key component, so it is necessary for the Oracle database administrator to check for shared pool contention.

In order to avoid performance degradation due to memory fragmentation in the shared pool, find the larger and more commonly executed objects in the database and pin them to the shared pool memory. This will prevent the reparse phase and fragmentation of the shared pool. Do this as soon as the instance starts using the database trigger *on database startup*.

The next example shows how to find the largest and most frequently executed objects and pin then into memory using a database startup trigger.

If this is an Oracle E-Business Suite database, use *$ad_top/sql/adxckpin.sql* to find objects that are candidates to be pinned. Also, use the following query which is similar to the script above:

🖫   Code 7.31 – dbms_shared_pool.sql

```
conn sys@ora11g as sysdba

Connected to Oracle 11g Enterprise Edition Release 11.1.0.6.0
conn / as sysdba

set lines 79
column type format a12
column object format a36
column loads format 99990
column execs format 9999990
column kept format a4
column "total space (K)" format a20

select owner || '.' || name object
       , type
       , to_char(sharable_mem/1024,'9,999.9') "space(K)"
       , loads
       , executions execs
       , kept
from v$db_object_cache
where type in ('function','package','package body','procedure')
   and owner not in ('sys')
   and  to_char(sharable_mem/1024,'9,999.9') > 50
   and loads > 10
order by "space(K)",loads,owner, name
/
```

```
Obj Name                                TYPE          SPACE(K)  LOADS    Execs  KEPT
------------------------------------    ------------  --------  -----  -------  ----
apps.hxc_preference_evaluation          package body     107.8     82   142332  NO
apps.wf_xml                             package body     123.2     42     1372  NO
apps.hxc_time_entry_rules_utils_pkg     package body     128.5     54    30203  NO
apps.hxc_time_category_utils_pkg        package body     134.9     63    71400  NO
aaps.wf_engine                          package body     139.9     53   204171  NO
apps. hxc_alias_utility                 package body     141.0     14     2374  NO
apps.hxc_self_service_time_deposit      package body     141.8     62    26102  NO
apps.wf_mail                            package body     169.0     42     8126  NO
apps.wf_notification                    package body     170.3     53    41890  NO
apps.pa_otc_api                         package body     205.7     25      749  NO
sys.dbms_aqadm_sys                      package body     208.5     45     1136  NO
apps.pa_trx_import                      package body     265.1     51    11621  NO
```

This query shows the biggest and most frequently used objects in the database. They are perfect candidates to be pinned into the shared pool memory. To pin them, use the trigger below:

```
create or replace trigger trg_pinning_packages
  after startup on database
begin
  dbms_shared_pool.keep(name => 'apps.hxc_preference_evaluation');
  dbms_shared_pool.keep(name => 'apps.wf_xml');
  dbms_shared_pool.keep(name => 'apps.hxc_time_entry_rules_utils_pkg');
  dbms_shared_pool.keep(name => 'apps.hxc_time_category_utils_pkg');
  dbms_shared_pool.keep(name => 'apps.wf_engine');
  dbms_shared_pool.keep(name => 'apps.hxc_alias_utility');
  dbms_shared_pool.keep(name => 'apps.hxc_self_service_time_deposit');
  dbms_shared_pool.keep(name => 'apps.wf_mail');
  dbms_shared_pool.keep(name => 'apps.wf_notification');
  dbms_shared_pool.keep(name => 'apps.pa_otc_api');
  dbms_shared_pool.keep(name => 'sys.dbms_aqadm_sys');
  dbms_shared_pool.keep(name => 'apps.pa_trx_import');
end trg_pinning_packages;
```

It is also possible to pin cursors, sequences and triggers. First, create a cursor and use it. Next, identify the *address* and *hash_value* column values from the *v$open_cursor* view and use these values to pin this cursor into the shared pool memory.

```
--Create and open a cursor to pin it after.
set serveroutput on 90000000
declare
cursor c1 is
select object_name, object_type from dba_objects;
v_name varchar2(30);
v_type varchar2(30);

begin
dbms_output.enable(buffer_size => 10000000);
   open c1;
   if c1%isopen then
   loop

   fetch c1 into v_name, v_type;
   exit when c1%notfound;
   dbms_output.put_line(a => v_name ||v_type);
```

```
   end loop;
   end if;

end;
/
```

Now, query the *v$open_cursor* view to find the cursor created. Use the *keep* procedure with information returned by *address* and *hash_value* to pin this cursor into memory.

```
select
   user_name,
   address,
   hash_value
from
   gv$open_cursor
where
   sql_text like '%dba_objects%';

USER_NAME                      ADDRESS   HASH_VALUE
------------------------------ --------  ----------
pkg                            5A5A4084  3271523444

--Pin cursor into memory
exec sys.dbms_shared_pool.keep(name =>'5A5A4084, 3271523444',flag =>  'c');

--Check if the cursor is with status keep yes in memory
set lines 79
column type format a12
column "Obj Name" format a20
column loads format 99990
column "Execs" format 9999990
column kept format a4
column "total space (K)" format a20

select
   owner||'.' ||name "Obj Name" ,
   type,
   to_char(sharable_mem/1024,'9,999.9') "space(K)",
   loads,
   executions "Execs",
   kept
from
   v$db_object_cache
where
   type ='cursor'
and
   name like '%dba_objects%'
and
   kept='yes'
order by
   "space(K)",
   loads,
   owner,
   name
/

Obj Name                       TYPE       SPACE(K) LOADS   Execs KEPT
```

```
---------------------------------------- ------------- -------- ----- ------- ----
pkgG.dba_objects                         cursor             .0    1       0 NO
```

Sequences and triggers can also be pinned as follows:

```
    --First check if sequence is pinned or not
col owner for a10
col name for a15
col type for a10
col kept for a5
select
   owner,
   name,
   type,
   kept
from
   v$db_object_cache
where
   name='audses$';

OWNER        NAME             TYPE         KEPT
----------   ---------------  ----------   -----
sys          audses$          sequence     NO

--Now pin the sequence
begin
dbms_shared_pool.keep(name => 'sys.sudses$',flag => 'Q');
end;
/

--Check if it was pinned into memory
col owner for a10
col name for a15
col type for a10
col kept for a5
select
   owner,
   name,
   type,
   kept
from
   v$db_object_cache
where
   name='audses$';
```

```
OWNER        NAME             TYPE         KEPT
----------   ---------------  ----------   -----
sys          audses$          sequence     YES
```

There is also a procedure named *purge* that will clean data from the memory for a specified object. The target object must no longer be pinned in memory when using the *purge* procedure.

```
--Purge data from memory for a specified object

begin
```

```
--First un-pin the cursor
   dbms_shared_pool.unkeep(
       name => '5A5A4084, 3271523444',
       flag => 'C');

--Purging cursor data
   dbms_shared_pool.purge(
       name => '5A5A4084, 3271523444',
       flag =>'C' ,heaps => 0);

--Purging sequence
   dbms_shared_pool.purge(
       name => 'sys.audses$',
       flag => 'Q');

end;
/
```

If a user is executing a process that requires memory from the shared pool, and the RDBMS cannot find the needed space, an 'out of memory' message can be displayed to the user. To do this, configure the threshold using the *aborted_request_threshold* procedure. The value specified is in bytes and can range from 5000 bytes to 2 GBs.

```
--Setting shared pool out of memory threshold
begin
dbms_shared_pool.aborted_request_threshold(threshold_size =>10485760 );   --
10MB is the limit until ' out of memory'  message is displayed to the user
end;
/
```

Good information can be found on shared pool fragmentation in MOSC Note: "Resolving Shared Pool Fragmentation in Oracle 7". Although this note is for Oracle Database 7, its queries can still be used in 9i, 10g and 11g databases.

Package *dbms_utility*

For the most part, Oracle DBMS packages focus on one subject; in this regard, the *dbms_utility* package is out of the ordinary. This package has procedures and functions that work for different purposes like returning information about instances, databases and data blocks, analyzing database objects, converting data formats and more. The script responsible for its creation is *$ORACLE_HOME/rdbms/ admin/ dbmsutil.sql* and is called when the database is created.

I will not attempt examples for all procedures and functions; instead, the main and most commonly used features are used in the next sample. It is well known that *dbms_stats* and *analyze* (old fashioned) commands are used to analyze objects in a database. The *dbms_utility* also has its own procedures that can be used to help database administrators optimize their analysis process.

The *analyze_database* procedure is used to analyze all tables, indexes and clusters in a specified database.

🖫 Code 7.32 – dbms_utility_analyze.sql

```
conn sys@orallg as sysdba

Connected to Oracle 11g Enterprise Edition Release 11.1.0.6.0
conn / as sysdba

begin
   dbms_utility.analyze_database(
      method => 'estimate',
      estimate_rows => NULL,
      estimate_percent => 30,
      method_opt => 'for all columns size 20');
end;
/
```

The *analyze_part_object* procedure is used to analyze an object partition via parallelism.

```
begin
   dbms_utility.analyze_part_object(
      schema => 'pkg',
      object_name => 'tab_partitioned',
      object_type => 'T',
      command_type => 'E',
      command_opt => 'E',
      sample_clause => 'sample 30 percent');
end;
/
```

To analyze all objects of a specific schema, use the *analyze_schema* procedure.

```
begin
   dbms_utility.analyze_schema(
      schema => 'pkg',
      method => 'estimate',
      estimate_rows => NULL,
      estimate_percent => 20,
      method_opt => for all indexes');
end;
/
```

Other procedures can return information about databases, instances and data blocks, as in the next example. In a RAC environment, sometimes which instances are active needs to be known.

We can use the *active_instances* and *is_cluster_database* procedures to accomplish this task. As we see below, the code shows the same information as would be returned by querying the *gv$active_instances* table.

🖫 Code 7.33 – dbms_utility_db_info.sql

```
conn sys@ora11g as sysdba

Connected to Oracle 11g Enterprise Edition Release 11.1.0.6.0
conn / as sysdba

--Using query on v$active_instances
select
    *
from
    v$active_instances;

INST_NUMBER INST_NAME
----------- ----------------
          1 host1:SID1
          2 host2:SID1
          3 host3:SID3
          4 host4:SID4

--Using dbms_utility procedures
set serveroutput on
declare
    v_inst_table dbms_utility.instance_table;
    v_inst_count number;
begin
--First check if it is a cluster database
    if dbms_utility.is_cluster_database then
        dbms_utility.current_instances(
            instance_table => v_inst_table ,
            instance_count => v_inst_count );
        dbms_output.put_line(a => 'Logged in on  '|| v_inst_table.first|| '
instance.');
        dbms_output.put_line(a => 'This Cluster has
'||v_inst_count||'instances.');
        else
        dbms_output.put_line(a => ' This is a standalone database. Not a cluster
database!');
        end if;
end;
/

Logged in on  1 instance.
This Cluster has 4 instances.
```

Get database information using the *db_version* procedure.

```
set serveroutput on
declare
    v_version varchar2(15);
    v_compability varchar2(15);
begin
    dbms_utility.db_version(
        version => v_version,
        compatibility => v_compability);
    dbms_output.put_line(
            a => 'My database version is
    :'||v_version||'.');
```

```
    dbms_output.put_line(
           a => 'Compability is
           :'||v_compability||'.');
end;
/

My database version is :11.2.0.1.0.
Compability is          :11.2.0.0.0.
```

Other procedures that are very handy, in this case for transporting table data to CSV files, are *comma_to_table* and *table_to_comma*. Take a look at these examples.

For another example, let's suppose we have a table with one column which contains first and last names of database users and we need to separate these values with commas:

🖫 Code 7.34 – dbms_utility_comma.sql

```
conn sys@ora11g as sysdba

Connected to Oracle 11g Enterprise Edition Release 11.1.0.6.0
conn / as sysdba

--Create the first table
create table
   tab_users (
       full_name varchar2(60)
       );

--Insert some values on this table
insert into
   tab_users
values ('"Ronald","Reagan"');

insert into
   tab_users
values ('"Abraham","Lincoln"');

insert into
   tab_users
values ('"George","Washington"');

insert into
   tab_users
values ('"Thomas","Jefferson "');
commit;

--Query to check how is the data before split data
select
   *
from
   tab_users;

FULL_NAME
------------------------------------------------------------
"Ronald","Reagan"
```

```
"Abraham","Lincoln"
"George","Washington"
"Thomas","Jefferson "
```

Next, we create a second table which will receive the data separated into two columns. Then create the procedure that will use the *comma_to_table* procedure in order to split the data and insert it into a new table.

```
create table
    tab_users_temp (
        first_name varchar2(30),
        last_name varchar2(30));

create or replace procedure prc_dbms_utility is
    v_tablen        binary_integer;
    v_tab dbms_utility.uncl_array;
begin
  for t_rec in (select * from tab_users)
  loop
    dbms_utility.comma_to_table(list => t_rec.full_name,tablen =>
v_tablen,tab =>  v_tab);

--The translate function is used to replace a sequence of characters in a
string with another set of characters

    v_tab(1) := translate(STR1 => v_tab(1),src =>  'A"',dest => ' ');
    v_tab(2) := translate(STR1 => v_tab(2),src =>  'A"',dest => ' ');

    insert into
       tab_users_temp
    (first_name,last_name)
    values
    (v_tab(1), v_tab(2));

  end loop;
  commit;
end prc_dbms_utility;

--Execute the procedure just created
exec load_c2t_test;

--Check data on new table and note that it is now separated
select
    *
from
    tab_users_temp;

FIRST_NAME                      LAST_NAME
------------------------------  ------------------------------
"Ronald"                        "Reagan"
"Abraham"                       "Lincoln"
"George"                        "Washington"
"Thomas"                        "Jefferson "
```

The *dbms_utility* can also be used to get a data block address. Many Oracle scripts will provide the file and block number, but then this information must be translated into the actual data block address (DBA) for the block; *dbms_utility* simplifies the process. For example, to dump file number 101, block 50, enter the following PL/SQL.

🖫 Code 7.35 – dbms_utility_make_data_block.sql

```
conn sys@ora11g as sysdba

Connected to Oracle 11g Enterprise Edition Release 11.1.0.6.0
conn / as sysdba

set serveroutput on
declare
v_address varchar2(30);
begin
select
   dbms_utility.make_data_block_address(file => 101,block => 50)
into
   v_address
from
   dual ;
   dbms_output.put_line(a => 'Data block address is:'||v_address);
end;
/
```

Also use *dbms_utility* to help compile objects in a schema. With the *compile_schema* procedure, use FALSE in the *compile_all* parameters to compile only the invalid objects.

🖫 Code 7.36 – dbms_utility_compile.sql

```
conn sys@ora11g as sysdba

Connected to Oracle 11g Enterprise Edition Release 11.1.0.6.0
conn / as sysdba

begin
   dbms_utility.compile_schema(
      schema =>'pkg' ,
      compile_all => FALSE,
      reuse_settings => FALSE);
end;
/
```

These were just a few representative examples of the many procedures and functions available within the *dbms_utility* package.

Package *dbms_warning*

The *dbms_warning* built-in package is used in 11g to manipulate the default PL/SQL warning messages in conjunction with the new 11g *plsql_warnings* parameter. It is possible to manage all PL/SQL warning messages by specifying the *plsql_warnings* initialization parameter and then suppressing or customizing these kinds of messages in a PL/SQL code.

With *dbms_warning*, the user can get the current values being used, set new values and delete settings in the session or system level. The next example shows how to use the *dbms_warning* package to manipulate PL/SQL warning messages. Specify to enable or disable diferent kinds of warnings or treat warnings of a specific category as errors by setting *plsql_warnings = 'Enable|Disable|Error Category1' [,'Enable|Disable|Error Category2']...*

There are four possible warning categories in the *plsql_warnings* initialization parameter or at the session level:

1. *all:* This sets warnings for all types

2. *severe:* Sets warning messages for wrong results and abnormal behavior.

3. *performance:* Warning messages involving performance problems

4. *informational:* Warning messages of the informational category

In the next example, how to use *dbms_warning* to change PL/SQL warning messages to set, get and suppress warning information will be shown.

⊞ Code 7.37 – dbms_warning.sql

```
conn sys@ora11g as sysdba

Connected to Oracle 11g Enterprise Edition Release 11.1.0.6.0
conn / as sysdba

--Getting warning values using dbms_warning package
select
    dbms_warning.get_category(
        warning_number => 5000)
from
    dual;

DBMS_WARNING.GET_CATEGORY(WARN
---------------------------------------------
severe

select
    dbms_warning.get_category(
        warning_number => 6000)
from
    dual;

DBMS_WARNING.GET_CATEGORY(WARN
---------------------------------------------
informational

select
    dbms_warning.get_category(
```

```
      warning_number => 7000)
from
   dual;

DBMS_WARNING.GET_CATEGORY(WARN
----------------------------------------------
performance
```

The function *get_warning_setting_cat* is used to get warning category settings for the current session.

```
select
   dbms_warning.get_warning_setting_cat(
      warning_category => 'performance')
from
   dual;

DBMS_WARNING.GET_WARNING_SETTI
----------------------------------------------
disable:performance

select
   dbms_warning.get_warning_setting_cat(
      warning_category => 'informational')
from
   dual;

DBMS_WARNING.GET_WARNING_SETTI
----------------------------------------------
disable:informational

select
   dbms_warning.get_warning_setting_cat(
      warning_category => 'severe')
from
   dual;

DBMS_WARNING.GET_WARNING_SETTI
----------------------------------------------
disable:severe
```

Using the *get_warning_setting_num* function will return a warning number setting in the current session if the specified warning is enabled or disabled. Here is an example:

```
select
   dbms_warning.get_warning_setting_num(
      warning_number => 5000)
from
   dual;

select
   dbms_warning.get_warning_setting_num(
      warning_number => 6000)
from
   dual;
```

```
select
   dbms_warning.get_warning_setting_num(
      warning_number => 7000)
from
   dual;


--Using get_warning_setting_string to get current session warning string
select
   dbms_warning.get_warning_setting_string
from
   dual;
```

Use the *add_warning_setting_%* procedure to modify current settings at the session or system level.

```
--Modify current settings at session or system level

begin

   dbms_warning.add_warning_setting_cat(
      warning_category => 'all',
      warning_value => 'enable',
      scope => 'session');
end;
/

begin
   dbms_warning.add_warning_setting_num(
      warning_number => 7203,
      warning_value => 'enable',
      scope => 'system');
end;
/

begin
   dbms_warning.set_warning_setting_string(
      value =>'disable:all' ,
      scope =>'system' );
end;
/

begin
   dbms_warning.set_warning_setting_string(
      value =>'disable:all' ,
      scope =>'session' );
end;
/
```

This shows how this warning setting influences the PL/SQL compilation warning message. The first step is to check current warning values. Then create a test procedure, enabling warnings at a session level, and after the procedure is compiled again, the warning messages appear.

💾 Code 7.38 – dbms_warning_example.sql

```
conn sys@ora11g as sysdba

Connected to Oracle 11g Enterprise Edition Release 11.1.0.6.0

conn / as sysdba

--Effectively using PL/SQL warning simple example
--Check actual warning value
select
  dbms_warning.get_warning_setting_string
from
  dual;

GET_WARNING_SETTING_STRING
------------------------------------
enable:all

--Create a test procedure
create or replace procedure prc_test_dbms_warning as
  v_var  varchar2(10) := 'xx';
begin
  if 2=2 then
    select 'xxx'
    into   v_var
    from   dual;
  else
    raise_application_error(-20000, 'v_var != 1!');
  end if;
end;
/

--Enable PL/SQL warning
exec dbms_warning.add_warning_setting_cat(warning_category =>
'ALL',warning_value => 'enable',scope => 'session');

--Check new value
select
  dbms_warning.get_warning_setting_string
from
  dual;

--Create procedure again and note error messages
create or replace procedure prc_test_dbms_warning as
  v_var  varchar2(10) := 'xx';
begin
  if 2=2 then
    select 'xxx'
    into   v_var
    from   dual;
  else
    raise_application_error(-20000, 'v_var != 1!');
  end if;
end;
/

--Get errors
show errors
```

Package dbms_warning

```
LINE/COL ERROR
-------- -----------------------------------------------------------------1/1
PLW-05018: unit prc_test_dbms_warning omitted optional AUTHID clause;
default value definer used
9/5      PLW-06002: Unreachable code
```

Now disable warnings in this procedure for errors *PLW-05018* and *PLW-06002* by using this *compile* option below or by using the *add_warning_setting_num* procedure.

```
alter procedure prc_test_dbms_warning compile plsql_warnings='enable:all,
disable:06002, disable:05018';
alter procedure prc_test_dbms_warning compile plsql_warnings='enable:all';

begin
   dbms_warning.add_warning_setting_num(
       warning_number => 06002,
       warning_value => 'disable',
       scope => 'session');
end;
/

alter procedure prc_test_dbms_warning compile ;
--At this time just one error will be showed
show errors

begin
   dbms_warning.add_warning_setting_num(
       warning_number => 05018,
       warning_value => 'disable',
       scope => 'session');
end;
/

alter procedure prc_test_dbms_warning compile ;
```

Finally, no error will be shown when compiling the test procedure after disabling warning messages using the *add_warning_setting_num* procedure as warning numbers will be suppressed.

Package *debug_extproc*

External procedures have a particular package used to debug their sessions called *debug_extproc*. In order to debug an external procedure, start an agent within the session. This package is not installed by default. If the package is needed, the script *dbextp.sql* must be executed. The script is located in both the Companion CD for Oracle 10g or the new Oracle Examples CD for Oracle 11g.

Now, follow this example which shows how to enable the *debug* process in an *external* procedure. First, run the *dbextp.sql* script which will create the *debug_extproc* package.

```
conn sys@ora11g as sysdba

Connected to Oracle 11g Enterprise Edition Release 11.1.0.6.0
conn / as sysdba

@?/plsql/demo/dbextp.sql
```

This next step is used in Oracle 10g. Start the *external* procedure agent. This connects to the *external* procedure and enables information about the process being used to be gathered.

```
begin
   debug_extproc.startup_extproc_agent;
end;
/
```

In Oracle 11g, start an agent using the new *agtctl* utility as in this example.

```
agtctl set max_dispatchers  2 my_agent1
agtctl set tcp_dispatchers  1 my_agent1
agtctl set max_task_threads 2 my_agent1
agtctl set max_sessions     5 my_agent1
agtctl unset listener_address my_agent1
agtctl set listener_address "(address=(protocol=ipc)(key=extproc))"
my_agent1
agtctl startup extproc my_agent1
```

The next step is to find the PID of this session that has an agent started.

```
ps -ef | grep extproc

ora11g    23783    1  0 18:59 ?        00:00:00 extprocep_agt1 -mt
```

Now use the *gdb executable* to attach the *extproc* to the session that has an agent started.

```
gdb  extprocep_agt1 23783
GNU gdb Fedora (6.8-27.el5)

Copyright (C) 2008 Free Software Foundation, Inc.
License GPLv3+: GNU GPL version 3 or later
<http://gnu.org/licenses/gpl.html>
This is free software: you are free to change and redistribute it.
There is no warranty, to the extent permitted by law.  Type "show copying"
and "show warranty" for details.
This GDB was configured as "i386-redhat-linux-gnu"...
extprocep_agt1: No such file or directory.

Attaching to process 23783
Reading symbols from /u01/app/oracle/product/11.2.0/db11g/bin/extproc...(no
debugging symbols found)...done.
```

```
Reading symbols from
/u01/app/oracle/product/11.2.0/db11g/lib/libagtsh.so...(no debugging symbols
found)...done.
Loaded symbols for /u01/app/oracle/product/11.2.0/db11g/lib/libagtsh.so
...

...
Loaded symbols for /lib/libresolv.so.2

(no debugging symbols found)
0x00ab5402 in __kernel_vsyscall ()
(gdb)
```

Use the *break* command to insert a breakpoint.

```
(gdb) break extprocep_agt1
Function "extprocep_agt1" not defined.
Make breakpoint pending on future shared library load? (y or [n]) y
Breakpoint 1 (extprocep_agt1) pending.
(gdb)
```

Now run the *external* procedure so the agent can gather the debug information.

```
select
    external_program('ORACLE_HOME')
from
    dual;
```

After that, the agent connects the *external* procedure called by Oracle to the debugger. Now find the errors and determine how to fix them using the debugger. In this example, Linux *gdb* was used. It may be necessary to refer to the debugger's documentation for specific actions that can be performed from here.

Package *dbms_random*

The next example uses the *dbms_random* function to randomize a series of numbers from which a character string is then constructed. From the random number obtained with *dbms_random*, take the three numbers from the third position and check if they exist within 33 and 125, the allowable numbers for ASCII printable characters. After all the work with *dbms_random*, we figured out that it would have been easier just to cycle through the possible values for the varrays in a nested looping structure. Of course, that would have led to a non-random ordered table. For the work we were doing, it would have been OK to do it that way, but we can see other situations where the *dbms_random* technique would be beneficial.

My thought was to use varray types and populate them with the various possible values, then use *dbms_random.value* to generate the index values for the various varrays. The *count* column was just a truncated call to *dbms_random* in the range of 1 to 600. All of this was placed into a procedure with the ability to give it the number of required values.

Code 7.40 – dbms_random.sql

```
conn sys@ora11g as sysdba

Connected to Oracle 11g Enterprise Edition Release 11.1.0.6.0
conn / as sysdba

create or replace procedure load_random_data(cnt in number) as
  v_rand number;
begin

 dbms_random.initialize (123456);
 for i in 1..1000 loop
 v_rand := dbms_random.value;
 insert
 into rand values (i,v_rand);
 end loop;
end;
/
```

The *dbms_random* function is deprecated by *dbms_crypto*.

Summary

This chapter has shown how and when to use almost all packages designed for management and monitoring tasks with regard to their day-to-day database administrative work. In the next chapter, Data Warehouse packages will be explained and demonstrated.

Oracle Data Warehouse Packages

A DWH (Data Warehouse) database normally holds summarized operational data pertaining to an entire enterprise. Usually, data is loaded through a clean-up and aggregation process, such as an ETL process (Extraction Transformation and Load), with predetermined intervals such as daily, monthly or quarterly. One of the key concepts in data warehousing is that the data is stored along a timeline. A data warehouse must support the needs of a large variety of users. A DWH may contain summarized as well as atomic data. A DWH may combine the concepts of OLTP, OLAP and DSS into one physical data structure. Major operations in a DWH are usually reported with a low to medium level of analytical processing.

A data warehouse contains detailed, nonvolatile, time-based information. Usually, data marts are derived from data warehouses. A data warehouse design needs to be fairly straightforward as many users will query the data warehouse directly. However, only 10% of the queries in a DWH are ad-hoc in nature with 90% being canned query or reports.

Data warehouse design and creation is an interactive and evolving process; it is never entirely finished. For a DWH to succeed, the user community must be intimately involved from design through implementation. Generally, data warehouses are denormalized structures. A normalized database stores the greatest amount of data in the smallest amount of space. In a data warehouse, storage space is sacrificed for speed via denormalization.

Many of the time-honored concepts are bent or completely broken when designing a data warehouse. An OLTP designer may have difficulty in crossing over to data warehousing design. In fact, a great OLTP designer may find DWH to be frustrating and difficult. Many object-related concepts are implemented in a DWH design. A source for DWH designers may be found in a pool of OO (Object-Oriented) developers.

These next pages will introduce some packages that can be used in data warehouse environments.

Package *dbms_advanced_rewrite*

The main purpose of this package is to provide a route for an SQL statement to follow a specific execution plan. Sometimes it is not possible to change the application code. Rather than using an inferior plan which is experiencing performance issues, this package should be implemented to allow a materialized view plan to be invoked. Oracle has named this functionality Advanced Query Rewrite Using Equivalence. More information about this can be found in the Oracle Database Data Warehousing Guide.

This example will show how simple it is to change the path of an SQL statement to a new one that is performing better. First, the user must have *execute* privilege on the *dbms_advanced_rewrite* package. The initialization parameter *query_rewrite_enabled* must be *TRUE* and *query_rewrite_integrity* must be *trusted* or *stale_tolerated*.

Connect as *sysdba* and grant the necessary privileges to *pkg* user. Check if the initialization parameters have the correct values and change them if necessary.

🖫 Code 8.1 – dbms_advanced_rewrite.sql

```
conn sys@ora11g as sysdba

Connected to:
Oracle 11g Enterprise Edition Release 11.2.0.1.0 - Production
With the Partitioning, Oracle Label Security, OLAP, Data Mining,
Oracle Database Vault and Real Application Testing options

--Grant privileges to pkg user
grant execute on dbms_advanced_rewrite to pkg;
grant create materialized view to pkg;

--Change the initialization parameters
alter system set query_rewrite_enabled=TRUE scope=both;
alter system set query_rewrite_integrity=trusted scope=both;
```

Suppose that the application has a view named *sales_v1* that is performing a full table scan. Since it has a *full* hint inside of it, create another view without this hint. The second view will be *sales_v2*.

```
create view sales_v1
as
select /*+ full (sales)*/
   amount_sold + (amount_sold * 0.035) as amount
from
   sales
where
  prod_id=10;

create view sales_v2
as
```

```
select
   amount_sold + (amount_sold * 0.035) as amount
from
   sales
where
  prod_id=10;
```

Check the explain plan for both views and note that the first one is doing a FTS.

```
--First view
explain plan for
select * from sales_v1;
select * from table(dbms_xplan.display);

PLAN_TABLE_OUTPUT
--------------------------------------------------------------------------------
Plan hash value: 1550251865
--------------------------------------------------------------------------------
| Id  | Operation           | Name  | Rows  | Bytes | Cost (%CPU)| Time     | Ps
--------------------------------------------------------------------------------
|   0 | select statement    |       |   165 |  1485 |  1376   (1)| 00:00:17 |
|   1 |  partition range all|       |   165 |  1485 |  1376   (1)| 00:00:17 |
|*  2 |   table access full | sales |   165 |  1485 |  1376   (1)| 00:00:17 |
--------------------------------------------------------------------------------
Predicate Information (identified by operation id):
---------------------------------------------------
   2 - filter("prod_id"=10)

14 rows selected

--Second view
explain plan for
select * from sales_v2;
select * from table(dbms_xplan.display);
plan_table_output
--------------------------------------------------------------------------------
Plan hash value: 511273406
--------------------------------------------------------------------------------
| Id  | Operation                            | Name          | Rows  | Bytes | Co
--------------------------------------------------------------------------------
|   0 | select statement                     |               |   165 |  1485 |
|   1 |  partition range all                 |               |   165 |  1485 |
|   2 |   table access by local index rowid  | sales         |   165 |  1485 |
|   3 |    bitmap conversion to rowids       |               |       |       |
|*  4 |     bitmap index single value        | sales_prod_bix|       |       |
--------------------------------------------------------------------------------
Predicate Information (identified by operation id):
---------------------------------------------------
   4 - access("PROD_ID"=10)

16 rows selected
```

Since the application code cannot be changed, use the *declare_rewrite_equivalence*
procedure from the *dbms_advanced_rewrite* package as follows:

```
begin
   dbms_advanced_rewrite.declare_rewrite_equivalence(
      name => 'my_first_equivalence',
      source_stmt => 'select * from sales_v1',
      destination_stmt => 'select * from sales_v2',
      validate => FALSE,
      rewrite_mode => 'recursive');

end;
/
```

Check if the rewrite equivalence was created properly by querying the *dba_rewrite_equivalences* view.

```
col owner            for a10
col name             for a20
col source_stmt      for a30
col destination_stmt for a30

select
    *
from
    dba_rewrite_equivalences;

OWNER      NAME                 SOURCE_STMT                  DESTINATION_STMT
REWRITE_MODE
---------- -------------------- ---------------------------- ------------------------------------
-----
pkg        my first equivalence select * from sales_v1       select * from sales_v2
recursive
```

Finally, test the explain plan again for the first command. It is best to get the plan for the second view rather than the first one.

```
explain plan for
select * from sales_v1;
select * from table(dbms_xplan.display);

PLAN_TABLE_OUTPUT
-------------------------------------------------------------------------------------
Plan hash value: 511273406
-------------------------------------------------------------------------------------
| Id | Operation                          | Name           | Rows | Bytes | Co
-------------------------------------------------------------------------------------
|  0 | select statement                   |                |  165 |  1485 |
|  1 |  partition range all               |                |  165 |  1485 |
|  2 |   table access by local index rowid| sales          |  165 |  1485 |
|  3 |    bitmap conversion to rowids     |                |      |       |
|* 4 |     bitmap index single value      | sales_prod_bix |      |       |
-------------------------------------------------------------------------------------
Predicate Information (identified by operation id):
-------------------------------------------------------
   4 - access("PROD_ID"=10)

16 rows selected
```

That was a simple example showing what *dbms_advanced_rewrite* can do.

It is also possible to use this package in conjunction with OLAP function, as in the next example.

One of the options available for the Enterprise Edition of Oracle 10g is the OLAP Option, a multidimensional calculation engine that allows the DBA to perform OLAP analysis on multidimensional datatypes. By using the OLAP Option, DBAs working on data warehousing projects can choose to store their detail level data in normal Oracle relational tables, and then store aggregated data in OLAP Option analytic workspaces for further multidimensional analysis.

Starting with the Oracle 9i OLAP Option, access can be provided to these analytic workspaces with SQL statements by using the new *olap_table* function.

```
select product, city, sales,
  from table(olap_table('my_first_aw duration session',
    'sales_table',
    '',
    'dimension category from product
    dimension country from geography
    measure sales from sales
    ));
```

However, it was not possible to use these analytic workspaces as replacements for materialized views if the idea was to take advantage of query rewrite as the query rewrite mechanism in Oracle 9i would never recognize the *olap_table* function as being one that could provide the aggregated answers to the users' original query. Oracle 10g addresses this shortcoming by providing a new feature called query equivalence.

Query equivalence allows us to declare that two SQL statements are functionally equivalent and that the target statement should be used in preference to the source statement. By using the query equivalence feature, we can produce a custom SQL query, in this instance by using the *olap_table* feature to retrieve summary data from an analytic workspace, and have the query used to satisfy a regular SQL statement that summarizes via the usual SUM() and GROUP BY clauses.

Taking our previous example, we might want my analytic workspace to be used to provide a specific summary for a SQL query. In this case, my SQL query might be:

```
select
    category,
    country,
    sum(sales)
from
    product p,
    geography g,
    sales s
where
    s.product_id = p.product_id
and
    s.geography_id = p.geography_id
group
    by p.category,
    g.country;
```

To declare that the analytic workspace query is functionally equivalent to the previous query, issue the command:

```
    dbms_advanced_rewrite.declare_rewrite_equivalence (
    'my_second_equivalence',
    'select
```

```
        category,
        country,
        sum(sales)
    from
        product p,
        geography g,
        sales s
    where
        s.product_id = p.product_id
    and
        s.geography_id = p.geography_id
    group by
        p.category,
        g.country',
      ' select
          product,
          city,
          sales,
        from
          table(olap_table('my_first_aw duration session',
                           'sales_table',
        '',
        'dimension category from product
        dimension country from geography
        measure sales from sales))');
```

Query equivalence can be used to substitute any SQL or DML statement for another, including use of the new SQL MODEL clause, and is particularly useful when SQL is generated by an application and cannot be changed. But there is a different way to phrase the query, perhaps using new data structures such as an OLAP Option analytic workspace that has been created.

In order to drop the rewrite equivalence, use the *drop_rewrite_equivalence* procedure.

```
begin
    dbms_advanced_rewrite.drop_rewrite_equivalence(
        name => 'My_First_Equivalence');
end;
/
```

Package *dbms_cube*

Oracle 10g introduced some new OLAP capabilities using the built-in analytical workspaces of the Oracle database. There are many new PL/SQL and XML-based interfaces that aid in the creation of workspaces based on the cubes, dimensions, measures, and calculations defined in the OLAP database catalog. These new interfaces can be used by the new packages provided or by Oracle Enterprise Manager to define and build analytic workspaces. This removes the need for the user to learn OLAP DML commands. This is now the familiar territory of PL/SQL packages and OEM!

Oracle 10g also provided significant help with performance enhancements. New parallel capabilities are provided for aggregate and *SQL* import operations, making it much faster to load and materialize analytic workspaces from relational database information. 11g also provides many hierarchy-related improvements.

OLAP data can be stored in either relational tables or multi-dimensional data types held within an analytic workspace. Among its many functions, the *dbms_cube* package can be used to create and populate analytic workspaces by using the *build* procedure.

The first step is to verify that OLAP is already installed and is valid in the database. To do so, follow MOSC Note: 296187.1 in Oracle Support. After confirming that OLAP is installed, move on to some examples of how to create materialized views and dimensions using the cubes packages.

How to Create a Cube using a Materialized View

To see how to use a sube with a materialized view, we start by creating a materialized view that will be used for this example.

💾 Code 8.2 – dbms_cube.sql

```
conn sys@ora11g as sysdba

Connected to:
Oracle 11g Enterprise Edition Release 11.2.0.1.0 - Production
With the Partitioning, Oracle Label Security, OLAP, Data Mining,
Oracle Database Vault and Real Application Testing options

create materialized view "pkg"."cal_month_sales_mv" ("calendar_month_desc",
"dollars")
   on prebuilt table without reduced precision
   using index
   refresh force on demand
   using default local rollback segment
   using enforced constraints enable query rewrite
   as select    t.calendar_month_desc
   ,         sum(s.amount_sold) as dollars
   from      sales s
   ,         times t
   where     s.time_id = t.time_id
   group by t.calendar_month_desc
;

alter table
   "pkg"."cal_month_sales_mv"
modify
   ("calendar_month_desc" not null enable);
```

Now, we make a cube under the materialized view that we just created by using the *create_mview* procedure of the *dbms_cube* package. Then we check the explain plan of the materialized view query, and note that it is performing a full table scan.

```
--Check explain plan before creating the cube
explain plan for
select    t.calendar_month_desc
   ,         sum(s.amount_sold) as dollars
   from      sales s
   ,          times t
   where     s.time_id = t.time_id
   group by t.calendar_month_desc
;
select * from table(dbms_xplan.display);
```

```
--Before creating mview the plan is like below:
PLAN_TABLE_OUTPUT
-------------------------------------------------------------------------------     Plan hash
value: 2607197432

--------------------------------------------------------------------------------------------
| Id  | Operation              | Name     | Rows  | Bytes | Cost (%CPU)| Time     | Pstart| Pstop |
--------------------------------------------------------------------------------------------
|   0 | select statement       |          |    60 |  2220 |  1413   (2)| 00:00:17 |       |       |
|   1 |  hash group by          |          |    60 |  2220 |  1413   (2)| 00:00:17 |       |       |
| * 2 |   hash join             |          |  1460 | 54020 |  1412   (2)| 00:00:17 |       |       |
|   3 |    view                 | vw_gbc_5 |  1460 | 30660 |  1395   (2)| 00:00:17 |       |       |
|   4 |     hash group by       |          |  1460 | 18980 |  1395   (2)| 00:00:17 |       |       |
|   5 |      partition range all|          |  918K |   11M |  1377   (1)| 00:00:17 |     1 |    28 |
|   6 |       table access full | sales    |  918K |   11M |  1377   (1)| 00:00:17 |     1 |    28 |
|   7 |    table access full    | times    |  1826 | 29216 |    17   (0)| 00:00:01 |       |       |
--------------------------------------------------------------------------------------------

Predicate Information (identified by operation id):
---------------------------------------------------

   2 - access("item_1"="T"."time_id")

19 rows selected.
```

```
--Create the cube

declare
v_mview varchar2(40);
begin
v_mview :=  dbms_cube.create_mview(mvowner => 'pkg',mvname =>
'cal_month_sales_mv',sam_parameters => 'build=immediate');
end;
/
```

After creating the cube, check the explain plan again. This shows that the materialized view that has just been created is running automatically.

```
--After creating mview the new plan is this one below
PLAN_TABLE_OUTPUT
--------------------------------------------------------------------------------
Plan hash value: 826791475

--------------------------------------------------------------------------------
| Id  | Operation       | Name     | Rows  | Bytes | Cost (%CPU)| Time
|
--------------------------------------------------------------------------------
|   0 | select statemnt |          |  8168 |  215K |    30   (4)|
00:00:01 |
```

```
|   1 | hash group by                          |                   | 8168 | 215K|  30   (4)|
00:00:01 |
|*  2 |   mat_view rewrite cube access uter | cb$cal_month_sales | 8168 | 215K|  29   (0)|
00:00:01 |
------------------------------------------------------------------------------------
```

If it is necessary to refresh a cube or any stale dimensions before refreshing, use the *build* procedure. Following are two examples on the correct syntax for using the *build* procedure based either on dimensions or cubes:

```
--Building dimension examples
begin
   dbms_cube.build(script =>
'cal_month_sales_aw.times_dim_d1_end_of_cal_mon3');
end;
/

--Building cube example
begin
   dbms_cube.build(
       script => 'pkg.times',
       method => 'C',
       refresh_after_errors => FALSE,
       parallelism => 2,
       atomic_refresh => FALSE,
       automatic_order => TRUE,
       add_dimensions => FALSE,
       scheduler_job => 'job_name',
       master_build_id => 1);
end;
/
```

Confusing as it may be, to build something is not the purpose of the procedure named *build*; rather, it is used to load data inside a cube or a dimension. Here is some information on the commands that can be used:

- *clear [values | leaves | aggregates]*: This command prepares the cube for data refresh. If used in dimensions, it deletes keys and, consequently, data values for cubes using this dimension.

- *values*: If this option is used, all data in the cube is cleared. All facts will need to be reloaded. Also, aggregates need to be recomputed. Supports complete refresh method.

- *leaves*: Clears only detail data and not aggregates. Only aggregates for changed or new facts need to be recomputed, though all facts must be reloaded.

- *aggregates*: This option clears all aggregates but maintains detail data. Aggregates must be recomputed.

- *load [synch | no synch]*: This command loads data into a dimension or cube. Only two options are available. They are:

  - *synch*: This option correlates relational data sources with dimension keys.

- *no synch*: This option loads dimension keys but will not delete pre-existing keys.

- *solve*: This option is used to aggregate a cube using specified rules.

- *compile*: This option can only be used with dimensions. It creates the supporting structure for a dimension.

- *analyze*: This option calls the *analyze* procedure of the *dbms_aw_stats* package in order to analyze cubes or dimensions.

- *execute olap dml* string: This is used to execute a DML command in a specified analytic workspace.

- *execute plsql* string: This option can be used to execute a PL/SQL program or script of a database.

- *model model_name*: This option is used to execute a previously created model.

- *aggregate using [measure]*: This option generates aggregate values for cubes.

With Oracle 11g, it is possible to export and import analytic workspaces using XML templates and these procedures:

- *export_xml*: Used to export OLAP metadata from an XML format to a CLOB

- *export_xml_to_file*: Used to export OLAP metadata to a file in XML format

- *import_xml*: Used to create, modify or drop an analytic workspace within an existing template

- *validate_xml*: Used to validate the analytic workspace without making changes within a database

Take a look at the examples below:

📁 Code 8.3 – dbms_cube_xml.sql

```
conn sys@ora11g as sysdba

Connected to:
Oracle 11g Enterprise Edition Release 11.2.0.1.0 - Production
With the Partitioning, Oracle Label Security, OLAP, Data Mining,
Oracle Database Vault and Real Application Testing options

--Export to XML file
begin
   dbms_cube.export_xml_to_file(
      object_ids => 'pkg',
      output_dirname => 'exp_dbms',
      output_filename => 'my_exp_cube.xml');
end;
/

--Validate XML metadata
```

```
begin
   dbms_cube.validate_xml(
      dirname=>'exp_dbms',
      filename=>'my_exp_cube.xml');
end;
/

--Import metadata
begin
   dbms_cube.import_xml(dirname => 'exp_dbms',filename =>
'my_exp_cube.xml');
end;
/
```

Package *dbms_cube_advise*

While the *dbms_cube* package is designed to create, load and process data in cubes and dimensions, *dbms_cube_advise* is used to check if a cube's materialized view supports a fast refresh and query rewrite. The important function of this package is *mv_cube_advice*. It is used to generate missing objects and/or to verify that all requirements are met.

Here is an example:

🖫 Code 8.4 – dbms_cube_advise.sql

```
conn sys@ora11g as sysdba

Connected to:
Oracle 11g Enterprise Edition Release 11.2.0.1.0 - Production
With the Partitioning, Oracle Label Security, OLAP, Data Mining,
Oracle Database Vault and Real Application Testing options

set linesize 200
col sqltext for a100
col "Recom Type" for a30
col "Cube Name" for a15
col "Name Master Table" for a12
select
   decode(advicetype,
      1,'Create NOT NULL constraint',
      2,'Create PK on master table',
      3,'Create PK on master view',
      4,'Create FK on master table',
      5,'Create FK on master view',
      6,'Create relational dimensions',
      7,'Create mview log',
      8,'Compile mview') "Recom Type",
   apiobject "Cube Name",
   sqlobject "Name Master Table",
   sqltext "SQL Command"
from
   table(dbms_cube_advise.mv_cube_advice(owner => 'pkg',objName =>
'cal_month_sales',reqType => '0'));
```

The results would look like this:

```
Recom Type                   Cube Name        Name Master Table SQL Command
--------------------------   ---------------  ----------------- ----------------Create NOT NULL
constraint     cal_month_sales sales             alter table "pkg"."sales" modify ( "time_id"
constraint "COAD_NN000105" not null
Create NOT NULL constraint     cal_month_sales TIMES             alter table "pkg"."times" modify (
"calendar_month_id" constraint "COAD_NN000106"
Create NOT NULL constraint     cal_month_sales times             alter table "pkg"."times" modify (
"calendar_quarter_id" constraint "COAD_NN0001
Create NOT NULL constraint     cal_month_sales times             alter table "pkg"."times" modify (
"calendar_year_id" constraint "COAD_NN000108"
Create NOT NULL constraint     cal_month_sales times             alter table "pkg"."times" modify (
"time_id" constraint "COAD_NN000109" not null
Create PK on master table      cal_month_sales times             alter table "pkg"."times" modify
("time_id" constraint "COAD_PK000110" primary k
Create PK on master table      cal_month_sales sales             sales           alter table
"pkg"."sales" add constraint "COAD_PK000111" primary key (time_id) r
Create FK on master table      cal_month_sales sales             alter table "pkg"."sales" modify
("time_id" constraint "COAD_FK000112" reference
Create relational dimensions   times_dim_d1     times_dim_d1     create dimension
"pkg"."times_dim_d1"
                                                                  level "month" is
("pkg"."times"."calen

Compile mview                  cal_month_sales cb$cal_month_sales alter materialized view
"pkg"."cb$cal_month_sales" compile
```

The *mv_cube_advice* function generates recommendations for a cube's materialized view. It determines which constraints, SQL dimension objects and materialized view logs would benefit a query rewrite in order to enable a faster refresh. This is the primary function of the Materialized View Advisor feature found in Analytic Workspace Manager. A few other functions and packages of *dbms_cube_advise* are described below:

- *trace*: This procedure is used to turn on/off diagnostic messages in server output for the *mv_cube_advice* function.

🖫 Code 8.5 – dbms_cube_advise_trace.sql

```
conn sys@ora11g as sysdba

Connected to:
Oracle 11g Enterprise Edition Release 11.2.0.1.0 - Production
With the Partitioning, Oracle Label Security, OLAP, Data Mining,
Oracle Database Vault and Real Application Testing options

set serverout on format wrapped
execute dbms_cube_advise.trace(1);

dbms_coad_diag: Changing diagLevel from [0] to [1]

.

--Execute the same advise function
set linesize 200
col sqltext for a100
col "Recom Type" for a30
col "Cube Name" for a15
col "Name Master Table" for a18
select
   decode(advicetype,
      1,'Create NOT NULL constraint',
```

```
      2,'Create PK on master table',
      3,'Create PK on master view',
      4,'Create FK on master table',
      5,'Create FK on master view',
      6,'Create relational dimensions',
      7,'Create mview log',
      8,'Compile mview') "Recom Type",
   apiobject "Cube Name",
   sqlobject "Name Master Table",
   sqltext "SQL Command"
from
   table(dbms_cube_advise.mv_cube_advice(owner => 'pkg',objName =>
'cal_month_sales',reqType => '0'));
```

After the normal query results, diagnostic messages like these will appear:

```
20100611 10:37:23.155957000 dbms_coad_diag NOTE: Parameter mvOwner   : pkg
20100611 10:37:23.156923000 dbms_coad_diag NOTE: Parameter mvName    : cb$cal_month_sales
20100611 10:37:23.157031000 dbms_coad_diag NOTE: Parameter factTab   : pkg.sales
20100611 10:37:23.157055000 dbms_coad_diag NOTE: Parameter cubeName  : cal_month_sales
20100611 10:37:23.157074000 dbms_coad_diag NOTE: Parameter cnsState  : rely disable novalidate
20100611 10:37:23.157093000 dbms_coad_diag NOTE: Parameter NNState   : disable novalidate
20100611 10:37:23.157117000 dbms_coad_diag NOTE: Begin NN:
20100611 10:37:23.625093000 dbms_coad_diag NOTE: End   NN:
20100611 10:37:23.625156000 dbms_coad_diag NOTE: Begin PK:
20100611 10:37:23.842807000 dbms_coad_diag NOTE: End   PK:
20100611 10:37:23.842907000 dbms_coad_diag NOTE: Begin FK:
20100611 10:37:23.980269000 dbms_coad_diag NOTE: End   FK:
20100611 10:37:23.980326000 dbms_coad_diag NOTE: Begin RD:
20100611 10:37:24.849280000 dbms_coad_diag NOTE: End   RD:
20100611 10:37:24.849339000 dbms_coad_diag NOTE: Begin CM:
20100611 10:37:24.851761000 dbms_coad_diag NOTE: End   CM:
```

Note that additional diagnostic information was added at the end of the query results. This can help to diagnose any issues found through the recommendations function.

Another procedure of the *dbms_cube_advise* package is *set_cns_exception_log*. It identifies the name of an exception log used when validated constraints generated by *mv_cube_advice* are executed. Here is more information about some analytic workspace objects and their properties:

- *dba_aws:* Shows information about all analytic workspaces in a database

- *dba_aw_obj:* Shows information about all objects found in analytic workspaces

- *dba_aw_prop:* Shows analytic workspace properties

- *dba_aw_ps:* Shows space used by each analytic workspace

- *dba_cubes:* Shows information about cubes

Here are *sys* tables used internally (do not change data in these tables):

```
--Shows all analytic workspace in database
select * from sys.aw$;
--Shows information of programs that can be used to create metadata catalogs
select * from sys.aw$awmd;
--Can be used to get information about summary space used
```

```
select * from sys.aw$awreport;
--Shows tracking data about access to aggregate cells
select * from sys.aw_track$;
--History of all pages
select * from sys.ps$;
```

Good scripts related to OLAP are available to download at this Oracle link: http://www.oracle.com/technology/products/bi/olap/olap_ dba_scripts.zip. For example, this script shows how much space an analytic workspace is consuming in the database:

```
set pages 500 lines 110
bre on report;
comp sum lab "Total Disk:" of mb on report;

col awname format a40 heading "Analytic Workspace"
col tablespace_name format a20 heading "Tablespace"
col mb format 999,999,990.00 heading "On Disk MB"

select
    dbal.owner||'.'||substr(dbal.table_name,4) awname,
    sum(dbas.bytes)/1024/1024 as mb,
    dbas.tablespace_name
from
    dba_lobs dbal,
    dba_segments dbas
where
        dbal.column_name = 'awlob'
    and
        dbal.segment_name = dbas.segment_name
group by
    dbal.owner,
    dbal.table_name,
    dbas.tablespace_name
order by
    dbal.owner,
    dbal.table_name;
```

For further information regarding OLAP Administration, check out the Oracle OLAP User's Guide 11g Release 1 (11.1).

Packages *dbms_data_mining* and *dbms_data_mining _transform*

One of the new features in Oracle 9i was Oracle Data Mining, a data mining engine which allowed data analysts and application developers to perform a range of data mining algorithms on data held in the Oracle database. Oracle 9i came with a number of mining algorithms such as Adaptive Bayes Networks, Clustering and Association

Rules, together with a Java API, to allow ODM functions to be included in Java applications.

Whilst this was useful for Java programmers, it was not all that relevant for PL/SQL programmers and to remedy this, Oracle 10g came with a new package called *dbms_data_mining* that provides PL/SQL access to the data mining engine.

Like the Java API, *dbms_data_mining* allows for building a data mining model, testing it and then applying the model to provide scores or predictive information for an application. One of the key differentiators for Oracle data mining is that mining models can be applied directly to data in the database. There is no need to extract the data and then separately load it into the mining engine, meaning that data mining can now be carried out in real time. The Oracle data mining engine can be pointed at any schema in the database. If the data needs processing beforehand to place continuous and discrete values into range bins, there is also a new accompanying package, *dbms_data_mining_transform*, to carry this out automatically.

Oracle provides a graphical tool named Oracle Data Miner. This can be downloaded at http://www.oracle.com/technology/products/bi/ odm/index.html. Further information on Oracle data mining can be found in "Oracle Data Mining Concepts" at http://tahiti.oracle.com.

The data mining packages *dbms_data_mining* and *dbms_data_mining_tranform* provide many procedures and functions for managing data mine information. Some of them will be presented in the next example.

There should be some familiarity with Oracle data mining as some objects are a prerequisite for using the *dbms_data_mining* and *dbms_data_mining_transform* packages. A complete Oracle by Example of ODM can be found through this link: http://www.oracle.com/technetwork/database/options/odm/odm-samples-194497.html. The first example will show how to create, drop, rename, export, import and get information about mining models.

🖫 Code 8.6 – dbms_data_mining.sql

```
conn sys@ora11g as sysdba

Connected to:
Oracle 11g Enterprise Edition Release 11.2.0.1.0 - Production
With the Partitioning, Oracle Label Security, OLAP, Data Mining,
Oracle Database Vault and Real Application Testing options

begin
    dbms_data_mining.create_model(
        model_name => 'my_first_model',
        mining_function => dbms_data_mining.feature_extraction,
        data_table_name => 'tab_my_tab_exemple',
```

```
            case_id_column_name => 'cust_id',
            target_column_name => NULL,
            settings_table_name => 'my_new_settings_1',
            settings_schema_name => 'pkg',
            xform_list => NULL);
end;
/

--Dropping a model
begin
    dbms_data_mining.drop_model(model_name => 'my_first_model',force =>
TRUE);
end;
/

--Rename a model
begin
    dbms_data_mining.rename_model(
        model_name => 'my_first_model',
        new_model_name => 'my_first_model_new_name');
end;
/
```

Here are some important points on exporting a model. During the process of the import or export procedures, temporary tables with the names *dm$p_model_expimp_temp*, *dm$p_model_import_temp*, and *dm$p_model_tabkey_temp* are created. Located in the owner's schema, they contain internal information about export or import processes. Be sure that the object directory is already created in the database.

In this example, only two models will be exported. If it is necessary to export all models, leave *model_filter* blank.

The command below will export all models for the user that is currently connected.

```
begin
    dbms_data_mining.export_model(
        filename => 'my_first_exp_data_mining',
        directory => 'exp_mining_dir',
        model_filter => 'name in (''nmf_model_1'', ''svm_model_2'')',
        filesize => NULL,
        operation => NULL,
        remote_link => NULL,
        jobname => NULL);
end;
/
```

A dump file named *my_first_exp_data_mining* is generated in the directory specified by *exp_mining_dir*. This example shows how to import a model connected as sys, mapping source schema to a different target schema.

```
begin
   dbms_data_mining.import_model(
      filename => 'my_first_exp_data_mining',
      directory => 'exp_mining_dir',
      model_filter => NULL,
      operation => NULL,
      remote_link => NULL,
      jobname => NULL,
      schema_remap => pkg_target);
end;
/
```

The next examples show how to add, remove and get information about the cost mode matrix. The process of adding a cost mode matrix associates the classification model with the cost matrix table.

```
begin
   dbms_data_mining.add_cost_matrix(
      model_name => 'my_first_exp_data_mining',
      cost_matrix_table_name => 'costs_nb',
      cost_matrix_schema_name => NULL);
end;
/

--Remove cost mode matrix
begin
   dbms_data_mining.remove_cost_matrix(
      model_name => 'my_first_exp_data_mining');
end;
/
```

There are other functions that can be used to gather information about models. They are described below:

```
--Return XML object with information about Decision Tree Model
select
   *
from
   table(dbms_data_mining.get_model_details_xml(model_name =>
'my_first_model'));


--Return coefficient statistics for a Generalized Linear Model
select
   *
from
   table(dbms_data_mining.get_model_details_glm(model_name =>
'my_first_model'));

--Return information about k-Means Clustering Models
select
   *
from
   table(dbms_data_mining.get_model_details_km(
         model_name => 'my_first_model',
```

```
            cluster_id => NULL,
            attribute => NULL,
            centroid => NULL,
            histogram => NULL,
            rules => NULL,
            attribute_subname => NULL));

--Return information about Naive Bayes Model
select
    *
from
    table(dbms_data_mining.get_model_details_nb(model_name =>
'my_first_model'));

--Return information about Non-Negative Matrix Factorization Model
select
    *
from
    table(dbms_data_mining.get_model_details_nmf(model_name =>
'my_first_model'));

--Return information about O-Cluster Clustering Model
select
    *
from
    table(dbms_data_mining.get_model_details_oc(
            model_name =>  'my_first_model',
            cluster_id => NULL,
            attribute => NULL,
            centroid => NULL,
            histogram => NULL,
            rules => NULL);

--Return information about a linear Support Vector Machine Model
select
    *
from
    table(dbms_data_mining.get_model_details_svm(model_name =>
'my_first_model'));

--Return statistics information about a model
select
    *
from
    table(dbms_data_mining.get_model_details_global(model_name =>
'my_first_model'));

--This function was replaced by data dictionary view
dba|all|user|_mining_model_settings.
select
    *
from
    dba_mining_model_settings;

--This function was replaced by data dictionary view
DBA|all|user|_mining_model_attributes
select
    *
```

Packages dbms_data_mining and dbms_data_mining
_transform

```
from
   dba_mining_model_attributes;

--Return information about transformation definitions associated with a
model
select
   *
from
   table(dbms_data_mining.get_model_transformations(model_name =>
'my_first_model'));
```

While *dbms_data_mining* is used to create, drop, change and get information about data mining models, *dbms_data_mining_transform* is used to prepare data for mining.

In the next examples, operations like *create*, *insert*, *stack* and *xform* will be found. They are used to transform columns of data for mining. The operations are briefly described here, followed by examples:

- *create*: This operation creates a transformation table used for transformation of data such as binning, column removal, normalization, outlier treatment and missing value treatment.

- *insert*: This operation populates a transformation table in a specified data source.

- *stack*: This operation adds to a list of transformation instructions. This stack can be used in the *create_model* procedure.

- *xform*: This operation creates a view based on table data which contains transformed columns.

Procedures starting with *create_%* are responsible for creating definition tables and procedures starting with *insert_%* are responsible for inserting transformation instructions into definition tables. There are also the procedures *stack_%* used to add expressions to the transformation definition stack and *xform_%* to create views that can add, remove or transform values and expressions.

Code 8.7 – dbms_data_mining_transform.sql

```
conn sys@ora11g as sysdba

Connected to:
Oracle 11g Enterprise Edition Release 11.2.0.1.0 - Production
With the Partitioning, Oracle Label Security, OLAP, Data Mining,
Oracle Database Vault and Real Application Testing options

--Procedure to create a table that will be filled with attribute information
to be excluded from mining process.
begin
   dbms_data_mining_transform.create_col_rem(
      rem_table_name => 'tab_transf_def',
      rem_schema_name => 'pkg');
end;
```

```
/
--Procedure to create a view that removes columns specified from data table.
begin
dbms_data_mining_transform.xform_col_rem(
   rem_table_name => 'tab_transf_def',
   data_table_name => 'tab_data',
   xform_view_name => 'view_1',
   rem_schema_name => 'pkg',
   data_schema_name => 'pkg',
   xform_schema_name => ' pkg ');
end;
/


--Procedure to produce bin boundaries at equal intervals in ordered data
begin
   dbms_data_mining_transform.insert_bin_num_eqwidth(
      bin_table_name => 'tab_bin',
      data_table_name => 'tab_data',
      bin_num => 10,
      exclude_list => dbms_data_mining_transform.column_list(
                                    'cust_id',
                                    'affinity_card',
                                    'bookkeeping_application',
                                    'bulk_pack_diskettes',
                                    'flat_panel_monitor',
                                    'printer_supplies',
                                    'y_box_games',
                                    'os_doc_set_kanji'),
      round_num => 4
      bin_schema_name => 'pkg',
      data_schema_name => 'pkg');
end;
/


--Update stack definition using expression in xform_list
begin
   dbms_data_mining_transform.stack_norm_lin(
      norm_table_name => 'tab_norm',
      xform_list => '({expr} - {shift})/{scale}',
      norm_schema_name => '');
end;
/
```

Package *dbms_dimension*

It used to always be a challenge to describe dimensions, and we used to depend on dictionary tables such as *dba_dimensions* and *dba_dim_attributes*. The Oracle Enterprise Manager (OEM) package was also useful for describing the structure of a dimension.

With the 10g release, there is a new way of describing dimensions using the package *dbms_dimension*. The *describe_dimension* procedure can be used in the *dbms_dimension* package for this purpose. The following statement executes the procedure.

```
execute dbms_dimension.describe_dimension('sales.mydim');
```

A dimension can also be validated by using the *validate_dimension* procedure of the *dbms_dimension* package. This procedure is similar to the old *dbms_olap.validate_dimension* procedure. Whenever the *validate_dimension* procedure encounters any errors, the errors are written to the *dimension_exceptions* table. Therefore, before we run the *validate_dimension* procedure, we need to create a local table, *dimension_exceptions*. The *utldim.sql* script needed to create this table is available in the Oracle Home directory *($ORACLE_HOME/rdbms/admin* on Unix).

In the next example, these two procedures will be used to describe and validate a dimension owned by *pkg* user.

🖫 Code 8.8 – dbms_dimension.sql

```
conn sys@ora11g as sysdba

Connected to:
Oracle 11g Enterprise Edition Release 11.2.0.1.0 - Production
With the Partitioning, Oracle Label Security, OLAP, Data Mining,
Oracle Database Vault and Real Application Testing options

set serveroutput on
begin
   dbms_dimension.describe_dimension(
      dimension => 'promotions_dim');
end;
/

  dimension pkg.promotions_dim
    level category is pkg.promotions.promo_category_id
    level promo is pkg.promotions.promo_id
    level promo_total is pkg.promotions.promo_total_id
    level subcategory is pkg.promotions.promo_subcategory_id

    hierarchy promo_rollup (
            promo child of
            subcategory child of
            category child of
            promo_total
    )
     attribute category level category determines
pkg.promotions.promo_category
    attribute promo level promo determines pkg.promotions.promo_begin_date
    attribute promo level promo determines pkg.promotions.promo_cost
    attribute promo level promo determines pkg.promotions.promo_end_date
    attribute promo level promo determines pkg.promotions.promo_name
    attribute promo_total level promo_total determines
pkg.promotions.promo_total
```

```
    attribute subcategory level subcategory determines
pkg.promotions.promo_subcategory
```

Next, we use the *validate_dimension* procedure to verify that the relationships for a dimension are valid.

```
begin
   dbms_dimension.validate_dimension(
      dimension => 'promotions_dim',
      incremental => TRUE,
      check_nulls => TRUE,
      statement_id => 'Validating dim promotions_dim');
end;
/



--Check if the procedure finds any error
select
   *
from
   dimension_exceptions;
```

Now we check for errors regarding relationships using one of these tables described below:

```
SQL> desc  mview$_exceptions
```

Name	Type	Nullable	Default	Comments
owner	varchar2(30)			
table_name	varchar 2(30)			
dimension_name	varchar 2(30)			
relationship	varchar 2(11)			
bad_rowid	*rowid*			

```
SQL> desc  dimension_exceptions
```

Name	Type	Nullable	Default	Comments
statement_id	varchar2(30)	Y		
owner	varchar 2(30)			
table_name	varchar 2(30)			
dimension_name	varchar 2(30)			
relationship	varchar 2(11)			
bad_rowid	*rowid*			

This single package is created using *dbmssum.sql* that can be found in the *$ORACLE_HOME/rdbms/admin* directory and it overrides the *validate_dimension* that was on the *dbms_olap* package on older database versions.

Package *dbms_mview*

Oracle materialized views are one of the single most important SQL tuning tools and they are a true silver bullet, allowing for pre-joining complex views and pre-compute summaries for superfast response time.

Oracle materialized views were first introduced in Oracle 8 as snapshots and were enhanced to allow very fast dynamic creation of complex objects. Oracle materialized views allow sub-second response times by pre-computing aggregate information, and Oracle dynamically rewrites SQL queries to reference existing Oracle materialized views.

Without Oracle materialized views, unnecessary repeating large-table full-table scans as summaries are computed over and over. Once Oracle materialized views have been enabled, Oracle provides several methods for invoking query rewrite. Query rewrite is generally automatic, but it can be explicitly enabled by using *alter session*, *alter system*, or SQL hints:

- *alter {session | system} disable query rewrite*

- *select / *+rewrite(mv1)*/...*

In Oracle, if *refresh fast* is specified for a single-table aggregate Oracle materialized view, a materialized view log must have been created for the underlying table, or the refresh command would fail. When creating an Oracle materialized view, there is the option of specifying whether the refresh occurs manually (*on demand*) or automatically (*on commit, dbms_job*). To use the fast warehouse refresh facility, specify the on demand mode. To refresh the Oracle materialized view, call one of the procedures in *dbms_mview*. The *dbms_mview* package provides three types of refresh operations:

1. *dbms_mview.refresh:* Refreshes one or more Oracle materialized views

2. *dbms_mview.refresh_all_mviews:* Refreshes all Oracle materialized views

3. *dbms_mview.refresh_dependent:* Refreshes all table-based Oracle materialized views

Following, find some examples of how to use the *dbms_mview* package and when to use its procedures. The first example shows how to reorganize a table using two procedures. These procedures should be executed from time to time in order to optimize performance and reduce disk I/O utilization.

🖫 Code 8.9 – dbms_mview_reorganization.sql

```
conn sys@ora11g as sysdba

Connected to:
Oracle 11g Enterprise Edition Release 11.2.0.1.0 - Production
With the Partitioning, Oracle Label Security, OLAP, Data Mining,
```

```
begin
   dbms_mview.begin_table_reorganization(tabowner => 'pkg',tabname =>
'cal_month_sales_mv');
end;
/

begin
   dbms_mview.end_table_reorganization(tabowner => 'pkg',tabname =>
'cal_month_sales_mv');
end;
/
```

If estimating the size of a materialized view prior to creating it is chosen, use the *estimate_mview_size* procedure as follows:

💾 Code 8.10 – dbms_mview_estimate.sql

```
conn sys@ora11g as sysdba

Connected to:
Oracle 11g Enterprise Edition Release 11.2.0.1.0 - Production
With the Partitioning, Oracle Label Security, OLAP, Data Mining,
Oracle Database Vault and Real Application Testing options

declare
   v_num_rows number;
   v_num_bytes number;
begin
   dbms_mview.estimate_mview_size(
      stmt_id => 'test_estimate',
      select_clause => 'select
                            department_id,
                            job_id,
                            sum(salary)
                        from
                            emp
                        group by
                            department_id,
                            job_id',
      num_rows => v_num_rows,
      num_bytes => v_num_bytes);
      dbms_output.put_line(a => 'Number of rows is:'||v_num_rows);
      dbms_output.put_line(a => 'Number of bytes is:'||v_num_bytes);
end;
/

Number of rows is:1
Number of bytes is:54
```

Another package option is useful for gleaning materialized view details. To know what kind of refresh is supported, simply run the *explain_mview* procedure and it will show this information. The results will be stored in a table named *mv_capabilities_table*, created by the *utlxmv.sql* script. It is also possible to load the results into an array as in this next example.

Package dbms_mview   **435**

Code 8.11 – dbms_mview_explain_mview.sql

```
conn sys@ora11g as sysdba

Connected to:
Oracle 11g Enterprise Edition Release 11.2.0.1.0 - Production
With the Partitioning, Oracle Label Security, OLAP, Data Mining,
Oracle Database Vault and Real Application Testing options
create table tab_array_results (
   v_array_results sys.explainmvarraytype);

declare
 v_mview_ddl varchar2(1000) := 'create materialized view emp_sum
                                tablespace tbs_data
                                refresh on demand
                                enable query rewrite
                                as
                                select
                                    department_id,
                                    job_id,
                                    sum(salary)
                                from
                                    emp
                                group by
                                    department_id,
                                    job_id';

 v_mv_array sys.ExplainMVArrayType;
begin
  dbms_mview.explain_mview(
     mv => v_mview_ddl,
     msg_array =>  v_mv_array);

  insert into
     tab_array_results
  values
  (v_mv_array);
  commit;
end;
/
```

Now simply query the *tab_array_results* table to find information regarding the materialized view specified in this example.

Another procedure, *explain_rewrite*, is used to identify why a query failed to rewrite or why the optimizer is choosing a specific materialized view. Take a look at the next example. The results will be stored in a table named *rewrite_table* created by the *utlxrw.sql* script found in *$ORACLE_HOME/rdbms/admin* directory.

Code 8.12 – dbms_mview_explain_rewrite.sql

```
conn sys@ora11g as sysdba

Connected to:
Oracle 11g Enterprise Edition Release 11.2.0.1.0 - Production
With the Partitioning, Oracle Label Security, OLAP, Data Mining,
Oracle Database Vault and Real Application Testing options
```

```
begin
   dbms_mview.explain_rewrite(
      query => 'select
                                department_id,
                                job_id,
                                sum(salary)
                        from
                                emp
                        group by
                                department_id,
                                job_id',
      mv => 'emp_sum',
      statement_id => 'My_First_Explain_Rewrite');
end;
/
```

Now check if the query is using a materialized view by querying *rewrite_table* as follows:

```
set linesize 140
col statement_id    for a30
col mv_owner        for a5
col mv_name         for a10
col mv_in_msg       for a8
col message         for a40
col original_cost   for 99
col rewritten_cost  for 99

select
   statement_id,
   mv_owner,
   mv_name,
   message,
   pass,
   mv_in_msg,
   original_cost,
   rewritten_cost
from
   rewrite_table
where
   pass='yes';

STATEMENT_ID                   MV_OW MV_NAME    MESSAGE                                  PAS MV_IN_MS
ORIGINAL_COST REWRITTEN_COST
------------------------------ ----- ---------- ---------------------------------------- --- --------
------------- --------------
My_First_Explain_Rewrite       pkg   emp_sum    QSM-01209: query rewritten with material yes emp_sum
3             2                                  ized view, emp_sum, using text match alg
                                                 orithm
```

Oracle Database automatically purges log data from materialized views; although in some situations, the snapshot log may grow to a huge size. The most common scenario where this problem happens is when the master table has more than one snapshot. If one of the snapshots is not configured with an automatic refresh, the file size may become unwieldy.

Package dbms_mview

Here are some purge examples that can be very useful with materialized views. This next procedure is used to purge rows from a materialized view log. Use the *num* parameter with a value of three to delete the rows required for refreshing the three least recently refreshed materialized views.

The last parameter, *flag,* is used to make sure that rows will be deleted from the materialized view log for at least one materialized view.

🖫 Code 8.13 – dbms_mview_purge_log.sql

```
conn sys@ora11g as sysdba

Connected to:
Oracle 11g Enterprise Edition Release 11.2.0.1.0 - Production
With the Partitioning, Oracle Label Security, OLAP, Data Mining,
Oracle Database Vault and Real Application Testing options

begin
   dbms_mview.purge_log(
       master => 'tab_master',
       num => 3,
       flag => 'delete');
end;
/
```

Commonly used in data warehouse environments, the following procedure will purge data from the direct loader log once they are no longer needed by any materialized view.

🖫 Code 8.14 – dbms_mview_purge_direct_load_log.sql

```
conn sys@ora11g as sysdba

Connected to:
Oracle 11g Enterprise Edition Release 11.2.0.1.0 - Production
With the Partitioning, Oracle Label Security, OLAP, Data Mining,
Oracle Database Vault and Real Application Testing options

begin
   dbms_mview.purge_direct_load_log;
end;
/
```

This next procedure will purge only rows from a specified materialized view log. It must be executed on the master site. Use the *dba_registered_mviews* view for the information needed to perform this procedure.

🖫 Code 8.15 – dbms_mview_purge_mview_from_log.sql

```
conn sys@ora11g as sysdba

Connected to:
Oracle 11g Enterprise Edition Release 11.2.0.1.0 - Production
```

```
With the Partitioning, Oracle Label Security, OLAP, Data Mining,
Oracle Database Vault and Real Application Testing options

select
   owner,
   name,
   mview_site
from
   dba_registered_mviews;

begin
   dbms_mview.purge_mview_from_log(
      mviewowner => 'pkg',
      mviewname => 'cal_month_sales_mv',
      mviewsite => '');
end;
/
```

To refresh a list of materialized views all at once, use the *dbms_mview.refresh* procedure. The next example will refresh two materialized views from different users while using different refresh methods; *complete* and *fast refresh* in this instance.

🖫 Code 8.16 – dbms_mview_refresh.sql

```
conn sys@ora11g as sysdba

Connected to:
Oracle 11g Enterprise Edition Release 11.2.0.1.0 - Production
With the Partitioning, Oracle Label Security, OLAP, Data Mining,
Oracle Database Vault and Real Application Testing options

begin
   dbms_mview.refresh(
      list =>'pkg.cb$times_dim_d1_cal_rollup,
             sh.fweek_pscat_sales_mv' ,
      method =>'cf' ,
      refresh_after_errors => TRUE,
      purge_option => 2,
      parallelism => 2,
      atomic_refresh => FALSE,
      nested => TRUE);
end;
/
```

If there is a site with a large number of materialized views and all stale materialized views need to be refreshed, use the *dbms_mview.refresh_all* procedure from the next example:

```
set serveroutput on
declare
v_failures binary_integer;
begin
   dbms_mview.refresh_all_mviews(
      number_of_failures => v_failures,method => 'cf',refresh_after_errors
=> TRUE);
```

```
      dbms_output.put_line(a => 'Failures on this refresh:'||v_failures);
end;
/
```

```
Failures on this refresh:0
```

The *dbms_mview.refresh_dependent* procedure can be used to refresh all materialized views that are dependent on a master table.

Note: There are additional properties specified in Oracle Database PL/SQL Packages and Types Reference regarding this procedure.

```
set serveroutput on
declare
v_failures binary_integer;
begin
   dbms_mview.refresh_dependent(
      number_of_failures => v_failures,
      list => 'sh.sales,
               pkg.test,
               pkg.time',
      method => 'c',
      nested => TRUE);
   dbms_output.put_line(
      a => 'Failures on this refresh:'||v_failures);
end;
/
```

There is also an internal procedure named *dbms_mview.refresh_mv*. Its utilization is not recommended unless specifically requested by Oracle support.

```
begin
   dbms_mview.refresh_mv(
      pipename => 'my_pipe_example',
      mv_index => 2,
      owner => 'pkg',
      name => 'mv_name',
      method => 'c',
      rollseg => NULL,
      atomic_refresh => NULL,
      env => NULL,
      resources => NULL);
end;
/
```

Materialized views are registered automatically by Oracle upon their creation. If, for some reason, an error is received during the registration process, register or unregister a materialized view or snapshot using the following procedure:

Code 8.17 – dbms_mview_register_unregister.sql

```
conn sys@ora11g as sysdba

Connected to:
Oracle 11g Enterprise Edition Release 11.2.0.1.0 - Production
With the Partitioning, Oracle Label Security, OLAP, Data Mining,
Oracle Database Vault and Real Application Testing options

--Register mview
begin
dbms_mview.register_mview(
   mviewowner => 'pkg',
   mviewname => 'mview_name',
   mviewsite => 'dbms',
   mview_id => sysdate,
   flag => dbms_mview.reg_rowid_mview,
   qry_txt => 'select department_id, job_id, sum(salary) from emp group by
department_id, job_id');
end;
/

--Unregister mview
begin
   dbms_mview.unregister_mview(
      mviewowner => 'pkg',
      mviewname => 'mview_name',
      mviewsite => 'dbms');
end;
/
```

Keep in mind that the processes of register/unregister shown above are not normally necessary.

Package *dbms_olap*

Oracle provides advisory functions in the *dbms_olap* package if there is doubt about which materialized views to create. These functions help in designing and evaluating materialized views for query rewrite. This package is still supported; however, most of its functionality was improved by other packages, so if a new application is being developed, it is recommended that those other packages be used instead.

Old procedures like *add_filter_item*, *create_id*, *estimate_mview_size*, *validate_dimension* and others were deprecated and replaced by new procedures in packages *dbms_advisor*, *dbms_dimension* and *dbms_mview*. In Oracle 11g, there are just three procedures. They are demonstrated in the next example.

The procedure *validate_dimension* is included for backward compatibility. However, it is preferred to use the new *dbms_dimension.validate_dimension*.

```
conn sys@ora11g as sysdba

Connected to:
Oracle 11g Enterprise Edition Release 11.2.0.1.0 - Production
With the Partitioning, Oracle Label Security, OLAP, Data Mining,
Oracle Database Vault and Real Application Testing options

begin
   dbms_olap.validate_dimension(
       dimension_name => 'my_view_name',
       dimension_owner => 'pkg',
       incremental => TRUE,
       check_nulls => TRUE);
end;
/
```

The *estimate_mview_size* procedure shown next is identical to its counterpart located in the *dbms_mview* package.

```
declare
v_rows number;
v_bytes number;
begin
   dbms_olap.estimate_mview_size(
       stmt_id => 'Test Estimate',
       select_clause => 'select
                             sum(sal),
                             emp_group
                          from
                             emp
                          group by
                             emp_group',
       num_rows => v_rows,
       num_bytes => v_bytes);
   dbms_output.put_line(a => 'Number of rows:'||v_rows);
   dbms_output.put_line(a => 'Number of bytes:'||v_bytes);
end;
/
```

The *set_logfile_name* procedure is used to rename the default *refresh.log* file when refreshing a materialized view.

```
begin
   dbms_olap.set_logfile_name(
       filename => '/tmp/my_mview_Refresh_Logfile.log');
   dbms_mview.refresh(;
   commit;
end;
/
```

As previously mentioned, *dbms_olap* was divided between different packages, and thus, *dbms_olap* has become a package with very few procedures.

Package *dbms_refresh*

This package provides another method for refreshing materialized views. It has the advantage of refreshing not only one, but a group of materialized views simultaneously. While the *dbms_mview.refresh* procedure can be used to refresh a single materialized view, the *dbms_refresh* package can be used to refresh all materialized views that belong to the same group.

It has procedures to create groups to be refreshed, add/remove materialized views to/from a group, add/remove a materialized view group, change the refresh interval of a group, refresh a group manually and automatically specify interval times.

Now a complete example will be shown in which a group will be created, materialized views added and removed to and from the group, how the group is refreshed and lastly, how to drop the group. First, create the materialized views that will be used in this example:

🖫 Code 8.19 – dbms_refresh.sql

```
conn sys@ora11g as sysdba

Connected to:
Oracle 11g Enterprise Edition Release 11.2.0.1.0 - Production
With the Partitioning, Oracle Label Security, OLAP, Data Mining,
Oracle Database Vault and Real Application Testing options

create table
   tab_dbms_refresh
tablespace
   tbs_data as
select
   *
from
   sys.source$;

alter table
   tab_dbms_refresh
add constraint
   pk_tab_dbms_refresh primary key (obj#, line);

create materialized view log on
   tab_dbms_refresh
with primary key;

col log_owner for a5 Heading "Owner"
col master for a15 Heading "Master Table"
col log_table for a15 Heading "Log Table"
col primary_key for a5 Heading "PK"
select
   log_owner,
   master,
   log_Table,
   primary_key
```

```
from
   dba_mview_logs
   where master='tab_dbms_refresh';;

select
   owner,
   mview_name
from
   dba_mviews
where
   mview_name like 'my_view%';

create materialized
   view my_view_1
tablespace tbs_data
refresh complete
as
select
   s.obj# ,
   count(s.line)
from
   tab_dbms_refresh s
group by
   s.obj#;

create materialized
   view my_view_2
tablespace tbs_data
refresh complete
as
select
   s.obj# ,
   count(s.line)
from
   tab_dbms_refresh s
group by
   s.obj#;

create materialized
   view my_view_3
tablespace tbs_data
refresh complete
as
select
   s.obj# ,
   count(s.line)
from
   tab_dbms_refresh s
group by
   s.obj#;
```

Now a procedure named *make* is used to create a materialized view group.

```
begin
   dbms_refresh.make(
      name => 'my_refresh_group_1',
      list => 'my_view_1',
      next_date => sysdate,
```

```
        interval => 'systimestamp + 1/24',
        implicit_destroy => FALSE,
        lax => TRUE,
        job => 0,
        rollback_seg => NULL,
        push_deferred_rpc => NULL,
        refresh_after_errors => NULL,
        purge_option => NULL,
        parallelism => 2,
        heap_size => NULL);
end;
/
```

Verify that the materialized view group was created and which materialized views belong to it by querying the *dba_snapshot* and *dba_refresh* views. Alternately, the *sys.rgroup$* table and *dba_rgroup* view can be used.

```
select
    r.rname "refresh group",
    sn.name "mview name"
from
    dba_snapshots sn,
    dba_refresh r
where
    sn.refresh_group = r.refgroup;

select
    *
from
    sys.rgroup$;

select
    *
from
    dba_rgroup;
```

Suppose that we want to add more materialized views to the group created above. To do so, we use the *dbms_refresh.add* procedure. This will add the other two materialized views created in the group above. Now check the group again:

```
begin
    dbms_refresh.add(
        name => 'my_refresh_group_1',
        list => 'my_view_2,my_voew
._3');
        commit;
end;
/


select
    r.rname "refresh group",
    sn.name "mview name"
from
    dba_snapshots sn,
```

```
   dba_refresh r
where
   sn.refresh_group = r.refgroup;
```

```
Refresh Group                    MView Name
-----------------------------    -----------------------------
my_refresh_group_1               my_view_1
my_refresh_group_1               my_view_2
my_refresh_group_1               my_view_3
```

Next, use the *dbms_refresh.change* procedure to change the refresh interval of a specified group. First, check the existing interval. Then make the change and check the interval values again.

```
col "interval"       for a20
col "mview Name"     for a20
col "refresh group"  for a20

select
   r.rname "refresh group",
   sn.name "mview Name" ,
   r.interval "interval"
from
   dba_snapshots sn,
   dba_refresh r
where
   sn.refresh_group = r.refgroup;

begin
   dbms_refresh.change(
      name => 'my_refresh_group_1',
      next_date => sysdate,
      interval => 'systimestamp +1/12',
      parallelism => 4);
      commit;
end;
/

col "interval"       for a20
col "mview Name"     for a20
col "refresh group"  for a20

select
   r.rname "refresh group",
   sn.name "Mview name" ,
   r.interval "interval"
from
   dba_snapshots sn,
   dba_refresh r
where
   sn.refresh_group = r.refgroup;
```

In order to refresh the entire group, use the *dbms_refresh.refresh* procedure as follows:

```
select
   mview_name,
```

```
   to_char(last_refresh_date,'rrrr-mm-dd hh24:mi:ss')
from
   dba_mviews
where
   mview_name like 'my_view%';

begin
   dbms_refresh.refresh(name => 'my_refresh_group_1');
end;
/
```

If it is necessary to remove a materialized view from a group, use the *dbms_refresh.subtract* procedure as in the command below. Before the drop, check if the materialized view actually exists in the group from which it should be removed.

```
col "interval"      for a20
col "mview name"    for a20
col "refresh group" for a20

select
   r.rname "refresh group",
   sn.name "mview name" ,
   r.interval "interval"
from
   dba_snapshots sn,
   dba_refresh    r
where
   sn.refresh_group = r.refgroup;

begin
   dbms_refresh.subtract(
      name => 'my_refresh_group_1',
      list => 'my_view_1');
   commit;
end;
/
```

Use the *dbms_refresh.destroy* procedure if a refresh group needs to be removed. It is necessary to connect as the group owner in order to remove a materialized refresh group.

```
begin
   dbms_refresh.destroy(name => 'my_refresh_group_1');
   commit;
end;
/
```

Occasionally, there may be a need to recreate the materialized view in another database and to export a materialized view group. Use the *user_export* procedure to generate the DDL command of a specified group number, as in the next example.

```
declare
   v_out varchar2(2000);
```

Package dbms_refresh   **447**

```
begin
   dbms_refresh.user_export(
      rg# => 2,mycall => v_out);
   dbms_output.put_line(a => 'mycall is:'||v_out);
end;
/
```

Alternatively, use *dbms_refresh.user_export_child* to recreate a given group by generating the DDL command of this type.

Summary

In this chapter, packages pertaining to data warehousing were explained and exemplified. How to use the most important procedures and functions of packages such as *dbms_advanced_rewrite*, *dbms_cube*, *dbms_cube_advise*, *dbms_data_mining*, *dbms_data_mining_transform*, *dbms_dimension*, *dbms_mview*, *dbms_olap* and *dbms_refresh* was illustrated.

In the next chapter, packages that are used to manage Real Application Cluster databases will be introduced.

RAC and Distributed Transactions

Oracle touts itself as the unbreakable database and claims that using their Real Application Clusters (RAC) can provide architecture with guaranteed continuous availability. The RAC product supersedes the older cluster product, Oracle Parallel Server (OPS). RAC databases are becoming more and more popular because they provide availability, performance and scalability in one package. This bypasses the need of making any changes in the application code or processes.

This chapter will examine two packages that are relevant with Real Application Cluster and Distributed Transactions. They are useful in the day-to-day setting of a RAC Database Administrator.

Package *dbms_service*

There are at least three known utilities that can be used to manage services in an Oracle RAC environment: Database Configuration Assistant (DBCA), Server Control (SRVCTL) and the *dbms_service* package. Like the first two utilities listed, the *dbms_service* package can administer services but, unlike DBCA and *srvctl*, *dbms_service* works with one node at a time rather than all nodes in a cluster. In the first example, how to create, delete, start, and stop services in RAC and single instance databases will be shown.

It is important to note that some of the main procedures of this package are deprecated in Oracle 11g Release 2 for RAC database instances. This is because the *dbms_service* package will not make any updates in the Cluster Ready Services (CRS) attributes that are necessary in this version; the service control (*srvctl*) utility should be used instead.

Imagine that we have a Real Application Cluster database with three instances. The plan is to create three services obeying the following rules:

- *srv_prod*: This service is used by production users. It always connects to the first instance of RAC.

- *srv_cust*: This service is used by certain customers who only need to execute select queries on the database every time.

- *srv_low.* This service is utilized by users who have low priority over the RAC database. It offers less CPUs and memory.

Code 9.1 – dbms_service.sql

```
conn sys@oral1g as sysdba

Connected to:
Oracle 11g Enterprise Edition Release 11.2.0.1.0 - Production
With the Partitioning, Oracle Label Security, OLAP, Data Mining,
Oracle Database Vault and Real Application Testing options

--Creating services
begin
dbms_service.create_service(
    service_name => 'srv_prod',
    network_name => 'dbms1',
    goal => dbms_service.goal_throughput,
    dtp => FALSE,
    aq_ha_notifications => NULL,
    failover_method => dbms_service.failover_method_basic,
    failover_type => dbms_service.failover_type_session,
    failover_retries => 3,
    failover_delay => 5,
    clb_goal => dbms_service.clb_goal_short);
end;
/

begin
dbms_service.create_service(
    service_name => 'srv_cust',
    network_name => 'dbms2',
    goal => dbms_service.goal_none,
    dtp => FALSE,
    aq_ha_notifications => NULL,
    failover_method => dbms_service.failover_method_none,
    failover_type => dbms_service.failover_type_select,
    failover_retries => 2,
    failover_delay => 10,
    clb_goal => dbms_service.clb_goal_long);
end;
/

begin
dbms_service.create_service(
    service_name => 'srv_low',
    network_name => 'dbms3',
    goal => dbms_service.goal_none,
    dtp => TRUE,
    aq_ha_notifications => NULL,
    failover_method => dbms_service.failover_method_none,
    failover_type => dbms_service.failover_type_select,
    failover_retries => 2,
    failover_delay => 20,
    clb_goal => NULL);
end;
/
```

Here are descriptions of each parameter in this procedure:

- *service_name->*: Name of service to be created

- *network_name->*: In which instance this service will connect to

- *goal->*: The workload management chosen (*service_time*, throughput or none)

- *dtp->*: A distributed transaction service to be used with XA connections

- *aq_ha_notifications->*: Is a service that receives HA events from an AQ. For example, a TimesTen configuration.

- *failover_method->*: TAF failover method

- *failover_type->*: TAF failover type

- *failover_retries->*: TAF failover retries

- *failover_delay->*: TAF failover delay

- *clb_goal->*: Connection Load Balancing method

Now check the services just created by querying the *dba_services* view.

```
set linesize 140
col name              for a10 heading "name"
col network_name      for a10 heading "net name"
col failover_method   for a10 heading "TAF method"
col failover_type     for a8  heading "TAF type"
col failover_retries  for 99  heading "TAF retries"
col goal              for a10 heading "goal"
col clb_goal          for a20 heading "cluster load bal"

select
   name,
   network_name,
   failover_method,
   failover_type,
   failover_retries,
   goal,
   clb_goal
from
   dba_services
where name like 'srv%';
```

Suppose we want to change a service by disallowing it to use a distributed transaction and changing the failover retries from two to five. This can be done by using the *modify_service* procedure as in the next example:

```
begin
   dbms_service.modify_service(
   service_name => 'srv_low',
   goal => dbms_service.goal_none,
   dtp => FALSE,
```

```
   aq_ha_notifications => NULL,
   failover_method => dbms_service.failover_method_none,
   failover_type => dbms_service.failover_type_select,
   failover_retries => 5,
   failover_delay => 20,
   clb_goal => NULL);
end;
/
```

To delete a service, just use the *delete_service* procedure as follows:

```
begin
   dbms_service.delete_service(
      service_name => 'srv_low');
end;
/
```

Use *start_service* and *stop_service* to start or stop a service. If it is running in a RAC database, by default it will stop/start the service in the local instance where the command is being executed.

```
--Starting a service in a single instance database
begin
   dbms_service.start_service(
      service_name => 'srv_prod',
      instance_name => NULL);
end;
/

--Starting a service in a specific instance
begin
   dbms_service.start_service(
      service_name => 'srv_low',
      instance_name => 'dbms2');
end;
/

--Starting a service in all instances of a RAC database
begin
   dbms_service.start_service(
      service_name => 'srv_cust',
      instance_name => dbms_service.all_instances);
end;
/

--Check if service is up or down by querying v$active_services view
col name        for a15 Heading "name"
col network_name for a10 Headind "net name"

select
   name,
   network_name
from
   v$active_services
where name like 'srv%';
```

```
Name            Net Name
--------------- ----------
srv_cust        dbms2
srv_prod        dbms1
srv_low         dbms3
```

It is also possible to stop a service in a single database instance, in a specific instance or in all RAC instances. Here is an example of each:

```
--Stopping a service in a single instance database

begin
    dbms_service.stop_service(service_name => 'srv_prod',instance_name =>
NULL);
end;
/

--Stopping a service in a specified instance
begin
    dbms_service.stop_service(service_name => 'srv_low',instance_name =>
'dbms2');
end;
/

--Stopping a service in all RAC instances
begin
    dbms_service.stop_service(service_name => 'srv_low',instance_name =>
dbms_service.all_instances);
end;
/
```

The next and last example of this package shows the *disconnect_session* procedure. It can be used to disconnect all sessions of a specific service from all instances. There are two options when using this procedure: disconnect immediately or after the session transactions have finished.

Disconnecting all sessions of service with *srv_cust* from all instances after session transactions has finished:

```
begin
    dbms_service.disconnect_session(
        service_name => 'srv_cust',
        disconnect_option => 0);
end;
/
```

Disconnecting all sessions of the *srv_cust* service from all instances immediately.

```
begin
    dbms_service.disconnect_session(
        service_name => 'srv_cust',
        disconnect_option => 1);
end;
```

Here are some useful views for getting information pertaining to Oracle Services:

- *gv$active_services*: Shows the active services in a database

- *gv$services*: Shows information about services in a database

- *v$service_wait_class*: Shows the wait information for each service

- *dba_services*: Shows all services in a database

- *dba_hist_service_wait_class*: Shows historical information about the wait event class for each service that was tracked by the Workload Manager

- *dba_hist_service_name*: Shows historical information about services tracked by the Workload Manager

- *dba_hist_service_stat*: Displays historical information about service statistics tracked by the Workload Manager

By the same token, other Oracle utilities can be used to manage services as mentioned before. Oracle Enterprise Manager Database or Grid Control offers easy access for managing services. SRVCTL is a little more complicated, but a reliable method for working with Oracle Services.

Package *dbms_xa*

IT environments are becoming more and more complex. With multiple databases and applications communicating together, it can be difficult to manage without the proper resources.

One good example is when there are transactions traveling between different applications which must be committed to different databases like BPEL, Oracle E-Business Suite, Oracle Transportation Manager and/or Oracle Retail, Oracle XA provides an external interface used to interact with a transaction manager out of the database. It is used for committing transactions of different databases while maintaining data integrity. These database transactions are also known as distributed transaction processing (DTP).

The *dbms_xa* package provides an interface for working with XA via PL/SQL language. Certain privileges are necessary for a user to execute particular XA tasks:

1. To execute *xa_recover*, the user must have select privileges in the *dba_pending_transactions* view.

2. To manipulate XA transactions created by other users, the *force any transaction privilege* is required.

Advanced DBMS Packages

In the next example, how to create a distributed transaction from one session and commit to another session by using the *dbms_xa* package will be shown.

🔖 Code 9.2 – dbms_xa.sql

```
conn sys@ora11g as sysdba

Connected to:
Oracle 11g Enterprise Edition Release 11.2.0.1.0 - Production
With the Partitioning, Oracle Label Security, OLAP, Data Mining,
Oracle Database Vault and Real Application Testing options

--First create a test table
create table
   tab_dbms_xa (col1 number);

insert into
   tab_dbms_xa values (1);

commit;

select
   *
from
   tab_dbms_xa;
```

Now an XA transaction is created in the first session. This session will do an update and add two insertions on the test table, but will not commit. Note that the session timeout is increased, so there is more time to work with this sample.

```
--Setting timeout in session using xa_settimeout function. The value
specified is in number of seconds.
declare
  v_sess_timeout  pls_integer;
begin
  v_sess_timeout := dbms_xa.xa_settimeout(seconds => 10000);
end;
/


set serveroutput on
declare
  v_my_transaction  pls_integer;
  v_xa_xid      dbms_xa_xid := dbms_xa_xid(3322);
  v_xa_exception exception;
  v_ora_error pls_integer;
begin
```

Notice that the *xa_start* function is used to associate the current session with a transaction and that the *tmnoflags* constant is set to inform that it is a new transaction.

```
  v_my_transaction   := dbms_xa.xa_start(
                          xid => v_xa_xid,
                          flag => dbms_xa.tmnoflags);
```

Package dbms_xa   **455**

```
--Check if XA transaction is OK
  if v_my_transaction <> dbms_xa.xa_ok then
    v_ora_error := dbms_xa.xa_getlastoer();
    dbms_output.put_line(a => 'Attention! Oracle Error - ORA-' ||
v_ora_error || ' obtained. XA Process failed!');
    raise v_xa_exception;
  else dbms_output.put_line(a => 'XA Process ID 3322 started');
  end if;

--DML Operations
  update
    tab_dbms_xa
  set
    col1=11 ,
    col2='Value updated on Session 1.'
  where
    col1=1;

  insert into
    tab_dbms_xa
  values (2,'Value inserted on Session 1.');

  insert into
    tab_dbms_xa
  values (3,'Value inserted on Session 1.');
```

Suspending a transaction is done using *xa_end* and *tmsuspend*. This enables the transaction to be caught later by another session.

```
v_my_transaction   := dbms_xa.xa_end(
                         xid => v_xa_xid,
                         flag =>  dbms_xa.tmsuspend);

--Check if XA transaction is OK
  if v_my_transaction <> dbms_xa.xa_ok then
    v_ora_error := dbms_xa.xa_getlastoer();
   dbms_output.put_line(a => 'Attention! Oracle Error - ORA-' || v_ora_error
|| ' obtained. XA Process failed!');
    raise v_xa_exception;
    else dbms_output.put_line(a => 'XA Process ID 3322 is working!');
  end if;

  exception
    when others then
      dbms_output.put_line(a => 'A XA problem occur. Please check the error
('||v_my_transaction||') and try again. This transaction will be rolled back
now!');
      v_my_transaction := dbms_xa.xa_end(xid => v_xa_xid,flag =>
dbms_xa.tmsuccess);
      v_my_transaction := dbms_xa.xa_rollback(xid => v_xa_xid);

      if v_my_transaction <> dbms_xa.xa_ok then
        v_ora_error := dbms_xa.xa_getlastoer();
        dbms_output.put_line(a => 'A problem occur while trying to rollback
the transaction. Please try to fix error '||v_my_transaction||', ORA-' ||
v_ora_error || '.');
        raise_application_error(-20001, 'ORA-'||v_ora_error|| ' error when
```

```
trying to rollback a transaction');
    end if;
    raise_application_error(-20002, 'ORA-'||v_ora_error||' Transaction was
rolled back successfully!');
end;
/
```

Now there is a transaction identified by *XID=3322*. Another session will now be opened to make changes to this transaction before it is committed. To check that the transaction is created and active, use the query below:

```
select
   state,
   flags,
   coupling
from
   gv$global_transaction
where
   globalid = dbms_xa_xid(3322).gtrid;

STATE                                    FLAGS COUPLING
-------------------------------------- ---------- ---------------
active                                       0 tightly coupled
```

Here, the *xa_start* function is used with the *tmresume* constant to join an existing transaction; in this case, the transaction with *XID=3322*.

```
set serveroutput on
declare
  v_my_transaction  pls_integer;
  v_xa_xid      dbms_xa_xid := dbms_xa_xid(3322);
  v_xa_exception exception;
  v_ora_error pls_integer;
begin

  v_my_transaction  := dbms_xa.xa_start(
                          xid => v_xa_xid,
                          flag => dbms_xa.tmresume);

  --Check if XA transaction is OK
  if v_my_transaction <> dbms_xa.xa_ok then
     v_ora_error := dbms_xa.xa_getlastoer();
     dbms_output.put_line(a => 'Attention! Oracle Error - ORA-' ||
                          v_ora_error || ' obtained. XA Process failed!');
     raise v_xa_exception;
  else
     dbms_output.put_line(
        a => 'XA Process ID 3322 started - ####### Step 1 ##########');
  end if;

  --DML operations on test table
  dbms_output.put_line(
     a => '########## Inserting a new value in test table ##########');
  insert into tab_dbms_xa values (4,'Value inserted on Session 2.');
```

In order to detach from a session, the *tmsuccess* constant is used with the *xa_end* function, shown here:

```
  v_my_transaction   := dbms_xa.xa_end(
                        xid => v_xa_xid,
                        flag =>  dbms_xa.tmsuccess);
  --Check if XA transaction is OK
  if v_my_transaction <> dbms_xa.xa_ok then
    v_ora_error := dbms_xa.xa_getlastoer();
    dbms_output.put_line(a => 'Attention! Oracle Error - ORA-' ||
                        v_ora_error || ' obtained. XA Process failed!');
    raise v_xa_exception;
  else
    dbms_output.put_line(a => 'XA Process ID 3322 started - ####### Step 2
##########');
  end if;

  exception
    when others then
      dbms_output.put_line(a => 'A XA problem occur. Please check the error
('||
                        v_my_transaction||') and try again. This
transaction will be rolled back now!');
      v_my_transaction := dbms_xa.xa_end(
                        xid => v_xa_xid,
                        flag =>  dbms_xa.tmsuccess);
      v_my_transaction := dbms_xa.xa_rollback(
                        xid => v_xa_xid);

      if v_my_transaction != dbms_xa.xa_ok then
        v_ora_error := dbms_xa.xa_getlastoer();
        dbms_output.put_line(a => 'A problem occur while trying to rollback
the transaction. Please try to fix the error '||
                        v_my_transaction||', ORA-' || v_ora_error ||
'.');
        raise_application_error(-20001, 'ORA-'||v_ora_error|| ' error when
trying to rollback a transaction');
      end if;

      raise_application_error(-20002, 'ORA-'||v_ora_error||
       ' Transaction was rolled back successfully!');
end;
/
```

At this point, if the *tab_dbms_xa* table is checked, it will not show the lines created/updated yet. This is because no commit has been made. In the third session shown next, it will be made.

```
declare
 v_my_transaction  pls_integer;
 v_xa_xid       dbms_xa_xid := dbms_xa_xid(3322);
 v_xa_exception exception;
 v_ora_error pls_integer;

begin
```

Here, the *xa_commit* function is used and all changes are finally stored in the *tab_dbms_xa* table.

```
    dbms_output.put_line('Using xa_commit function to commit changes!');
    v_my_transaction  := dbms_xa.xa_commit(
                            xid => v_xa_xid,
                            onephase =>  true);

  --Check if XA transaction is OK
  if v_my_transaction <> dbms_xa.xa_ok then
    v_ora_error := dbms_xa.xa_getlastoer();
    dbms_output.put_line(a => 'Attention! Oracle Error - ORA-' ||
                        v_ora_error || ' obtained. XA commit Process
failed!');
    raise v_xa_exception;
  else dbms_output.put_line(a => 'XA Process ID is working and was commited
successfully!');
  end if;

    exception
      when others then
        dbms_output.put_line(a => 'A XA problem occur. Please check the error
('||
                            v_my_transaction||') and try again. This
transaction will be rolled back now!');
        v_my_transaction := dbms_xa.xa_end(xid => v_xa_xid,flag =>
dbms_xa.tmsuccess);
        v_my_transaction := dbms_xa.xa_rollback(xid => v_xa_xid);

        if v_my_transaction <> dbms_xa.xa_ok then
          v_ora_error := dbms_xa.xa_getlastoer();
          dbms_output.put_line(a => 'A problem occur while trying to rollback
the transaction. Please try to fix the error '||
                            v_my_transaction||', ORA-' || v_ora_error ||
'.');
          raise_application_error(-20001, 'ORA-'||v_ora_error|| ' error when
trying to rollback a transaction');
        end if;

        raise_application_error(-20002, 'ORA-'||v_ora_error||
          ' Transaction was rolled back successfully!');
end;
/
```

Lastly, check the *tab_dbms_xa* table to get the results created in the first sessions and committed in the third session.

```
select
    *
from
    tab_dbms_xa;

    COL1 COL2
---------- ------------------------------------------------------
      11 Value updated on Session 1.
       2 Value inserted on Session 1.
```

```
3 Value inserted on Session 1.
4 Value inserted on Session 2.
```

If an error occurs when using distributed transactions like the loss of the network connection, the transaction may become lost. They may be found in views like *dba_2pc_pending*, *dba_2pc_neighbors*, *dba_pending_transactions* or *v$global_transactions*. When these lost transactions need to be purged, use a script like the one below:

```
select
   'commit force '''||local_tran_id||''';'
from
   dba_2pc_pending;

select
   'exec dbms_transaction.purge_lost_db_entry('''||local_tran_id||''');'
from
   dba_2pc_pending
where
   state='forced commit';

exec dbms_transaction.purge_lost_db_entry('123.544.7');'

--Always commit after command above
commit;
```

This will find all pending transactions, commit and then purge them if they are still hanging. Make sure to commit after purging the transaction.

Summary

Good things come in small packages, and the packages in this chapter are no exception. Despite there only being two, their importance should not be underestimated. To learn the concept and manage services is one of the main duties of a DBA nowadays thanks to increasing Real Application Cluster environments that demand this knowledge. Also, the way that Oracle 11g works with distributed transactions has been ameliorated by the creation of the *dbms_xa* package, as demonstrated in this chapter.

As with this chapter, the next one is small but equally as important, pertaining to packages of the Oracle Data Guard feature.

Oracle Data Guard Packages

Oracle Data Guard was conceived as a disaster recovery solution. It holds a copy of the primary database in a standby mode, ready to become the production database in case of a disaster. Oracle Data Guard is created to provide a standby database that can be used to protect Oracle data from failure, disasters, data corruptions and human error.

Some companies are using the new Oracle Extended Real Application Cluster and ASM of Oracle 11g as a disaster recovery solution, commonly known as Geo-Cluster. This is only advisable when sites are in close proximity to each other. For companies whose standby sites are located further than 100 kilometers (about 60 miles), it is advisable to use Oracle Data Guard. In Oracle Database version 11gR2, up to 30 standby sites can be housed.

This chapter will present two packages: *dbms_dg* is used to warn Data Guard Broker to initiate a failover and *dbms_logstdby* which is used to manage the logical standby database.

Package *dbms_dg*

Introduced in Oracle 11g, the *dbms_dg.initiate_fs_failover* procedure provides a new method used to initiate a Fast-Start Failover based upon the requirement of specific conditions. This package is housed within the Data Guard Broker, which holds all services pertaining to the monitoring of the primary database. The Data Guard Broker initiates the failover to a standby database in the case of any planned or unplanned outage.

The following example will show how a scenario would play out when Data Guard Broker is working within the Disaster Recovery scheme.
So assume that we already have a Data Guard Broker configured with *db_orig* as the primary database and *db_targ* as the standby database. The first step needed in order for this package to work is to enable fast start failover. It is done with a single step as follows:

Code 10.1 – dbms_dg.sql

```
conn sys@ora11g as sysdba
```

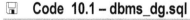

```
Connected to:
Oracle 11g Enterprise Edition Release 11.2.0.1.0 - Production
With the Partitioning, Oracle Label Security, OLAP, Data Mining,
Oracle Database Vault and Real Application Testing options

--Enable fast start failover
--Where db_org is the primary site and db_targ is the standby site
dgmgrl> edit database 'db_orig' set property FastStartFailoverTarget =
'db_targ';
dgmgrl> edit database 'db_targ' set property FastStartFailoverTarget =
'db_orig';
```

Now, choose the protection mode to be used and set this with the command example
below:

```
--Enable maximum protection mode
dgmgrl> edit database 'db_orig' set property LogXptMode=sync;
dgmgrl> edit database 'db_disre' set property LogXptMode=sync;
dgmgrl> edit configuration set protection mode as MaxAvailability;
```

The failover process will begin once the time specified by the *faststartfailoverthreshold*
parameter is reached. In this example, the time used is 45 seconds.

```
dgmgrl> edit configuration set property FastStartFailoverThreshold=45;
```

Next, enable the fast-start failover and start the observer:

```
--Now enable fast-start failover
dgmgrl> enable fast_start failover;
dgmgrl> start observer;
```

Now use the following command to check the fast-start failover environment:

```
dgmgrl> show fast_start failover;

Fast-Start Failover: enable
 Threshold:            45 seconds
 Target:               db_orig
 Observer:             dbms.f2c.com.br
 Lag Limit:            40 seconds
 Shutdown Primary:     TRUE
 Auto-reinstate:       TRUE

Configurable Failover Conditions
 Health Conditions:
   Corrupted Controlfile        YES
   Corrupted Dictionary         YES
   Inaccessible Logfile          NO
   Stuck Archiver               YES
   Datafile Offline             YES

 Oracle Error Conditions:
   ORA-01578
```

In addition to these automatic methods that guide to the fast-start failover, we can create my own customized conditions. In the example below, we will use a specific value of an application timeout metric to obligate a failover.

```
set serveroutput on
declare
    v_status integer;
    v_threshold number; --This value can be from any table that record
application timeout values for example.
begin
    --Choose when the failover will happens here
    if v_threshold > 100 then
        status := dbms_dg.initiate_fs_failover(condstr => 'Failover
Requested');
    end if;

    if v_status := '16646' then
        dbms_output.put_line('Fast-Start Failover Disabled!');
    else
        dbms_output.put_line('Fast-Start Failover Successfully! ORA-
'||v_status');
    end if;

end;
/
```

There are some optional database initialization parameters that can be used to configure Data Guard. They are described here:

- *faststartfailovermyshutdown*: If set to TRUE, the primary database will be overthrown if the value of *v$database.fs_failover_status* column is stalled for a time larger than the value specified in the *faststartfailoverthreshold* parameter. Its default value is TRUE.

- *faststartfailoverlaglimit*: This parameter specifies a maximum lag time in seconds; the standby is allowed to fall behind the primary in terms of redo applied. Beyond this time, a FSF will not be allowed. The minimum value is 10 seconds.

- *faststartfailoverautoreinstate*: If it is not necessary to reinstate the primary database after a fast-start failover, set this parameter to FALSE.

- *observerconnectidentifier*: It is possible to change the connection identifier being used by the Data Guard Broker observer by changing this parameter.

Package *dbms_logstdby*

Oracle Data Guard provides options for physical and logical standby database creation. This package can be used to configure and manage a logical standby database by enabling tasks, such as skipping tables to be replicated, controlled access on specific tables, supplemental log configuration and managing parameter configurations.

The *logstdby_administrator* role, created with Oracle 9i, is granted to users who will be managing logical standby databases. In the next example, it will be shown how and when to use this package when administering a Disaster Recover database. we will be using Oracle Data Guard with a logical standby database in this scenario.

Use the *apply_set* procedure to change the parameter values of SQL Apply in a logical standby database. In this example, the number of applier servers will be changed to 90.

Also, the option to delete the archived redo log files if they have already been applied on logical standby database will be enabled by setting the *log_auto_delete* parameter to TRUE.

🖫 Code 10.2 – dbms_logstdby.sql

```
conn sys@ora11g as sysdba

Connected to:
Oracle 11g Enterprise Edition Release 11.2.0.1.0 - Production
With the Partitioning, Oracle Label Security, OLAP, Data Mining,
Oracle Database Vault and Real Application Testing options

--Use apply_set procedure to change parameter values of SQL Apply in a
logical standby database
begin
    dbms_logstdby.apply_set(inname => 'maxservers',value => '100'); --increse
max servers limit
end;
/

begin
    dbms_logstdby.apply_set(inname => 'apply_servers',value => '90'); --set
new value
    dbms_logstdby.apply_set(inname => 'log_auto_delete',value => 'TRUE');
end;
/
```

Information can be found about when the value was actually modified by querying the view:

```
select
    event_time,
    status
from
    dba_logstdby_events
/

EVENT_TIME   STATUS
---------- ------------------------------------------------------------
```

```
8/26/2010 1 apply_set: max_servers changed to 100
8/26/2010 1 apply_set: max_servers changed to 100
8/26/2010 1 apply_set: max_servers changed to 100
8/26/2010 1 apply_set: max_servers changed to 100
8/26/2010 1 apply_set: apply_servers changed to 10
8/26/2010 1 apply_set: log_auto_delete changed to TRUE
8/26/2010 1 apply_set: apply_servers changed to 90
8/26/2010 1 apply_set: log_auto_delete changed to TRUE
```

In order to restore the parameters default value, use the *apply_unset* procedure.

```
begin
    dbms_logstdby.apply_unset(inname => 'apply_servers');
end;
/

--Check parameters values on dba_logstdby_parameters
select
    name,
    value
from
    dba_logstdby_parameters
/
```

To build the Log Miner dictionary, connect to Oracle as sysdba, open the database and put the database in a quiesce state. Then the dictionary can be created using the following statement:

```
--Build Log Miner dictionary and record supplemental metadata that will be
used by SQL Apply process use the build procedure
--First open the database and quiesce it
alter database open;
alter database quiesce restricted;
begin
    dbms_logstdby.build;
end;
/
```

The *instantiate_table* procedure is used to refresh a logical standby database table with values from the primary database. It will drop the table into the logical standby database if it already exists. Check if the table to be instantiated has any *skip* configured in it:

```
--Check for skips being used
select
    statement_opt,
    owner,
    name
from
    dba_logstdby_skip;

STATEMENT_OPT                       OWNER      NAME
------------------------------- ---------- ----------
```

```
schema_ddl                          pkg          jobs
```

If there is skip information on the table, remove it by using the *unskip* procedure as follows:

```
begin
   dbms_logstdby.unskip(
      stmt => 'schema_ddl',
      schema_name => 'pkg',
      object_name => 'jobs');
end;
/
```

Finally, execute the *instantiate* procedure using the database link pointing to the logical standby database.

```
begin
   dbms_logstdby.instantiate_table(schema_name => 'pkg',table_name =>
'jobs',dblink => 'db_disre');
end;
/
```

Sometimes it may be necessary to find out which archive redo log files were already applied in a logical standby database and can be removed because they are no longer needed by the SQL Apply process. To perform this task, on the logical standby use the *purge_session* procedure.

```
begin
   dbms_logstdby.purge_session;
end;
/
```

Use the view below to locate archives that can be deleted:

```
select
   *
from
   dba_logmnr_purged_log
/
```

After finding the archives, delete them at the OS level because this procedure will not do it automatically.

If my logical standby database has become the primary database, and we want additional logical standby databases to work correctly, we will want to run the *rebuild* procedure. This will record important metadata information required for other logical standby databases. We can run it as follows:

```
begin
```

```
    dbms_logstdby.rebuild;
end;
/
```

My next example will demonstrate how to use the *skip* procedure. When configured, SQL Apply replicates all data executed on a primary database to a standby database except data that is marked to be skipped. There are many possible ways to specify which data to skip. For example, it is possible to prevent a certain table from being replicated using the *skip* procedure. We can also direct SQL Apply to not replicate any DDL commands made in a certain schema. Here are examples of both:

🖫 Code 10.3 – dbms_logstdby_skip.sql

```
conn sys@ora11g as sysdba

Connected to:
Oracle 11g Enterprise Edition Release 11.2.0.1.0 - Production
With the Partitioning, Oracle Label Security, OLAP, Data Mining,
Oracle Database Vault and Real Application Testing options

--Skipping DML on tab_salary table
begin
    dbms_logstdby.skip(
        stmt => 'dml',
        schema_name => 'pkg',
        object_name => 'tab_salary');
end;
/

--Skipping all DDL made in PKG schema
begin
    dbms_logstdby.skip(
        stmt => 'schema_ddl',
        schema_name => 'pkg',
        object_name => 'tab_salary');
end;
/

--Check for skips being used
col name for a10
col owner for a10
select
    statement_opt,
    owner,
    name
from
    dba_logstdby_skip;
```

Here is a practical example. Suppose we have my datafiles in a directory different from the source primary database '/*u02*/*oradata*/*primdb*' and target standby database '/*u03*/*oradata*/*stdbydb*'. In this case, if it were a *physical* standby database, when we create a tablespace in the primary database, it would have been created in the standby database automatically if the *standby_file_management* initialization parameter was set to

---

auto. This works with both physical and logical standby databases. Another parameter, called *db_file_name_convert*, would specify where these datafiles are to be created in the standby database. Note that this parameter only works with physical standby databases.

Despite this, we can achieve a similar functionality with the next example. In order to force datafiles to be created in another directory, we use the following procedure:

💾 Code 10.4 – dbms_logstdby_replace_dtfs.sql

```
conn sys@ora11g as sysdba

Connected to:
Oracle 11g Enterprise Edition Release 11.2.0.1.0 - Production
With the Partitioning, Oracle Label Security, OLAP, Data Mining,
Oracle Database Vault and Real Application Testing options

--Procedure to create datafiles in a different directory on standby database
create or replace procedure proc_replace_dfs_location(
                         v_old_statement in varchar2,
                         v_schema    in varchar2,
                         v_name      in varchar2,
                         v_xidusn    in number,
                         v_xidslt    in number,
                         v_xidsqn    in number,
                         v_action    out number,
                         v_new_statement out varchar2) as
begin
  v_new_statement := replace(
                      srcstr => v_old_statement,
                      oldsub =>  '/u02/oradata/primdb',
                      newsub =>  '/u03/oradata/stdbydb');

  v_action := dbms_logstdby.skip_action_replace;

exception
  when others then
     v_action    := dbms_logstdby.skip_action_error; --Raise an error that
halts SQL Apply process
     v_new_statement := NULL;
end proc_replace_dfs_location;


begin
   dbms_logstdby.skip(
      stmt => 'create tablespace',
      proc_name => 'proc_replace_dfs_location');
end;
/
```

Now every time a tablespace is created in the primary database with its datafiles in directory *'/u02/oradata/primdb'*, they will be placed in the *'/u03/oradata/stdbydb'* directory of the standby database.

Summary

Despite being a small chapter, these two packages are very important; especially when using a logical standby database in a Disaster Recovery scenario. In the next chapter, packages pertaining to Oracle Streams, part of Oracle High Availability Solutions, will be introduced.

Oracle Streams

By design, Oracle RAC has always had a latency issue when the RAC nodes are geographically distributed. In these cases, many shops use Oracle Streams for back-and-forth replication. For most configurations, Oracle Streams are cheaper, i.e. licensing costs, than RAC and Oracle Streams allow for back-and-forth replication between two active production servers.

Stream replications work by using queues that store Data Definition Language and Data Manipulation Language. They then propagate these changes to the target database. It is also possible to create rules that manipulate data before they are propagated to the destination target.

Despite being an advanced replication tool, Oracle Streams is not the best choice for a Disaster Recovery solution. In some cases, such as using complex applications like Oracle E-Business, SAP, JD Edwards and PeopleSoft, it is not easy or even possible to keep Streams working for this purpose. In these cases, the best High Availability and Disaster Recovery solution is still Oracle Data Guard with the Oracle Real Application cluster.

One advantage of Oracle Streams is the ability to configure replication in a heterogeneous environment like Oracle and SQL Server. The following pages will show some of the main packages that can be used to create, configure and manage Oracle Streams.

Package *dbms_apply_adm*

This package was originally introduced with Oracle Database 9i and is one of the packages used to create and manage a Streams environment. It is triggered by the *$?/rdbms/admin/dbmsapp.sql* script that is called by *catproc.sql* after the database is created. Basically, Oracle Streams are comprised of three main processes: the *capture*, *propagation* and *apply* processes. The *dbms_apply_adm* package can be used, among other things, to create, alter, drop and change parameters of the *apply* processes.

There are some parameters that can be changed by the *set_parameter* procedure. Each *apply* process can be modified in a way that will allow it to work properly. Next, we will explain some procedures of *dbms_apply_adm* in more detail. To run these next examples, a basic configuration with Streams replication must be made. For help with the initial steps, refer to Oracle's documentation. Also, a book on the subject that can be helpful is *Oracle Streams* from Madhu Tumma.

Some initialization parameters must be specified before using Streams:

- *compatible*: This parameter must be set to 10.1.0 or higher.

- *global_names*: This must be set to TRUE so that if databases have the same name, they can be identified when a database link is created between them.

- *job_queue_processes*: This parameter specifies how many processes will be used in jobs. The minimum recommended value is 4.

- *parallel_max_servers*: A minimum value of 2 must be specified for this parameter because it is used by *capture* and *apply* processes.

- *open_links*: This parameter should be set to a value of 4 (default) or higher. It is used to specify how many open connections one remote session may have.

- *streams_pool_size*: In version 10g Release 2, this parameter can be 0 if *sga_target* is being used; otherwise, start with a value equal to 10% of *shared_pool_size* and tune from that value if needed.

- *timed_statistics*: There are some dynamic time statistic views that can be used to gather information on a *streams* process. In order to gather this information, this parameter must be set to TRUE.

In order to check the recommended configuration for Oracle Streams, take a look at Oracle Support Note, "10gR2 Streams Recommended Configuration [ID 418755.1]".

The first step is to create a simple table replication configuration between two databases, *sourcedb* and *targetdb*.

🖫 Code 11.1 – dbms_apply_adm.sql

```
conn sys@ora11g as sysdba

Connected to:
Oracle 11g Enterprise Edition Release 11.2.0.1.0 - Production
With the Partitioning, Oracle Label Security, OLAP, Data Mining,
Oracle Database Vault and Real Application Testing options

--Create schema example on both source and target databases
create user str_schema identified by 123;
grant connect,resource to str_schema;
```

Create a Streams administrator users who will manage the Streams Replication Configuration. First on *sourcedb* is user *str_source* and then on *targetdb*, the user is *str_target*.

```
--Sourcedb (sourcedb)
conn / as sysdba

create user
    str_source
identified by 123;

alter user
    str_source
default tablespace users
temporary tablespace temp
quota unlimited on users;

grant
    connect,
    resource,
    aq_administrator_role,
    dba
to str_source;

begin
    dbms_streams_auth.grant_admin_privilege('str_source');
end;
/

commit;

--Target DB (targetdb)

create user
    str_target
identified by 123;

alter user
    str_target
default tablespace users
temporary tablespace temp
quota unlimited on users;

grant
    connect,
    resource,
    aq_administrator_role,
    dba
to str_target;

begin
    dbms_streams_auth.grant_admin_privilege('str_target');
end;
/

commit;
```

Now we will create the Streams queue tables and database links that will be used.

```
connect str_source/123@sourcedb

begin
    dbms_streams_adm.set_up_queue(
      queue_table => 'streams_queue_table',
      queue_name  => 'streams_queue',
      queue_user  => 'str_source');
end;
/

--Create database links on source database
conn sys/manager@sourcedb as sysdba
create public database link
  targetdb using 'targetdb';

conn str_source/123@sourcedb
create database link targetdb
  connect to str_target identified by "123"
  using 'targetdb';

--Create database links on target database
conn str_target/123@targetdb
create database link sourcedb
  connect to str_source identified by "123"
  using 'sourcedb';

conn system/manager@targetdb
create public database link
  sourcedb using 'sourcedb';


--Create Stream Queue on Target Database
connect str_target/123@targetdb
begin
    dbms_streams_adm.set_up_queue(
      queue_table => 'streams_queue_table',
      queue_name  => 'streams_queue',
      queue_user  => 'str_target');
end;
/
```

Now the schema rules need to be created in the *apply* process of the target database. These rules will be used to configure what will be replicated. In this case, every DDL and DML command will be replicated to the target database in the *apply* process.

```
--Adding schema rules on target database. The schema str_schema will be used
in this example.
conn str_target/123@targetdb
begin
    dbms_streams_adm.add_schema_rules(
      schema_name    => 'str_schema',
      streams_type   => 'apply',
      streams_name   => 'stream_apply',
      queue_name     => 'str_target.streams_queue',
```

```
      include_dml     => TRUE,
      include_ddl     => TRUE,
      source_database => 'sourcedb');
end;
/
```

Next, the *capture* process and propagation rules are created on the source database as follows:

```
--Now capture process will be created in source database
conn str_source/123@sourcedb
begin
  dbms_streams_adm.add_schema_rules(
    schema_name     => 'str_schema',
    streams_type    => 'capture',
    streams_name    => 'stream_capture',
    queue_name      => 'str_source.streams_queue',
    include_dml     => TRUE,
    include_ddl     => TRUE,
    source_database => 'sourcedb');
end;
/

--The propagation rule will be created on source database as follows:
begin
  dbms_streams_adm.add_schema_propagation_rules(
    schema_name             => 'str_schema',
    streams_name            => 'stream_propagate',
    source_queue_name       => 'str_source.streams_queue',
    destination_queue_name  => 'str_target.streams_queue@targetdb',
    include_dml             => TRUE,
    include_ddl             => TRUE,
    source_database         => 'sourcedb');
end;
/
```

Before starting the *apply* process, tables from the source database must exist on the target database. If they already exist, just instantiate the objects as follows:

```
conn str_source/123@sourcedb
set serveroutput on
declare
    v_inst_scn number; -- variable to hold instantiation scn value
    begin
        v_inst_scn := dbms_flashback.get_system_change_number();
        dbms_output.put_line(a => 'The instantiation number is: ' ||
v_inst_scn);
end;
/

The instantiation number is: 9336013
```

After getting the instantiation number from the source database, use the *set_schema_instantiation_scn* procedure of the *dbms_apply_adm* package to mark the replication to start from that point.

```
connect str_target/123@targetdb
begin
   dbms_apply_adm.set_schema_instantiation_scn(
     source_schema_name   => 'str_schema',
     source_database_name => 'sourcedb',
     recursive            => TRUE,
     instantiation_scn    => 9336013 );
end;
/
```

With the *set_parameter* procedure, it is possible to change many *apply* parameters. Now set the *disable_on_error* parameter to a value of *n*, so the *apply* process will not stop if an apply error happens.

```
conn str_target/123@targetdb
begin
  dbms_apply_adm.set_parameter(
    apply_name => 'stream_apply',
    parameter  => 'disable_on_error',
    value      => 'n');
end;
/
```

Now the *capture* and *apply* processes can be started on the source and target database by using the following commands:

```
--Start capture process on source database
conn str_source/123@sourcedb
begin
  dbms_capture_adm.start_capture(capture_name => 'stream_capture');
end;
/

--Start apply process on target database
conn str_target/123@targetdb
begin
   dbms_apply_adm.start_apply(apply_name => 'stream_apply');
end;
/
```

With the Streams configuration finished, run some tests by executing the DDL and DML commands and check the replication.

```
 --Check how many rows are in source and target table
conn str_schema/123@sourcedb

--Create tab_jobs table
create table tab_jobs (
```

```
      job varchar2(10),
      area varchar2(30),
      min_sal number,
      max_sal number);

select
   count(*)
from
   tab_jobs;

conn str_schema/123@targetdb
select
   count(*)
from
   str_schema.tab_jobs;

--Insert rows on source table
conn str_schema/123@sourcedb
insert into tab_jobs values ('DBA', 'Oracle Database',10000, 20000);
insert into tab_jobs values ('DBA', 'SQL Server Database',7000, 12000);
insert into tab_jobs values ('DBA', 'MySQL Database',8000, 10000);
```

Check for *capture* and *propagation* processes by querying the *dba_capture* and *dba_propagation* views in the source database. Check for *apply* processes by querying *dba_apply* in the target database.

Now that there is an Oracle Streams environment, continue to work with some *dbms_apply_adm* procedures. Use the *create_apply* procedure to create an *apply* process in the target database. Before creating the *apply* process, make sure to create the queue table that will be used with the *create_apply* procedure.

⊟ Code 11.2 – dbms_apply_create_apply.sql

```
conn sys@ora11g as sysdba

Connected to:
Oracle 11g Enterprise Edition Release 11.2.0.1.0 - Production
With the Partitioning, Oracle Label Security, OLAP, Data Mining,
Oracle Database Vault and Real Application Testing options

--First create the anydata type queue table
begin
   dbms_streams_adm.set_up_queue(
      queue_table => 'tab_anydata_queue',
      storage_clause => 'tablespace users',
      queue_name => 'tab_anydata_queue');
end;
/

--You can check queue table created by querying dba_queue_tables as follows:
col owner for a10
col ueue_table for a20
col type for a8
col object_type for a35
select
```

```
   owner,
   queue_table,
   type,
   object_type
from
   dba_queue_tables
where
   owner='str_target';

OWNER        QUEUE_TABLE                         TYPE      OBJECT_TYPE
----------   ----------------------------------  --------  ------------
str_target streams_queue_table                   object    sys.anydata

str_target tab_anydata_queue                     object    sy.anydata

--Now create the apply process using the queue table created above
begin
   dbms_apply_adm.create_apply(
      queue_name => 'str_target.streams_queue',
      apply_user => 'str_target',
      apply_name => 'apply_1',
      source_database => 'sourcedb',
      apply_database_link => NULL); --This is used just in case of
heterogeneous replication. This should be the database link to a non-Oracle
Database in that case.
end;
/

--Check apply procces by querying dba_apply view
col apply_name for a15
col queue_name for a15
col queue_owner for a10
col status for a10
select
   apply_name,
   queue_name,
   queue_owner,
   status
from
   dba_apply;

APPLY_NAME        QUEUE_NAME        QUEUE_OWNE STATUS
---------------   ---------------   ---------- ----------
stream_apply      streams_queue     str_target enabled
apply_1           streams_queue     str_target disabled
```

The *apply* process just created is still disabled and does not have any rules applied to it yet as covered in the previous example. Here it is seen how and when to utilize some other procedures of the *dbms_apply_adm* package.

🖫 Code 11.3 – dbms_apply_all.sql

```
conn sys@ora11g as sysdba

Connected to:
Oracle 11g Enterprise Edition Release 11.2.0.1.0 - Production
With the Partitioning, Oracle Label Security, OLAP, Data Mining,
```

```
--Delete all apply errors for a specific apply process using
delete_all_errors procedure
begin
   dbms_apply_adm.delete_all_errors(
      apply_name => 'stream_apply');
end;

--Delete a specific error transaction using delete_error procedure
begin
   dbms_apply_adm.delete_error(
      local_transaction_id => '1.4566.3343');
end;
/

--Drop an apply process and their unused rules  using drop_apply procedure
begin
   dbms_apply_adm.drop_apply(
      apply_name => 'apply_1',
      drop_unused_rule_sets => TRUE);
end;
/

--Create and drop object dependency to define parent-child relationship
between two objects at destination database
begin
   dbms_apply_adm.create_object_dependency(
      object_name => 'hr.tab_child',
      parent_object_name => 'hr.tab_parent');
end;
/

--Drop object dependency
begin
   dbms_apply_adm.drop_object_dependency(
      object_name => 'hr.tab_child',
      parent_object_name => 'hr.tab_parent');
end;
/

--If you fix a problem and need to re-execute all transactions of an apply
process use the execute_all_errors procedure
begin
   dbms_apply_adm.execute_all_errors(
      apply_name => 'streams_apply',
      execute_as_user => TRUE);
end;
/

--Or just execute one error by using execut_error procedure
begin
   dbms_apply_adm.execute_error(
      local_transaction_id => '4.556.9812',
      execute_as_user => TRUE);
end;
/
```

```
--Use remove_stmt_handler to remove a statement DML handler for a specified
operation on a specified database object from apply process
begin
  dbms_apply_adm.remove_stmt_handler(
    object_name     => 'str_schema.tab_jobs',
    operation_name  => 'update',
    handler_name    => 'handler_1',
    apply_name      => 'streams_apply');
end;
/

--Set or unset change handler for specific operations in specific objects
using set_change_handler procedure
--Unset
begin
  dbms_apply_adm.set_change_handler(
    change_table_name    =>  'str_schema.tab_test_handle',
    source_table_name    =>  'str_schema.tab_jobs',
    capture_values       =>  '*',
    apply_name           =>  'apply$22',
    operation_name       =>  'delete',
    change_handler_name  =>  NULL);
end;
/

--Set
begin
  dbms_apply_adm.set_change_handler(
    change_table_name    =>  'str_schema.tab_test_handle',
    source_table_name    =>  'str_schema.tab_jobs',
    capture_values       =>  '*',
    apply_name           =>  'apply$22',
    operation_name       =>  'delete',
    change_handler_name  =>  'str_change_handler_$11');
end;
/
```

My final example will show how to fix an error in the *apply* process using procedures
of the *dbms_apply_adm* package. Suppose we have a table without primary keys in my
replication environment. We then create a primary key on the target database table.
The first duplicated row inserted in the source database table will hang on this
replication process which can be viewed in the *dba_apply_error* table.

To create the error, first create a primary key on the target table and then insert a row
in the source table.

🖫 Code 11.4 – dbms_apply_duplicated_rows.sql

```
conn sys@ora11g as sysdba

Connected to:
Oracle 11g Enterprise Edition Release 11.2.0.1.0 - Production
With the Partitioning, Oracle Label Security, OLAP, Data Mining,
Oracle Database Vault and Real Application Testing options
```

```
--On target database

alter table str_schema.tab_jobs
  add constraint pk_id primary key (job_id);

--On source database
insert into   str_schema.tab_jobs values ('XX','ZZZZZ',1000,2000);
commit;insert into   str_schema.tab_jobs values ('XX','ZZZZZ',1000,2000);
commit;

--On target database check error message
col apply_name for a15
col queue_name for a15
col queue_owner for a15
col source_database for a10
col local_transaction_id for a10
col source_transaction_id for a10
col message_number for 9999
col error_message for a60
select
    apply_name,
    queue_name,
    queue_owner,
    source_database,
    local_transaction_id,
    source_transaction_id,
    message_number,
    error_message
from
    dba_apply_error;
```

```
APPLY_NAME      QUEUE_NAME      QUEUE_OWNER     SOURCE_DAT LOCAL_TRAN SOURCE_TRA MESS ERROR_MESSAGE
--------------  --------------- --------------- ---------- ---------- ---------- ---- ---------
stream_apply    streams_queue   str_target      sourcedb   3.28.207   6.7.221       1 ORA-00001:
unique constraint (str_schema.pk_id) violated
```

In order to allow duplicated rows in this table, change a parameter for this *apply* process:

```
begin
    dbms_apply_adm.set_parameter(
        apply_name => 'stream_apply',
        parameter => 'allow_duplicate_rows',
        value => 'Y');
end;
/

--Drop the primary key on target table
alter table str_schema.tab_jobs
  drop constraint pk_id cascade;
```

Now execute the *execute_error* procedure informing the *local_transaction_id* discovered in the *dba_apply_error* view.

```
begin
    dbms_apply_adm.execute_error(
```

```
        local_transaction_id => '3.28.207');
end;
/
```

Now we can see the duplicated row and also replicate any duplicated rows in this table and/or *apply* process.

Here are some other *apply* process related views:

- *dba_apply*: Displays information on all *apply* processes in the database

- *dba_apply_errors*: Displays information about error transactions found in the *apply* processes

- *dba_apply_change_handlers*: Displays information about change handlers in all tables

- *dba_apply_conflict_columns*: Displays information about conflict handlers in all tables

- *dba_apply_dml_handlers:* Displays information about all DML handlers in a database

- *dba_apply_enqueue*: Displays information about apply enqueue for all rules

- *dba_apply_execute*: Displays information about the apply execute actions in a database

- *dba_apply_instantiated_global*: Displays information about databases with an instantiation

- *dba_apply_instantiated_objects*: Displays information about objects instantiated

- *dba_apply_instantiated_schemas*: Displays information about schemas instantiated

- *dba_apply_key_columns*: Displays information about substitute key columns

- *dba_apply_object_dependencies*: Displays information about all object dependencies in *apply* processes

- *dba_apply_parameters*: Displays information about all parameters of all *apply* processes

- *dba_apply_progress*: Displays information about the progress of all *apply* processes

- *dba_apply_spill_txn*: Displays information about spilled transactions in all *apply* processes

- *dba_apply_table_columns*: Displays information about all non-key columns for all tables in a database

- *dba_apply_value_dependencies*: Displays information about value dependencies in a database

---

Package dbms_apply_adm   **481**

Good information on printing errors and LCR messages is available in Oracle® Streams Concepts and Administration 11g Release 2 (11.2) Part Number E17069-04 where print procedures used to get further information regarding *apply* processes and their messages can be found.

Packages *dbms_aq* and *dbms_aqadm*

Advanced Queuing (AQ) is Oracle's implementation of a messaging system which can be used as a replacement for the *dbms_pipe* package and other bespoke solutions. The basic unit of the Oracle Advanced Queuing messaging system is a message with the most important element of the message being its contents or payload.

The payload of the advanced queuing message can be as simple or complicated as desired. In this case, the only concern is that the message has been sent. The particular contents are not important at this time, so the message is extremely simple.

Administration of queues within Oracle Advanced Queuing is done using the *dbms_aqadm* package and requires the *aq_administrator_role* to be granted to the administrator. Alternatively, all administration can be performed by a privileged user such as SYS or SYSTEM. With the payload object defined, the queue table is created using the *create_queue_table* procedure.

Once the queue table has been created, the individual queues are created and started using the *create_queue* and *start_queue* procedures, respectively. A single queue table can hold many queues as long as each queue uses the same type for its payload.

Messages are queued and dequeued within Oracle Advanced Queuing using the *dbms_aq* package. Access to this package can be granted using the *aq_user_role* role. However, access to it from a stored procedure is achieved by using the *job_chain_aq_setup.sql* script which grants the privilege on this object directly to the test user.

There are sets of tools and Oracle Features that make use of queue tables like Oracle Workflow, Oracle Streams, Oracle Advanced Replication, Oracle Alerts and more. In the next example, some procedures and functions of *dbms_aq* and *dbms_aqadm* will be shown. Suppose that we want to monitor and receive warnings and critical alerts when the number of blocked users in a database exceed five sessions.

The first step is to check the metric ID and then to set the metric value with my own values.

🖫 Code 11.5 – dbms_aq.sql

```
conn sys@ora11g as sysdba

Connected to:
Oracle 11g Enterprise Edition Release 11.2.0.1.0 - Production
With the Partitioning, Oracle Label Security, OLAP, Data Mining,
Oracle Database Vault and Real Application Testing options

--create usr_alert user that will be used on this example
create user usr_alert identified by manager;
grant dba to usr_alert ;

begin
   dbms_server_alert.set_threshold(
      metrics_id => 9000,
      warning_operator => dbms_server_alert.operator_ge,
      warning_value => '2',
      critical_operator => dbms_server_alert.operator_ge,
      critical_value => '5',
      observation_period => 1,
      consecutive_occurrences => 1,
      instance_name => NULL,
      object_type => dbms_server_alert.object_type_session,
      object_name => NULL);
end;
/
```

Check the thresholds created by querying *dba_thresholds*.

```
select
   *
from
   dba_thresholds;
```

These alerts are stored by default in the *alert_qt* table in Oracle 11g; in 10g, they are stored in the *alert_que* table. The MMON process checks for exceeded threshold limits and creates a new alert for each one. In order to dequeue the alert generated, it is necessary to create an agent using the *create_aq_agent* procedure of the *dbms_aqadm* package:

```
begin
   dbms_aqadm.create_aq_agent(
      agent_name=> 'locked_users_alert');
end;
/
```

Check the created agent by querying *dba_aq_agents*.

```
select
   agent_name
from
   dba_aq_agents;
```

Next, add a subscriber to the alert just created by using the *add_subscriber* procedure of the *dbms_aqadm* package as:

```
begin
   dbms_aqadm.add_subscriber(
      queue_name=>'alert_queue',
      subscriber => aq$_agent('locked_users_alert','',0)
      );
end;
/

--or
declare
v_subscriber sys.aq$_agent;
begin
   v_subscriber := sys.aq$_agent('subs_alert_lock_2', '', 0);
   dbms_aqadm.add_subscriber(
      queue_name=>'alert_que',
      subscriber => v_subscriber);
end;
/
```

Now enable database access to the added subscriber by using the *enable_db_access* procedure of the *dbms_aqadm* package:

```
begin
   dbms_aqadm.enable_db_access(
      agent_name =>'locked_users_alert',
      db_username=>'usr_alert');
end;
/
```

Check which users have privileges to which agent by querying the *dba_aq_agent_privs* view as follows:

```
select
   agent_name,
   db_username
from
   dba_aq_agent_privs;
```

Next, grant *dequeue* privileges to the dbms user with the *grant_queue_privilege* procedure in the *dbms_aqadm* package.

```
begin
   dbms_aqadm.grant_queue_privilege(
      privilege =>'dequeue',
      queue_name => 'alert_que',
      grantee=>'system',
      grant_option=>false);
end;
/
```

Now that the agent and subscriber were created and the user that will dequeue messages has the right privileges, the *dequeue* process will be created.

```
--First simulate some locks

--Open 2 sessions and execute the same update without commit

create table tab_lock (col1 number);
insert into tab_lock values (1);

update tab_lock set col1=2 where col1=1;

set serveroutput on
declare
  v_dequeue_options       dbms_aq.dequeue_options_t;
  v_message_properties dbms_aq.message_properties_t;
  v_alert_type_message          alert_type;
  v_message_handle      raw(16);
  v_message_1             aq.message_typ;
  type msgidtab is table of raw(16) index by binary_integer;
  msg_id msgidtab;
  dq_msg_id raw(16);


cursor c_msgs_id is
select msg_id
  from aq$alert_qt
 where msg_state = 'ready';


begin
  v_dequeue_options.consumer_name := 'locked_users_alert';
  v_dequeue_options.wait          := 1;
  v_dequeue_options.navigation    := dbms_aq.first_message;
  dbms_aq.dequeue(queue_name          => 'sys.alert_que',
                  dequeue_options     => v_dequeue_options,
                  message_properties => v_message_properties,
                  payload             => v_alert_type_message,
                  msgid               => v_message_handle);
  dbms_output.put_line('alert message dequeued:');
  dbms_output.put_line(' timestamp: ' ||
v_alert_type_message.timestamp_originating);
  dbms_output.put_line(' message type: ' ||
v_alert_type_message.message_type);
  dbms_output.put_line(' message group: ' ||
v_alert_type_message.message_group);
  dbms_output.put_line(' message level: ' ||
v_alert_type_message.message_level);
  dbms_output.put_line(' host id: ' || v_alert_type_message.host_id);
  dbms_output.put_line(' host network addr: ' ||
v_alert_type_message.host_nw_addr);
  dbms_output.put_line(' reason: ' ||
                       dbms_server_alert.expand_message(userenv('language'),

v_alert_type_message.message_id,

v_alert_type_message.reason_argument_1,
```

```
v_alert_type_message.reason_argument_2,

v_alert_type_message.reason_argument_3,

v_alert_type_message.reason_argument_4,

v_alert_type_message.reason_argument_5));
  dbms_output.put_line(' sequence id: ' ||
v_alert_type_message.sequence_id);
  dbms_output.put_line(' reason id: ' || v_alert_type_message.reason_id);
  dbms_output.put_line(' object name: ' ||
v_alert_type_message.object_name);
  dbms_output.put_line(' object type: ' ||
v_alert_type_message.object_type);
  dbms_output.put_line(' instance name: ' ||
v_alert_type_message.instance_name);
  dbms_output.put_line(' suggested action: ' ||
                    dbms_server_alert.expand_message(userenv('language'),

v_alert_type_message.suggested_action_msg_id,

v_alert_type_message.action_argument_1,

v_alert_type_message.action_argument_2,

v_alert_type_message.action_argument_3,

v_alert_type_message.action_argument_4,

v_alert_type_message.action_argument_5));
  dbms_output.put_line(' advisor name: ' ||
v_alert_type_message.advisor_name);
  dbms_output.put_line(' Scope: ' || v_alert_type_message.scope);

end;
```

Having such a tool to send and receive messages, with methods to queue and track them, is key to ensuring the mission-critical messages are delivered and processed, even if the communication channel is temporarily disrupted. So it clearly has many real life applications. This is just one of many tasks that can be accomplished with *dbms_aq* and *dbms_aqadm* packages.

How and when to use these *enqueue* and *dequeue* packages for the specific tasks is now apparent.

Package *dbms_capture_adm*

One of the main processes of a Streams configuration, the *capture* process, is responsible for capturing changes from the redo log files. If the information is not in the redo log, it can capture changes from the archived log files instead. This package can be used to start, stop, create and change the configuration of the *capture* process in a Streams environment.

Although *dbms_streams_adm* can create *capture* processes with rules, *dbms_capture_adm* creates a *capture* process with more control by manually specifying the rules that are needed. It accomplishes this via another package named *dbms_rule_adm*. In the next examples, how to instantiate a table, schemas and all tables of a database will be shown. Also to be introduced is how to create, drop, alter, start and stop a *capture* process.

For this example, a *capture* process will be created, parameters will be changed, additional information added and then the process will be started, stopped and dropped.

🖫 Code 11.6 – dbms_capture_adm.sql

```
conn sys@ora11g as sysdba

Connected to:
Oracle 11g Enterprise Edition Release 11.2.0.1.0 - Production
With the Partitioning, Oracle Label Security, OLAP, Data Mining,
Oracle Database Vault and Real Application Testing options

--Create a tablespace for streams data if it didn't exists
create tablespace
   tbs_streams_data
datafile size 200M;

--Create a queue table for capture process
begin
   dbms_aqadm.create_queue_table(
      queue_table=> 'str_source.tab_capture',
      queue_payload_type=> 'sys.anydata',
      sort_list=> '',
      comment=> 'Queue table for capture process.',
      multiple_consumers=> TRUE,
      message_grouping=> dbms_aqadm.transactional,
      non_repudiation => dbms_aqadm.none,
      storage_clause=> ' tablespace "tbs_strea,s_data" pctfree 10 pctused 0
initrans 1 maxtrans 255 storage ( initial 64K next 0K minextents 1
maxextents 2147483645 pctincreaste 0)',
      compatible=> '8.1',
      primary_instance=> '0',
      secondary_instance=> '0');
      commit;
end;
/

--Create a new queue for the capture process
begin
   dbms_aqadm.create_queue(
      queue_name => 'str_source.q_capture',
      queue_table => 'str_source.tab_capture',
      comment => 'queue for capture process');
```

```
      commit;
end;
/

--Create the capture process using the queue just created above

begin
   dbms_capture_adm.create_capture(
      queue_name => 'str_source.q_capture',
      capture_name => 'str_source.capture_1');
commit;
end;
/

--Change the paralelism of a capture process
begin
   dbms_capture_adm.set_parameter(
      capture_name => 'str_source.capture_1',
      parameter => 'parallelism',
      value => 4);
end;
/
```

Check all parameters of the *capture* processes by querying the *dba_capture_parameters* view:

```
set linesize 140
col parameter for a30
col value for a5
select
   *
from
   dba_capture_parameters
where
   capture_name = '"str_source"."capture_1"'
and
   parameter ='parallelism'
/
```

The next step is to start, stop and finally drop the *capture* process using the *dbms_capture_adm* package.

```
begin
   dbms_capture_adm.start_capture(
      capture_name => 'str_source.capture_1');
end;
/

--Check if it is started
select
   capture_name,
   status
from
   dba_capture
/
```

```
--Stop capture process
begin
    dbms_capture_adm.stop_capture(
        capture_name => 'str_source.capture _1',
        force => TRUE);
end;
/

--Drop capture process
begin
    dbms_capture_adm.drop_capture(
        capture_name => 'str_source.capture _1',
        drop_unused_rule_sets => TRUE);
end;
/
```

The next code shows how to use the procedure *include_extra_attribute*. This instructs a *capture* process to include specified additional attributes in the Logical Change Records (LCRs) beyond those commonly captured such as *row_id*, *serial#*, *session$*, *thread#*, *tx_name* and *username*.

This procedure may help in auditing or to just filter information that will be used in an *apply* process.

In the example below, how to add *username* as an extra attribute for the LCR being captured is reviewed.

🖫 Code 11.7 – dbms_capture_adm_extra_att.sql

```
conn sys@ora11g as sysdba

Connected to:
Oracle 11g Enterprise Edition Release 11.2.0.1.0 - Production
With the Partitioning, Oracle Label Security, OLAP, Data Mining,
Oracle Database Vault and Real Application Testing options

--Include extra attribute - username and session#
begin
    dbms_capture_adm.include_extra_attribute(
        capture_name => 'str_source.capture _1',
        attribute_name => 'username',
        include => TRUE);
end;
/

begin
    dbms_capture_adm.include_extra_attribute(
        capture_name => 'str_source.capture _1',
        attribute_name => 'session#',      include => TRUE);
end;
/

--You can use dba_capture_extra_attributes view to check which attributes a
capture process is using
```

Package dbms_capture_adm   **489**

```
col attribute_name for a10
select
    capture_name,
    attribute_name,
    include
from
    dba_capture_extra_attributes
where
    capture_name='"str_source"."capture_1"';

CAPTURE_NAME                         ATTRIBUTE_ INCLUDE
----------------------------------  ---------- -------
"str_source"."capture_1"            row_id     NO
"str_source"."capture_1"            serial#    NO
"str_source"."capture_1"            session#   YES
"str_source"."capture_1"            thread#    NO
"str_source"."capture_1"            tx_name    NO
"str_source"."capture_1"            username   YES

--Exclude extra attribute session#
begin
    dbms_capture_adm.include_extra_attribute(
        capture_name => 'str_source.capture_1',
        attribute_name => 'username',
        include => FALSE);
end;
/
```

Instantiation is a process of marking a table point from which a *replication* process will begin. When a table is instantiated, the SCN that is used by an *apply* process appears. That *apply* process will start the *replication* process for all records that occur after this SCN.

Object instantiation is a prerequisite for Oracle Streams configuration. The *dbms_capture_adm* package has procedures that address this. The final examples of this package will show how to instantiate a table, all objects of a specific schema, or even all database tables at once. Here is a technique almost always used when just a small set of tables need to be replicated.

Code 11.8 – dbms_capture_adm_instantiation.sql

```
conn sys@ora11g as sysdba

Connected to:
Oracle 11g Enterprise Edition Release 11.2.0.1.0 - Production
With the Partitioning, Oracle Label Security, OLAP, Data Mining,
Oracle Database Vault and Real Application Testing options

create table
    str_source.tab_test_replic(
        emp_id number,
        first_name varchar2(30),
        last_name varchar2(30));
```

```
--Table Instantiation adding supplemental logging for all columns
begin
   dbms_capture_adm.prepare_table_instantiation(
      table_name => 'str_source.tab_test_replic',
      supplemental_logging => 'all');
end;
/
```

All tables which are prepared for instantiation in a database can be checked by querying the *dba_capture_prepared_tables* view as follows:

```
select
   table_owner,
   table_name,
   timestamp
from
   dba_capture_prepared_tables
/
```

```
ABLE_OWNER       TABLE_NAME       TIMESTAMP
---------------  --------------   -----------
str_source       tab_test_replic  10/10/2010
```

Next, instantiate all tables of a specified schema. This process will also instantiate all future tables created automatically.

```
--Schema instantiation adding supplemental logging for key columns (primary
keys, unique keys, bitmap indexes,and foreign keys columns)

begin
   dbms_capture_adm.prepare_schema_instantiation(
      schema_name => 'str_source',
      supplemental_logging => 'keys');
end;
/
```

In order to check all schemas prepared for instantiation, use a query of *dba_capture_prepared_schemas* as below:

```
select
   schema_name,
   timestamp
from
   dba_capture_prepared_schemas;

SCHEMA_NAME                     TIMESTAMP
------------------------------  -----------
str_source                      10/10/2010
```

Finally, use *prepare procedure_global_instantiation* for all tables of the local database to be instantiated. All future tables created will automatically be prepared for instantiation.

```
begin
    dbms_capture_adm.prepare_global_instantiation(
        supplemental_logging => 'keys');
end;
/
```

Use the following query to check if the database is instantiated as a whole.

```
select
    *
from
    dba_capture_prepared_database;
```

```
TIMESTAMP   SUPPLEMENTAL_LOG_DATA_PK SUPPLEMENTAL_LOG_DATA_UI SUPPLEMENTAL_LOG_DATA_FK
SUPPLEMENTAL_LOG_DATA_ALL
----------- ------------------------ ------------------------ ------------------------ --------------
-----------
10/10/2010  explicit                 explicit                 explicit                 NO
```

As shown, *dbms_capture_adm* provides methods to instantiate objects by specifying just one table, all tables of a schema, or all tables of the database. There are other methods to instantiate objects like using export and import utilities, Data Pump and also Oracle RMAN, but they are beyond the scope of this book.

Package *dbms_aqelm*

Oracle Advanced Queue asynchronous notification allows Advanced Queue subscribers to receive notifications without needing to be connected to the database. There are four different mechanisms that can be used to send notifications: PL/SQL Callback procedure, OCI Callback procedure, email notification or by sending notifications to a specific HTTP address.

This package provides a method of sending Oracle Streams Advanced Queue asynchronous notifications via e-mail or a http address. Through this package, the hosts, port, proxy user and the notification(s) to be sent can be configured. In the next example, how to gather values, how to send a notification and how to change configuration values of ports, proxies and hosts will be viewed.

🖫 Code 11.9 – dbms_aqelm.sql

```
conn sys@ora11g as sysdba

Connected to:
Oracle 11g Enterprise Edition Release 11.2.0.1.0 - Production
With the Partitioning, Oracle Label Security, OLAP, Data Mining,
Oracle Database Vault and Real Application Testing options
```

```
--Set mail configurations
begin
   dbms_aqelm.set_mailhost(mailhost => 'smtp.myhost.com');
   dbms_aqelm.set_mailport(mailport => 25);
   dbms_aqelm.set_proxy(proxy => 'proxy.myhost.com');
   dbms_aqelm.set_sendfrom(sendfrom => 'paulo.portugal@f2c.com.br');
end;
/

--Get mail configuration
set serveroutput on
declare
v_mailhost varchar2(100);
v_port     number;
v_sendfrom varchar2(50);

begin
   dbms_aqelm.get_mailhost(v_mailhost);
   dbms_aqelm.get_mailport(v_port);
   dbms_aqelm.get_sendfrom(v_sendfrom);
   dbms_output.put_line(a => ' Mail host is:'||v_mailhost);
   dbms_output.put_line(a => ' Port is      :'||v_port);
   dbms_output.put_line(a => ' Send from    :'||v_sendfrom);
end;
/

--Sending notification using send_mail
begin
   dbms_aqelm.send_email(
      sendto => 'paulo.portugal@f2c.com.br',
      text => 'Testing email from send_mail!');
end;
/

--Sending notification to a URL
declare
v_statuscode varchar2(100);
begin
   dbms_aqelm.http_send(
      url => 'http://10.10.10.1/',
      what => 'test sending URL ',
      what1 => 10,
      status_code => v_statuscode);
   dbms_output.put_line(a => 'Status code is: '||v_statuscode);
end;
/
```

Another frequent task with AQ is trying to find out the active subscribers. Check the subscribers that have been configured to receive notifications by querying the *sys.reg$* table.

```
select
   subscription_name,
   location_name
from
   sys.reg$;
```

```
SUBSCRIPTION_NAME                         LOCATION_NAME
-----------------------------------       ---------------------------------------
"str_source"."streams_queue":aq$_p@"str_  plsql://sys.dbms_isched.event_notify
target"."streams_queue"@targetdb
```

Information about the subscription was obtained and can always be checked using the *reg$* table.

Package *dbms_hs_passthrough*

Oracle Streams is a powerful tool which can be configured in a heterogeneous environment; for example, with a replication between an Oracle Database and a SQL Server database. This package provides the functionality to send a command directly to a non-Oracle database.

Several SQL commands can be navigated across non-Oracle databases: *create table*, *alter table*, *select*, *update*, *delete* and many others. It is also possible to use bind variables within these commands as will be shown in the following examples.

We are creating a Streams replication environment with an Oracle source database and the destination is an SQL Server database. we want to create the table that will be replicated on the SQL Server to begin configuring my Streams replication. This example will show one of the main procedures of *dbms_hs_passthrough* (*execute_immediate*) used to run any non query SQL in the non-Oracle database immediately.

In this example, we create a table in an SQL Server database by using a database link named *sqlserverdb* configured with a transparent gateway.

🖫 Code 11.10 – dbms_hs_passthrough.sql

```
conn sys@ora11g as sysdba

Connected to:
Oracle 11g Enterprise Edition Release 11.2.0.1.0 - Production
With the Partitioning, Oracle Label Security, OLAP, Data Mining,
Oracle Database Vault and Real Application Testing options

declare
ret integer;
begin
ret := dbms_hs_passthrough.execute_immediate@sqlserverdb(
'create table str_dest.test_table
(id_inst                     int NOT NULL,
id_role_inst         char(2) NOT NULL,
id_direct_status          tinyint,
flg_generate_title   numeric(1))');
end;
/
commit;
--Add primary key on a table on a non-oracle database
declare
```

```
ret integer;
begin
ret := dbms_hs_passthrough.execute_immediate@sqlserverdb(
'alter table str_dest.test_table
add constraint tit_cont_tit_ser_plan_dt_mod_1
primary key nonclustered(
id_inst)');
end;
/
```

In the second example, we will execute a query using bind variables that are specified by the *bind_variable* procedure of the *dbms_hs_passthrough* package. This is one of many procedures available to deal with bind variables when using this package.

🖫 Code 11.11 – dbms_hs_passthrough_variable.sql

```
conn sys@ora11g as sysdba

Connected to:
Oracle 11g Enterprise Edition Release 11.2.0.1.0 - Production
With the Partitioning, Oracle Label Security, OLAP, Data Mining,
Oracle Database Vault and Real Application Testing options

--Using bind variables in a query
declare
v_cursor binary_integer;
v_ret binary_integer;
v_id integer;
v_first_name varchar2(30);
v_last_name varchar2(30);
v_bind_id integer;
v_bind_first_name varchar2(30);
begin
    v_cursor:=dbms_hs_passthrough.open_cursor@sqlserver;
    dbms_hs_passthrough.parse@sqlserver(v_cursor,'select id, first_name,
last_name from test_table where id = ? and first_name = ?');
    v_bind_id := 10
    v_bind_first_name := 'paulo'
    dbms_hs_passthrough.bind_variable@sqlserver(v_cursor,1,v_bind_id);

dbms_hs_passthrough.bind_variable@sqlserver(v_cursor,2,v_bind_first_name);
    begin
        v_ret:=0;
        while (true)
        loop
            v_ret:=dbms_hs_passthrough.fetch_row@sqlserver(v_cursor,false);
            dbms_hs_passthrough.get_value@sqlserver(v_cursor,1,v_id);
            dbms_hs_passthrough.get_value@sqlserver
(v_cursor,2,v_first_name);
            dbms_hs_passthrough.get_value@sqlserver
(v_cursor,3,v_last_name);
dbms_output.put_line('First Name '||v_first_name);
dbms_output.put_line(Last Name '||v_last_name);
        end loop;
        exception
        when no_data_found then
        begin
```

```
            dbms_output.put_line('no more rows found!');
            dbms_hs_passthrough.close_cursor@sqlserver(v_cursor);
        end;
    end;
end;
/
```

Note that when querying data from a non-Oracle database, the *execute_immediate* procedure cannot be used; instead, use procedures to open and fetch a cursor in order to get a *query* value.

Packages *dbms_mgwadm* and *dbms_mgwmsg*

Oracle Streams enable the propagation between two Oracle Stream Advanced Queues. This is an Oracle-Oracle configuration. Oracle Messaging gateway is a feature that makes the communication between Oracle Streams Advanced Queue and non-Oracle applications like Websphere and other applications tools possible.

For the purpose of configuring Messaging Gateway, two packages were created: *dbms_mgwadm* and *dbms_mgmsg*. In the next codes, how to configure Messaging Gateway to be used in conjunction with Websphere will be reviewed. The Oracle Messaging gateway has two main components: the Agent and the *dbms_mgwadm* administration package. The first thing to do is to create these packages by running the *catmgw.sql* script which is found in the *$ORACLE_HOME/mgw/admin* directory.

Next, configure the *listener.ora* and *tnsnames.ora* in order to start the Messaging Gateway Agent. Some examples of how they should be configured are below:

🖫 Code 11.12 – dbms_mgw.sql

```
conn sys@ora11g as sysdba

Connected to:
Oracle 11g Enterprise Edition Release 11.2.0.1.0 - Production
With the Partitioning, Oracle Label Security, OLAP, Data Mining,
Oracle Database Vault and Real Application Testing options

--Check your listener.ora and tnsnames.ora and validate if they have the
proper values necessary to start the agent

--tnsnames.ora
mgw_agent=
(description =
 (address_list =
  (address = (protocol=ipc)(key=extproc)))
  (connect_data = (sid=mgwextproc) (presentation=RO)))


agent_service =
(description =
```

```
  (address_list =
  (address=
  (protocol=ipc) ( key=extproc)))
  (connect_data =
  (sid=sourcedb)(presentation=RO)))


--listener.ora
listener =
  (description =
    (address = (protocol = tcp)(host = 10.10.10.113)(port = 1521))
    (address = (protocol = ipc)(key  =extproc))

  )

sid_list_listener =
  (sid_list =
  (sid_desc =
     (global_dbname = dbms)
     (ORACLE_HOME = /u01/app/oracle/product/11.2.0/db11g)
     (sid_name = dbms)
  )
  (sid_desc=
   (sid_name= mgwextproc)

(envs="ld_library_path=/u01/app/oracle/product/11.2.0/db11g/jdk/jre/lib/i386
:/u01/app/oracle/product/11.2.0/db11g/jdk/jre/lib/i386/server:/u01/app/oracl
e/product/11.2.0/db11g/lib")
    (ORACLE_HOME=/u01/app/oracle/product/11.2.0/db11g)
    (program = extproc))
    )
```

Check the *mgw.ora* file that is used by the agent. This file is located in the *$ORACLE_HOME/mgw/admin* directory and will look something like the lines below:

```
set
ld_library_path=/u01/app/oracle/product/11.2.0/db11g/jdk/jre/lib/i386:/u01/a
pp/oracle/product/11.2.0/db11g/jdk/jre/lib/i386/server:/u01/app/oracle/produ
ct/11.2.0/db11g/rdbms/lib:/u01/app/oracle/product/11.2.0/db11g/lib

log_directory=/u01/app/oracle/product/11.2.0/db11g/mgw/log
log_level = 0
set
classpath=/u01/app/oracle/product/11.2.0/db11g/jdbc/lib/ojdbc5.jar://u01/app
/oracle/product/11.2.0/db11g/jdk/jre/lib/i18n.jar://u01/app/oracle/product/1
1.2.0/db11g/jdk/jre/lib/rt.jar://u01/app/oracle/product/11.2.0/db11g/sqlj/li
b/runtime12.jar://u01/app/oracle/product/11.2.0/db11g/jlib/orai18n.jar://u01
/app/oracle/product/11.2.0/db11g/jlib/jta.jar://u01/app/oracle/product/11.2.
0/db11g/rdbms/jlib/jmscommon.jar://u01/app/oracle/product/11.2.0/db11g/rdbms
/jlib/aqapi.jar:/opt/mqm/java/lib/com.ibm.mqjms.jar:/opt/mqm/java/lib/com.ib
m.mq.jar:/opt/mqm/java/lib/:/opt/mqm/java/lib/connector.jar
```

Create a user that will have Messaging Gateway permissions and configure connection information used by the agent to connect to the database.

```
create user mgw identified by mgw;

grant connect,mgw_agent_role  to mgw;
begin
    dbms_mgwadm.db_connect_info(
        username => 'mgw',
        password => 'mgw',
        database => 'sourcedb');
end;
/
```

To check agent information, query the *mgw_gateway* view.

```
col agent_database for a10
col agent_status for a10
col agent_user for a10
col max_connections for 99
select
    max_memory,
    max_connections,
    agent_user,
    agent_database,
    agent_status
from
    mgw_gateway;
```

Now start the agent by using the *start_agent* procedure. Note that after starting the *agent_status*, the column on table *mgw$_gateway* will change in value from 0 to 1.

```
begin
    dbms_mgwadm.startup;
end;
/

--Shutdown the agent
begin
    dbms_mgwadm.shutdown(
        sdmode => dbms_mgwadm.shutdown_immediate);
end;
/
```

Now it is time to create a particular queue table and a queue for this process. After this has been created, start the queue.

```
begin
    dbms_aqadm.create_queue_table(
        queue_table => 'mgw_q_table',
        multiple_consumers=>TRUE,
        queue_payload_type =>'sys.anydata' ,
        compatible => '8.1');
        dbms_aqadm.create_queue(
        queue_name => 'mgw_q',
        queue_table => 'mgw_q_table');
end;
```

```
/
--Start the queue
begin
    dbms_aqadm.start_queue (queue_name => 'mgw_q');
end;
/
```

Now that the queue has been created and started, the next step will be creating the link that is responsible for connecting the database to the Websphere application. This link is created using the *create_msgsystem_link* procedure:

```
declare
    v_mgw_properties sys.mgw_properties;
    v_mgw_mq_properties sys.mgw_mqseries_properties;
begin
    v_mgw_mq_properties := sys.mgw_mqseries_properties.construct();
    v_mgw_mq_properties.max_connections := 5;
    v_mgw_mq_properties.interface_type :=
dbms_mgwadm.mqseries_base_java_interface;
    v_mgw_mq_properties.username := 'webuser';
    v_mgw_mq_properties.password := 'web123';
    v_mgw_mq_properties.hostname := '10.10.10.114';
    v_mgw_mq_properties.port        := 5522;
    v_mgw_mq_properties.channel   := 'system.def.svrconn';
    v_mgw_mq_properties.queue_manager := 'mgw_q_manager';
        v_mgw_mq_properties.outbound_log_queue := 'mgw_out_log_q';
    v_mgw_mq_properties.inbound_log_queue :=  'mgw_in_log_q';

    dbms_mgwadm.create_msgsystem_link(
        linkname => 'mgw_link',
        properties => v_mgw_mq_properties,
        options => v_mgw_properties,
        comment => 'This is the link to connect to Websphere.' );
end;
/
```

The link just created can be checked by querying the *mgw$_links* table or *mgw_links* view as follows:

```
col link_name for a10
select
    link_name,
    agent_name
from
    mgw$_links;

select
    link_name,
    link_type,
    agent_name
from
    mgw_links;
After creating the link, we register the non-Oracle queue in the Messaging
Gateway.
```

```
begin
   dbms_mgwadm.register_foreign_queue(
      name => 'mgw_fk_queue',
      linkname => 'mgw_link',
      provider_queue => 'mgw_fk_queue',
      domain => dbms_mgwadm.domain_queue,
      comment => 'Foreign Link Test.');
end;
/
```

Check the foreign queue by querying the *mgw_foreign_queues* view:

```
col name for a14
col provider_queue for a15
select
   name,
   link_name,
   provider_queue,
   domain
from
   mgw_foreign_queues;


NAME           LINK_NAME    PROVIDER_QUEUE   DOMAIN
-------------- ----------   ---------------- ------
mgw_fk_queue   mgw_link     mgw_fk_queue     queue
```

Finally , after creating the link that will guide messages to Websphere, a job is created using the *create_job* procedure which replaced the old *add_subscriber* and *schedule_propagation*. This job is created using the following scripts.

```
begin
   dbms_mgwadm.create_job(
      job_name => 'mgw_job',
      propagation_type => dbms_mgwadm.outbound_propagation,
      source => 'sys.mgw_q',
      destination => 'mgw_fk_queue@mgw_link',
      enabled => TRUE,
      poll_interval => 10,comments => 'My test mgw Job.');
end;
/

--Check the subscriber using the mgw_subscribers view.
col subscriber_id for a10
col queue_name for a10
col destination for a22
select
   subscriber_id,
   propagation_type,
   queue_name,
   destination,
   status
from
   mgw_subscribers;

--Check job created
```

```
col job_name for a10
col source for a10
col status for a10
select
    job_name,
    propagation_type,
    source,
    destination,
    enabled,
    link_name,
    status
from
    mgw_jobs;
```

While *dbms_mgwadm* is used to create and manage Messaging Gateway configurations, *dbms_mgwmsg* is a package used to convert message bodies; for example, converting a *sys.anydata* object, encapsulating a *lcr* to a *sys.xmltype* or functions like *nvarray_find_name* used to find a name-value array for an element.

Package *dbms_propagation_adm*

The *propagation* process is responsible for sending enqueued messages from the source queue to the destination queue. A queue can participate in many *propagation* processes at once. One single source queue can propagate events to multiple destination queues. Likewise, a single destination queue may receive events form multiple source queues.

The rules for the *propagation* process are specified as follows: these rules can be defined at the table, schema or global level. They can propagate or discard row changes from DML and DDL commands.

The *dbms_propagation_adm* package provides procedures that enable propagation process management. With this package, it is possible to create, alter, stop, start and drop a *propagation* process. Meanwhile, packages *dbms_rule* and *dbms_rule_adm* enable the rule creation and rule evaluation to be used in the propagation process. In my example of this package, a rule that converts the owner of objects is created and will be used in a *propagation* process.

The first step is to create a rule that will change the owner of an object. Suppose that the owner in *sourcedb* is *str_source* and the owner in *targetdb* is *str_target*. In this example, the Streams owner is the *stradmin* database user. Create the function that will be used in rule. This function will change the object owner to *str_target*.

🖫 Code 11.13 – dbms_propagation_rule.sql

```
conn sys@ora11g as sysdba

Connected to:
```

```
create or replace function str_source.transf_function(in_any in sys.anydata)
   return sys.anydata -- my user is "str_source"
  is
  v_lcr    sys.lcr$_row_record;
  ret    pls_integer;
  objnm varchar2(30);
begin
  ret    := in_any.getobject(v_lcr);
  objnm := v_lcr.get_object_name;
  v_lcr.set_object_owner('"str_target"');
  return sys.anydata.convertobject(v_lcr);
end;
/

show errors;
```

Now create the rule set and the rule using the PL/SQL block below; specifying the function created above.

```
begin
        dbms_rule_adm.create_rule_set(
             rule_set_name=>'str_source.my_test_rule_set',
             evaluation_context=>'sys.streams$_evaluation_context') ;
end ;
/

declare
        action_ctx sys.re$nv_list ;
        ac_name varchar2(30) := 'streams$_transform_function' ;
begin
        action_ctx := sys.re$nv_list(sys.re$nv_array()) ;
        action_ctx.add_pair(ac_name,
sys.anydata.convertvarchar2('str_source.transf_function')) ;  --change to my
user"stradmin"
        dbms_rule_adm.create_rule(
             rule_name=>'str_source.rule_test',
             condition=>':dml.get_object_owner() = ''str_source'' and ' ||
':dml.is_null_tag() = ''Y''',
             evaluation_context=>'sys.streams$_evaluation_context',
             action_context => action_ctx) ;

        dbms_rule_adm.add_rule(
             rule_set_name=>'str_source.my_test_rule_set',
             rule_name=>'str_source.rule_test');
end ;
/
```

Confirm that the rule was created by querying the *dba_rules* and *dba_rule_set_rules* views:

```
set linesize 140
col rule_set_name for a18
```

```
col rule_owner for a10
col rule_name for a9
 col rule_condition for a80
select
   rs.rule_set_name,
   r.rule_owner,
   r.rule_name,
   r.rule_condition
from
   dba_rules r,
   dba_rule_set_rules rs where
   rs.rule_name  = r.rule_name and
   rs.rule_owner = r.rule_owner
   and rs.rule_set_name='my_test_rule_set'
order by
   rs.rule_set_name,
   r.rule_name;

RULE_SET_NAME      RULE_OWNER RULE_NAME RULE_CONDITION
----------------   ---------- --------- --------------------------------------------------------
my_test_rule_set   str_source rule_test :dml.get_object_owner() = 'str_source' and :dml.is_null_tag()
= 'Y'
```

Lastly, initiate the *propagation* process by specifying the rule just created. This will tell Streams that all objects belonging to the user *str_source* in *sourcedb* will belong to user *str_target* in *targetdb*.

```
begin
   dbms_propagation_adm.create_propagation(
      propagation_name => 'Prop_Test',
      source_queue => 'str_source.streams_queue',
      destination_queue => 'str_target.streams_queue',
      destination_dblink => 'targetdb',
      rule_set_name => 'my_test_rule_st');
end;
/
```

Now all propagated objects will have their owner changed from *str_source to str_target* as specified by the new rule.

There are other procedures and functions in these three packages. We will touch upon some of the more important ones here.

🖫 Code 11.14 – dbms_propagation_and_rules.sql

```
conn sys@ora11g as sysdba

Connected to:
Oracle 11g Enterprise Edition Release 11.2.0.1.0 - Production
With the Partitioning, Oracle Label Security, OLAP, Data Mining,
Oracle Database Vault and Real Application Testing options

--Stop a propagation process

begin
```

```
   dbms_propagation_adm.stop_propagation(propagation_name =>
'prop_test',force => TRUE);
end;
/

--Start a propagation process
begin
   dbms_propagation_adm.stop_propagation(propagation_name =>'prop_test'
,force => TRUE);
end;
/

--Add, alter or remove a rule set for a propagation process

--Remove rule set
begin
   dbms_propagation_adm.alter_propagation(
      propagation_name => 'prop_test',
      rule_set_name => 'my_test_rule_set',
      remove_rule_set => TRUE);
end;
/

--Drop a propagation process and their unused rule sets
begin
   dbms_propagation_adm.drop_propagation(
      propagation_name => 'prop_test',
      drop_unused_rule_sets => TRUE);
end;
/
```

In the case below, we create a table alias for table *test_table*, which was just created. If the rules just created need to be evaluated in their context, use the code shown here:

```
set serveroutput on
declare
v_true_rules   sys.re$rule_hit_list;
v_maybe_rules sys.re$rule_hit_list;
rnum        integer;

begin
   dbms_rule.evaluate(
   rule_set_name => 'str_source.my_test_rule_set',
   evaluation_context => 'my_tab_alias_ctx',
   true_rules =>v_true_rules,
   maybe_rules =>  v_maybe_rules);


for rnum IN 1..v_true_rules.count loop
      dbms_output.put_line('Using rule '||
    v_true_rules(rnum).rule_name);
      end loop;

end;
/
```

Next to be covered are two packages that have to do with Streams administration.

Packages *dbms_streams* and *dbms_streams_admin*

Despite these two packages having similar names, they provide different functionalities regarding Streams configuration and management. The first package, *dbms_streams*, can be used to execute tasks such as converting *anydata* objects into Logical Change Record (*lcr*) objects, gather information about streams like stream names, types and attributes and set tags for redo entries.

The second package, *dbms_streams_adm*, provides procedures and functions for configuring Oracle Streams. It also adds and removes rules for *capture*, *propagation* and *apply* processes. With this package, it is even possible to dequeue at a table, schema or database level.

In the next example, we will show how to set a tag using the *dbms_streams* package. Then we will locate the tag using both *dbms_logmnr* and *get_tag* functions.

🖫 Code 11.15 – dbms_streams_tag.sql

```
conn sys@ora11g as sysdba

Connected to:
Oracle 11g Enterprise Edition Release 11.2.0.1.0 - Production
With the Partitioning, Oracle Label Security, OLAP, Data Mining,
Oracle Database Vault and Real Application Testing options

--First find out which archive are being used, by querying the
v$archived_log table
select
    max(sequence#),
    name
from
    v$archived_log
group by
    name;

--/u02/oradata/archives/1_27_729104245.dbf

--Set the tag using set_tag procedure of dbms_streams package
begin
    dbms_streams.set_tag(tag =>
'74657374746E675F64626D735F73747265616D735F7061636B61676573');
    commit;
end;
/

--use dbms_logmnr to find the replication marker, and see the tag
begin
    dbms_logmnr.add_logfile('/u02/oradata/archives/1_28_729104245.dbf');
    dbms_logmnr.add_logfile('/u02/oradata/archives/1_29_729104245.dbf');
```

```
   dbms_logmnr.add_logfile('/u02/oradata/archives/1_30_729104245.dbf');
   dbms_logmnr.start_logmnr(options=>dbms_logmnr.DICT_FROM_ONLINE_CATALOG);
end;
/

begin
   dbms_logmnr.start_logmnr;
end;
/

select * from v$logmnr_contents where operation='replication marker';


--Get tag using get_tag function
set serveroutput on
declare
 v_tag raw(2000);
begin
   v_tag := dbms_streams.get_tag;
   dbms_output.put_line('My tag is = ' ||
                         utl_raw.cast_to_varchar2(rawtohex(v_tag)));
end;
/

select
   utl_raw.cast_to_varchar2(
      dbms_streams.get_tag)
from
   dual;
```

So say we want to execute certain items in specific situations of an *apply* process. We want the process to differ based on the *update*, *delete* or *insert* commands being replicated. To accomplish this, we will make use of the *get* functions of the *dbms_streams* package.

First, create a table that will be used for this test. Create the table in both source and target databases.

🖫 Code 11.16 – dbms_streams_get.sql

```
conn sys@ora11g as sysdba

Connected to:
Oracle 11g Enterprise Edition Release 11.2.0.1.0 - Production
With the Partitioning, Oracle Label Security, OLAP, Data Mining,
Oracle Database Vault and Real Application Testing options

create table stradmin.tab_test_get_str (
   col1 number,
   col2 varchar2(10),
   col3 varchar2(20));

alter table
   stradmin.tab_test_get_str
add constraint
   pk_col1
```

```
primary key
  (col1);
```

Create a procedure to get the system change number of this table.

```
    variable scn number;

create or replace procedure stradmin.insert_reg (p_scn out number) is
  cursor c1 is
    select * from stradmin.tab_test_get_str;
  c1_rec c1 % rowtype;
  scn     number;
begin
  scn := dbms_flashback.get_system_change_number();
  dbms_flashback.enable_at_system_change_number(query_scn => scn);
  dbms_flashback.disable;

  commit;

  dbms_output.put_line('scn table tab_test_get_str = ' || scn);
  p_scn := scn;

exception
  when others then
    dbms_flashback.disable;
    raise;
end;
/
commit;
set serveroutput on

begin
insert_reg (:scn);
end;
/
```

Now include this table in the replication environment using the following commands:

```
conn stradmin/stradmin@strsource;

begin
  dbms_streams_adm.add_table_rules(table_name     =>
'stradmin.tab_test_get_str',
                                   streams_type => 'capture',
                                   streams_name => 'rep_capture_ora',
                                   queue_name     =>
'stradmin.streams_queue');
end;
/

begin
  dbms_streams_adm.add_table_rules(table_name     =>
'stradmin.tab_test_get_str',
                                   streams_type => 'apply',
                                   streams_name =>
'rep_apply_to_SQLServer_ORA',
```

```
                                         queue_name    =>
'stradmin.streams_queue');
end;
/

--Set table instantiation
declare
v_scn number;
begin
  dbms_apply_adm.set_table_instantiation_scn(
     source_object_name => 'stradmin.tab_test_get_str',
     source_database_name => 'sourcedb',
     instantiation_scn => :SCN,
     apply_database_link => 'targetdb');
end;
/
```

A procedure containing actions to follow in each case of an *update*, *delete* or *insert* command will be created:

```
create or replace procedure proc_dml_handler_tab_test(in_any in sys.AnyData)
is
  lc_lcr       sys.lcr$_row_reocrd;
  lc_rc        pls_integer;
  lc_command   varchar2(10);
  lc_ob_owner  varchar 2(30);
  lc_ob_name   varchar 2(30);
  lc_intError  integer := 0;
  lc_varErrmsg varchar 2(4000);
  lc_retorno   number;
  lc_cont_exec varchar 2(50);
  lc_valor_binary_aux   varchar2(100)  := NULL;
  lc_command_sql_server varchar2(32000);
  lc_binary              number;
  lc_binary_aux          number;
  lc_valor_binary        number;
begin
  lc_rc       := in_any.getobject(lc_lcr);
  lc_ob_owner := lc_lcr.get_object_owner();
  lc_ob_name  := lc_lcr.get_object_name();
  lc_command  := lc_lcr.get_command_type;

  execute immediate alter session set nls_numeric_characters='',.,''';

  lc_cont_exec := 'Step 1';

  if lc_command = 'update' then

     --Do update things here


  elsif lc_command = 'delete' then
     --Do delete things here
End if;

  if lc_ob_name = 'tab_test_get_str' then
```

```
if  lc_command = 'update' then

    --Delete columns from a row of LCR if the command is an update

    if lc_lcr.get_value('new','col1') is NOT NULL then
        lc_lcr.delete_column('col1');
      end if;
      if lc_lcr.get_value('new','col2') is NOT NULL then
        lc_lcr.delete_column('col2');
      end if;
      if lc_lcr.get_value('new','col3') is NOT NULL then
        lc_lcr.delete_column('col3');
      end if;

    else
    --Delete columns for update command in any case

      lc_lcr.delete_column('col1');
      lc_lcr.delete_column('col2');
      lc_lcr.delete_column('col3');

      end if;

  end if;

  if lc_command = 'update' or lc_command = 'insert' then
    lc_lcr.set_values('new', NULL);
  else
    lc_lcr.set_values('old', NULL);
  end if;

  lc_lcr.set_command_type('update');
  lc_lcr.set_object_name('stradmin');
  lc_lcr.add_column('new', 'col1', anydata.Convertnumber(1));

  lc_lcr.execute(true);
exception
  when others then
    lc_intError  := sqlcode;
    lc_varErrmsg := sqlerrm;
    raise_application_error(-20001,
                     lc_varErrmsg || ' # ' || lc_cont_exec || ' - '
||
                     'Error in stradmin.proc_dml_handler_tab_test ');
end;
/
```

Next, create the DML handler for each command type linking it to the procedure we just created:

```
begin
  dbms_apply_adm.set_dml_handler(object_name        =>
'stradmin.tab_test_get_str',
                                 object_type        => 'table',
                                 operation_name     => 'insert',
                                 error_handler      => FALSE,
                                 user_procedure     =>
```

```
'stradmin.proc_dml_handler_tab_test',
                                apply_database_link => NULL,
                                apply_name          => NULL);
end;
/

begin
  dbms_apply_adm.set_dml_handler(object_name      =>
'stradmin.tab_test_get_str',
                                object_type       => 'table',
                                operation_name    => 'delete',
                                error_handler     => FALSE,
                                user_procedure    =>
'stradmin.proc_dml_handler_tab_test',
                                apply_database_link => NULL,
                                apply_name          => NULL);
end;
/

begin
  dbms_apply_adm.set_dml_handler(object_name      =>
'stradmin.tab_test_get_str',
                                object_type       => 'table',
                                operation_name    => 'update',
                                error_handler     => FALSE,
                                user_procedure    =>
'stradmin.proc_dml_handler_tab_test',
                                apply_database_link => NULL,
                                apply_name          => NULL);
end;
/
```

The example above can be used in cases where there is a need to transform data while it is being replicated. It can also be used as a template for other general cases.

The *dbms_streams_admin* package contains a set of subprograms. These can be used to create queues, manage Streams metadata, add table, schema and global rules, generate Streams replication scripts and more.

How to Easily Configure Streams Replication

The next example will show how to quickly create a Streams configuration for tablespace *tbs_1*. All objects that exist in *tbs_1* will be part of the replication process.

First we create the Streams users on both the source and target databases:

🖫 Code 11.17 – dbms_streams_asm.sql

```
conn sys@ora11g as sysdba

Connected to:
Oracle 11g Enterprise Edition Release 11.2.0.1.0 - Production
With the Partitioning, Oracle Label Security, OLAP, Data Mining,
```

```
conn sys/manager@sourcedb as sysdba

create user
   dbms_str_user
identified by
   dbms_str_user;

grant
   create database link,
   unlimited tablespace,
   connect,
   resource,
   aq_administrator_role,
   create any directory,
   dba
to
   dbms_str_user;

begin
   dbms_streams_auth.grant_admin_privilege(
          grantee => 'dbms_str_user');
end;
/

commit;
```

Now create tablespace tbs_1 as well as one table inside it to be used with this example.

```
create tablespace
   tbs_1
datafile size
   10M;

alter user dbms_str_user default tablespace tbs_1;

conn dbms_test_user@sourcedb

create table tab_str_test(
             col1 number,
             col2 varchar2(10)) tablespace tbs_1;

alter table tab_str_test add primary key (col1);

insert into tab_str_test values (1,'A');
insert into tab_str_test values (2,'B');
commit;
```

Create the local directory where scripts will be stored. In addition, we also need to create an object directory which points where the tablespace datafile is located.

```
--sourcedb
create or replace directory
   script_dir as
```

```
            '/u01/app/oracle/admin/sourcedb';

grant
   read,
   write on directory script_dir to public;


create or replace directory
   tbs_dir_source as
      '/u02/oradata/sourcedb/datafile';

grant
   read,
   write on directory tbs_dir_source to public;

--Targetdb
create or replace directory
   script_dir as
      '/u01/app/oracle/admin/targetdb';

grant
   read,
   write on directory script_dir to public;

create or replace directory
   tbs_dir_target as
      '/u02/oradata/targetdb/datafile/';

grant
   read,
   write on directory tbs_dir_target to public;
```

Create a database link in the source database pointing to the target database. Create a reciprocal link in the target, pointing to the source database. Make sure that there is the *service_name* in *tnsnames.ora*.

```
--sourcedb
drop database link targetdb;
create database link
   targetdb
connect to
   dbms_str_user
identified by
   dbms_str_user
using
   'targetdb';

--Targetdb
drop database link sourcedb;

create database link
   sourcedb
connect to
   dbms_str_user
identified by
   dbms_str_user
```

```
using
   'sourcedb';
```

Finally, use *maintain_simple_tts* to clone the tbs_1 tablespace from *sourcedb* to *targetdb*. Since we am using *script_name* parameters, it will generate a script with all the steps necessary to create the replication on the tbs_1 tablespace. This procedure must be executed on the capture database.

```
begin
   dbms_streams_adm.maintain_simple_tts(
      tablespace_name => 'tbs_1',
      source_directory_object => 'tbs_dir_source',
      destination_directory_object => 'tbs_dir_target',
      source_database => 'sourcedb',
      destination_database => 'targetdb',
      script_name => 'my_script1.sql',
      script_directory_object => 'script_dir');
end;
/
```

If the tasks should actually be executed rather than just creating the scripts, use the command below:

```
begin
   dbms_streams_adm. maintain_simple_tts(
      tablespace_name => 'tbs_1',
      source_directory_object => 'tbs_dir_source',
      destination_directory_object => 'tbs_dir_target',
      source_database =>'sourcedb',
      destination_database => 'targetdb',
      perform_actions => TRUE,
      bi_directional => TRUE);
end;
/
```

There are some good views used to help solve problems that may happen when configuring Oracle Streams using *dbms_streams_adm* package. Learn how to fix a problem on the next example.

How to Find and Fix Problems in Streams Configuration

If errors are encountered while executing any *maintain* procedures of the *dbms_streams* package and an attempt is made to run additional procedures without first fixing the exiting error, a message like this will be received:

Code 11.18 – dbms_streams_views.sql

```
conn sys@ora11g as sysdba

Connected to:
Oracle 11g Enterprise Edition Release 11.2.0.1.0 - Production
```

With the Partitioning, Oracle Label Security, OLAP, Data Mining,
Oracle Database Vault and Real Application Testing options

```
begin
   dbms_streams_adm.maintain_simple_tts(
      tablespace_name => 'tbs_1',
      source_directory_object => 'tbs_dir_source',
      destination_directory_object => 'tbs_dir_target',
      source_database => 'sourcedb',
      destination_database => 'targetdb',
      script_name => 'my_script1.sql',
      script_directory_object => 'script_dir');
end;
```

```
ORA-23622: Operation sys.dbms_streams_adm.maintain_simple_tts is in
progress.
ORA-06512: at "sys.dbms_sys_error", line 105
ORA-06512: at "sys.dbms_streams_mt", line 2608
ORA-06512: at "sys.dbms_streams_mt", line 7721
ORA-06512: at "sys.dbms_streams_adm", line 2426
ORA-06512: at line 2
```

```
SQL>
```

To remedy this, check *dba_recoverable_script_errors* to determine the error number and
get the block number of that error.

```
select
   script_id,
   block_num,
   error_message,
   error_creation_time
from
   dba_recoverable_script_errors
where
   error_creation_time > systimestamp -1/24;
SCRIPT_ID                     BLOCK_NUM ERROR_MESSAGE
ERROR_CREATION_TIME
------------------------------ --------- -----------------------------------------------------------
----------------------- ----------------
94CDA13FFD84CDE6E0400A0A710A1D8F        4 ORA-26723: user "dbms_str_user" requires the role "DBA"
11/11/2010 19:31:16
```

In the previous scenario, note that the user has to have the DBA privileges. In some
cases, further investigation is needed using the *dba_recoverable_script_blocks* view.

```
set long 10000
select
   script_id,
   block_num,
   status,
   forward_block,
   undo_block
from
   dba_recoverable_script_blocks b
where
```

```
b.block_num=4
and
script_id='94CDB67BB22F03BFE0400A0A710A1FF7';
```

This query shows the *forward block* script and *undo block* script. To execute one of these blocks, run the *recover_operation* procedure.

```
begin
    dbms_streams_adm.recover_operation(
        script_id => '94F0120925608F08E0400A0A710A217D',
        operation_mode => 'purge');
end;
/
```

How to configure Streams Replications for an entire tablespace using *maintain_simple_tts* has now been shown. The database and schema replication can also be configured by using the *maintain_schemas* and *maintain_global* procedures.

Package *dbms_streams_auth*

As with any of Oracle's tools, Streams have a security level; this is managed through the *dbms_streams_auth* package. Within this package, the database administrator can grant and revoke Streams Administration privileges to users. There is also an option that can be used to grant administrative privilege to a remote user for managing local databases through a database link.

This is a fairly straightforward package, so we will show all procedures using a single example.

How to Grant and Revoke Streams Administrative Privileges

Rather than assigning a privilege, a script is created that will be used at a later time.

🖫 Code 11.19 – dbms_streams_auth.sql

```
conn sys@ora11g as sysdba

Connected to:
Oracle 11g Enterprise Edition Release 11.2.0.1.0 - Production
With the Partitioning, Oracle Label Security, OLAP, Data Mining,
Oracle Database Vault and Real Application Testing options

--Just create scripts to be executed at a later time
begin
    dbms_streams_auth.grant_admin_privilege(
        grantee => 'dbms_str_user',
        grant_privileges => TRUE,
```

```
      file_name => 'str_admin_grant.sql',
      directory_name => 'dir1');
end;
/
```

The output of this script contains a lot of select and execute grants for many objects used when configuring Oracle Streams. The output is as follows:

```
[ora11g@dbms sourcedb]$ cat str_admin_grant.sql
-- rule privileges section
grant execute on dbms_rule_adm to "dbms_str_user"
/
-- rule privileges section
grant execute on dbms_rule_adm to "dbms_str_user"
/
begin
  dbms_rule_adm.grant_system_privilege(
    privilege => dbms_rule_adm.create_evaluation_context_obj,
    grantee => '"dbms_str_user"',
    grant_option => TRUE);
end;
/
begin
  dbms_rule_adm.grant_system_privilege(
    privilege => dbms_rule_adm.create_rule_set_obj,
    grantee => '"dbms_str_user"',
    grant_option => TRUE);
end;
/
```

How to generate a script to revoke administrative privilege from a user is shown here:

```
    --Revoke admin privileges script
begin
   dbms_streams_auth.revoke_admin_privilege(
      grantee => 'dbms_str_user',
      revoke_privileges => TRUE,
      file_name => 'str_admin_revoke.sql',
      directory_name => 'dir');
end;
 /
```

The procedure that grants/revokes remote administration privileges for users to manage streams replication on remote databases via database links is:

```
begin
   dbms_streams_auth.grant_remote_admin_access(
      grantee => 'dbms_str_user');
end;
/


begin
   dbms_streams_auth.revoke_remote_admin_access(
```

```
        grantee => 'dbms_str_user');
end;
/
```

To check the administration privilege of a user (local or remote) on a database, check the *dba_streams_administrator* view as below:

```
--Check who is Streams Administrator
select
   *
from
   dba_streams_administrator;
```

```
USERNAME                       LOCAL_PRIVILEGES ACCESS_FROM_REMOTE
------------------------------ ---------------- ------------------
str_source                     YES              YES
strmadmin                      YES              YES
dbms_str_user                  YES              YES

SQL>
```

Note that there is a column named *access_from_remote* which indicates whether or not a user has remote privilege access to a local Streams Administration.

Package *dbms_streams_advisor_adm*

Oracle is always creating tools that help manage and administer databases and their features. This is the case for Oracle Streams. There is a tool, named Oracle Streams Performance Advisor, that basically is nothing more than using the *dbms_streams_advisor_adm* package.

This package is used to generate a report containing performance advice regarding a database Streams configuration. It is used in conjunction with views and shows the information gathered by this package. It is designed to help the user work more efficiently toward producing better performance within a Streams environment.

Information about enqueue rate, current queue size, capture rate, send rate, bandwidth, latency, message apply rate, transaction apply rate and more are gathered. The results can be found in views like:

- *dba_streams_tp_component*: This view displays information about each component of Streams for each database

- *dba_streams_tp_component_link*: This view displays information on how flow messages are moving between Oracle Streams components

- *dba_streams_tp_component_stat*: Displays temporary information on performance statistics and session statistics of Oracle Streams components

- *dba_streams_tp_database*: This view shows information on each database that has an Oracle Streams component

- *dba_streams_tp_path_bottleneck*: Displays information about components that are experiencing poor performance, decreasing the overall flow messages in a Stream path. A Streams path is a flow of messages from the source database to the target database.

- *dba_streams_tp_path_stat*: This view shows performance statistics about each Streams path

There are other views used to temporarily show information. They only last for the session's lifetime. The one purpose of *dbms_streams_advisor_adm* is to gather all performance advisor information. When *analyze_current_performance* is executed, it takes snapshots which are used to gather information that is calculated and assessed by the Streams Performance Advisor.

In my next example, we will show how to gather statistics from the Streams Performance Advisor by using the *dbms_streams_advisor_adm* package.

How to Get Streams Performance Information

First execute the *analyze_current_performance* procedure, then check the results by querying certain views.

💾 Code 11.20 – dbms_streams_advisor_adm.sql

```
conn sys@ora11g as sysdba

Connected to:
Oracle 11g Enterprise Edition Release 11.2.0.1.0 - Production
With the Partitioning, Oracle Label Security, OLAP, Data Mining,
Oracle Database Vault and Real Application Testing options

begin
    dbms_streams_advisor_adm.analyze_current_performance;
end;
/
```

Use the views below to check all performance information generated by the *dbms_streams_advisor_adm* package.

```
--Check each component in each database
select * from dba_streams_tp_component;

--Check how message flow between each component
col "db" for a10
col "dest_db" for a10
select
    source_component_name "name",
```

```
        source_component_db "db",
        source_component_type "type",
        destination_component_name "dest_name",
        destination_component_db "dest_db",
        decode (position, 1,'Capture',
                          2,'Queue',
                          3,'Propag. Sender',
                          4,'Propag. Receiver',
                          5,'Queue', 'NULL') "Start Component"
from
    dba_streams_tp_component_link;

--Check information about performance statistics and session statistics
select * from dba_streams_tp_component_stat;

--Check databases that have Streams components
select * from dba_streams_tp_database;

--Check who is the bootleneck
select * from dba_streams_tp_path_bottleneck;

--Check statistics about each streams path
select * from dba_streams_tp_path_stat;

select * from dba_streams_tp_database;
```

This package enables Streams Administrator to find which components are causing performance degradation; thus facilitating the solution to the problem.

Package *dbms_streams_messaging*

Another package frequently used by Streams Administrators is *dbms_streams_messaging*. This will enable the enqueue and dequeue of messages from and into an *anydata* queue. The package *dbms_streams_messaging* cannot be used to enqueue or dequeue messages from a buffered queue. In this case, use the *dbms_aq* package.

Here are the procedures of this package:

1. *dequeue*: This procedure is used by the message client to dequeue messages from a specified queue.

2. *enqueue*: This procedure is used to enqueue messages for the current database user to a specified queue. The current user must be associated with an advanced queue agent. In addition, the name of the agent must match the user name. There is a procedure which is used to automatically create this agent, *set_up_queue* from the *dbms_streams_adm* package that was already presented in this chapter.

The next example will demonstrate how to create a process which will dequeue messages via the messaging client.

How to Enqueue and Dequeue Messages

The first step is to create a type and table that will be used in this example.

💾 Code 11.21 – dbms_streams_messaging.sql

```
conn sys@ora11g as sysdba

Connected to:
Oracle 11g Enterprise Edition Release 11.2.0.1.0 - Production
With the Partitioning, Oracle Label Security, OLAP, Data Mining,
Oracle Database Vault and Real Application Testing options

--First create a message type on tabe tab_str_test

create or replace type
   dbms_str_user.type_tab_str_test
as object (col1 number,
           col2 varchar2(10)
)
/

--Create the table
create table dbms_str_user.tab_str_test
    (col1 number,
       col2 varchar2(10),
        primary key (col1));
```

Next, create database links from one database to another.

```
--sourcedb to targetdb
create database link targetdb
  connect to dbms_str_user identified by dbms_str_user
  using 'targetdb';

--targetdb to sourcedb
create database link sourcedb
  connect to dbms_str_user identified by dbms_str_user
  using 'sourcedb';
```

Now create an *anydata* queue on both source and target databases.

```
--Create queue table
begin
   dbms_aqadm.drop_queue_table(
     queue_table => 'my_queue_table',
     force => TRUE,
     auto_commit => TRUE);

   dbms_aqadm.create_queue_table(
     queue_table => 'my_queue_table',
     queue_payload_type => 'sys.anydataA',
     storage_clause => ' tablespace tbs_streams_data',
     sort_list => 'priority,enq_time',
     multiple_consumers => TRUE,
```

Advanced DBMS Packages

```
        message_grouping => dbms_aqadm.transactional,
        comment => 'My test queue table.',
        compatible => '10.0');
end;
/

--Create anydata queue using queue table created above (on source and target
database)
begin
    dbms_streams_adm.set_up_queue(
        queue_table => 'my_queue_table',
        storage_clause => 'tablespace tbs_streams_data',
        queue_name => 'my_anydata_queue',
        queue_user => 'dbms_str_user',
        comment => 'my anydata queue.');
end;
/
```

Create the propagation used to send information to *targetdb* through a database link.

```
begin
    dbms_propagation_adm.drop_propagation(
        propagation_name => 'prop_tab_str_test',
        drop_unused_rule_sets => TRUE);

    dbms_propagation_adm.create_propagation(
        propagation_name => 'prop_tab_str_test',
        source_queue => 'dbms_str_user.my_anydata_queue',
        destination_queue => 'dbms_tr_user.my_anydata_queue',
        destination_dblink => 'targetdb');
end;
/
```

Next, we create a trigger, which will enqueue messages in my message system. Note that every time a row is inserted into the *tab_str_test* table, it is also enqueued in *my_anydata_queue*:

```
create or replace trigger dbms_str_user.trg_enqueue
  after insert on dbms_str_user.tab_str_test
  referencing old as old new as new
  for each row
declare
  message dbms_str_user.type_tab_str_test;
begin
  message := dbms_str_user.type_tab_str_test(col1 => :new.col1,
                                             col2 => to_char(:new.col2));
  dbms_streams_messaging.enqueue(queue_name =>
'dbms_str_user.my_anydata_queue',
                                 payload    =>
anydata.convertobject(message));
end trg_enqueue;
/
```

Now we need to dequeue messages using the *dequeue* procedure. First, a message client is created using the *add_message_rule* procedure of the *dbms_streams_adm* package. Note that a rule is specifying that only messages with *col1 > 1* will be dequeued.

```
begin
  dbms_streams_adm.add_message_rule (
    message_type    => 'dbms_str_user.type_tab_str_test',
    rule_condition => ':msg.col1 > 1',
    streams_type    => 'dequeue',
    streams_name    => 'dbms_str_user_cons2',
    queue_name      => 'dbms_str_user.my_anydata_queue');
end;
/
```

The next step is to create a procedure which will dequeue messages from the queue created.

```
create or replace procedure prc_dequeue as
  v_steps             varchar2(30);
  v_have_messages     boolean := TRUE;
  msg                 sys.anydata;
  v_message           dbms_str_user.type_tab_str_test;
  v_int               pls_integer;
  v_dequeue_options dbms_aq.dequeue_options_t;
  v_message_id raw(16);
begin
  v_steps := 'first message';
  v_dequeue_options.wait := dbms_aq.no_wait;

  while (v_have_messages) loop
    begin
      dbms_streams_messaging.dequeue(
        queue_name    => 'dbms_str_user.my_anydata_queue',
        streams_name => 'dbms_str_user_consumer',
        payload       => msg,
        navigation    => v_steps,
        wait          => dbms_streams_messaging.no_wait,msgid =>
v_message_id);


    commit;
      if msg.gettypename() = 'dbms_str_user.type_tab_str_test' then
        v_int := msg.getobject(v_message);
        dbms_output.put_line(a => 'value for col1: ' || v_message.col1);
        dbms_output.put_line (a => 'value for col2: ' || v_message.col2);
      end if;
      v_steps := 'next message';
      commit;
    exception
      when sys.dbms_streams_messaging.endofcurtrans then
        v_steps := 'next transaction';
      when dbms_streams_messaging.nomoremsgs then
        v_have_messages := false;
        dbms_output.put_line(a => 'No more messages.');
        dbms_output.put_line('The error code was = ' || sqlcode);
        dbms_output.put_line('The error message was ' || sqlerrm);
```

Advanced DBMS Packages

```
    when others then
      dbms_output.put_line('The error code was = ' || sqlcode);
      dbms_output.put_line('The error message was ' || sqlerrm);
        raise;
    end;
  end loop;
end;
/
```

Finally, perform some insert operations, check values in the queue and use the procedure to dequeue the messages.

```
--Insert some values
truncate table tab_str_test;
select * from tab_str_test;
insert into tab_str_test values (1,'Test1');
insert into tab_str_test values (2,'Test2');
insert into tab_str_test values (3,'Test3');
commit;

--Check if values inserted are on queue table
select
    q_name,
    msgid,
    enq_time,
    enq_uid,
    sender_name,
    deq_time,
    deq_uid
    from
my_queue_table;
```

Run the procedure to dequeue the messages and check the output displayed:

```
set serveroutput on
begin
    prc_dequeue;
end;
/

--Check queue table again on columns starting with deq%
select
    q_name,
    msgid,
    enq_time,
    enq_uid,
    sender_name,
    deq_time,
    deq_uid
    from
my_queue_table;
```

These examples have shown a simple way to dequeue messages from a queue table. Other methods include the *dbms_aq* package covered earlier in this chapter.

Package dbms_streams_messaging   **523**

Summary

In this chapter, we have shown how to use nearly all packages pertaining to Oracle Streams and Replication. We have introduced packages used to configure Streams Replications at the table, schema or database level, packages used to create rules to be followed by a propagations process, packages used to create, capture and apply propagation processes, packages to grant Streams administration privileges and others.

The next chapter will show how to use the most important packages of the Oracle HTML DB and XDB feature.

Oracle HTML DB and XML DB

Introduction

Oracle Application Express (ApEx, formerly called HTML DB) is one of the most exciting web application development tools on the market. HTML-DB Application Express is a true Rapid Application Development environment that can take an idea from concept to a working production level application in a very short period of time and this book can help with understanding the underlying packages that make this possible.

Oracle XML DB is another Oracle technology used to store and manage XML data in the database. Oracle provides native support to XML data. The packages that will be presented in this chapter make reference to both the XML and HTML DB. We will show the main procedures of these packages regarding the installation and management of these technologies.

There are some steps that need to be made before using these features as they are not installed by default. To have access to the XML packages, it is necessary to install the XML DB option by using the *catqm.sql script* found in *$ORACLE_HOME/rdbms/admin*. In the same way, to use HTML DB packages, Oracle Application Express needs to be installed. This is a more advanced installation where ApEx, ApEx Listener and one HTTP Server (in my case, I just downloaded OC4J Containers) need to be installed. The step-by-step installation guide can be found in Oracle® Application Express Installation Guide Release 4.0 Part Number E15513-01.

Next, how to use the most important and useful packages that concern HTML DB and XML DB will be revealed.

Package *htmldb_custom_auth*

This package provides the user with procedures and functions that are related to authentication and session management. Among other things, this package offers functions and procedures that could be used to get the session id, check existence of an item in a page, get authentication username, perform login and authentication and more.

The following are some examples of these functions and procedures. Use the *application_page_item_exists* function to check if an item exists in a page. If it exists, a TRUE value is returned; otherwise, it returns FALSE.

⊟ Code 12.1 – htmldb_custom_auth.sql

```
conn sys@ora11g as sysdba

Connected to:
Oracle 11g Enterprise Edition Release 11.2.0.1.0 - Production
With the Partitioning, Oracle Label Security, OLAP, Data Mining,
Oracle Database Vault and Real Application Testing options

begin
  if  htmldb_custom_auth.application_page_item_exists(p_item_name =>
'item1') then
      dbms_output.put_line(a => 'Exist.');
  else
      dbms_output.put_line(a => 'Does not exist.');
  end if;
end;
```

If we want to check if the current page is public or not, we use the *current_page_is_public* function. It returns TRUE if it is public or FALSE if is not.

```
begin
   if htmldb_custom_auth.current_page_is_public then
      dbms_output.put_line(a => 'Is a public page');
  else
      dbms_output.put_line(a => 'Is not a public page');
   end if;
end;
/
```

If we want to define a user session setting the user and session id, use the *define_user_session* procedure. To get the *user* and *session id* values, use the *get_user* and *get_session_id* functions.

```
declare
v_user varchar2(30);
v_session_id number;
begin
   htmldb_custom_auth.define_user_session(p_user => 'user1',p_session_id =>
10);
   select
      htmldb_custom_auth.get_user
   into
      v_user
   from
      dual;
```

```
select
    htmldb_custom_auth.get_session_id
into
    v_session_id
from
    dual;
dbms_output.put_line(
    a => 'User: '||v_user||' - Session ID:'||v_session_id);
end;
/
```

If we need to get cookie properties in the current session, we use the *get_cookie_props*
procedure.

```
set serveroutput on
declare
v_cookie_name varchar2(50);
v_cookie_path varchar2(100);
v_cookie_domain varchar2(20);
v_secure boolean;
begin
    htmldb_custom_auth.get_cookie_props(
        p_app_id => 1,
        p_cookie_name => v_cookie_name,
        p_cookie_path => v_cookie_path,
        p_cookie_domain => v_cookie_domain,
        p_secure => v_secure);
    dbms_output.put_line(a => 'Cookie Name:'||v_cookie_name);
    dbms_output.put_line(a => 'Cookie Pah:'||v_cookie_path);
    dbms_output.put_line(a => 'Cookie Domain:'||v_cookie_domain);

  --secure means the "Flag to set secure property of cookie."
  if v_secure then
      dbms_output.put_line(a => 'Cookie Secure!');
  else
      dbms_output.put_line(a => 'Cookie NOT Secure!');
  end if;
end;
/
```

To get LDAP attributes for a current authentication scheme in the current
application, use the *get_ldap_props* procedure.

```
set serveroutput on
declare
v_ldap_host varchar2(30);
v_ldap_port number;
v_use_ssl varchar2(10);
v_ldap_use_exact_dn varchar2(30);
v_ldap_dn varchar2(30);
v_search_filter varchar2(30);
v_ldap_edit_function varchar2(30);
begin
    htmldb_custom_auth.get_ldap_props(
        p_ldap_host => v_ldap_host,
        p_ldap_port => v_ldap_port,
```

```
      p_use_ssl => v_use_ssl,
      p_use_exact_dn => v_ldap_use_exact_dn,
      p_ldap_dn => v_ldap_dn,
      p_search_filter => v_search_filter,
      p_ldap_edit_function => v_ldap_edit_function);
   dbms_output.put_line(a => 'LDAP host                :  '||v_ldap_host);
   dbms_output.put_line(a => 'LDAP port                :  '||v_ldap_port);
   dbms_output.put_line(a => 'LDAP Use SSL             :  '||v_use_ssl);
   dbms_output.put_line(a => 'LDAP use exact DN        :
'||v_ldap_use_exact_dn);
   dbms_output.put_line(a => 'LDAP DN                  :  '||v_ldap_dn);
   dbms_output.put_line(a => 'LDAP Search Filter       :  '||v_search_filter);
   dbms_output.put_line(a => 'LDAP Edit Function       :
'||v_ldap_edit_function);
end;
/
```

HTML DB has a sequence that can be used to generate the next session id. To do this, run the *get_next_session_id* function.

```
set serveroutput on
declare
   v_next_session_id number;
   v_current_session_id number;
begin
   select
      htmldb_custom_auth.get_next_session_id,
      htmldb_custom_auth.get_session_id into    v_next_session_id ,
v_current_session_id
   from
      dual;

   dbms_output.put_line(a => 'Next Session ID    :'||v_next_session_id);
   dbms_output.put_line(a => 'Current Session ID :'||v_current_session_id);
end;
/
```

To get the current username registered with the current HTML DB session, use the *get_username* function.

```
set serveroutput on
declare
   v_username varchar2(30);
begin
   select
      htmldb_custom_auth.get_username
   into
      v_username
   from
      dual;
   dbms_output.put_line(a => 'Username is:'||v_username);
end;
/
```

To get the security group id of the workspace for the current user, use the *get_security_group_id* function.

```
set serveroutput on
declare
v_sec_group_id number;
begin
   select
      htmldb_custom_auth.get_security_group_id
   into
      v_sec_group_id
   from
      dual;
   dbms_output.put_line(a => 'Security Group Number is:'||v_sec_group_id);
end;
/
```

To know if a session is valid or not, use the *is_session_valid* function:

```
set serveroutput on
begin
   if htmldb_custom_auth.is_session_valid then
      dbms_output.put_line(a => 'Is a valid session!');
   else
      dbms_output.put_line(a => 'Is NOT a valid session!');
   end if;
end;
/
```

There are procedures used to log in, log out and authenticate a user session registration. These are the *login* and *logout* procedures. See some examples below:

```
--login
begin
   htmldb_custom_auth.login(
      p_uname => 'pportugal',
      p_password => 'XXX112',
      p_session_id => 'dbms_session',
      p_app_page => ':1');
end;
/

--logout
begin
--p_next_app_page_sess indicates the application and page id, where the user
will be redirected to, after logout, in this case, application 300, page 5
   htmldb_custom_auth.logout(
      p_this_app => '300',
      p_next_app_page_sess => '300:5');
end;
/
```

While the *login* procedure makes the session authentication, the *post_login* procedure will make session registration.

Package htmldb_custom_auth

```
begin
   htmldb_custom_auth.post_login(
      p_uname => 'pportugal',
      p_session_id => 'dbms_session',
      p_app_page => ':1',
      p_preserve_case => TRUE);
end;
/
```

To see if a session id exists, use the *session_id_exists* function. It returns TRUE if it exists or FALSE if not.

```
begin
   if htmldb_custom_auth.session_id_exists then
      dbms_output.put_line('Session ID exist.');
   else
      dbms_output.put_line('Session ID dos not exist.');
   end if;
end;
/
```

All these procedures and functions are used to manage session and user authentication and registration with Oracle Application Express.

Package *htmldb_item*

The *htmldb_item* package can be used to create specific page items. The normal way, of course, is to create them on the application page using the wizards. However, if the need ever arises to create them in a web application dynamically at runtime, this is how it is done.

The most common use for the *htmldb_item* package is in a report or tabular form. The most common of all the procedures is the *checkbox* procedure. This procedure is used extensively in the information on checkboxes. A few of the *htmldb_item* procedures are outlined below. With the examples provided, users should have enough information to go the ApEx documentation and be able to use the rest of the dynamic page item procedures.

With this package, for example, we can create checkboxes, different types of lists, text areas, radio groups and pop ups such as creating checkboxes dynamically in a query using the following command:

🖫 Code 12.2 – htmldb_item.sql

```
conn sys@ora11g as sysdba

Connected to:
Oracle 11g Enterprise Edition Release 11.2.0.1.0 - Production
With the Partitioning, Oracle Label Security, OLAP, Data Mining,
```

```
--Use the command below to create a check box enabled for all employees on
table emp_del
select
   htmldb_item.checkbox(
      p_idx => 2,
      p_value => employee_id,
      p_attributes => 'checked') " ",
      first_name,
      last_name
from
   hr.emp_del
order by 1;


--Or this other command that create a check box just for users that have the
salary greather than 100.
select
   htmldb_item.checkbox(p_idx => 1,p_value => employee_id,p_attributes =>
'checked') " ",
   first_name,
   last_name
from
   hr.emp_del
where
   salary > 100
order by 1;
```

Parameters for the *htmldb_item* package:

- *p_idx*: This indicates the ID number of the global *htmldb_application* variable. The range of values is one to 50. A ten produces a page item with the name *f10*. It can then be referenced with *htmldb_application.g_f10*.

- *p_value*: This is the value of the checkbox. This is the return value that will be in the *g_f10* array if the checkbox is checked when the page is submitted.

- *p_attributes*: HTML tags can be added here.

- *p_checked_values*: These are the default values to be checked. A valid value here is 4:5:2:4.

- *p_checked_values_delimiter*: This is the character used as the delimiter for the *p_checked_values* parameter.

To create a date popup function dynamically, use the *date_popup* function. The next example shows how to create a date popup function for the *hiredate* column of the *emp_del* table.

```
select htmldb_item.date_popup(p_idx        => 10,
                   p_row        => rownum,
                   p_value      => add_months(sysdate, rownum),
                   p_date_format => 'DD-MON-YY HH24:MI')
```

Package htmldb_item

```
from all_objects
where rownum < 5;
```

Use the *display_and_save* function to display an item as text and save its value to the session state.

```
select
    htmldb_item.display_and_save(
        p_idx => 10,
        p_value => object_id)
from
    dba_objects
where rownum < 10;

HTMLDB_ITEM.DISPLAY_AND_SAVE(P
-----------------------------------------------------------------
<input type="hidden" name="f10" value="20" /><span>20</span>
<input type="hidden" name="f10" value="46" /><span>46</span>
```

To dynamically generate hidden fields, use the function named *hidden* and to generate text fields, use the function named *text*. Both are used on next example:

```
select object_id,
       htmldb_item.hidden(
           p_idx => 1,
           p_value => object_id) ||
       htmldb_item.text(
           p_idx => 2,
           p_value => object_name) Object_ID_Name
  from dba_objects
 where rownum < 5
 order by 1;
```

There are some functions used to generate select lists. They are exemplified below:

```
--To generate a static select list use select_list function and to
select
    htmldb_item.select_list(
        p_idx        => 1,
        p_value      => 'y',
        p_list_values => 'yes;y,no;n')
  from dba_objects
where rownum < 5;

--To generate select list from a list of values (LOV) use
select_list_from_lov function
select
    htmldb_item.select_list_from_lov(
        p_idx   => 2,
        p_value => object_name,
        p_lov   => 'ob_name_flow_lov')
from
    dba_objects;

--To generate very large select lists from a list of values use
```

Advanced DBMS Packages

```
select_list_from_lov_xl funtion.
select
   htmldb_item.select_list_from_lov_xl(
      p_idx   => 2,
      p_value => object_name,
      p_lov   => 'ob_name_flow_lov')
from
   dba_objects;

--To generate a select list from a query use select_item_from_query function
select htmldb_item.select_list_from_query(p_idx   => 2,
                                          p_value => object_name,
                                          p_query => 'select distinct
object_name from dba_objects')
from
   dba_objects
where rownum < 5;
```

Also, to generate text fields from the list of values or from a query, use the functions below:

```
--Text functions

--Simple text function
select
   htmldb_item.text(
      p_idx => 2,
      p_value => object_name) object_name,
   htmldb_item.text(
      p_idx => 3,
      p_value => object_type) object_type
   from dba_objects
where rownum < 5;

--Text from LOV
select
   htmldb_item.text_from_lov(
      p_value => object_id,
      p_lov => 'obj_id_obj_name_lov') o
from
   dba_objects;
```

To generate a radiogroup from a SQL query, use the *radiogroup* function:

```
select distinct
   htmldb_item.radiogroup(
      p_idx            => 1,
      p_value          => object_type,
      p_selected_value => 1,
      p_display        => object_type)
from
dba_objects;
```

Popups and popup keys can also be created from different sources like the LOV query. See the next examples:

Package htmldb_item

```
--Popup_from_lov
select
   htmldb_item.popup_from_lov(
      p_idx      => 1,
      p_value    => object_name,
      p_lov_name => 'lov1')
  from dba_objects;

--popup_from_query
select
   htmldb_item.popup_from_query(
      p_idx      => 1,
      p_value    => username,
      p_lov_query => 'select username from dba_users')
  from dba_users

--popupkey_from_lov
select
   htmldb_item.popupkey_from_lov(
      p_idx => 1,
      p_value => object_id,
      p_lov_name => 'lov1')
from
   dba_objects;

--popupkey_from_query
select
   htmldb_item.popupkey_from_query (
   p_idx => 1,
   p_value => object_id,
   p_lov_query => 'select object_name, object_id from dba_objects')
from dba_objects;
```

All these functions are automatically used when running APEX wizards to create pages. The intention here is to see how to use them when the specific needs are not fully met by the APEX wizards.

Package *htmldb_util*

The *htmldb_util* packages provide several procedures that can be used in ApEx or in stored procedures within the database. The ApEx development environment provides other methods for performing the same functionality as many of these functions do. However, when developing stored procedures, the same functionality is available through the use of the *htmldb_util* package.

Some procedures and functions of this package are described below. All these procedures and functions described here are excerpts from *Easy HTML-DB Oracle Application Express* by Michael Cunningham and Kent Crotty.

- *clear_app_cache*:   This procedure clears all session states for the application provided in the parameter.

- *clear_page_cache*: This procedure clears the session state in the current application for the page provided in the parameter.

- *clear_user_cache*: This procedure clears the cache for the current user. It also removes all preferences for the user. The added benefit of this procedure is it will clear the cache for all applications in which the user has session state. The downfall is it clears the preferences. CAUTION: Doing this for the development login will reset any preferences that have been set, such as the View being set to Icon or Details for the page definition and other attribute pages.

- *get_current_user_id*: This returns the ID number of the currently logged in user.

- *get_email*: This returns the email stored in the database for the provided username. This procedure can be used with the *htmldb_mail* package for sending mail.

- *get_last_name*: This returns the last name of the username specified. There is also a *get_first_name* function to return the user's first name.

- *get_username*: This returns the username of the user ID provided.

- *get_numeric_session_state*: This returns the value of session state converted to a number. ApEx provides a shorthand function to the same thing, named *nv*.

- *get_preference*: This returns the value of a preference for the user provided.

- *get_session_state*: This returns the value of an item in session state. ApEx provides a shorthand function to do the same thing, named *v*.

- *remove_preference*: This removes a stored preference for the username provided.

- *remove_sort_preference*: This removes the sorting preferences stored for the user. The sorting preferences keep track of how a user sorted a report in a prior visit to the web page. This is a way for APEX to sort the report the same way the next time the user visits the web page.

- *set_preference*: This procedure stores a value for the user in persistent session state. The persistent session state is called a preference. The next time the user visits the application, the preference can be restored.

- *set_session_state*: This procedure sets the session state for an item. This is valuable because it allows the session state of page items to be set from within a stored procedure.

- *string_to_table*: This converts a delimited string into a PL/SQL array. This function is primarily used when working with checkboxes, multi-select lists and radio buttons.

- *table_to_string*: This function is the partner to *string_to_table*. It converts an array into a delimited string. When selecting data from a database table, this function can be used to set the session state for checkboxes, multi-select lists and radio buttons.

- *url_encode*. This converts special characters to *hexadecimal* value.

The next example uses some of these procedures and packages:

🖫 Code 12.3 – htmldb_util.sql

```
conn sys@ora11g as sysdba

Connected to:
Oracle 11g Enterprise Edition Release 11.2.0.1.0 - Production
With the Partitioning, Oracle Label Security, OLAP, Data Mining,
Oracle Database Vault and Real Application Testing options

--Clear app cache, of app 50 for current session
begin
   htmldb_util.clear_app_cache(p_app_id => '50');
end;
/

--Clear page cache for page ID 20
begin
   htmldb_util.clear_page_cache(p_page_id => '20');
end;
/

--Clear user cache from current session
begin
   htmldb_util.clear_user_cache;
end;
/

--Get current user id
select
   htmldb_util.get_current_user_id
from
   dual;

--Get email
select
   htmldb_util.get_email(p_username => 'pportugal')
from
   dual;

--Get last name

select
   htmldb_util.get_last_name(p_username => ' pportugal ')
from
   dual;

--Get numeric session state
set serveroutput on
declare
   v_item number;
begin
```

```
   select
      htmldb_util.get_numeric_session_state(p_item => 'item_test')
   into
      v_item
   from
      dual;
   dbms_output.put_line('Item number: '||v_item);
end;


--Get   preference
set serveroutput on
declare
   v_preference number;
begin
   select
      htmldb_util.get_preference(p_preference => 'my_pref',p_user =>
'pportugal')
   into
      v_preference
   from
      dual;
   dbms_output.put_line('Preference: '||v_preference);
end;

--Get session state
declare
v_session_state varchar2(30);
begin
   select
      htmldb_util.get_session_state(p_item => 'my_item')
   into
      v_session_state
   from
      dual;
   dbms_output.put_line(a => 'Session state:'||v_session_state);
end;
/

--Remove preference
begin
   htmldb_util.remove_preference(
      p_preference => 'my_pref',
      p_user => :app_user);
end;
/

--Remove sort preference
begin
   htmldb_util.remove_sort_preferences(
      p_user => :app_user);
end;
/

--Remove user account
begin
   htmldb_util.remove_user(p_user_id => '3343');
end;
/
```

```
or

begin
   htmldb_util.remove_user(p_user_name => ' pportugal ');
end;
/

--Set preference in a persistent session state
begin
   htmldb_util.set_session_state(
      p_name => 'my_item',
      p_value => 'myvalue');
end;
/

--Return a PL/SQL array given a string
set serveroutput on
declare
   v_array htmldb_application_global.vc_arr2;
begin
   v_array := htmldb_util.string_to_table(p_string => 'blue:red:green');
for z in 1..v_array.count loop
   htp.print(v_array(z));
   dbms_output.put_line(a => v_array(z));
end loop;
end;
```

Like any other *html_db* package, all procedures and functions of this *htmldb_util* are used automatically when invoking *html_db* wizards to create and modify pages.

Package *dbms_xdb*

One of the main packages related to Oracle XML DB is *dbms_xdb*. Within this package, it is possible to manage and configure resources for XML DB and also administer security privileges. Once XML DB is installed on the database, this package and the others about XDB that will be covered later on in this chapter can be used. In order to install XML DB, run the *catqm.sql* script. This script can be found in the *$ORACLE_HOME/rdbms/admin* directory.

To check if XML DB is already installed on the database, just query the *dba_registry* view. This view shows information about all components that are loaded into the database. Some useful and practical examples will be shown below so the reader can gain some knowledge on XML DB management.

The *dbms_xdb* package contains more than eighty procedures and functions and thus, as it is not possible to show one example for each one of them, some of most useful and most important will be shown in the next example.

First to be shown is how to create folders for the XML database.

💾 Code 12.4 – dbms_xdb_folders.sql

```
conn sys@ora11g as sysdba

Connected to:
Oracle 11g Enterprise Edition Release 11.2.0.1.0 - Production
With the Partitioning, Oracle Label Security, OLAP, Data Mining,
Oracle Database Vault and Real Application Testing options

--Folder examples
--Create a new folder resource
declare
    v_return boolean;
begin
    v_return := dbms_xdb.CreateFolder(abspath => '/usr');
commit;
end;
/

--Check if the resource is a folder or a container
set serveroutput on
declare
    v_return boolean;
begin
    if dbms_xdb.isFolder(abspath => '/usr') then
        dbms_output.put_line(a => 'Is a folder or container!');
    else
        dbms_output.put_line(a => 'Is not a folder or container!');
    end if;
end;
/
```

The next example shows some procedures and functions used to create, delete, rename and manage resources.

💾 Code 12.5 – dbms_xdb_resources.sql

```
conn sys@ora11g as sysdba

Connected to:
Oracle 11g Enterprise Edition Release 11.2.0.1.0 - Production
With the Partitioning, Oracle Label Security, OLAP, Data Mining,
Oracle Database Vault and Real Application Testing options

--Resources
--Create a new resource files
declare
v_res boolean;
carsxmlstring varchar2(300):=
'<?xml version="1.0"?>
<cars>
    <car carno="1" modelno="10" carname="X" carcolor="blue"/>
    <car carno="2" modelno="20" carname="Y" carcolor="red"/>
    <car carno="3" modelno="30" carname="W" carcolor="green"/>
    <car carno="4" modelno="40" carname="Z" carcolor="yellow"/>
```

```
</cars>';
modelsxmlstring varchar2(300):=
'<?xml version="1.0"?>
<models>
   <model modelno="10" modelname="sport"/>
   <model modelno="20" modelname="luxury"/>
   <model modelno="30" modelname="SUVs"/>
   <model modelno="40" modelname="sedan"/>
   <model modelno="50" modelname="truck"/>
</models>';
begin
v_res := dbms_xdb.createResource(abspath => '/usr/tmp/cars.xml',data =>
carsxmlstring);
v_res := dbms_xdb.createResource(abspath => '/usr/tmp/models.xml',data =>
modelsxmlstring);
end;
/

--Check if a resource exists or not
declare
   v_result boolean;
begin
   if dbms_xdb.ExistsResource(abspath => '/usr/tmp/models.xml') then
      dbms_output.put_line(a => 'Resource exists!');
   else
      dbms_output.put_line(a => 'Resource does not exists!');
   end if;
end;
/

--Delete a resource
select * from xdb.resource_view r where r.any_path like '%models%';
begin
   dbms_xdb.DeleteResource(abspath => '/usr/tmp/models.xml');
   commit;
end;
/

--RenameResource
select
   any_path
from
   xdb.resource_view r
where
   r.any_path like '%cars%';

begin
   dbms_xdb.RenameResource(
      srcpath => '/usr/tmp/cars.xml',
      destfolder => '/usr/tmp/',
      newname => 'cars2.xml');
   commit;
end;
/

select
   any_path
from
   xdb.resource_view r
```

```
where
   r.any_path like '%cars%';


select * from dba_objects where object_name like '%xml_temp_instance%'

--Add user defined attrubutes to a resource
declare
v_return boolean;
v_data varchar2(300):=
'<?xml version="1.0"?>
<cars>
   <car carno="5" modelno="50" carname="Z1" carcolor="orange"/>
</cars>';
begin
   dbms_xdb.appendResourceMetadata(abspath => '/usr/tmp/cars2.xml',data
=>xmltype(v_data));
end;
/


--Use getResource to get xdb resource information
set serveroutput on
declare
   v_xdb_res          dbms_xdbresource.xdbresource;
   v_create_date      dbms_xdbresource.xdbresource;
   v_res_mime_type    varchar2 (20);
begin
   v_xdb_res := dbms_xdb.getresource (abspath => '/usr/tmp/cars2.xml');
   dbms_output.put_line('-----------------------------');
   dbms_output.put_line('Content Type:
'||dbms_xdbresource.getcontenttype(v_xdb_res));
   dbms_xdbresource.setcontenttype (v_xdb_res, 'text/plain');
end;
/


--Delete all metadata for a resource
begin
   dbms_xdb.purgeResourceMetadata(abspath => '/usr/tmp/cars2.xml');
end;
/


--Change the owner for a resource
begin
   dbms_xdb.changeOwner(abspath => '/usr/tmp/cars2.xml',owner =>
'xdb',recurse => TRUE);
end;
/
```

It is possible to lock and unlock resources to work with them when necessary and it is also possible to check if the resource is locked. Find in the next example some of the lock procedures and functions of the *dbms_xdb* package.

🖫 Code 12.6 – dbms_xdb_locks.sql

```
conn sys@ora11g as sysdba
```

Package dbms_xdb

```
Connected to:
Oracle 11g Enterprise Edition Release 11.2.0.1.0 - Production
With the Partitioning, Oracle Label Security, OLAP, Data Mining,
Oracle Database Vault and Real Application Testing options

--Find next more examples now about how to lock, unlock discover locks in
resources.

--Lock examples
declare
    v_lock boolean;
begin
    if dbms_xdb.LockResource(abspath => '/usr',depthzero => TRUE,shared =>
FALSE) then
    dbms_output.put_line(a => 'Resource locked!');
else
    dbms_output.put_line(a => 'Resource unlocked!');
end if;
    commit;
end;
/
```

If we try to execute the command above one more time, it will generate a message like this:

```
ORA-31102: Already locked in exclusive mode. Cannot add lock.
ORA-06512: at "XDB.DBMS_XDB", line 3
ORA-06512: at line 4

--To unlock the resource use UnlockResource function
declare
    v_lock boolean;
begin
    v_lock := dbms_xdb.UnlockResource(abspath => '/usr');
    dbms_output.put_line(a => 'Resource unlocked!');
    commit;
end;
/

--Discover locks
set serveroutput on
declare
    v_lock dbms_xdbresource.XDBResource;
begin
    v_lock := dbms_xdb.LockDiscovery(abspath =>  '/usr',xmltype(v_lock));
    dbms_output.put_line(a => 'Lock: '||v_lock);
end;
/

--Return a resource lock token based on a given path
set serverutput on
declare
    v_lock varchar2(30);
begin
    dbms_xdb.GetLockToken(
        abspath => '/usr/tmp/cars2.xml',
        locktoken => v_lock);
```

```
      dbms_output.put_line(a => 'Lock:'||v_lock);
end;
/

--Get a session lock token list
set serveroutput on
declare
    v_tokenlist xdb.locktokenlisttype;
begin
    select dbms_xdb.GetLockTokenList into v_tokenlist from dual;
    dbms_output.put_line(a => 'Token list:'||v_tokenlist);
end;
/
```

By default, the XML database is configured with http port set to 8080 and FTP port to 2100. To change these values or get the actual value, use the corresponding functions shown next.

Code 12.7 – dbms_xdb_ftp_http.sql

```
conn sys@ora11g as sysdba

Connected to:
Oracle 11g Enterprise Edition Release 11.2.0.1.0 - Production
With the Partitioning, Oracle Label Security, OLAP, Data Mining,
Oracle Database Vault and Real Application Testing options

--Set FTP and HTTP port
begin
    dbms_xdb.setFTPPort(new_port => 2122);
    dbms_xdb.setHTTPPort(new_port => 8089);
end;
/


--Get new values
declare
    v_ftpport number;
    v_httpport number;
begin
    select dbms_xdb.getFTPPort into v_ftpport from dual;
    select dbms_xdb.getHTTPPort into v_httpport from dual;
    dbms_output.put_line(a => 'FTP port:'||v_ftpport);
    dbms_output.put_line(a => 'HTTP port:'||v_httpport);
end;
/
```

Some procedures are used to set parameters of a listener end point that corresponds to the XML DB HTTP server. It is possible to set HTTP and HTTP2 listeners with the follow procedures:

Code 12.8 – dbms_xdb_listener.sql

```
conn sys@ora11g as sysdba
```

```
Connected to:
Oracle 11g Enterprise Edition Release 11.2.0.1.0 - Production
With the Partitioning, Oracle Label Security, OLAP, Data Mining,
Oracle Database Vault and Real Application Testing options

--Set listener endpoint
begin
   dbms_xdb.setlistenerendpoint(
   endpoint => 2,
   host => '10.10.10.113',
   port => 1443,
   protocol => 2);
end;
/
```

Check if the XML database is running with secure settings by using the query below:

```
col "Protocol" for a10
col "Port Number" for a11
select
    extractValue(value(x),'/httpconfig/http2-protocol',
'xmlns="http://xmlns.oracle.com/xdb/xdbconfig.xsd"') "Protocol",
    extractValue(value(x),'/httpconfig/http2-port',
'xmlns="http://xmlns.oracle.com/xdb/xdbconfig.xsd"') "Port Number"
from
table(xmlsequence(extract(xdburitype('/xdbconfig.xml').getXML(),'/xdbconfig/
sysconfig/protocolconfig/httpconfig'))) x
/

Protocol   Port Number
---------- -----------
tcps       1443
```

To check the listener endpoint, use the procedure below:

```
declare
    v_port number;
    v_protocol number;
    v_host varchar2(50);
begin
    dbms_xdb.getListenerEndPoint(endpoint => 2,host => v_host,port =>
v_port,protocol => v_protocol);
    dbms_output.put_line(a => 'Host    :'||v_host);
    dbms_output.put_line(a => 'Port    :'||v_port);
    dbms_output.put_line(a => 'Protocol:'||v_protocol);
end;
/

Host    :10.10.10.113
Port    :1443
Protocol:2
```

Sometimes the storage tablespace for XDB objects needs to be changed and *dbms_xdb* provides a procedure to check and another to change all XDB objects to another tablespace. The following shows how to do that.

How to Check Current XDB Tablespace and Change It

First, use the *getxdb_tablespace* procedure to check what is the current tablespace being used by the XDB database.

💾 Code 12.9 – dbms_xdb_tablespace.sql

```
conn sys@ora11g as sysdba

Connected to:
Oracle 11g Enterprise Edition Release 11.2.0.1.0 - Production
With the Partitioning, Oracle Label Security, OLAP, Data Mining,
Oracle Database Vault and Real Application Testing options

--Get current XDB tablespace
declare
    v_xdbtbs varchar2(30);
begin
    select dbms_xdb.getxdb_tablespace into v_xdbtbs from dual;
    dbms_output.put_line(a => 'Actual XDB tablespace is:'||v_xdbtbs);
end;
/

--Create another tablespace
create tablespace tbs_xdb_new datafile size 200M;

--Change XDB tablespace using movexdb_tablespace procedure as follows:
begin
    dbms_xdb.movexdb_tablespace(new_tablespace => 'tbs_xdb_new');
end;
/

--Check new tablespace again with this simple query
select
    dbms_xdb.getxdb_tablespace
from
    dual;
```

These examples above were just an useful introductory sample of more than eighty procedures and functions that compose the *dbms_xdb* package and are used to manage the XDB database.

Package *dbms_xdbt*

As the XML database stores information in a different manner from a normal database schema, Oracle provides some performance improvements by offering the *dbms_xdbt* package that supports the index creation on XML DB when the information is like Microsoft Word documents and other binary data.

In order to create the *dbms_xdbt* package, the XDB feature must be installed. When it is installed, it automatically calls for *dbmsxdbt.sql* scripts that can be found in the *$ORACLE_HOME/rdbms/admin* directory. Next are some examples of how to create and synchronize indexes and create preferences for these indexes.

How to Create Indexes for XML DB

In next example, we will show how to create an index using the *createindex* procedure and also how to optimize and synchronize this index. Before creating an index, preferences must be created. The procedure responsible for creating preferences is *createpreferences*. When it is executed, it calls all other preferences procedures like *createdatastorepref, createfilterpref, createiexerpref, createstoplistpref, createwordlistpref, createstoragepref,* and *createsectiongrouppref.*

💾 **Code 12.10 – dbms_xdbt_index.sql**

```
conn sys@ora11g as sysdba

Connected to:
Oracle 11g Enterprise Edition Release 11.2.0.1.0 - Production
With the Partitioning, Oracle Label Security, OLAP, Data Mining,
Oracle Database Vault and Real Application Testing options

begin
    xdb.dbms_xdbt.createPreferences;
    xdb.dbms_xdbt.createIndex;
end;
/
```

Configure auto sync by using the *configureautosync* procedure.

```
begin
    xdb.dbms_xdbt.configureautosync;
end;
/
```

The command above will create and schedule a job with the following code:

```
xdb.dbms_xdbt.autosyncjobbycount('xdb$ci',2,'50M');
```

To sync an index manually, use the *autosyncjobbycount* procedure:

```
begin
    xdb.dbms_xdbt.autosyncjobbycount(
        myIndexName => 'xdb$ci',
        myMaxPendingCount =>2 ,
        myIndexMemory => '50');
end;
/
```

There are other methods related to preference creation, but all of them are inside the *createpreference* procedure.

Package *dbms_xdbz*

To keep the XML database secure, Oracle provides different methods of security like row-level and column-level security and also fine-grained access control for XML DB resources. Before starting to explain what the *dbms_xdbz* package is and when and how to use it, it is necessary to have at least a basic knowledge of what is understood by ACL and ACE when the subject is the XML database.

Access Control Lists (ACLs) are a technique used to protect XML DB resources from being accessed by unauthorized users. All resources, when created, receive an ACL associated within it and ACLs can also be created later and associated to an already created resource. All ACLs are stored in *xdb$acl* tables on the XDB schema.

Access Control Entry (ACE) is an entry in ACL in the form of an XML element. It is responsible for granting or denying access to XML resources. Taking the explanation above in consideration, it is time to start demonstrating some examples of this package usage.

A principal is a user or role that will either receive or have the privilege revoked to access a XML resource. Find below the procedures that are used to reset, set, delete, add and change an application principal.

Code 12.11 – dbms_xdbz_app_principal.sql

```
conn sys@ora11g as sysdba

Connected to:
Oracle 11g Enterprise Edition Release 11.2.0.1.0 - Production
With the Partitioning, Oracle Label Security, OLAP, Data Mining,
Oracle Database Vault and Real Application Testing options

--Application principal
--Add an Application user or role to XML DB.
declare
   v_res boolean;
begin
   v_res :=   xdb.dbms_xdbz.add_application_principal(name => 'SH');
   dbms_output.put_line(a => 'Added application principal!');
   commit;
end;
/

--Setting application principal
declare
v_res boolean;
begin
```

```
   v_res := xdb.dbms_xdbz.set_application_principal(
                                    principal_name => 'SH',
                                    allow_registration =>
TRUE);
   commit;
   dbms_output.put_line(a => 'Application principal set!');
end;
/

--Delete all information about an Application user or role.
declare
   v_res boolean;
begin
   v_res :=   xdb.dbms_xdbz.delete_application_principal(name => 'SH');
   commit;
   dbms_output.put_line(a => 'Application principal deleted!');
end;
/
```

Also on the *dbms_xdbz* package are two purge procedures used to purge cache information. They are exemplified below:

💾 Code 12.12 – dbms_xdbz_purge.sql

```
conn sys@ora11g as sysdba

Connected to:
Oracle 11g Enterprise Edition Release 11.2.0.1.0 - Production
With the Partitioning, Oracle Label Security, OLAP, Data Mining,
Oracle Database Vault and Real Application Testing options

--Purges the shared cache of GUIDs to Application user or roles names
mappings.
declare
   v_res boolean;
begin
   v_res := xdb.dbms_xdbz.purgeApplicationCache;
end;
/

--Purge LDAP nickname cache
declare
   v_res boolean;
begin
   v_res := xdb.dbms_xdbz.purgeLdapCache;
end;
/
```

There are also validating procedures inside the *dbms_xdbz* package that can be used to validate ACLs before using them. For example, suppose that we want to add privileges to an ACL but want to check if the ACL is valid before it.

Take a look on this next example that shows a simple way to validate an ACL. First create an ACL, add a privilege to it and assign this ACL with host www.rampant.cc.

🖫 Code 12.13 – dbms_xdbz_validate.sql

```
conn sys@ora11g as sysdba

Connected to:
Oracle 11g Enterprise Edition Release 11.2.0.1.0 - Production
With the Partitioning, Oracle Label Security, OLAP, Data Mining,
Oracle Database Vault and Real Application Testing options

begin
  dbms_network_acl_admin.create_acl(acl         => 'www_ramp.xml',
                                    description => 'www rampant acl',
                                    principal   => 'xdb',
                                    is_grant    => true,
                                    privilege   => 'connect');
  dbms_network_acl_admin.add_privilege(acl         => 'www_ramp.xml',
                                       principal => 'xdb',
                                       is_grant  => true,
                                       privilege => 'resolve');
  dbms_network_acl_admin.assign_acl(acl  => 'www_ramp.xml',
                                    host => 'www.rampant.cc');
end;
/
commit;


--Now, suppose that we want to give XDB the connect privilege everywhere.
Use the pl/sql block below:

declare
  v_acl_path varchar2(500);
  v_acl_id   raw(16);
begin
  -- Look for the ACL currently assigned to '*' and give flows_xxxxxx
  -- the "connect" privilege if flows_XXXXXX does not have the privilege
yet.
  select acl
    into v_acl_path
    from dba_network_acls
   where host = '*'
     and lower_port is null
     and upper_port is null;

  select sys_op_r2o(extractvalue(p.res, '/Resource/XMLRef'))
    into v_acl_id
    from xdb.xdb$acl a, path_view p
   where extractvalue(p.res, '/Resource/XMLRef') = ref(a)
     and equals_path(p.res, v_acl_path) = 1;

  --Now use validateACL procedure to check if ACL being used is valid
  dbms_xdbz.validateacl(acloid => acl_id);

  --Finally, check and give the privilege to the user
  if dbms_network_acl_admin.check_privilege(acl       => acl_path,
                                            user      => 'SH',
                                            privilege => 'connect') is null
then
    dbms_network_acl_admin.add_privilege(acl       => acl_path,
                                         principal => 'SH',
```

```
                                        is_grant   => TRUE,
                                        privilege => 'connect');
   end if;
exception
   when no_data_found then
      dbms_network_acl_admin.create_acl(acl          => 'www_ramp.xml',
                                        description => 'ACL that grant connect
everywhere',
                                        principal   => 'SH',
                                        is_grant    => TRUE,
                                        privilege   => 'connect');
      dbms_network_acl_admin.assign_acl(acl => 'www_ramp.xml', host => '*');
end;
```

Check all ACLs created by querying the *dba_network_acls* view that shows the network host, the ACL path, upper and lower port range.

The next packages have to do with XML management and document manipulation.

Packages *dbms_xmldom* and *dbms_xmlparser*

The *dbms_xmldom* and *dbms_xmlparser* packages are two of the many API packages used to access and manage XMLType data. Document Object Model (DOM) is a representation for a XML document that is kept dynamically in memory. With DOM, it is possible to define the logical structure of documents and how they are accessed and managed.

While *dbms_xmldom* is used to access XMLType data, *dbms_xmlparser* is used to access the content and the XML documents structure. Within these packages it is possible, among other things, to create XMLType tables and views, access the XMLType data and manipulate XMLType data.

As these packages contain more than two hundred and fifty functions, procedures and constraints, it will not be possible to exemplify all of them in this chapter. Instead, the example below will use some of these procedures and functions from both packages. In this example, some procedures and functions of the *dbms_xmldom* package will be used to create a DOM document into a table and manipulate this data.

A *xmltype* table is created and after that, some value is inserted into this table. Procedures used to create an element node and manipulate the data of the element created are explained later.

Code 12.14 – dbms_xmldom_dom_doc.sql

```
conn sys@ora11g as sysdba

Connected to:
```

```
Oracle 11g Enterprise Edition Release 11.2.0.1.0 - Production
With the Partitioning, Oracle Label Security, OLAP, Data Mining,
Oracle Database Vault and Real Application Testing options

create table
   tab_test_xmldom of
xmltype;

declare
  v_doc        dbms_xmldom.domdocument;
  v_doc_node      dbms_xmldom.domnode;
  v_dom_element    dbms_xmldom.domelement;
  v_buffer        varchar2(300);
  v_dom_node      dbms_xmldom.domnode;
  v_variable       XMLType;
  v_chil_node dbms_xmldom.domnode;
  v_node_list   dbms_xmldom.domnodelist;
  v_var2       varchar2(100);
  v_elem dbms_xmldom.domelement;
  v_doc1 dbms_xmldom.domdocument;
  v_n_element dbms_xmldom.domnode;
begin
  v_variable :=
xmltype('<tab_test_xmldom><car>audi_a4</car></tab_test_xmldom>');
  v_doc   := dbms_xmldom.cument(v_variable);
  v_doc_node := dbms_xmldom.makenode(v_doc);
  dbms_xmldom.writetobuffer(n => v_doc_node,buffer =>  v_buffer);
  dbms_output.put_line(a => 'Before change:' || v_buffer);

  v_dom_element := dbms_xmldom.getdocumentelement(doc => v_doc);
  v_node_list  := dbms_xmldom.getelementsbytagname(elem =>
v_dom_element,name =>  'car');
  v_dom_node      := dbms_xmldom.item(nl => v_node_list,idx =>  0);
  v_chil_node := dbms_xmldom.getFirstChild(n => v_dom_node);

  dbms_xmldom.setnodevalue(n => v_chil_node,nodevalue =>  'audi_a8');
  dbms_xmldom.writetobuffer(n => v_doc_node,buffer =>  v_buffer);
  dbms_output.put_line(a => 'After change:' || v_buffer);


  v_doc1 := dbms_xmldom.newdomdocument;
  v_elem := dbms_xmldom.createelement(doc => v_doc,tagName =>  'CAR');
  v_n_element := dbms_xmldom.makenode(v_elem);
  dbms_output.put_line('node name = ' || dbms_xmldom.getnodename(n =>
v_n_element));
  dbms_output.put_line('node value = '|| dbms_xmldom.getnodevalue(n =>
v_n_element));
  dbms_output.put_line('node type = ' || dbms_xmldom.getnodetype(n =>
v_n_element));

  dbms_xmldom.freedocument(doc => v_doc);
  insert into tab_test_xmldom values (v_variable);

end;
/

--Check the table values
SQL>
 select * from
```

```
  tab_test_xmldom;

SYS_NC_ROWINFO$
-----------------------------------------------------------------------
<tab_test_xmldom>
  <CAR>audi_a8</CAR>
</tab_test_xmldom>
```

Here are the procedures and functions used in the last example:

- *newdomdocument*: Procedure that processes the XMLType document and creates an instance

- *makenode*: Function used to create a handle for the object

- *writetobuffer*: Function used to write the document to a varchar buffer

- *getdocumentelement*: This function gets the document element

- *getelementsbytagname*: This function gets an element based on its tag name

- *getfirstchild*: Function used to retrieve the first child of a node being used

- *setnodevalue*: Procedure used to set the value of the node being used

- *writetobuffer*: This procedure writes contents of a document into a buffer using the database character set

- *freedocument*: This procedure frees a *dom* document object

Much more can be done with the *dbms_xmldom* package, but it is beyond the scope of this book. Instead, the focus will be on another XML package previously presented, *dbms_xmlparser*.

XML elements, known also as storage units, contain parsed or unparsed data. A parsed object may contain common character data or markup language. These markups are used to describe the storage layout and logical structure of the object. The *dbms_xmlparser* package allows access to XML documents, enabling the user to get their structure and content and access or modify the document's elements and attributes.

The next example will show how to parse an XML document using the *dbms_xmlparser* package. A table containing XML data is created. Then this table is used in a function that checks if the XML inside the table is formed correctly or not.

First, create a test table named *tab_xml_parse*.

📇 Code 12.15 – dbms_xmlparser.sql

```
conn sys@ora11g as sysdba
```

```
Connected to:
Oracle 11g Enterprise Edition Release 11.2.0.1.0 - Production
With the Partitioning, Oracle Label Security, OLAP, Data Mining,
Oracle Database Vault and Real Application Testing options

--First create the test table named tab_xml_parse
create table tab_xml_parse (
  col1 varchar2(200),
  col2 clob);
```

Now create a directory which will hold an XML file to be inserted into the newly created table.

```
create directory dir_xml_docs AS '/tmp';

grant read,write at dir_xml_docs to public;
```

Create a procedure to insert the XML data from the file to the table *tab_xml_parse.*

```
create or replace procedure prc_insert_xml_to_table (v_directory in
varchar2,
                               v_file_name in varchar2,
                               v_char_set in varchar2)
is
  v_xmlfile bfile;
  v_myclob clob;
  v_dest integer := 1;
  v_source integer := 1;
  v_language_context integer := dbms_lob.default_lang_ctx;
  v_warning_message integer;
begin

  insert into
    tab_xml_parse
    (col1,
     col2)
  values
    (v_file_name,
     empty_clob())
  returning col2 into v_myclob;

  v_xmlfile := bfilename(directory => v_directory,
                   filename => v_file_name);

  dbms_lob.open(file_loc => v_xmlfile);

  dbms_lob.loadclobfromfile(dest_lob => v_myclob,
                      src_bfile =>  v_xmlfile,
                      amount =>  dbms_lob.getlength(v_xmlfile),
                      dest_offset => v_dest,
                      src_offset =>  v_source,
                      bfile_csid => nls_charset_id(v_char_set),
                      lang_context => v_language_context,
                      warning =>  v_warning_message);
  dbms_lob.close(file_loc => v_xmlfile);
```

```
end prc_insert_xml_to_table;
/
```

Use the procedure created above to insert XML data into the table.

```
begin
    prc_insert_xml_to_table(
        v_directory => 'dir_xml_docs',
        v_file_name => 'itunesLib.xml',
        v_char_set => 'utf8');
end;
/

--Query table and check results
select * from tab_xml_parse;
```

Create the function to check whether or not the XML document is formed properly.

```
create or replace function func_check_xml (v_xmlfile clob) return boolean is
    v_parser dbms_xmlparser.parser;
    v_err varchar2(200);
    v_xml_parse_err exception;
    pragma exception_init(v_xml_parse_err,-31011);
begin
    v_parser := dbms_xmlparser.newparser;
    dbms_xmlparser.parseclob(v_parser,v_xmlfile);
    dbms_xmlparser.freeparser(v_parser);
    return true;
exception
    when v_xml_parse_err then
dbms_output.put_line('Erro while parsing!!!!');
        dbms_xmlparser.freeparser(v_parser);
        v_err := sqlerrm;
        dbms_output.put_line(v_err);
        return false;
end func_check_xml;
/
```

Lastly, execute the function to check if the XML data inside the *tab_xml_parse* table is in a correct format.

```
set serveroutput on
declare
    v_xmlfile clob;
    v_is_ok boolean;
    indoc varchar2(2000);
    myparser dbms_xmlparser.parser;
    indomdoc dbms_xmldom.domdocument;
    innode dbms_xmldom.domnode;
    buf varchar2(2000);
begin
    select col2 into v_xmlfile
    from tab_xml_parse
    where col1 = 'itunesLib.xml';
    v_is_ok := func_check_xml(v_xmlfile);
```

Advanced DBMS Packages

```
    if v_is_ok then
      dbms_output.put_line('The XML document is OK!');
    else
      dbms_output.put_line('The XML document is wrong!!');
    end if;

--Another example inside this block
    dbms_output.put_line(a => '######################');
    dbms_output.put_line(a => '# Another example      #');
    indoc := '<car><name>bwm m3</name></car>';
-- Construct a parser instance
    myparser := dbms_xmlparser.newparser;
--Parse XML documents
    dbms_xmlparser.parsebuffer(p => myparser,doc =>  indoc);
--Obtain the DOMDocument interface
    indomdoc := dbms_xmlparser.getdocument(p => myparser);
    innode := dbms_xmldom.makenode(doc => indomdoc);
    dbms_xmldom.writetobuffer(n => innode,buffer =>  buf);
    dbms_output.put_line(a => buf);
    dbms_xmldom.freedocument(doc => indomdoc);
    dbms_xmlparser.freeparser(p => myparser);
    dbms_output.put_line(a => '######################');

end;
/
```

Some of the main procedures and functions of *dbms_xmlparser* were used in the last example. Here are their functions:

- *newparser*. Used to return a new parser instance

- *parseclob*. Used to parse XML stored in a CLOB

- *freeparser*. Used to free a parser object

- *parserbuffer*. This function parses an XML stored in a document

- *getdocument*. Returns the node of a tree built by parse in a document

There are many other functions and packages in *dbms_xmlparser*. Further information can be found by consulting tahiti.oracle.com.

Packages *dbms_xmlgen* and *dbms_xmlquery*

How can data be transformed in a table to XML format? Just as we can select and format into HTML code, and this is what takes place behind the scenes in iSQL*Plus, we can select from a table and have the output be well-formed XML. We use the *dbms_xmlgen.getxml* function to accomplish this.

The syntax is select *dbms_xmlgen.getxml('your query here* from dual and with spool and SQL*Plus settings set correctly, the output is a dump of data in XML format. Where

---

is this useful? Anywhere or anytime we need to transform data into XML format, the *getxml* function can be used.

Of particular note, Oracle's new reporting tool Business Intelligence Publisher is intimately tied to XML. In fact, report or template development is largely driven by having an XML file representation of data to start with. Dump a portion of the data into XML format, load the XML data into an RTF document in Word, call the table wizard, and a report template is created just like that.

Of course, much more can take place with respect to manipulating the data. Oracle recommends that data selection and formatting, as much as possible, be done via the *select* statement as opposed to forcing the RTF processing engine to manipulate the data. The RDBMS engine is obviously much more powerful than what Microsoft Word has to offer. Oracle recommends that *dbms_xmlgen* be used over *dbms_xmlquery*.

Would it not be fantastic if data could be simply pulled from Oracle preformatted with XML tags? Many Oracle shops use XML for data transfer, web services, reports, and the Oracle data can be easily tagged using the *dbms_xmlgen* package. Oracle's XML Publisher product can retrieve XML from an HTTP feed and use it to generate rich reports with graphs, images, and other content and then mail, fax, print, or FTP them. All that is needed is the XML.

Oracle gives the *dbms_xmlgen* package for formatting Oracle output in XML. The *dbms_xmlgen* package generates XML on-the-fly using any query desired; in addition, it is extremely easy to use from either the SQL prompt or in code, as it is just a simple query. Below are some useful examples for creating XML data using both the *dbms_xmlgen* and *dbms_xmlquery* packages. Run this simple query:

Code 12.16 – dbms_xmlgen.sql

```
conn sys@ora11g as sysdba

Connected to:
Oracle 11g Enterprise Edition Release 11.2.0.1.0 - Production
With the Partitioning, Oracle Label Security, OLAP, Data Mining,
Oracle Database Vault and Real Application Testing options

select
   owner,
   table_name
from
   dba_tables
where
   owner='system'
and
   rownum <2;

OWNER                              TABLE_NAME
---------------------------------  ------------------------------
```

```
system                              aq$_internet_agents

select
   dbms_xmlgen.getXML('select owner,table_name from dba_tables where
owner=''system'' and rownum <2') query_xml
from
   dual;

QUERY_XML
-----------------------------------------------------------------------
<?xml version="1.0"?>
<rowset>
 <row>
  <owner>system</owner>
  <table_name>aq$_internet_agents</table_name>
 </row>
</rowset>
```

It is very easy to generate XML data from a query using the *getxml* procedure.

Now examine more advanced XML tagging with *dbms_xmlgen*. Most XML has sub-nodes for each main node. For instance, what if we wanted to pull XML for every department, and a sub-node for every employee under it? We can use the cursor function!

🖫 Code 12.17 – dbms_xmlgen_getxml.sql

```
conn sys@ora11g as sysdba

Connected to:
Oracle 11g Enterprise Edition Release 11.2.0.1.0 - Production
With the Partitioning, Oracle Label Security, OLAP, Data Mining,
Oracle Database Vault and Real Application Testing options

 select department_id, department_name,
  cursor(select first_name, last_name
  from employees e
  where e.department_id = d.department_id) emp_row
  from departments d
  where rownum < 4

DEPARTMENT_ID DEPARTMENT_NAME                   EMP_ROW
------------- ------------------------------    --------------------
           10 Administration                    cursor statement : 3

cursor statement : 3


FIRST_NAME           LAST_NAME
-------------------- ------------------------
Jennifer             Whalen

           20 Marketing                         cursor statement : 3

cursor statement : 3

FIRST_NAME           LAST_NAME
-------------------- ------------------------
Michael              Hartstein
Pat                  Fay
```

```
     30 Purchasing                    cursor statement : 3

cursor statement : 3

FIRST_NAME            LAST_NAME
--------------------  ------------------------
Den                   Raphaely
Alexander             Khoo
Shelli                Baida
Sigal                 Tobias
Guy                   Himuro
Karen                 Colmenares
```

The results do not look too impressive at the SQL prompt. However, watch as we surround it with a call to *dbms_xmlgen.getxml*:

```
select dbms_xmlgen.getxml('
 select department_id, department_name,
 cursor(select first_name, last_name
 from employees e
 where e.department_id = d.department_id) emp_row
 from departments d
 where rownum < 4
 ') from dual
```

```
<?xml version="1.0"?>
<rowset>
 <row>
  <department_id>10</department_id>
  <department_name>administration</department_name>
  <emp_row>
   <emp_row_row>
    <first_name>Jennifer</first_name>
    <last_name>Whalen</last_name>
   </emp_row_row>
  </emp_row>
 </row>
 <row>
  <department_id>20</department_id>
  <department_name>marketing</department_name>
  <emp_row>
   <emp_row_row>
    <first_name>Michael</first_name>
    <last_name>Hartstein</last_name>
   </emp_row_row>
   <emp_row_row>
    <first_name>Pat</first_name>
    <last_name>Fay</last_name>
   </emp_row_row>
  </emp_row>
 </row>
 <row>
  <department_id>30</department_id>
  <department_name>Purchasing</department_name>
  <emp_row>
   <emp_row_row>
    <first_name>Den</first_name>
    <last_name>Raphaely</last_name>
   </emp_row_row>
```

```
  <emp_row_row>
   <first_name>Alexander</first_name>
   <last_name>Khoo</last_name>
  </emp_row_row>
  <emp_row_row>
   <first_name>Shelli</first_name>
   <last_name>Baida</last_name>
  </ emp_row_row >
  < emp_row_row >
   <first_name>Sigal</first_name>
   <last_name>Tobias</last_name>
  </ emp_row_row >
  < emp_row_row >
   <first_name>Guy</first_name>
   <last_name>Himuro</last_name>
  </ emp_row_row >
  < emp_row_row >
   <first_name>Karen</first_name>
   <last_name>Colmenares</last_name>
  </ emp_row_row >
  </emp_row>
 </row>
</rowset>
```

Note that we did not change the query syntax in any way. But check out the great XML results! We have each *department* as a *row* tag, and the cursor we created gives me an *emp_row* node containing recurring *emp_row_row* nodes.

Tips for Using *dbms_xmlgen*

The *dbms_xmlgen* package can be extremely useful for quick retrieval of web records. Simply make a page that accepts input, such as *department_id*, and pass it into the SQL query. If we direct the database response directly to the browser, we have an easy XML display program. The best part of *dbms_xmlgen* is used for quickly formatting reports. XML Publisher accepts standard XML and allows forming extremely detailed reports using templates made in Microsoft Word.

With standard SQL queries tagged using *dbms_xmlgen*, XML Publisher can have a full reporting suite that easily pulls Oracle data with XML tags, forms it into a PDF, DOC, XLS, or HTML report, and distributes the report via e-mail using its native e-mail capabilities. This is far easier than the traditional *utl_mail* or *utl_smtp* e-mail packages which required specialized invocation code. Next, some *dbms_xmlquery* examples will be given that compare them with the *dbms_xmlgen* package.

For example, the following issue came up for one of my forum users while creating a web service to return nested XML data. The data contains a special character that prevented IE 6.0 from displaying the XML output. By default, *xmlgen* generates an *xml header <?xml version = '1.0'?>*. By converting to *dbms_xmlquery*, we can set the XML header to a company standard encoding *<?xml version = '1.0' encoding = 'ISO-8859-*

1'?>, and the web service will work fine. This code is almost identical, though the irrelevant portions have been removed.

```
qryCtx := dbms_xmlquery.newcontext(v_prd_query);
    --
    --  Set the encoding tag to handle Unicode
    --
    dbms_xmlquery.setencodingtag(qryctx, 'ISO-8859-1');
    dbms_xmlquery.setrowsettag(qryctx, 'root');
    dbms_xmlquery.setrowtag(qryctx, v_bayer_group_tag);
    --
    --  Set up the bind variables.
    --  Note: dbms_xmlquerycannot handle a bind variable occurring more than
once.
    --
    dbms_xmlquery.setbindvalue (qryctx, 'cp_bayer_group',
upper(i_bayer_group));
    dbms_xmlquery.setbindvalue (qryctx, 'cp_filter1',
upper(i_filter));
    dbms_xmlquery.setbindvalue (qryctx, 'cp_filter2',      upper(i_filter));
    dbms_xmlquery.setbindvalue (qryctx, 'cp_filter3',      upper(i_filter));
    --
    --  Execute the query and put the results into the clob
    --
    o_results := dbms_xmlquery.getxml(qryctx);
    --
    --  close the context
    --
    dbms_output.put_line('close context');
    dbms_xmlquery.closecontext(qryctx);
```

The comment shows that multiple occurrences of a bind variable do not work in *dbms_xmlquery*. The following error will be received:

```
oracle.xml.sql.OracleXMLSQLException: Missing IN or OUT parameter at index::
2
```

This is where the index refers to which occurrence of a bind variable (starting at 0) failed. In this case, it was the third *bind_variable* occurrence that failed.

```
|| 'from    sde_bayer_code_pref_names_v bc' || chr(10)
    || '        ,(select bc2.type_code    AS type_code' || chr (10)
    || '                bc2.code_seq_id  AS code_seq_id' || chr(10)
    || '        from    sde_bayer_code_pref_names_v bc2' || chr (10)
    || '        where   upper(bc2.code) like upper(:cp_filter1)' || chr
(10)
    || '        union' || chr(10)
    || '        select sn2.type_code    AS type_code' || chr(10)
    || '                ,sn2.code_seq_id  AS code_seq_id' || chr(10)
    || '        from    sde_bayer_code_sci_names_v sn2' || chr(10)
    || '        where   upper(sn2.short_name) like upper(:cp_filter1 ||
:cp_filter2)' || chr(10)
```

So, *dbms_xmlgen* is faster, but does not allow for the specification of the encoding tag. *dbms_xmlquery* allows for the encoding tag as well as the specification of an id variable and value for each row in a rowset, but it cannot handle multiple ocurrences of the same bind variables.

Packages *dbms_xmlsave* and *dbms_xmlstore*

The *dbms_xmlsave* package can be used to upload XML data into a table. It requires a good bit of manual typing as each tag has to be quoted and concatenated. The *dbms_xmlstore* package allows uploading an XML file directly and inserting the contents into a table.

Both *dbms_xmlsave* and *dbms_xmlstore* are part of the Oracle XML SQL Utility (XSU). The main differences between them are that *dbms_xmlstore* is written in C and compiled in kernel form, so it is faster; *dbms_xmlstore* uses Simple API for XML to parse XML, providing higher scalability and consuming less memory than the *dbms_xmlsave* package. Another important difference between them is that some *dbms_xmlstore* functions like *insertxml*, *updatexml* and *deletexml* can have XMLType (from the *dbms_xmlstore* package) instances in addition to CLOB values, thereby offering a better integration with XML DB.

Here is an example of uploading a new record into the EMP table using the *dbms_xmlsave* package.

💾 Code 12.18 – dbms_xmlsave.sql

```
conn sys@ora11g as sysdba

Connected to:
Oracle 11g Enterprise Edition Release 11.2.0.1.0 - Production
With the Partitioning, Oracle Label Security, OLAP, Data Mining,
Oracle Database Vault and Real Application Testing options

declare
  insctx   dbms_xmlsave.ctxtype;
  n_rows   number;
  s_xml    varchar2 (32767);
begin
  s_xml :=
'<rowset>'
|| '<row>'
|| '<empno>7783</empno>'
|| '<ename>clark</ename>'
|| '<job>manager</job>'
|| '<mgr>7839</mgr>'
|| '<sal>2450</sal>'
|| '<deptno>10</deptno>'
|| '</row>'
||'</rowset>';
```

```
insctx := dbms_xmlsave.newcontext ('emp');
-- get the context handle
dbms_xmlsave.setrowtag (insctx, 'row');
n_rows := dbms_xmlsave.insertxml (insctx, s_xml);
-- this inserts the document
dbms_xmlsave.closecontext (insctx);
end;
/
```

A bit cumbersome, but it can be done.

In this example, table *emp3* is a copy of *emp*. The generated *xml* data file is named *emp3.xml* and is located in a directory object named *mydir* - *C:\Temp* in this example. Here is the procedure code to upload an *xml* file:

🖫 Code 12.19 – dbms_xmlstore.sql

```
conn sys@ora11g as sysdba

Connected to:
Oracle 11g Enterprise Edition Release 11.2.0.1.0 - Production
With the Partitioning, Oracle Label Security, OLAP, Data Mining,
Oracle Database Vault and Real Application Testing options

create or replace procedure insertxml
(dirname in varchar2,
 filename in varchar2,
 tablename in varchar2)
is
xmlfile bfile;
myclob clob;
insCtx dbms_xmlstore.ctxtype;
rows number;

begin
dbms_lob.createtemporary(myclob, TRUE, 2);

-- handle to the xml file on the OS
xmlfile := bfilename(upper(dirname),filename);

-- open file
dbms_lob.fileopen(xmlfile);

-- copy contents of file into empty clob
dbms_lob.loadFromFile
(myclob, xmlfile, dbms_lob.getLength(xmlfile));

-- context handle
insCtx := dbms_xmlstore.newcontext(upper(tableName));

-- this inserts the file
rows := dbmd_xmlstore.insertxml(insctx, myclob);
dbms_output.put_line(to_char(rows) || ' rows inserted');

-- close handle
dbms_xmlstore.closecontext(insctx);
```

```
end insertxml;
/
```

The process to upload a file is to execute the procedure and pass in the directory object name, the file name, and the target table.

Since *dbms_xmlstore* has advantages over *dbms_xmlsave*, it is recommended that it be used first. In Oracle 11g, *dbms_xmlsave* is not installed with XML DB; *dbms_xmlstore* is installed by default when installing the XML DB functionality.

Package *dbms_xmlschema*

The XSD (XML Schema Definition), is a database metadata generic Document Type Definition (DTD) that allows for storing XML documents. Once a document structured with a DTD is defined, it can be loaded into the XSD schema and used to validate the structure of XML documents.

XML schemas are used to check if XML instance documents are correspondent to their specification. XML schema can be stored in an XMLType storage model in one of three ways: structured storage, unstructured model CLOB or binary XML storage.

The *dbms_xmlschema* is a package that offers procedures and functions for managing XML schemas. A few of the things which can be accomplished with the *dbms_xmlschema* package are:

- Evolving an XML schema using *inplaceevolve* and *copyevolve* procedures

- Compiling a XML schema by using the *compileschema* procedure

- Registering and deleting XML schemas by using both the *registerschema* and *deleteschema* procedures, respectively

- Generating a XML schema using the *generateschema* procedure

Next are some examples of how and when to use the *dbms_xmlschema* procedures and functions.

This example will show how to register and delete a XML schema. The first step is to create directories where XML objects will be registered using the *dbms_xdb* package.

🖫 Code 12.20 – dbms_xmlschema_register_delete.sql

```
conn sys@ora11g as sysdba

Connected to:
Oracle 11g Enterprise Edition Release 11.2.0.1.0 - Production
With the Partitioning, Oracle Label Security, OLAP, Data Mining,
Oracle Database Vault and Real Application Testing options
```

```
declare
  v_return   boolean;
begin
  v_return := dbms_xdb.createfolder(abspath => '/dbms_book/');
  v_return := dbms_xdb.createfolder(abspath => '/dbms_book/schemas/');
  commit;
end;
/
```

Next, save the *test.xsd* file into the directory created above, by using Windows Explorer, for example, and register the schema using the *registerschema* procedure.

```
--test.xsd file
<test
  xmlns:xsi=http://www.w3.org/2001/XMLSchema-instance
  xsi:noNamespaceSchemaLocation=
    "http://localhost:8080/dbms_books/schemas/test.xsd">


begin
    dbms_xmlschema.registerschema(
        schemaURL => 'http://localhost:8080/dbms_book/schemas/test.xsd',
        schemaDoc => sys.UriFactory.getUri('/dbms_book/schemas/test.xsd'));
end;
/
```

To unregister a XML schema, use the *deleteschema* procedure:

```
begin
    dbms_xmlschema.deleteschema(schemaURL =>
'http://localhost:8080/dbms_book/schemas/test.xsd',
    delete_option => dbms_xmlschema.delete_cascade_force);
end;
/
```

Even after we use the *deleteschema* procedure, the XML schema will still have some information in the data dictionary. To completely remove an XML schema from any dictionary table, use *purgeschema*. The schema must have been registered for binary encoding and deleted using the hide mode.

🖫 Code 12.21 – dbms_xmlschema_purge.sql

```
conn sys@ora11g as sysdba

Connected to:
Oracle 11g Enterprise Edition Release 11.2.0.1.0 - Production
With the Partitioning, Oracle Label Security, OLAP, Data Mining,
Oracle Database Vault and Real Application Testing options

--Get the schema_id on dba_xml_schemas view
select
    schema_url,
    schema_id
```

```
from
    dba_xml_schemas;

--Purge the schema using purgeschema procedure
begin
    dbms_xmlschema.purgeschema(schema_id =>
'9681EC7762871E4EE0400A0A710A54FD');
end;
/
```

Check the *dba_xml_schemas* again; the row whose *schema_id* was just purged will not be found.

Now move to the next and final package, which does not pertain to XML, but rather, the explain plan.

Summary

This last chapter of the book has covered packages pertaining to Oracle HTML Database or Application Express and Oracle XML Database functionalities.

Packages presented in this chapter are used to create, delete and manipulate many different types of objects and documents in both XML and HTML environments.

Book Summary

After we finish watching a show at the theatre or opera, we just have an image of the final production. When we start to study or understand what happens behind the scenes, we start to give much more value to how much work has gone into it.

Although command line tools are becoming more and more difficult to be used, this book serves to give the reader some more detail in using command line examples and showing what happens on background when graphical user interfaces are being used by a database administrator or a development.

Packages presented in this book are part of the most interesting fields of Oracle Database Administration; for instance, performance and tuning, backup and recovery, tablespace management, security, concurrency, Real Application Cluster, Data Guard, Streams and others. It has packages from different Oracle Database versions and also covers the last Oracle 11g Release 2.

Index

About the Author

Paulo Portugal

Paulo Ferreira Portugal is a DBA with more than a decade of experience in IT and has worked as a DBA for 10 years. He is an Oracle Certified Master 11g, Oracle Certified Professional (9i, 10g and 11g); Oracle RAC 10g Certified Specialist; Oracle DBA 10g Certified Linux Administrator; Oracle Exadata Implementation Certified; IBM DB2 Certified (8 and 9 "Viper"); and an Oracle 11i Applications Database Administrator Certified Professional.

Currently, Paulo works as Senior Support Engineer for Oracle Brazil.

He has participated in the Oracle Beta Test 11i project using Data Guard, and is a specialist in High Availability tools like Oracle Data Guard, Oracle Streams and Oracle RAC. His clients in Brazil demand the most sophisticated services using tools like Oracle E-Business Suite 11i, Oracle OTM, Oracle Retail and Oracle BPEL with Oracle RAC 10g.

Paulo greatly enjoys what he does and is always improving his technical knowledge by attending events like Oracle Open World – San Francisco (2005, 2006 and 2011) and IBM Information on Demand – Los Angeles (2006) and Burleson Oracle RAC Cruise 2009.

Technical Editor

Gabriel Rosales

Gabriel Rosales, M.Sc. has over 10 years of IT and more than six of extensive experience with Oracle. Mr. Rosales has been an instructor at Oracle University for the Administration, Database Security and Oracle Tuning courses. He was awarded the best IT Project Manager Profile by the Costa Rican Chamber of ICTs in 2006.

Mr. Rosales holds a Masters Degree in IT with mention on Project Management from ULACIT and a Bachelor Degree in Computing Sciences from UCR. Currently, he is the DBA of Mercado de Valores, Costa Rica's most important private brokerage firm and is also an IT Masters Professor in ULACIT, one of the most recognized private universities of CR. Passionate about IT, Mr. Rosales also possesses important achievements and awards in areas such as educational software and C/C++ development. He has participated as a speaker in many respected forums, including Oracle OTN Tour Latin America 2010.

www.ingramcontent.com/pod-product-compliance
Lightning Source LLC
Chambersburg PA
CBHW081450050326
40690CB00015B/2742